The
Master
of the
Game

The
Master
of the
Game

Paul Nitze and
the Nuclear Peace

Strobe
Talbott

Alfred A. Knopf New York 1988

THIS IS A BORZOI BOOK PUBLISHED BY ALFRED A. KNOPF, INC.

Library of Congress Cataloging-in-Publication Data
Talbott, Strobe.
The master of the game: Paul Nitze and the nuclear peace.
Bibliography: p.
Includes index.
1. Nuclear arms control—United States—History.
2. Nuclear arms control—Soviet Union—History.
3. Nitze, Paul H.   I. Title.
JX1974.7.T264 1988   327.1′74′0924   88-45218
ISBN 0-394-56881-8

Manufactured in the United States of America

FIRST EDITION

To William Bundy and Sidney Drell,

two wise men

We shall now attempt to sketch the further steps in the history of the Glass Bead Game. Having passed from the musical to the mathematical seminaries . . ., the Game was so far developed that it was capable of expressing mathematical processes by special symbols and abbreviations. The players, mutually elaborating these processes, threw these abstract formulas at one another, displaying the sequences and possibilities of their science. This mathematical and astronomical game of formulas required great attentiveness, keenness, and concentration. Among mathematicians, even in those days, the reputation of being a good Glass Bead Game player meant a great deal; it was the equivalent of being a very good mathematician.

Magister Ludi by Hermann Hesse

At what point shall we expect the approach of danger? By what means shall we fortify against it? Shall we expect some transatlantic military giant to step the Ocean and crush us at a blow? Never! All the armies of Europe, Asia and Africa combined, with all the treasure of the earth (our own excepted) in their military chest, with a Bonaparte for a commander, could not by force take a drink from the Ohio, or make a track on the Blue Ridge, in a trial of a thousand years.

Abraham Lincoln, in an address before
the Young Men's Lyceum of Springfield,
Illinois, January 27, 1838

CONTENTS

PART TWO
Defense

This book—a sequel to *Endgame: The Inside Story of SALT II*, published in 1979, and *Deadly Gambits: The Reagan Administration and the Stalemate in Nuclear Arms Control*, published in 1984—is broader in scope and at the same time more personal in focus than either of its predecessors. It reviews the history of the nuclear age as represented by the career of one man. It is personal in another respect as well: My interest in the cluster of subjects I have dealt with here stems from my own experience of the Cuban missile crisis in October 1962. I was then sixteen and a student at the Hotchkiss School in Lakeville, Connecticut. At the height of the confrontation between John F. Kennedy and Nikita Khrushchev, the headmaster of Hotchkiss, William Olsen, summoned the entire student body to the school chapel and led us in a prayer for deliverance. Some time later, he announced a school holiday in honor of Paul Nitze, class of '24, who had been an advisor to President Kennedy during the crisis. For years afterward I associated Nitze's name with the world's closest approach to the brink of nuclear war—and with the statesmanship that had brought us back from the brink.

I did not meet Paul Nitze until more than a dozen years later, when I came to Washington as a correspondent for *Time*. In 1977 I began work on *Endgame*. Nitze was then outside the government but at the center of the public debate over SALT II. He was the most effective spokesman for the Committee on the Present Danger. I frequently attended his briefings and read his reports. While I was not persuaded by all of his criticisms of the emerging treaty, I was impressed by the man himself—by his mastery of the subject, the intensity and authority with which he made his case, and the sense of history he brought to discussion of a contemporary issue. When *Endgame* was published, Nitze invited me to his office and led me through his copy of the book page by page, explaining with great patience and in great detail, but also with relentless and reproving certitude, what he viewed as the shortcomings of my analysis. During those few hours, I was struck once again by the sheer forcefulness of his personality. I was intrigued by something else as well in our conversation: Underlying his critique of what he considered my overly favorable assessment of SALT II was an unstated but unmistakable conviction that he could have done better than the Carter

Administration in negotiating with the Soviets—and a no less obvious and passionate hope that he might still get a chance to try.

He got that chance, and in *Deadly Gambits* I chronicled his role as chief U.S. negotiator in the intermediate-range nuclear forces (INF) talks that ended with the Soviet walkout from the bargaining table in late 1983. A year later, it was clear that a new chapter in the story of nuclear diplomacy had begun, with the Strategic Defense Initiative (SDI) as a major factor and with Nitze as an even more important figure in the Nuclear and Space Talks (NST) than he had been in the INF negotiations. Hence the present book, which uses certain themes in Nitze's fortunes and views to explain the background of the agreements—and disagreements—between President Reagan and General Secretary Gorbachev.

In the pages that follow, then, I have focused on Nitze's role in the history of arms control. But that is only one facet of a multifaceted career. This book does not presume to be the biography that should, and doubtless will, be written about Nitze's varied and productive life. Nor was the book, at any stage or in any sense, authorized by Nitze. While he tried, when he deemed it appropriate, to be helpful to me as well as to other reporters, there were limits both to his cooperation and to his approval. He and I have continued to differ about a number of matters, including some that bear directly on his own career, such as his role in the fate of SALT II. I am all the more grateful to him, therefore, for his tolerance of a project that he must sometimes have felt to be dubious in concept and in substance. It should be noted, moreover, that he was frequently constrained by what he regarded as the legitimate requirements of confidentiality in government and diplomacy. Other sources, however, were often less constrained; and when I came to him with information that I had acquired elsewhere, he sometimes sought to set the record straight but sometimes refused comment, leaving me to my own devices.

Those devices were journalistic. If journalism of the kind that my colleagues and I practice in our week-to-week work is the first draft of history, this book—especially Part Two, on SDI and NST—may be considered an attempt at the second draft. I undertook the reporting and writing while the events described here were still in progress. Much of the official record will remain classified, and many of the participants will be barred from freely discussing their roles, for years to come. Early on, I approached a variety of people involved in, or likely to be knowledgeable about, SDI and NST. They agreed to speak to me on the condition that I would not identify them as sources.

For nearly four years, I kept in touch with many players while the game was under way. I frequently saw people shortly after a meeting in Washington or a negotiating session in Geneva. My informants' accounts were often based not just on fresh memory but on notes, memoranda of conversations, talking points, reporting cables, and other documents. I have used direct quotations when they were provided by sources with firsthand, immediate knowledge of what was said. Some quotations come from on-the-record interviews. In those cases, the sources are acknowledged in the book's endnotes.

• • •

An account of this kind necessarily leaves many sources who must remain anonymous, and so there are a number of people whom it is impossible to thank publicly for their help. They know who they are, and my gratitude to them is immense. But there are others I can acknowledge, and I wish to do so here. Quite a few were good enough not only to share with me their recollections, insights, and interpretations but also to look at portions of the manuscript—in some cases more than once, and in all cases with patience, generosity, and critical acumen.

I should first mention William Bundy and Sidney Drell, to whom this book is dedicated. Also: Harold Brown, who has been such an important theoretician and practitioner of national-security policy; McGeorge Bundy, who was at the right hand of President Kennedy during the Cuban missile crisis and at many other key moments, and who is soon to publish a landmark book on the role of nuclear weapons in high-level decisionmaking; David Callahan, a scholar who is currently at work on a more comprehensive study of Paul Nitze; Leslie Gelb, a fellow journalist who has served in government in important ways at critical times; James Goodby, an able diplomat and negotiator, more recently a fine teacher and author; Morton Halperin, who has been on the frontier of clear thinking about nuclear-arms policy; Thomas Halsted, a dedicated educator of the public on these issues; Richard Holbrooke and William Hyland, two friends who have been policymakers as well as editors—and who accordingly were able to give me double assistance; Michael Krepon, whose work in the crucial field of verification has set the standard for everyone else; Jan Lodal, whose guidance has benefited me since I first came onto the foreign-policy beat in Washington; Robert McNamara, himself a key figure in the history of the nuclear age, who did so much to make sound and sustainable policy out of the idea of deterrence; Janne Nolan, who shared with me her insights into the bureaucratic politics of SDI; John Rhinelander, who helped both in the negotiation of the antiballistic missile treaty in the seventies and in the defense of the treaty in the eighties; Gerard Smith, who has played such a distinguished role in arms control, including in many of the episodes recounted here; Ted Warner, who combines to a rare degree a knowledge of the Soviet

Union with expertise about the awesome hardware and the awful numbers; and James Woolsey, who possesses a deep understanding of the human subject of this book as well as of the political and military ones.

My thanks also to the Arms Control Association and to Spurgeon Keeny, its director and president; John Mendelsohn, vice-president; and James Rubin, assistant director. They answered numerous inquiries, provided me with considerable background material, and offered valuable comments on the manuscript. My associations with the Carnegie Endowment for International Peace, the Aspen Arms Control and Strategy Group, the Council on Foreign Relations, and the Center for International Security and Arms Control at Stanford University have given me an education in many of the problems discussed in this book as well as pleasant settings and excellent company in which to learn.

A number of Soviet institutions and individuals provided me with useful writings and conversation as well as showing me hospitality during my visits to Moscow. Of these I can mention the Institute for the Study of the USA and Canada, and particularly Georgi Arbatov, Radomir Bogdanov, Andrei Kokoshin, Mikhail Milshtein, Vladimir Pechatnov, Sergei Rogov, and Henry Trofimenko; and the Institute for World Economy and International Relations, particularly Aleksei Arbatov.

Others who helped me along the way: Michael Beschloss, Coit Blacker, Barry Blechman, Philip Bobbitt, Robert Bowie, John Bross, Barry Carter, Jimmy Carter, Lloyd Cutler, Lynn Davis, Douglas Dillon, Ralph Earle, Polly Fritchey, Sidney Graybeal, Richard Helms, Gregg Herken, Thomas Hughes, George Kennan, Anthony Lake, Thomas Longstreth, Charles Burton Marshall, Priscilla Johnson McMillan, Joseph Nye, Stanley Resor, James Schlesinger, Walter Slocombe, Paula Stern, Jeremy Stone, Cyrus Vance, Paul Warnke, and Thomas Watson. Thanks also to Steven Rearden and Ann Smith, who extended to me numerous courtesies even as they were hard at work assisting Paul Nitze in the preparation of his memoirs.

Michael Mandelbaum is one of the best editors and most influential teachers I have ever had. As in the past, he helped me not only to understand what has happened over the last forty years but to organize and present what I have learned. Anne Mandelbaum, too, helped me in a number of ways with her discriminating eye, finely tuned ear, and good sense.

This book, like its predecessors, stems directly from my reporting for *Time,* and some of its contents have appeared in its pages. The managing editor, Henry Muller, and the chief of correspondents, John Stacks, have been extraordinarily supportive in this as well as other ventures. Another colleague, Walter Isaacson, brought to bear on the manuscript the same wide-ranging intelligence and editorial skill that has made the Nation section of *Time* so gratifying to work for in recent years. His own work on the history of American foreign policy has been a model for me.

Special thanks to Lissa August and Martha Clark, who helped me both with my research on this book and with my administrative duties at *Time*. Other colleagues who eased my task with various indulgences and acts of assistance are Ann Blackman, Stan Cloud, Jim Jackson, Johanna McGeary, Bruce Nelan, Chris Redman, Barry Seaman, and Bruce van Voorst.

As with *Deadly Gambits,* I owe a huge debt of appreciation to my editors at Knopf, Ashbel Green and Charles Elliott. Along with my friend and advisor Mark Foster, they gave me support, encouragement, and advice when I most needed them. Melvin Rosenthal oversaw the copy-editing with great skill and intelligence as well as good humor.

Finally, a word about my wife, Brooke, and my sons, Devin and Adrian. I am grateful to them not only for putting up with another of my projects, with all the disruptions and impositions it meant for them, but for giving me a home and a life that make my work worthwhile.

S.T.
Washington, D.C.
August 8, 1988

The
Master
of the
Game

Strange Safety

Ronald Reagan was an exemplar of that uniquely American species of politician, the happy warrior. He came breezing into the presidency with a cheerful, willful disregard for the gloomier legacies of the past, particularly in foreign policy. As he saw it, his predecessors had let the world become too complicated and unfriendly; they had been too willing to accept its problems as intractable. That dreary resignation, bordering on defeatism, seemed to Reagan particularly to afflict conventional wisdom about the two biggest problems of all. One was the existence of another country: the Union of Soviet Socialist Republics. The other was a prodigy of modern science: the collaboration of physicists and engineers that allowed political leaders to order soldiers to detonate devices that split large atoms into smaller ones, releasing vast amounts of energy that then fused small atoms into larger ones, releasing even greater energy and causing destruction on a scale that man previously had been able to imagine only in his most extravagant myths.

For decades, the twofold object of American defense and diplomacy had been to make sure that the Soviet Union did not take over the world and that the thermonuclear bomb did not blow it up. These goals amounted to making the best of two bad but inescapable realities: the existence of the Soviet Union and the existence of the Bomb. That was not good enough for Reagan. He saw himself as the best combination of optimist, idealist, and pragmatist—a dreamer who could get things done, or at least could inspire the hope that they could be done someday. He was repeatedly accused in his 1980 presidential campaign of offering simple answers to complex problems. In reply, flashing his famous half-modest, half-cocky smile, Reagan pleaded guilty. "There *are* simple answers," he said. "There just aren't easy ones."

That was his bright side.

There was also a dark side. Reagan subscribed to a view of the Soviet Union and a reckoning of the Soviet-American military balance that were deeply pessimistic. At the core of his Administration's view of the world was the belief that the Soviet Union had attained military superiority over the United States. In March 1982, Reagan said at a news conference, "The truth of the matter is that on balance the Soviet Union does have a definite margin of superiority, enough so that there is risk and there is what I have called, as you all know, several times, 'a window of vulnerability.' ''

Other Presidents had come into office accusing their predecessors of letting the Soviets get ahead in certain categories of weaponry. Reagan was the first who asserted that the United States suffered from net inferiority and who believed, as he put it on a number of occasions, that "the Russians could just take us with a phone call." He meant that the Kremlin could have its way in a crisis merely by threatening attack. Reagan clung to that allegation long into his presidency. At a press conference in June 1986, he referred yet again to the Soviets' "superiority over us" and spoke of the need for the United States "to play catch-up."

Much of the rhetoric and thinking of the Administration seemed to rest on an assumption, largely unstated, that the contest between the superpowers was inherently unequal. According to this view, even if the United States were comparably armed, its relationship with the U.S.S.R. would still be unstable and, from the American standpoint, disadvantageous, for the Soviet Union's repressive political system and expansionist foreign policy predisposed it to the use of force. By contrast, the American preference for the marketplace over the battlefield restrained the United States from the use of force in its international behavior.

When, in a speech in Florida on March 8, 1983, Reagan spoke of the Soviet Union as "the focus of evil in the modern world," he was not just engaging in moralistic rhetoric for the benefit of an audience of evangelical Christians (although he was doing that as well); he was also expressing a deeply and widely held conviction that the Russian Bear armed with the Bomb posed a special threat not so much because of the nature of the Bomb as because of the nature of the Bear.

When Reagan contemplated his own country's nuclear arsenal, he, like most Americans, saw instruments of deterrence. This was a time-honored concept that George Washington explained in an address to the joint houses of Congress in 1790: "To be prepared for war is one of the most effectual means of preserving peace." The names that Americans gave their intercontinental ballistic missiles—Minuteman and Peacekeeper—suggested the heroes of American history, the citizens' militia that stood up to the British at Lexington and Concord, the sheriffs who faced down the bad guys in Dodge City or Tombstone. American ICBMs were the big sticks that allowed Uncle Sam to speak softly. When Americans saw gray, grainy pictures of Soviet rockets, however, they saw instruments not just of war but of surprise attack.

Reagan played on this subjective contrast with confidence and skill, but the more objective exercise of manipulating the numbers and technical details associated with nuclear weapons was beyond him. When drawn into the realm of facts, he often displayed stunning ignorance about the capabilities of the weapons over which he had authority.*

Reagan seemed to feel that imprecision hardly mattered because the facts themselves did not matter that much. Facts were details, and, as was often said in defense and even in admiration of him, Reagan was not a detail man. The President had a whole government full of experts to back him up with the facts when they would serve him. He was willing to listen to them when their numerology—their divination of the truth about prospects for war and peace from esoteric numbers—confirmed what he already knew in his gut: The Russians were bad; they were bad in ways that made their weapons more dangerous than similar American ones.

Reagan made no bones about rejecting the assumptions of the experts when he found them unpalatable. He found particularly objectionable the concept of deterrence as it had been redefined in the nuclear age: mutual deterrence based on mutual vulnerability to the threat of mutual destruction. That strange notion of safety meant being naked before a lethally armed enemy, and Reagan—again, like many of his countrymen—could never accept that idea.

For Reagan, the "catch-up" that he called for should be more than just a matter of having as many bombs as the Soviet Union. Real peace for the world and real safety for the United States could best be obtained by depriving the Russian Bear of his nuclear claws altogether. That was the fundamental appeal of an idea that Reagan unveiled on March 23, 1983, at the end of a speech on national television devoted to his defense program:

> Wouldn't it be better to save lives than to avenge them? . . . I believe there is a way. Let me share with you a vision of the future which offers hope. It is that we embark on a program to counter the awesome Soviet missile threat with measures that are defensive. . . . What if free people could live secure in the knowledge that their security did not rest upon the threat of instant [American] retaliation to deter a Soviet attack, that

---

*On one occasion Reagan said that cruise missiles could only be used "defensively." In fact, the jet-powered drones are designed to penetrate enemy defenses and attack targets deep inside the U.S.S.R. On another, he asserted that submarine-launched ballistic missiles could be recalled after they were fired—a capability not possessed by any ballistic missile. Well into his term he admitted, without apparent embarrassment, that he had not realized how much more of the Soviet nuclear deterrent was concentrated on land-based missiles than was the case for the United States—perhaps the single most important difference between the two arsenals. And he confessed—again, almost blithely—to having never understood what "this throw-weight business is all about." Throw-weight, the measure of the ability of ballistic missiles to hurl warheads, was nothing less than the bottom line in his own advisors' calculation of Soviet superiority; there was a discrepancy in firepower precisely because the Soviets did have so much of their throw-weight on large land-based missiles rather than smaller (though nonrecallable) submarine missiles and tiny (though highly offensive) cruise missiles.

we could intercept and destroy strategic ballistic missiles before they reached our own soil or that of our allies? . . . I call upon the scientific community in our country, those who gave us nuclear weapons, to turn their great talents now to the cause of mankind and world peace, to give us the means of rendering these nuclear weapons impotent and obsolete.

This was one of the most important presidential statements on the subject of nuclear weapons since Harry Truman had announced their existence. Here was a President proclaiming as a goal of American policy, if not quite to uninvent the Bomb, then the next best thing—to retire it forever.

That dream was, for the dreamer-in-chief himself, a way of reconciling the optimism that radiated through his personality and his political style with the gloom that underlay his view of the Soviet Union and the nuclear balance. The Strategic Defense Initiative (SDI)—immediately dubbed Star Wars—was the ultimate example of a simple answer to a difficult question. It was a way of reordering the Soviet-American military competition and nullifying once and for all what he saw as the U.S.S.R.'s inherent advantages in the nuclear arms race. Thanks to SDI, even as Reagan pounded away at the bad news of American strategic inferiority, there was an implication of good news just around the corner: Perhaps the world would not have to put up forever with the twin evils of Communist Russia and nuclear weapons; perhaps there would be no need to make terrible choices between being red and being dead.

Reagan gave his Star Wars speech almost exactly two weeks after his Evil Empire speech to the evangelicals in Florida. The close timing was significant. The Evil Empire speech had ended with a hope that Soviet Communism would prove to be "another sad, bizarre chapter in human history whose last pages even now are being written." Then came a quotation from Tom Paine: "We have it within our power to begin the world over again." This was not a conservative American President quoting a conservative Founding Father; it was the leader of what was already called the Reagan Revolution quoting a highly radical sentiment expressed by one of the firebrands of the American Revolution.

SDI was to be the cutting edge of the Reagan Revolution in national-security policy. If it worked, it might allow the United States to achieve victory over the Soviet Union once and for all, not through war but through the elimination of the Soviets' ability to threaten war. Unlike the power of the United States, of which force of arms was just one dimension, the power of the Soviet Union stemmed almost exclusively from its ability to do violence to its enemies. While the U.S.S.R.'s standing army and conventional weaponry were extremely formidable in their own right and the object of anxiety on the part of its neighbors, it was the Soviet Strategic Rocket Forces that made the U.S.S.R. what it was: the other superpower. Insofar as SDI succeeded in rendering nuclear weapons impotent and obsolete, it might do the same thing to the Soviet Union itself.

This was heady stuff. But SDI was beset by technological and conceptual flaws. Under close scrutiny, the idea of SDI began to look like an even stranger way of assuring safety than deterrence. Virtually no one in the U.S. government except Reagan believed in the vision of an America so thoroughly defended that nuclear weapons would rust away. SDI in its purest, presidentially sanctioned form was, from the outset, simultaneously a sacred cow and an embarrassment. Over time it became less of the first and more of the second. As Reagan's reputation for political surefootedness came into question, particularly in the wake of the Iran-Contra scandal of 1986–87, his favorite defense program became more susceptible to compromise, both in the politics of funding with the United States Congress and in the diplomacy of arms control with the Soviet Union.

As Reagan approached the end of his presidency, the kind of future he had envisioned in March 1983—a world without any nuclear weapons at all, a world in which peace depended on purely defensive rather than offensive devices—still figured in his rhetoric. But those who hoped to succeed him, Democrats and Republicans alike, were preparing to cope with a world in which there would still be a great many nuclear weapons. Indeed, even while Reagan was President, the United States had produced hundreds of new nuclear weapons a year. The future would entail finding unsimple answers to the unsimple questions that Reagan had tried to wave aside with the magic wand of SDI. By 1988, not only was the Reagan Administration still a long way from having established an entirely new system for keeping the peace— its quixotic attempt to do so made the old system look good by comparison.

Whether the President himself knew it or not, and whether he liked it or not, the legacy of the Reagan Administration was beginning to look less like a revolution and more like a restoration, a reinstatement of traditional ends and means in the way that the superpowers kept the nuclear peace—a return to reliance on the strange safety of mutual deterrence and a renewed effort through arms control to make that condition less strange and more safe.

The Silver Fox

Of those who brought about that restoration, the most persistent and prominent was Paul Henry Nitze. The story of SDI was largely the story of Nitze's tenacity and ingenuity on behalf of the progress in arms control that Ronald Reagan eventually made with Mikhail Gorbachev in 1988.

For most of Reagan's second term, Nitze served as ambassador-at-large

advisor to the President and to the secretary of state for arms
influence that goes with a government post is usually inversely
to the length of the title. Nitze was an exception to that rule.
. ..early four years, he was the gray eminence of nuclear diplomacy. He
played a central, sometimes decisive part in deliberations inside the Administration, in consultations with the U.S. Congress and America's allies, and
at meetings between Reagan and Gorbachev.

When Reagan and Gorbachev first met in 1985, the most publicized and
important of their sessions took place in the pool house of a villa on the
shore of Lake Geneva. The two leaders were one on one, with only their
interpreters present. At the beginning of that conversation, the President
handed the General Secretary a paper outlining the American terms for a
comprehensive agreement on how to regulate the superpower rivalry in the
acquisition and the deployment of strategic weapons. That paper was largely
the work of Paul Nitze. While Reagan and Gorbachev chatted, Nitze and
Secretary of State George Shultz were in the main villa, meeting with some
of Gorbachev's advisors.

Nitze was then seventy-eight years old; Reagan was seventy-four. Both
men were remarkably fit and vigorous. But they were vigorous in different
ways which reflected differences in their backgrounds and personalities.
Reagan's was the smooth, sometimes jaunty manner of someone who had
come a long way on a wink and a nod, who trusted in good luck and simple
virtues, including the virtue of simplicity itself. He had entered the fray of
national and international politics relatively easily yet relatively late in life,
too easily and too late for the complexities he found there to trouble or
change him greatly.

The contrast with Nitze was dramatic. If Reagan's style was easygoing
to the point of insouciance, Nitze's was marked by intensity. If Reagan
seemed to have reached the pinnacle of success by way of Main Street and
Easy Street, Nitze showed the signs of having traveled a longer, harder route.
He had gone from the Wall Street of the Depression to the Washington of
the New Deal. He had been involved in government since 1940, the year
that Ronald Reagan played George Gipp in *Knute Rockne, All American*. By
the time Reagan made his spectacular debut as a politician by winning the
governorship of California in 1966, Nitze had already been in and out of the
corridors of power for more than a quarter of a century. More than twenty
years later, when Reagan was in the White House, Nitze could say with
pride, "I've advised every President since Franklin Roosevelt, and all, to
some extent, have sought and taken that advice."

His early years were permeated with a potent combination of Old World
intellectuality, stiff-backed discipline, and noblesse oblige. He was born in
the Yankee college town of Amherst, Massachusetts, spent his early youth
on faculty row at the University of Chicago, and was educated—twice—at

Harvard University, as an undergraduate and later as a businessman taking a sabbatical so that he could grapple with the great issues of the day. His wife, Phyllis Pratt, who died in 1987, was an heiress of the Standard Oil fortune. Her favorite uncle, Harold Pratt, donated a mansion on Park Avenue in New York that became the home of the Council on Foreign Relations, the closest thing there was to a headquarters for the foreign-policy establishment.*

Nitze married and earned a great deal of money, but for most of his life, his real vocation was public service. He was the quintessential elder statesman, a role model for a number of government advisors and policymakers who were a generation or more younger than himself.

Toasting Nitze on the occasion of his 80th birthday, Shultz called him the finest public servant he had ever known. He praised his ability to outsit the Soviets when necessary and to find areas of compromise with them when possible: "Wise men come and wise men go, but decade after decade there is Paul Nitze." A year later, at three o'clock on the afternoon of Friday, January 15, 1988, Shultz arranged a surprise 81st birthday party for Nitze. Officials from agencies and departments all over town gathered in the mahogany-lined reception area outside the Secretary's office on the seventh floor of the State Department. Among those who came to pay homage were a few senior figures and battle-scarred veterans of the bureaucratic wars, including some of Nitze's most stubborn opponents. Edward Rowny, a retired general and former negotiator then on the fringes of policymaking, played "For He's a Jolly Good Fellow" on a harmonica. But the assemblage as a whole was surprisingly youthful. It was dominated by men and a few women in their thirties and forties, the technical experts and action officers who worked the longest hours on the hardest problems.

From the immediate neighborhood of Foggy Bottom were people like James Timbie, who had been laboring away almost anonymously in the bureaucracy for years, sometimes on behalf of policies that Nitze had opposed, but who was now working for him and with him. From the Pentagon, on the other side of the Potomac River and the other side of the battle lines that divided the Administration, had come an Army captain, Bruce Jackson, whose father had been an associate of Nitze's more than thirty years before. Jackson held views on SDI that Nitze had opposed in meetings earlier that same day, but Nitze respected Jackson's intellect and enjoyed his company.

While waiting for the cake, the guests clustered in small groups and, between songs and toasts, traded information, lobbied for their bosses' positions, explored the possibilities of interagency deals. The guest of honor

---

*The Long Island estate of another uncle, Herbert Pratt, became the weekend retreat for the Soviet mission to the United Nations.

himself was in the thick of the action. This was the so-called "working level" of the government, and it was here that Nitze enjoyed a special standing. A few days later, James Woolsey, a Washington attorney who had worked for Nitze, explained why:

"Paul has collected a kind of extended family over the years. He has had many protégés, but he has never expected them to sit at his feet and absorb his wisdom. He has always wanted them to challenge him, to argue with him, to roll up their sleeves and work alongside of him. He has hired people and promoted them precisely because they stood up to him. He has always been an aristocrat in his bearing and his background, but an intellectual egalitarian in the way he deals with people whom he considers worth the trouble—particularly younger people. He has a professorial style, but his is an open classroom. For him 'argumentative' is a compliment."

Another friend, Polly Fritchey, who had known Nitze for more than forty years, remarked, "If there is one image that sums up Paul Nitze for me, it is the scene of him surrounded by his four children and their friends, all arguing furiously. He's at the center of the argument but by no means having an easy time of it, and loving it all the more. The more disagreement, the better the discussion."

Nitze's contemporaries and juniors alike often felt that whatever the argument—whether they were on Nitze's side or not—it was important, at least in part, just because Nitze himself was engaged. Almost always, no matter how immediate or detailed the subject at hand, he conveyed a sense of history and of consequence. That was partially through his assertive manner and his conviction that details were important, sometimes all-important; but it was also because of his long, varied record of involvement in some of the biggest debates and toughest negotiations of the era.

On January 20, a few days after Nitze's 81st birthday, one of his former colleagues in government, Sidney Graybeal, was interviewed on television about the history of arms control. He was asked to assess the various practitioners of the craft. Graybeal declared Nitze to be "the best negotiator the United States has ever had . . . for two reasons: First, he has put arms control in its proper context—not as an end in itself but as a means to an end, consistent with our overall strategy and what we need for strategic stability. Second, he's a tremendous tactician, an excellent chess player who thinks about the third move in the game, who understands the Soviet objective and the American interest and how to work toward some common ground."

James Woolsey went still further in his praise. Nitze, he said, was "quite possibly the single most influential figure of the postwar period in setting American strategy and the approach to arms control. He is fond of saying that many good ideas are not new. Collective security and deterrence are old and good ideas. As much as anyone—perhaps more than anyone—he has put an enduring gloss on those ideas. He has shaped both issues and events, intellectually structuring the big problems of the age as well as dealing with them hands-on in more capacities and over a longer period than anyone else. There are people who have been more powerful at particular times, but no one who has done more to set the tone and context of policy over the whole period. It's all the more remarkable that he has done so either from outside the government or as a subcabinet official or an advisor.''

Nitze had played a long, influential, in some ways unique role in the drama of American national-security policy, but it was never a starring role. That fact may have been the key to his own darker side. For all his achievements and distinctions, his career as a public servant was also a saga of thwarted ambition, offended vanity, and swallowed pride. He almost never got the jobs he wanted when he wanted them. He was turned down for, or at the last minute deprived of, as many assignments as he received. He was constantly being sounded out for attractive jobs, or actually offered them, only to be blackballed by someone higher up in the government or off to one side in Congress.

Part of the reason was bad luck, of which Nitze had had more than his share—another difference between him and Reagan. At various times Nitze had run afoul of patronage, fashion, partisan politics, and the ambitions of other men. Yet some of his bad luck Nitze had unquestionably made for himself. He had a particular combination of confidence and determination which sometimes put people off, even scared them, including some who outranked him and were in a position to decide on what his own rank would be. Just as he treated many of his junior associates as intellectual peers, he was inclined to treat his bureaucratic superiors the same way—if not occasionally as inferiors; understandably, therefore, they sometimes regarded him as excessively independent, if not downright insubordinate. He had a reputation for arrogance and disregard of form. ''A loose cannon'' . . . ''A man in a hurry'' . . . ''Has his own agenda'' . . . ''Inclined to wander off the reservation'' . . . ''Not a team player'' . . . ''Needs to be managed.'' These were complaints and cautions that had echoed through the years among his colleagues—defenders as well as antagonists.

There was, then, among those with the power to grant him his wishes, a recurring reluctance to grant him his first wish, especially since he seemed so willing to settle for a second, less desirable alternative or even a third. So great was his desire to have a voice in the strategic debate that he accepted appointments below the level to which he aspired and for which he felt his talents and experience qualified him. That frequently meant working for people he considered beneath him in intellect, experience, energy, and even integrity. Nitze was, it was true, convinced that he could have a major impact even from lesser positions or, for long stretches of time, without any official position at all. Nonetheless, the many disappointments took their toll on him and accentuated the contrast between his style and Reagan's. Reagan, too, had experienced defeats along the way, but they did not seem to bother him; they did not show. With Nitze, they showed.

He seemed to be in a constant struggle with the world around him. He liked to speak of himself as being in fighting trim. He gave the impression that there was not an excess pound on his body, a misplaced thread in his suit, or a wasted word in his speech. His eyes had a slight squint, not because there was anything wrong with his vision but because he seemed always to be warily scrutinizing whatever was going on around him. His thin mouth often had a tight, downward cast, as though he were anticipating the sour taste of others' folly. This natural severity in his visage made his flashes of humor, exuberance, and mischievousness all the more striking. He took all things seriously, including his fun. He frequently flexed the muscles in his cheeks, a habit that contributed to the impression of great restlessness kept under great control. When he walked, he leaned forward, leading with his jaw; his pace was brisk, his shoulder blades jammed together, his chest out, his belly flat. As he entered his 80s, he was still an able skier, competitive equestrian, and all-around sportsman. "My body," he once remarked to Sidney Graybeal, a man seventeen years younger whom he had just trounced in tennis, "does what I tell it to."

The world, the nation, and the President were less obedient. But Nitze was still working on all three. There was often an air of embattlement about him. Sometimes it was an air of suppressed anger, even bitterness.

Nor was the anger always entirely suppressed. He was given to sporadic bursts of invective that jarred not only against the genteel traditions he normally embodied so well but against his own high regard for the cooler qualities of rationality, objectivity, and civility. These lapses seemed reminders that he had unwillingly spent crucial years of his life, and the nation's, on the sidelines. During these years he was, not surprisingly, rarely happy with the play of those on the field. He was sure he could do better. When excluded from power, he tended to be not just a critic of the incumbent administration but a savage, sometimes even seemingly vengeful opponent. He waged his side of these many struggles with a passion that sometimes carried him to extremes of *ad hominem* ferocity. Yet he was always fighting for more than just himself—and against more than just his adversaries of the moment. He was always, above all, a combatant in a battle of ideas.

Paul Nitze had a prominent role in the story of arms control. It was also an ambiguous role. The ambiguity followed a pattern: When outside the government, he was part of the problem afflicting arms control, an implacable obstructionist and sometimes even a character assassin of those who were trying to advance the process. When inside the government, he tended to be part of the solution—a dogged negotiator, an innovative deal maker, a bold infighter, a trusted counselor.

For ten years, from 1969 to 1979, the United States and the Soviet Union conducted the Strategic Arms Limitation Talks (SALT), producing two sets of agreements, SALT I in 1972 and SALT II in 1979. Nitze was a founding father of SALT even before the enterprise acquired an acronym. He was a negotiator and defender of SALT I, but he was then a sharp critic of SALT II. On the whole, those who cheered him in one act booed him in the next. And vice versa.

Opposition to SALT II had been one of the centerpieces of Ronald Reagan's campaign for the presidency. It was primarily because Nitze had been so forceful an antagonist of the treaty that he was invited to join the Reagan Administration. But there was much more to Nitze's role in the history of nuclear-weapons policy and arms control than spearheading the campaign against SALT II. Almost anyone who knew Nitze suspected that there was bound to be more to his role in the arms-control policies of the Reagan Administration than just serving obediently and passively as a symbol of its rejection of the past. He was too much of an activist for that, and he was too closely associated with the old regime—the post–World War II political, diplomatic, and military order—to be entirely comfortable in the new regime that proclaimed the Reagan Revolution.

The far right would never entirely trust Nitze because of his part in SALT I, while many liberals would never entirely forgive him for his opposition to SALT II. Nor did the Soviets know quite what to make of him. In the early seventies, when he was helping negotiate SALT I, they had associated him with the forces of light. Later in that same decade he had been a leader of what Moscow called "ruling circles hostile to the interests of world peace," "the military-industrial complex," "enemies of détente," even "warmongers." Because of his role in the SALT II debate, his appointment to the Reagan Administration in 1981 had been widely interpreted, in the West as well as in Moscow, as an example of letting the fox guard the chicken coop.

Yet four years later, as Reagan and Gorbachev met at the summit in Geneva, Nitze was the closest that arms control had to a friend in court in Washington—or as the Soviets (and surely he) would have preferred to put it, a representative of "more rational, sober-minded forces." Some Soviets referred to him as the silver fox. The nickname, originally coined by his fellow American negotiators in SALT I, was intended to suggest not preying on arms-control chickens but outsmarting anti–arms control hawks.

Among themselves, the Soviets also called him *starik,* which means literally "old man" but with connotations of authority and sagacity. If the Geneva summit were to lead anywhere, it would be because of a curious alliance between Nitze, as the man in the background writing some of Reagan's most important lines, and Gorbachev's own aides; agreement would come because his concept of American interests coincided, on critical points, with their understanding of Soviet interests. The Soviets, along with many Western Europeans and Americans, were counting on Nitze to save the Administration from itself, to rescue arms control from the stagnation into which it had fallen in the late seventies and to restore progress in the eighties.

Nitze was a Democrat in a Republican Administration, an East Coast patrician in a government originally dominated by West Coast parvenus, an Atlanticist surrounded by neo-isolationists, and, by 1987, an octogenarian struggling against men, many in their thirties and forties, who had higher rank, larger bureaucratic power bases, more formidable political patrons, and profoundly different views. Yet he battled on and, to a large extent, won.

For forty years he had been part of the mainstream of American thinking about how to manage the twin challenges of the Bomb and the Bear, although he tended toward the right bank of the mainstream and sometimes defined how far to the right that bank could be. But if Reagan was ignorant of much of the history of the nuclear age, or would have preferred to overlook it, Nitze was there as a constant reminder—a personification—of that history.

He was also a standard-bearer of certain themes in the strategic debate that had been going on for forty years. From the first days of the nuclear age, Nitze was convinced that nuclear weapons were useful instruments for the achievement of political and military ends, whether in a cold war or in a hot one. He believed that, despite the frightening scale of the destruction they could unleash and the difficulty in predicting what would happen in the event of their use, nuclear weapons could still be deployed—and, in extremis, detonated—to advance the interests of one superpower against the other. Moreover, he believed that differences in the size and composition of the Soviet and American nuclear arsenals mattered, both politically and militarily. He believed that even marginal advantages in favor of the United States enhanced deterrence, while marginal advantages in favor of the Soviet Union exacerbated the danger of a conflict that the West might lose, perhaps catastrophically.

Central to Nitze's life had been a concern with strategic vulnerability. His long career had been a kind of Paul Revere's ride to warn his government and his fellow citizens that they were in jeopardy from a Soviet attack. He was a detail man and a numbers man par excellence, an authority on the complex sums that supported Reagan's claim of Soviet superiority. Few could use the numbers to greater effect in briefings for the press and in congressional testimony. Moreover, like the President, Nitze had a gut feeling that the aggressive nature of the Soviet Union also had to be taken heavily into account when assessing the strategic balance.

In marked contrast to Reagan, however, Nitze was an operational pessimist, someone who believed that policy was largely a matter of making the best of a bad situation, of planning for the worst, while doing so in a way that would prevent it from happening. During the Truman Administration, when Reagan was still a movie actor and a Democrat, Nitze was in charge of long-range planning for the State Department. He asked some members of his staff to conduct a study on the chances of avoiding nuclear war in the indefinite future. The prognosis that came back was bleak: Sooner or later, given the irreconcilable differences between the United States and the Soviet Union and the hostile, predatory nature of Marxist ideology, there would be a nuclear war. So Nitze asked a different question: What if the United States conducted itself with maximum skill and wisdom for ten years? What were the chances of making it through those ten years? The task force revised upward the chances of avoiding war. Nitze then asked whether the first ten years of peace would increase the chances of a second ten years. The analysts said, yes, it would. Nitze drew a lesson for the maintenance of both the nuclear peace and his own peace of mind: "Try to reduce the dangers of nuclear war within the relevant future time period as best you can; you just get depressed if you worry about the long-term future."

Yet he could never free himself of such worry entirely; and often, over the years, he worried acutely as he believed he saw the strategic balance shifting in favor of an aggressive, disciplined, and deceitful enemy. During the Christmas holidays in 1985, a few weeks after President Reagan's first summit meeting with Mikhail Gorbachev in Geneva, Nitze took his grandchildren on a vacation to Aspen, Colorado. He had roots in Aspen; he had helped finance the development of the ski resort there, a venture that augmented his personal fortune. It was a place where he went to relax with his family. If there was anywhere he should have been able to savor a moment of satisfaction and calm, it was there.

Back in Washington, the mood was upbeat. The Administration was, for once, soft-pedaling the problems in the Soviet-American relationship and highlighting the opportunities. Other Administration officials had begun to claim that their defense policies had gone a long way toward closing the window of vulnerability and that Reagan had "brought Gorbachev to the table" because America was now able to "negotiate from strength."

Nitze was not so sanguine or so self-congratulatory. He knew that the numbers of weapons remained largely unchanged; and by his count they remained unfavorable to the West. During an interview with an Aspen television station on December 30, Nitze was almost morose. He was asked if he could say which side in the superpower rivalry had superiority.

"I think I can," he said. "I'm *sure* I can. The Soviets do in fact have nuclear superiority today. Our position has improved over the last five years but not reached that of the Soviet Union.'' He went on to dampen the optimism about Soviet-American relations that was suddenly flowing out of Washington. He wanted to persuade his audience that the superpower competition was going to be a long struggle, that there was no end in sight, that there would be no quick fixes and not much good news along the way. It was not a Reaganesque message.

Like Reagan, Nitze believed in the vulnerability of the United States to a militarily superior enemy. But the President and his advisor were concerned about vulnerability of quite different sorts. Reagan had a layman's visceral revulsion against the idea that the United States could be hit by enemy bombs, while Nitze had an expert's intellectual concern with problems of stability in the strategic competition. He worried about how many more bombs of what sort the enemy possessed and how the arithmetic of that inventory might translate into military or political advantage against the United States in a crisis. Unlike Reagan, Nitze accepted *absolute* vulnerability as part of the human condition in the nuclear age, although he was worried about imbalances in the *relative* vulnerabilities of the two sides: If the United States was more vulnerable to the Soviet Union than the other way around, the nuclear peace was less stable.

Nitze was never a true believer in SDI as a solution to the problem of either absolute or relative vulnerability. This was part of the reason for the sobriety bordering on melancholy that radiated from many of his statements, in marked contrast to Reagan's high spirits. Unlike the sixth of the Presidents he served, Nitze was not a happy warrior, for he recognized one of the biggest dilemmas of the age: that it did little good to dream of eliminating either nuclear weapons or the threat of a nuclear-armed Soviet Union; a way had to be found to live with both, and for him, that way had for many years included both deterrence and arms control.

Ronald Reagan came into office with a bias against arms control insofar as it was based on traditional deterrence, which in turn was based on mutual vulnerability. The standard by which Reagan seemed to judge arms-control initiatives was whether they were steps toward complete disarmament, therefore steps away from deterrence. Hence much of his distaste for SALT, a process and a series of agreements that embraced deterrence.

The standard by which Nitze judged arms-control agreements was whether they strengthened deterrence, particularly American deterrence of Soviet aggression—the only danger he considered real. Nitze was not always consistent in the way he applied that standard, but the standard itself remained the same. As a defender of SALT I, as an opponent of SALT II, and as a leader of the effort to improve on SALT in the Reagan Administration, Nitze believed that deterrence was the only game in town, and that arms control could and should serve to impose good and enforceable rules in that game. That was a far cry from Reagan's attempt to change the game altogether.

Eleven months after their first encounter in Geneva, Reagan and Gorbachev were together once again, in Reykjavik, Iceland. This time it was the Soviet leader who brought a piece of paper setting forth the terms of an ambitious arms-control deal. After intense discussions, Reagan and Gorbachev instructed their advisors to work through the night if necessary to hammer out an agreement.

Paul Nitze was the chief American representative in that session. It was an exhilarating experience, for which he had spent much of his long career preparing. For those ten hours, from 8:00 P.M. on Saturday night until 6:00 A.M. Sunday morning on October 11–12, 1986, he had moved out of the shadows. No longer was he simply one of a number of experts in the bureaucracy passing papers up through the system, hoping that the President would notice, agree, and act. Now he was the principal American at what turned out to be a critical juncture. While Reagan and Gorbachev slept nearby, their emissaries tried to cut the Gordian knot of arms control. The pressure, the stakes, and the risks were high.

Nitze's counterpart in the all-night talks was Sergei Akhromeyev, first deputy minister of defense, chief of the general staff of the armed forces of the U.S.S.R., marshal of the Soviet Union. Even dressed in civilian clothes, the sixty-six-year-old soldier possessed such bearing and authority that he looked and sounded every bit the embodiment of the military might of the other superpower.

Nitze was in his element. One of his favorite phrases—and activities—was to "work the problem," which meant to subject a disagreement or a puzzlement to exhaustive examination and discussion, look at it from many different angles, go back over it repeatedly until finally it yielded to an agreement or a solution. In his all-night bargaining session with Marshal Akhromeyev, Nitze made genuine progress in working the problem of arms control.

Reagan subsequently said on a number of occasions that "everything was on the table" at Reykjavik. In fact, more was on the table than Reagan himself seemed to realize. Not only were the negotiators dealing with the challenges posed by the burgeoning nuclear arsenals of the superpowers; at least by implication, they were reexamining and ultimately reaffirming the basis of the global nuclear peace and of America's guarantee to its European allies. They were also looking ahead to military systems that would not be available until the twenty-first century.

Afterward Nitze said that the Reykjavik meeting had been the most exciting three days of his life, "more fun than I've almost ever had." Yet the experience was, in the end, deeply frustrating. At the last minute and for many months afterward, the effort seemed to have come to naught.

Nitze described what he had been trying to do, during the all-night session with Akhromeyev and in his service to the Administration more generally, as "trying to make a silk purse out of a sow's ear." The silk purse was the most ambitious and beneficial agreement ever achieved in nuclear diplomacy between the United States and the Soviet Union. The sow's ear was SDI.

For five years, between 1983 and 1988, the nation and the world watched the spectacle of a President who confused nostrums with policies and dreams with strategy. The drama was played out between him and members of his government, many of whom felt compelled to feign enthusiasm for an idea that they considered extremely dubious. In the face of Reagan's stubborn attachment to SDI, his Administration became the scene of one of the most extraordinary episodes in the annals of American defense policy and diplomacy.

It was a bizarre instance of covert action, carried out almost entirely within the executive branch. The broad outlines of the operation, as well as the identity, motivation, and modus operandi of the various protagonists, were largely evident, almost a matter of public record. Yet the nature of what was going on remained obscure, the object of official obfuscation and therefore of public confusion.

Those conducting the clandestine activity were advisors to the President. Their target was the President himself. True to the spirit of covert operations, there was a large element of deception and dissembling in this struggle. For one faction, the real objective was a return to something close to traditional arms control (joint regulation of the arms race), only disguised as something new and better—indeed, something revolutionary and therefore, by definition, very untraditional. For the other faction, a bonus of the SDI program, if not the real objective, was the liquidation of arms control in any guise. But that purpose was itself disguised by rhetoric about holding arms control to higher standards than those that had been applied in the past.

This deception was deemed necessary largely because the President had his own objective in SDI, and it was compatible with neither of the competing ones that his advisors were trying, covertly, to impose on him. Ronald Reagan continued to believe very much in the original vision of March 1983: population defense so comprehensive and so close to being impregnable that the Soviet Union would have no choice but to cooperate in a transition to a new order in which defense would be the dominant, and eventually the sole, basis of Western security.

That was the President's sincere hope for SDI. Almost no one in his immediate employ shared that hope. So the objective of the game within the Administration—this deepest game that went on for five years between the two factions—was to finesse the longer-term implications of SDI while at the same time manipulating the shorter-term impact of the program in such a way as either to advance arms control or to stop it in its tracks.

Paul Nitze was the master of the game, the boldest and most persistent member of the arms-control-and-deterrence faction of the Reagan Administration; and as time went on, he was the most forthright and the most exposed to attack from the anti–arms controllers. From the beginning, Nitze set about to harness a presidential dream to the task of making reality a bit safer—the task to which he had devoted much of his life.

Just as Nitze's belief in American vulnerability had helped create the atmosphere in which SDI came about, his skepticism about large-scale strategic defenses helped bring the program down to earth, and his determination to "work the problem" helped bring SDI into the realm of the possible, where diplomats could use it to the immediate and practical advantage of the United States at the negotiating table with the Soviet Union.

For a while, the President's passionate belief in SDI, his government's lip service to the program, the Soviets' fulminations against it, and everyone else's fascination with the topic all had a preoccupying and distorting effect; they made it seem that SDI had ushered in a new era. In fact, the five years from 1983 to 1988 were an anomaly that ended with a grudging, largely implicit reaffirmation of the realities of the old era, one that had begun forty years before and that continues today. Paul Nitze had played an important part in those forty years, so it was fitting that he should also play an important part in re-establishing continuity after the strange interlude of SDI.

PART ONE

Offense

CHAPTER 1

Strength and Will

When, at the age of seventy, Paul Nitze sat down to tell his life story as part
of an oral history project conducted by the United States Air Force, he began
with the derivation of his name: "My father, who was one of the world's
greatest philologists, maintained that the origin of the name 'Nitze' was
the same Sanskrit writ from which the Greek word *nike* comes, and the
Greek word *nike* means 'victory.' So we have always taken pride in that
etymology."[1]

Victory was the objective of many endeavors to which Nitze devoted himself, not just as a military strategist but as a businessman, a bureaucrat, a
diplomat, a polemicist, and a theoretician. He was under no illusion that he
personally had always prevailed or that he had always been associated with
winning causes. Far from it. But part of his reason for pride seemed to be
that he believed that he, more than most people, understood the nature of
victory and of defeat, in the lives of both individuals and nations. He was
proud that, in the peculiar case of the nuclear age, he understood the dynamics of a struggle that probably could not be won but must not be lost.
The single most extraordinary thing about Nitze's life was his persistence—
his dogged refusal, in the face of repeated disappointment, frustration, and
sometimes outright rejection, to give up in the quest for influence in the
conduct of that struggle.

His recollections of his childhood reverberated with lessons about victory
and defeat, power and principle, authority and rebellion, aggression and
vulnerability. The anecdotes Nitze liked to tell about his life were rarely
without a moral, and the moral almost always had some application to statesmanship or strategy. He would frequently relate incidents from his youth to
a view of the world as a battleground where strength and willpower often
counted for more than rules, and where the rules that mattered were made
by the strong and enforced by the determined. He took satisfaction in having
many times surprised his elders and superiors, not always pleasantly, by
exerting his own will rather than doing the done thing. These were traits,
he said, that stood him in good stead when it came time for him to have a
say and a hand in the conduct of American foreign policy.

When Nitze was a small child, his father, William, was the head of the department of French literature at Amherst College in Massachusetts. He moved the family to Chicago, where he took up the post of chairman of the department of Romance languages and literatures at the University of Chicago. In the Nitze home, there was a great emphasis on the life of the mind and on the utility and virtues of rationality. Young Paul took to these values instinctively and at an early age. In 1988, his older sister Elizabeth recalled that, even as a three-year-old, Paul had been a "mathematical logician" and "hard-headed negotiator," who tried to explain, argue, and bargain his way out of trouble when he misbehaved.

But his youth also provided lessons in the limits of diplomacy and the uses of force. As a well-to-do boy from faculty row, Nitze had to pass a public school on his way to the private school he attended. One day, he stopped to watch some other boys playing marbles. The next thing he knew, he was on his back, being kicked and punched. From that moment, he was marked as a target for bullying and teasing. Finally, he tore up his stiff Buster Brown collar and joined an Italian street gang for self-protection. The leader of the gang was "the first charismatic leader" he ever saw in action. The high point of that "wonderful association," he later recalled, was when he proved himself as a member of the gang by stealing some tools from a construction site. It was, he added, an early instruction in "the basic truths about balance of power and the uses of force in the relationships of the real world. I didn't know it at the time, obviously, but I was forming a sense of the world that would influence greatly my views of the Soviet Union and how to deal with it."

Nitze's father was the scion of a prosperous German family that had emigrated to the United States after the Civil War. His mother, Anina, was also of German ancestry. Even in the relatively liberated environment of the University of Chicago, she created a sensation. She shocked the community by smoking cigarettes and asserting strong opinions about the music of Richard Strauss, the writings of Franz Kafka, and the dancing of her friend Isadora Duncan. Nitze said his mother was "by far the greatest influence in my life." She was small, dark, and brimming with "absolutely immense vitality and warmth and wit and energy, and loved me beyond any normal maternal love. It became overwhelming. At times I wanted to get away from it. It was too intense in a way."

The atmosphere in which Nitze grew up could be, by his own account, both stimulating and oppressive. He was "the oldest son of the oldest son of the oldest son of the oldest son of the Nitze family going back to the seventeenth century." With all those layers of primogeniture came a heavy weight of expectations—his own and his elders'—about how much he would accomplish: "I was allowed to do more or less what I wanted to do, although disappointment was easy to find, but only on those things where I was disappointed in myself, which was quite often." He was given "too much responsibility'' for his actions and his opinions: ''I always felt that I was asked to make up my mind as an adult on adult issues. . . . I was consulted as a full member of the family council right away from the age of seven on.''

Nitze was seven in 1914. That was the year when his family, which regularly took long trips to Europe, was in Munich just as England declared war on Germany. The Nitzes were hissed on the street for speaking English, so Nitze's father sewed an American flag on his sleeve to show that the family was American, not British.

All his life Paul Nitze has been fiercely resentful of aspersions on his patriotism, which occasionally accompanied attacks on him from the right. When, for his part, he was attacking others, as he did sometimes with stunning intemperance, he was given to using the epithet ''traitor'' or ''traitorous.'' The absurdity of the accusation made it, perhaps, all the more indicative of a sensitivity that may have stemmed from painful memories of being a German-American during World War I.

After the United States entered the war, his mother's brother, Paul Hilken, became a German agent and saboteur. Hilken, a tobacco exporter in Baltimore, was the paymaster of a spy ring on the East Coast and took part in a conspiracy to blow up a huge munitions depot on Black Tom Island in New York Harbor. Hilken subsequently turned state's evidence and avoided imprisonment, but the discovery of such a black sheep in its midst brought deep shame to the family.

At sixteen, Nitze was packed off to the genteel but highly competitive environment of Hotchkiss, a boarding school in rural Connecticut. Nitze cut loose. He and two other boys were ''sequestered'' for a series of violations of school rules, including staying out in a car too late with a girl. They were sentenced to a kind of house arrest and required every day to run ''the triangle,'' three miles of dusty country roads around the campus, while the other boys were at play. Nitze sent off for triangular key chain pendants which he handed out to his fellow miscreants as badges of honor. He formed the Sequestered Club. The headmaster called Nitze in to complain that he had seditiously turned what was supposed to be a punishment into an object of amusement and admiration around the school.

Later, when most of his fellow members of the Hotchkiss class of '24 went to Yale, Nitze chose Harvard instead. As he recalled years later, he was ''mightily turned off'' by a drunken and obnoxious Old Blue who spoke at a dinner in Chicago, while ''the Harvard fellow who spoke at the same occasion was more sensible—although less witty—than the Princetonian.''

''In those days,'' he recalled, ''grades didn't count. Harvard was more like a European university. You just tried to absorb wisdom. We all drank too much, had girls, and a rich, glorious life.'' He fell in with the fast crowd, joined the most elite of the Harvard clubs, Porcellian, and skipped his final examination in the history of economic thought so that he could attend a party in Newport, Rhode Island: "I distinguished myself by getting the lowest mark ever given at Harvard, which was a zero."

But even in his delinquencies and his pursuit of fun, there was an almost reckless intensity, a determination to push and to prove himself, to exert his strength and will in defiance of what others thought he could, or should, do. In his senior year, he buckled down to make up for the course he had flunked so spectacularly. "Just the fear of failure really drove me." He contracted hepatitis, then celebrated his recovery by getting drunk and accepting a bet that he and a friend could paddle a canoe from Ipswich, Massachusetts, to the New York Yacht Club. They made the trip in eight arduous days. Returning in triumph, he entered an impromptu track meet and collapsed in the middle of a sixty-yard dash. He spent several months in the hospital and almost died.

Nitze took an early interest in world affairs, and, in his mind, looming beyond his ancestral homeland of Germany was always Russia. Somewhere between the Sanskrit and the German, his name and therefore his forebears, he believed, had been Slavic. He had a Russian nurse as a child. An uncle on his father's side had been a scientist who was invited by the czar to study the geology of the Ural Mountains; his grandfather served as the Russian consul in Baltimore. Among the subjects on which Nitze, at the age of ten, was expected to express adult opinions around the dinner table in Chicago was the Russian Revolution of 1917.

His first direct exposure to the Soviet Union was brief, accidental, and illegal. After graduating from Harvard in 1928, he and a companion set off on a walking tour of northern Finland. They got lost in the fog and crossed a desolate portion of the Soviet frontier. They encountered a man in a boat on a lake who came to the shore and told them in German where they were and how they had better walk briskly back in the opposite direction. Nitze would not step foot on Soviet soil again for nearly thirty years.

Nitze's only connection with the early days of American policy toward the Soviet Union was similarly haphazard.

He might have followed his father and become an academic, but he found that profession rarefied and remote. Recalling the scholars he had known growing up, he said, "The thing that I couldn't get over was that here was a group that I thought was the most admirable group of men one could imagine, and they were having no impact upon the things that were going on in the world that seemed to me to be the most tragic and important. At that point I rather felt that I didn't want to follow in the footsteps of these people, admirable as they were, because they did not have a real impact upon affairs."

In 1929 he joined the New York investment firm of Dillon, Read and

Company just before the Crash, thus becoming "the last man hired in Wall Street for many years thereafter." He gravitated toward economics and business, he said, because it was a "field where one could be closer to the levers of power—to put it frankly, the levers of influence." He thrived in the depths of the Great Depression, acquiring the reputation of a prodigy as an investment banker.

In 1932, shortly before his marriage to Phyllis Pratt, Nitze was sharing bachelors' quarters with Sidney Spivak, one of his closest friends then and for years afterward. One day, Nitze was riding the Lexington Avenue subway and found himself sitting next to a wealthy, flamboyant man of the world who was bubbling over with stories about his personal friendships with various Bolsheviks and commissars. He was William Bullitt, who had been a young aide to Woodrow Wilson at the Versailles peace conference after World War I and had undertaken an official mission to Moscow in 1919. Bullitt had later been married for a while to Louise Bryant, the widow of the American Communist John Reed. When Nitze met him, Bullitt had recently returned from Europe, where he had been collaborating with Sigmund Freud on a study of Wilson and the Great War. Bullitt was now looking for a way to attach himself to the presidential campaign of Franklin Roosevelt.

Nitze invited Bullitt home for dinner with Spivak, who was working for FDR and agreed to introduce Bullitt to the candidate's advisors. A year later, President Roosevelt appointed Bullitt the first U.S. ambassador to Moscow. Bullitt underwent the classic disillusionment of an American Russophile in the thirties: his romanticism about the Revolution quickly gave way to horror at the emergence of the Stalinist police state and the vigorous machinations of Bolshevism's international arm, the Comintern. He left Moscow in 1936 bitterly anti-Soviet, in his own sentiments and in his recommendations to Washington.

Meanwhile, Nitze was developing his own notions of Communism from an intense study of totalitarianism as it was taking root in both Germany and Russia. He read a book, took a trip, and went back to school. Together, these three experiences constituted a Saul-on-the-road-to-Damascus conversion from businessman to statesman.

Nitze often said that Oswald Spengler's *The Decline of the West* was one of the most powerful influences of his life. He had read the work in college; then, on a salmon fishing expedition in Canada in the summer of 1936, he reread it "with care, word by word, while waiting for a fish to appear." Perhaps nothing in Nitze's biography more dramatically distinguishes him from Ronald Reagan. Even if Reagan had been widely read—and even if he had been able to penetrate the often convoluted, murky prose of Spengler's famous work—he almost certainly would have recoiled from its message. Both in its title and in its thesis, the book was deeply pessimistic. For just that reason it was an appropriate primer for Nitze, who spent much of his career worrying about the decline of the West and the imminence of danger from the East.

Spengler propounded a deterministic, cyclical theory of history and concluded that only those states that were able to exert absolute power would be able to resist the general decline of European civilization. There was an underlying premise, common to much of Nitze's own thinking in later years, that dictatorships were more disciplined, calculating, orderly, and determined—in a word, more *serious*—than democracies. By extension to the international politics of the thirties, the Spenglerian view held that the Western nations would be at a potentially fatal disadvantage in a conflict with the political system and military machine of a Hitler—or of a Stalin. And conflict was clearly coming.

In 1937, at the age of thirty, having just been made a vice-president of Dillon, Read, Nitze took a leave of absence and made an extended tour of Germany with his family. He saw a country that was recovering from unemployment and the disastrous effects of hyperinflation. But it was also a nation in the midst of an experiment that intrigued Nitze as much as it repelled him: the imposition of a leader's concept of strength and will on an entire society. He witnessed Adolf Hitler galvanizing crowds with his rhetoric about national destiny. A Berlin businessman to whom Nitze had a letter of introduction missed their appointment because he had been arrested by the Gestapo. A Jewish banker whom Nitze had known for years was too frightened to meet with him. Nitze later said he had been appalled by the terror. But he also found the Nazi youths he met, with their slogan of "Strength through joy," to be "tough, arrogant, and damned impressive."

Nitze returned to the United States, but not to his former life. Much to the dismay of his boss, Clarence Dillon, he took a full year's sabbatical at Harvard. Dillon asked if he would learn anything that would increase his potential value to the firm. Nitze said no, he was going to study sociology, religion, philosophy, and history. "There were big issues, big questions, big problems in the world. I wanted to come to terms with them. I couldn't do that making money at Dillon, Read. . . . My peers all recognized that I could do it as well as the next man, so there wasn't any need any longer to prove anything to myself about being able to do that." Nitze's reading of Spengler and his visit to Germany compelled him to try to understand better "the world social and political scene. I felt myself confused and inadequate in trying to estimate what was apt to happen in the future."

He rented a house for his family on Chestnut Street in Boston and threw himself into the study of St. Augustine, historical texts, and the theories that contemporary scholars were devising to explain the modern world. He attended lectures by the chairman of the sociology department, Pitirim Sorokin, a White Russian emigré who had been a high official in the short-lived provisional government of Alexander Kerensky. Sorokin was a living example of the fragility of Western liberalism in the face of revolutionary dictatorship. He was given to sweeping generalizations, with a heavy dose of religious mysticism. Like Spengler, he saw history as cyclical. As different ideas and forms of society clashed, exacerbating the contradictions within them and the tensions among them, man found himself in the "crisis of our age"; civilization gave way to the "law of the jungle" in the form of war and revolution. Sorokin saw the rise of authoritarianism in the thirties, including the consolidation of Stalinism in his native Russia, as a logical outgrowth of the disintegration of an "overripe" old order.

Nitze fell under the influence of two younger scholars. One was political scientist George Sawyer Pettee; the other, the distinguished sociologist Robert Merton. Pettee's book *The Process of Revolution*, published in 1938, was a highly academic meditation on the consequences of breakdown in the economic and social order: Revolution grows out of disorder; the revolutionary new order is imposed by force, sustained by terror, and can be imposed on other societies if they are in a state of weakness and susceptibility. Pettee concentrated heavily on the Russian case, and he noted numerous similarities between Nazism and Bolshevism. He saw Marxism as inherently militaristic and predatory. As an antidote to what he called "helpless drift," Pettee urged "intelligent adaptation," "scientific understanding of circumstances," "operating concepts which correspond to reality," and "control"—all ideas that appealed to Nitze and phrases that became part of his vocabulary in later years and other contexts.

Merton was already launched on a career dedicated to making sociology a hard science, an objective, precise codification of universally applicable theorems and principles. Like Sorokin and Pettee, Merton was studying Marxism-Leninism. As Nitze summarized the lesson he learned from Merton: "Action is influenced by objectives, and will makes a difference." Communist ideologists made no secret of their objective—the eventual domination of the world—and Soviet behavior in the late 1930s suggested that the U.S.S.R. was emerging from a period of internal consolidation to one of international expansion.

The juxtaposition of Nitze's visit to Germany and his sabbatical at Harvard cemented in his mind the similarities between the Nazi and Soviet forms of tyranny. They were, he said, "very comparable and in many ways compatible evils."

In 1938 Nitze returned to Wall Street. He briefly established his own investment firm, the Paul H. Nitze Company, but in the course of trying to go it alone he worked himself to exhaustion and a breakdown in his health. He went back to Dillon, Read. The president of the firm by then was James Forrestal, a friend and mentor of Nitze's.

That year Neville Chamberlain attempted to head off war by meeting Hitler at Munich and acquiescing in the German annexation of the Sudeten-land. Nitze remembered the event as "a rude but enduring lesson" that the United States must oppose foreign tyrannies firmly—if necessary, forcefully. In fact, however, it took a while—and even ruder events—for him to see that the lesson applied clearly to the challenge of Hitler. As with many other Americans, Nitze's initial reaction to the specter of war in Europe was to embrace a brand of isolationism that was peculiar to that period and that side of the Atlantic. The sentiment combined disdain for Britain and awe, tinged with grudging respect, for Germany.

Nitze's case was especially troublesome. His pessimism about the decline of the West, his outright admiration for the "damned impressive" side of what he had seen of the Third Reich, and his conversational pugnacity all led him to make statements before America's entry into the war that caused him trouble afterward. On top of all that, there was his German background. For years afterward he had to fend off accusations that he had gone beyond being just another America-Firster. An FBI file that appeared in a background check on Nitze in 1960 contained both the charge and the defense:

> In 1940, Vincent Astor, New York financier, advised that Nitze, at a small dinner party, said that he would rather see America under the dictatorship of Hitler than under the British Empire if either alternative became necessary.
>
> James Forrestal, former Secretary of Defense, now deceased, advised that he had heard that Nitze had attended a dinner party in 1940 and had made remarks concerning Hitler and his activities. Forrestal stated he was positive Nitze did not mean to be pro-German but meant that he knew Germany was well organized and could not be easily defeated. Mr. Forrestal indicated he had known Nitze for many years and considered him one hundred percent American and neither pro-German nor pro-Nazi.

Once the war had begun in Europe, Forrestal went to Washington to serve as one of President Roosevelt's special administrative assistants. In June 1940, while on a business trip in Louisiana, Nitze received a telegram: "BE IN WASHINGTON MONDAY MORNING. FORRESTAL." Nitze obeyed. With Dillon, Read still paying his salary, he served initially as Forrestal's aide. Later he was a consultant on the military draft to the War Department, financial director of the office of the coordinator of Inter-American Affairs, head of the metals and minerals branch of the Board of Economic Warfare, and chief of overseas procurement for the Foreign Economic Administration. Nitze's hard-charging style led Forrestal once to warn, "Paul, you always act too rapidly. When you decide that something ought to be done, you want to do it right today. Down here in Washington you can't get things done that way."

Many years later, Nitze remembered this remonstration with a touch of pride.

His relationship with Forrestal remained close, not least because they shared a conviction that, even at the outset of the struggle against Nazism, the world faced at least as great a danger from Bolshevism. Nitze gave Forrestal a copy of Pettee's book: "It was his first systematic exposure to the theoretical approach to the problem of Communism."

The other great trauma of those years was Pearl Harbor. It wrenched Nitze, and the nation, out of isolationism. Moreover, just as Munich had shaken a generation's trust in diplomacy as an effective means of dealing with an aggressive dictatorship, Pearl Harbor seemed to implant in Nitze's mind what became one of the grand obsessions of his life: strategic vulnerability. In the age of modern weaponry, the two great oceans that separated the United States from Asia and Europe provided far less protection than had long been assumed. Even though the continental United States remained, on December 7, 1941, and throughout the war, beyond the enemy's reach, the island of Oahu in the mid-Pacific was still U.S. territory, and the fleet stationed there was considered both vital and safe. Suddenly, Battleship America could be sunk at its moorings. Partly for that reason, isolationism gave way to internationalism; but it was internationalism rooted in a new sense of insecurity, a sense that what Abraham Lincoln had said could never happen—"Shall we expect some transatlantic military giant to step the ocean and crush us at a blow? Never!"—was now possible.

The Japanese sneak attack had deprived the United States in a few hours of a large part of the arsenal on which it depended for defense—and, indeed, for deterrence. The nightmare scenario of a Soviet nuclear first strike against the United States that drove the strategic debate of the postwar period was largely an updating of the script enacted on that infamous Sunday morning. The American battleships in Pearl Harbor had many of the characteristics later ascribed to strategic nuclear weapons. Battleships were the principal means for projecting American power around the globe to protect allies and intimidate enemies. What happened to them became, in retrospect, a vivid and gruesome warning of what it would be like to have America's bombers and intercontinental ballistic missiles destroyed on their runways and in their silos.

Calipers on the Rubble

For the United States, World War II began with an image that has haunted the modern age: the bolt-from-the-blue attack that destroys much of a nation's capacity to make—and therefore to deter—war. Four years later, it ended with another such image: the mushroom cloud rising over the radioactive ruins of a city.

According to one of the clichés of the second half of the twentieth century, nuclear war is an abstraction, a hypothetical proposition. Experts can debate what would happen, but they cannot know. Ideas about what nuclear war would be like are necessarily matters of guesswork, fear, and faith, since no one has ever seen what one actually looks like. That uncertainty is arguably part of what deters the world from ever finding out.

Yet the truism is not entirely true. The United States did wage nuclear war against the Japanese Empire. The episode was brief, the weapons primitive. But the deaths, the radiation burns, the blindness from seeing the fireball, the peculiar cancers from the fallout, the incinerated houses, smashed buildings, pretzeled railroad tracks, charred bridges—the mushroom clouds themselves—they were all real. For that brief moment at the very beginning of the nuclear age, nuclear war was an event in the world of facts. And Paul Nitze was there, literally standing amid the rubble, pondering the facts, trying to figure out what it all meant and how the world had changed.

By far the most important American motivation in using the atomic bomb against Japan was to hasten the end of World War II. That objective was more than sufficient to drive both the development of the bomb and the decision to drop it. But there was, in the back of the minds of some of those who had a hand in the attacks on Hiroshima and Nagasaki, another, secondary purpose: to intimidate the Soviet Union and establish the United States as the unchallenged guarantor of the postwar order. In that, America was less successful, for the principal effect on Stalin of the American A-bomb program was to stimulate the Soviet A-bomb program. A pattern was already in place, and it would extend unbroken to the competition and debate over strategic offenses and defenses in the 1980s.

Within days after the American nuclear attack on Japan, Stalin summoned the scientists who had been working on the Soviet equivalent of the Manhattan Project. "The equilibrium has been destroyed," he said. "Provide the bomb—it will remove a great danger from us."[2] The choice of words was revealing not just of Stalin's frame of mind at that moment but of the Soviet mentality for decades to come. "Equilibrium" has long since become part of nuclear jargon; the Russian word for security *(bezopasnost)* literally means "absence of danger." Important aspects of equilibrium and security exist in the eye of the beholder; each is something that one side sees as being in jeopardy when the other side makes a major scientific or military advance.

The Soviet Union was determined to match the United States in nuclear weaponry no matter what the cost. As it was, the cost was not all that great.

Nuclear weapons were extraordinarily powerful but comparatively cheap. It was within the means of a modern industrial country, even one as inefficient as the U.S.S.R., to have many. Thus, matching the United States in nuclear strength was an imperative of Soviet policy from the outset; and because of the extraordinary cost-effectiveness of nuclear weaponry, sooner or later that goal was bound to be achieved.

The inevitability and complexity of a bipolar nuclear order was evident in the aftermath of the atomic bombing of Hiroshima and Nagasaki. Almost immediately, a group of academics began work under the auspices of Yale University on a book that was published in 1946, titled *The Absolute Weapon*. The editor and principal contributor, Bernard Brodie, concluded that there was something profoundly paradoxical about these new weapons:

> The first and most vital step in any American security program for the age of atomic bombs is to take measures to guarantee to ourselves in case of attack the possibility of retaliation in kind. The writer in making that statement is not for the moment concerned about who will *win* the next war in which atomic bombs are used. Thus far the chief purpose of our military establishment has been to win wars. From now on its chief purpose must be to avert them. It can have almost no other useful purpose.

Some of the implications in this passage were reassuring, others disturbing. Once American monopoly of the Bomb gave way to Soviet-American competition, war would no longer be an option. That was reassuring. But Brodie's statement went further. These two nations, which in the pre-nuclear era would almost certainly have gone to war against each other, would now instead hold each other hostage with their nuclear weapons.

The concept of mutual vulnerability as an inescapable consequence of the Bomb had been around longer than the weapon itself. When the Danish physicist Niels Bohr arrived at Los Alamos, New Mexico, in 1943 to advise in the secret work going on there, he brought with him an idea that made that work seem ethically and intellectually more justifiable. Bohr told the senior American scientist, J. Robert Oppenheimer, that the new weapon would not just transform war but require mankind to transcend its age-old habit of making war. A historian of the development of the A-bomb, Richard Rhodes, summarized Bohr's message:

> By the necessity, commonly understood, to avoid triggering a nuclear holocaust, the *deus ex machina* [of the Bomb] would have accomplished then what men and nations had been unable to accomplish by negotiation or by conquest: the abolition of major war. Total security would be indistinguishable from total insecurity. A menacing standoff would be maintained suspiciously, precariously, at the brink of annihilation. Be-

fore the Bomb, international relations had swung between war and peace. After the Bomb, major war among nuclear powers would be self-defeating. . . . The pendulum now would swing wider: between peace and national suicide; between peace and total death.

During the days of deepest secrecy and suspense surrounding the Manhattan Project, Bohr believed that Franklin Roosevelt should warn Stalin that the American development of the weapon was underway and that the United States and the Soviet Union must lay the foundation of confidence for negotiations on postwar "safeguards." Thus, in Bohr's mind at least, the idea of nuclear weaponry gave birth to the idea of Soviet-American nuclear arms control well before the Trinity test of the first fission explosion.

In September 1945, little more than a month after the U.S. nuclear attack on Japan, another of the physicists who had made the bomb, Leo Szilard, spoke to a symposium at the University of Chicago. "We are in an armament race," he said, according to the notes of another participant. "If Russia starts making atomic bombs in two or three years—perhaps five or six years—then we have an armed peace, and it will be durable peace."[3]

Bohr, Szilard, and Brodie were making the same point: nuclear weapons made possible a new kind of war but also made essential a new kind of peace. Oppenheimer took that point and pressed it throughout the rest of his career. He predicted that the arms race would lead to a "strange stability." He meant that even if—as he then feared and as has since occurred—the Soviet and American arsenals were to grow exponentially, they would still hold each other in check. In 1953 Oppenheimer said that the nuclear-armed great powers "may be likened to two scorpions in a bottle, each capable of killing the other, but only at the risk of his own life." In 1955 Winston Churchill said, "It may be that we shall by a process of sublime irony have reached a stage in this story where safety will be the sturdy child of terror, and survival the twin brother of annihilation." In the 1980s McGeorge Bundy, a onetime presidential national security advisor who was writing a history of decision-making in the nuclear age, coined the phrase "existential deterrence" for the nuclear standoff between the superpowers; and William Hyland, a senior government analyst and policymaker in the seventies who later became the editor of *Foreign Affairs,* spoke of "inherent deterrence." These were all refinements of Bohr's presentiment before the Bomb came into existence and Brodie's insight just after.

Common sense told Brodie that a nuclear deterrent must, in order to deter, be highly capable. If it was to pose "the possibility of retaliation in kind," it must also be nearly invulnerable. But in a lifetime of thinking and writing on this subject, Brodie kept circling back to the point that he had made so forcefully in 1946: in a basic respect, nuclear weapons defied common sense; since the Bomb was a weapon too powerful and too unpredictable to use, it was an instrument not only of deterrence but also of *self*-deterrence.[4]

Paul Nitze was in the forefront of those who felt that Brodie's formulation of the problem failed to provide the United States with the basis for sound policy. He worried that self-deterrence might turn out to be self-defeat. Would both superpowers be self-deterred, or only the one that had the benefit of Brodie's wisdom? Brodie disavowed any interest in who would win a nuclear war. But what if the Soviets were less uninterested? How to make the threat of retaliation credible as a basis for deterrence if it was—inherently, existentially—*in*credible? Unless the United States was willing to follow through on that threat, was not even the one "useful purpose" that Brodie assigned to nuclear weapons itself dubious?

In short, must not the United States have an answer to another question that has reverberated through the strategic debate of the last forty years: What if deterrence fails? Embedded in Brodie's famous passage was a deeply pessimistic answer to that question. If, in the unpredictable and perhaps unmanageable course of what started as an orderly-sounding nuclear "exchange," the political and military authorities of one or both sides either were killed or lost their ability to transmit orders to their forces, conflict would become chaos, and chaos could lead to cataclysm. The world might be destroyed. In any event, there would be terrifying uncertainty about whether statecraft could intervene and stop the war in time to make peace, not to mention victory, possible.

Nitze was concerned that the Soviets would maintain their concept of victory. Unlike Brodie and the others who saw nuclear weapons as ushering in a new age—as representing a profound, merciful discontinuity in the history of warfare and therefore in the history of man—Nitze believed that nuclear weapons represented continuity. Despite what had happened at Hiroshima and Nagasaki, the world was still, in Nitze's view, governed by Karl von Clausewitz's famous maxim: War remained a means of pursuing policy by other means. Those means now included nuclear weapons. Surely the Soviets regarded them that way; and for purposes of deterring the Soviets, Americans must learn to see them that way, too.

Nitze objected to the vocabulary used by Brodie and other early theoreticians of deterrence. He found their choice of words symptomatic of sloppy thinking and a kind of morbid sentimentality. He believed that Brodie "let himself get mired down in words like 'absolute.' I don't believe in 'never'; I don't believe in 'inevitable,' and I don't believe in 'absolute weapons.' I think absolutist pronouncements lead to disaster."

Brodie's thesis was, in its essence, the assertion of a paradox: Nuclear weapons are too destructive to use. "My mind," Nitze once wrote, "shies away from straight contradiction or paradox. I still remain to be persuaded that contradiction is necessary.'' The very idea of paradox, said Nitze, whether ''in science or in humanity,'' offended his belief in the significance of reliable evidence and in the power of ''thought,'' ''will,'' and ''common sense.''

For his own thinking and discussion of the problems posed by nuclear weapons, Nitze preferred the vocabulary and intellectual methods of the hard sciences. Mathematics provided a large measure of certitude and left little room for ambiguity. As an antidote to whatever ambiguity or paradox survived the onslaughts of logic, he was intrigued by the theory of ''complementarity.'' This concept, developed by Niels Bohr, served originally to reconcile apparent contradictions in nuclear physics, such as the discovery that light can be described with equal accuracy as made up of waves and as made up of particles.

In 1953, in an address to his son Peter's graduating class at the Groton School, Nitze developed this theme. No doubt speaking well over the heads of the prep school seniors before him, he said that ''the complementarity of opposites''—''the concurrent application of complementary ideas which to our senses seem contradictory''—was a basic law of the universe, applicable to both physics and human affairs. Nearly a quarter-century later, Nitze resorted to similar terminology when he tried to articulate a credo for his life and thought: ''You have to follow Heraclitus' definition of truth: Truth and beauty are to be found in the tension between opposites. It is difficult for people to keep in mind the complementariness of opposing principles. They finally get tired of it and want something simpler.''[5]

His taste in music also reflected a desire to see order imposed on chaos and contradictions reconciled. His mother made him study piano as a child, and he took up the instrument again as an adult. His taste, both as an accomplished amateur pianist and as an avid concert-goer, ran to the ingenious way in which Johann Sebastian Bach reconciled great complexity with great tidiness and precision. All Nitze's life, he derived not just esthetic enjoyment but intellectual inspiration and emotional solace from Bach. In the busiest and most difficult days of 1987—when his wife was dying, and when diplomacy with the Soviet Union and internecine struggles between the State Department and the Pentagon were at fever pitch—Nitze slipped away from Washington to attend a Bach festival in Bethlehem, Pennsylvania. ''For me there's truth and beauty in the *order* of that music,'' he said. Bach was able to interweave melodies with the highly constrictive rules of baroque harmony and counterpoint—the musical equivalent of complementarity.

• • •

Niels Bohr had gone one step further in his own ruminations about complementarity than Paul Nitze seemed willing to go. The great physicist came to believe that the peril of nuclear weapons being used as instruments for waging war and the possibility of their very existence preventing their own use might be complementary. That idea anticipated Bernard Brodie's attempt to resolve the apparent contradiction between strategies for fighting war and doctrines for assuring deterrence, between the Bomb's twin identities as the absolute weapon and the absolutely unusable weapon.

For Nitze, Brodie's proposition had the effect not of resolving or overcoming ambiguity and paradox but of letting them have the upper hand, confounding reason and paralyzing will. Nitze resisted the notion that any physical phenomenon, especially one that could be exploited and measured by man, should inspire helplessness, awe, or fatalism. Moreover, he believed that Brodie's conclusion was "contrary to available evidence."

Nitze had firsthand familiarity with that evidence. When Brodie's *The Absolute Weapon* appeared in 1946, Nitze was vice-chairman of the U.S. Strategic Bombing Survey in the Pacific. The group had been formed two years before at the direction of the White House and supervised by the War Department. Its members were civilians, drawn mainly from the ranks of industry, business, and academia. Nitze had joined the survey because he was not getting along with his boss at the Foreign Economic Administration. The survey's charge was to conduct an impartial investigation of the role that American air power had played in bringing the Axis powers to their knees. The group traveled first to Europe, where it toured a number of heavily bombed German cities, then to Japan.

By the time he arrived at Hiroshima and Nagasaki, Nitze was already an experienced observer of what bombs could do. He had seen places in Germany where more people were killed by conventional explosives than by the A-bombs dropped on Japan. Nitze was one of the principal authors of a number of survey reports. "I'm proud of that work," he said nearly forty years later. "I think everything that I wrote there stands up today. Our task was to measure precisely the physical effects and other effects as well, to put calipers on it, instead of describing it in emotive terms. I was trying to put quantitative numbers on something that was considered immeasurable."

Nitze saw it as his task to demystify the Bomb, to treat it as another weapon rather than the Absolute Weapon. While others believed that nuclear weaponry was truly something new under the sun, Nitze believed that the measurements of the survey at Hiroshima and Nagasaki showed the effects to be roughly the equivalent of an incendiary bombing raid by 220 B-29s. The summary report of the Pacific Survey asked, then answered, a key question:

Does the existence of atomic bombs invalidate all conclusions relative to air power based on pre-atomic experience? It is the Survey's opinion that many of the pre-existing yardsticks are revolutionized, but that certain of the more basic principles and relationships remain. . . . Any attempt to produce war-decisive results through atomic bombing may encounter problems similar to those encountered in conventional bombing.

Nor did Nitze and his colleagues believe that the A-bombing of Hiroshima and Nagasaki had been "war-decisive": "It is the Survey's opinion that certainly prior to 31 December 1945, and in all probability prior to 1 November 1945, Japan would have surrendered even if the atomic bombs had not been dropped."

These two passages, along with reams of supporting data from the engineers, scientists, and doctors who made up the staff of the survey, did not endear the authors either to the leaders of the Air Force, who believed that a fleet of strategic bombers gave America a decisive and permanent edge in any future conflict, or to those theorists of nuclear weaponry who believed that the A-bomb had not only transformed the nature of war but made war obsolete. Nitze had little use for either group. One exaggerated the ability of nuclear-armed air power to win wars; the other, represented by Brodie, exaggerated the ability of nuclear weapons to deter wars.

While others had been stunned by the extent of the destruction in Hiroshima and Nagasaki, Nitze was impressed by the number of survivors, particularly in Nagasaki, where tunnel shelters provided reasonably effective protection, even at ground zero. He concluded that if the citizens had been warned, and if there had been more civil defense, many more would have survived. Buildings designed and constructed to withstand earthquakes had ridden out the shock waves. It seemed to him that the bombs had not broken the will of the populace to go on fighting. He noted that the regional government had issued a call for an "aroused fighting spirit to exterminate the devilish Americans."

Most subsequent analysis of the course of events within the Japanese government in August 1945 contradicted the survey's conclusion: The nuclear attack had indeed been "war-decisive." The very day after the attack on Nagasaki, the Japanese government issued a statement substantially agreeing to unconditional surrender. Whatever Nitze's eyes, instincts, and instruments told him on the scene, and whatever his report told the world, the Bomb had indeed ended the war. The question was whether it had ended *all* war between nuclear-armed states. Nitze's answer, then and later, was an emphatic "no"—or at least "not necessarily." He looked on Hiroshima and Nagasaki as a dramatization not so much of what must never again happen as of what could indeed happen again—something for which preparations must now be made.*

One of his recommendations in the survey report was that the United States initiate a civil defense program appropriate to the atomic age. Shortly after the war, when skyscrapers were sprouting up around New York, Nitze tried to persuade the city planner Robert Moses that there should be bomb shelters in all new buildings constructed in the future. Moses dismissed the suggestion. The American public was eager to put behind it the war that had just ended and to put out of its mind altogether the danger of another, far more horrible war in the future.

Nitze reluctantly came to accept Moses's reading of the popular mood, but the logic of civil defense remained compelling. He and his wife had a nineteen-hundred-acre estate, Causein Manor, in Charles County, Maryland, about forty-five minutes by car from Washington, or fifteen minutes by helicopter during his Pentagon days in the sixties. It was a working farm as well as a place for rest and recreation, and it was one of the great joys of his life. He loved overseeing the production of corn, soybeans, and wheat and raising cattle, pigs, and sheep. He loved gathering his four children—Heidi, Peter, William, and Nina—as well as other relatives and his many friends for vigorous, often athletic afternoons followed by wide-ranging, disputatious seminars on world affairs over long cocktail hours and sumptuous country meals. In addition to the barns, the stables, the bridle paths, the swimming pool, the tennis court, the beach house on the bank of the Potomac River, and the guest houses, the premises also included a bomb shelter, which for some years he kept well stocked with emergency provisions. When he was teased about the shelter by a friend who had come for the weekend, he remarked, "I want the Nitze children to be saved so that they can continue the human race." He did not seem to be entirely joking.

---

*In 1981, Nitze explained his difference with Brodie this way:

> Bernard Brodie took the view . . . that war in the nuclear age was *unthinkable* and that the whole purpose of policy must be solely and absolutely to avoid it. Our view in the U.S. Strategic Bombing Survey was more complex. We thought it highly desirable and highly probable that a capability to use nuclear weapons would deter any future war. . . . It was clear to all of us who were working on the problem that deterrence would emerge as the important concept for policymaking. However, we qualified this concept on three different points: a) deterrence could not be wholly counted on to succeed; b) policy had to be prepared to deal with the contingency that deterrence might fail, and c) the quality of deterrence depended upon one's ability to deal with the potential failure of deterrence. The vital factor is that one's ability to deal with the contingency of deterrence failing be understood by the other side.
>
> In preparing contingency policies we thought that, while much had changed from the pre-nuclear era, the basic principles of military strategy were not entirely laid to waste. They were deeply modified, but they still should play a major role in the development of military strategy in the nuclear era. . . . A warfighting capability is needed in order to have reliable deterrence.[6]

Two Men on a Train

It was a prevailing belief on the right in the early 1980s that the Soviet challenge and the required American response were both essentially military: The Soviet Union threatened American interests with its armed forces, and the United States must protect itself and its allies by building up its own armed strength. Nuclear weapons were integral to both halves of the equation: the Soviets might, if they felt they could get away with it, use their conventional military superiority, backed by nuclear weapons, to exert political pressure and perhaps even to commit aggression; therefore the United States must be prepared to retaliate.

An opposing view held that the possibility of nuclear war was a threat distinct from, although obviously related to, that of Soviet intimidation and aggression. The greatest peril was not that the Soviet Union would start a war but that the military and political competition between the superpowers would get out of hand and the two nuclear-armed giants would stumble together into catastrophe. The challenge, many believed, was therefore not so much to strengthen the American arsenal through a military buildup as to reduce the risk of war through Soviet-American cooperation in keeping the military competition under control. That meant largely arms control.

By 1980, the year that Ronald Reagan won election to the presidency, the basic issue of whether to give priority to an American defense buildup or to Soviet-American arms control was highly polarized, and the opposing sides were personified by Paul Nitze and George F. Kennan.

By then Kennan was one of the nation's most respected scholars and statesmen. He was the leading light of the American Committee on East-West Accord. While the Reagan Administration in general and Nitze in particular placed virtually the entire blame for the threat of nuclear war on the other superpower, the committee accepted, on behalf of the United States, a shared responsibility both for the problem and for the compromises that would be necessary to achieve a solution. In the Reagan era, the Committee on East-West Accord stood for the loyal opposition. Not a single one of its nearly three hundred members—many of them distinguished citizens and former government officials—joined the Administration when it came into office in 1981.

Kennan was three years older than Nitze. They had been friends and colleagues at the State Department in the late forties, until they fell out over some of the same issues that would divide them, and the country, in the eighties. On November 13, 1986, Nitze was among the guests who gathered at the Smithsonian Institution in Washington for a black-tie dinner to honor

Kennan. Two hours earlier, Nitze had been hard at work at the State Department, a few blocks away, helping Secretary of State George Shultz prepare for an upcoming round of negotiations with the Soviets; Kennan had come down from Princeton, New Jersey. In a speech opening the ceremonies, Shultz used the occasion to praise not only the guest of honor, Kennan, but Nitze as well. Shultz cited Nitze's place at his side as proof of the continuity between the Reagan Administration and the earliest, wisest counsels of the postwar era. During the elegant dinner and the gracious toasts, everyone was eager to link Nitze and Kennan to a single tradition of public service. Nitze and Kennan themselves recalled the beginning of their friendship over forty years before, inquired after each other's health, and exchanged assurances that, despite all, they had never been all that far apart on the important issues.*

In fact, they were, and had been for decades, very far apart indeed on the most important issues of the age. Kennan, like Brodie, saw the Bomb as revolutionary in its impact, ushering in a new era in which war was no longer an option for either the United States or the Soviet Union. He was appalled by what Nitze called "the Strategic Bombing Survey point of view." As for the Soviet Union, Kennan came to champion the hope that new realities of international politics, conspicuously including the Bomb, would effectively temper the inherent Soviet impulses toward expansion. On that score, too, he and Nitze were polar opposites in the great strategic debate.

But they had started out close together. In fact, Kennan had helped inculcate in Nitze's mind the image of the Soviet Union as a menace that must be countered by military as well as political means. The two men had first met by chance on a train in 1944, during World War II. Nitze was then based in Washington, supervising overseas procurement for the Federal Economic Administration, although he would soon be going abroad with the Strategic Bombing Survey. Kennan was the number two American diplomat in Moscow, deputy to Ambassador Averell Harriman; he had returned to the United States for consultations. Nitze and Kennan fell into conversation on subjects in which both were deeply interested: Communist Russia and the prospects for Soviet-American relations after the war. Nitze was eager to hear the impressions of someone who had studied Stalinist Russia firsthand.

Kennan had come home, as he recalled, "to impress on Washington the full ugliness of what we were up against." He did not regard Stalin as

---

*On May 8, 1987, Kennan again came down from Princeton and Nitze again took time off from his work at the State Department. They met for a lunch in honor of Marshall Shulman, a fellow veteran of the Truman Administration with whom Nitze had sharply disagreed over the years. That occasion was sponsored by the American Committee on East-West Accord, only as a sign of the times the group had now changed its name to the American Committee on U.S.-Soviet Relations—"accord," it was felt, had an unfashionable and even accommodationist ring.

"Uncle Joe" or accept the wishful thinking, then widespread in the West, that America's wartime alliance with Stalin would flow smoothly into post-war cooperation. He believed, as he put it then and later, that the Soviet Union was "run by a bunch of thugs" and that Stalin would be "big trouble" after the war.

Thus, Nitze's long and complex relationship with Kennan began on a note of shared concern about the Soviet threat and doubts about America's ability to muster a hard-headed—and, if necessary, hard-hitting—response. Kennan was, in those days, far more militant than most of his countrymen on the issue of the Soviet threat, but not more than his new acquaintance. As Kennan recalled somewhat ruefully many years later, "Perhaps I spoke too eloquently to Paul during our chance encounter on the train."[7]

Whatever Kennan said to Nitze on the train, and however he may have regretted it later, it was not a momentary outburst. It was a sustained, heartfelt message, one that Nitze accepted at the time and continued to believe long after Kennan had modified it to the point of repudiation.

After the war, when Nitze was in Japan pondering the effects of the Bomb, Kennan was still in Moscow, pondering the behavior of the U.S.S.R. By 1946, events seemed to have caught up with his wartime warnings to Washington. Stalin was determined to establish Soviet domination over Eastern Europe. While the other allies were demobilizing, the Red Army set out to incorporate into the Soviet empire the nations that it had supposedly liberated from the Nazis. Soviet expansionism was the casus belli of the Cold War, just as it would be the principal concern of American foreign policy in the 1980s. Ambassador Harriman hurried home to alert the new American President, Harry Truman, to the "barbarian invasion of Europe."

In February 1946, Stalin delivered a speech providing what some read as strong evidence for the suspicion that the Soviet Union would unleash World War III the moment it felt it could get away with it. Stalin was addressing a meeting on the eve of elections to the Supreme Soviet. A comparison of what he actually said with what people in the West understood him to mean offers a paradigm of Soviet-American relations: One side conjures up the worst case of what might happen; the other side interprets that worst case to confirm its own most alarming reckoning of the enemy's intentions. Stalin was speaking about the outcome of World War II and the prospects for the postwar period. He cited Lenin's thesis that "military catastrophes" are inevitable, given the nature of international capitalism and imperialism. Even with the Great Patriotic War now behind them, the Soviet people must be prepared for the possibility of future wars instigated by the enemy camp; it was necessary to reconstruct the Soviet Union's economy and rebuild its strength in order to "guarantee the homeland against all possible contingencies."

Some Soviets who listened to Stalin's speech on the radio recall putting their heads in their hands. The postwar period would entail prewar privation. It was, in a sense, Stalin's own opening salvo of the Cold War, and it came a month before Winston Churchill's "Iron Curtain" speech in Fulton, Missouri.

At the time, Nitze took Stalin's ominous references to "all possible contingencies" as a military threat. Nitze called on his friend James Forrestal, then secretary of the navy, and said the speech was "a delayed declaration of war against the United States." Forrestal agreed, but warned that no one else in the executive branch did. So Nitze discovered. The under secretary of state, Dean Acheson, accused him of "just seeing mirages."[8]

In his own reading of Stalin's speech, George Kennan saw something more than a mirage, though something less than a threat of war. That same month, February 1946, apologizing "in advance for this burdening of telegraphic channel," Kennan composed what became famous as the Long Telegram. In Kennan's view, the sources of Soviet conduct could best be understood in terms of psychopathology: "At [the] bottom of [the] Kremlin's neurotic view of world affairs is [a] traditional and instinctive Russian sense of insecurity." He stressed that "Soviet power, unlike that of Hitlerite Germany, is neither schematic nor adventuristic. It does not work by fixed plans." He warned that "hysterical anti-Sovietism" would only stir up Soviet paranoia, the source of so much Soviet misconduct. He prescribed a remedy that was indirect and largely nonmilitary: "World Communism is like [a] malignant parasite which feeds only on diseased tissue." Therefore, the United States should concentrate on restoring to health those nations on which Stalin, and his successors, might otherwise prey. Read in retrospect, the last passage of the telegram is especially rich in presentiments of debates that would flare in later years—and of Kennan's own position in those debates: "Finally we must have courage and self-confidence to cling to our own methods and conceptions of human society. After all, the greatest danger that can befall us in coping with this problem of Soviet Communism, is that we shall allow ourselves to become like those with whom we are coping."

The implication was that the United States should not necessarily fight fire with fire; it should not let itself be drawn into a military confrontation or even necessarily into a peacetime arms race. Significantly, nowhere in the five-thousand-odd words of his cable to Washington was there any mention of the atomic bomb, either as a means available to the United States for making the Soviet Union behave or in any other context. Kennan was trying to promote the revitalization of his own craft, diplomacy, as the best instrument for dealing with the paranoiacs in the Kremlin.

But in the early months of 1946, cables from Moscow were not read for their nuances. Kennan's depiction of the Soviet Union as a dangerous enemy was by now far more compatible with the mood in Washington than his earlier warnings had been. The Long Telegram had a sensational impact on the thinking of his superiors and on Kennan's career. Harriman sent the cable to Forrestal, who was already Nitze's promoter and now became Kennan's as well. Forrestal made sure that President Truman read the dispatch. The White House counsel, Clark Clifford, used the document as the basis of an influential paper he wrote for the President, outlining the coming U.S.-Soviet confrontation. Kennan became the man of the hour. He was recalled to Washington to serve as the first deputy commandant for foreign affairs at the National War College.

One of his fellow civilians on the faculty was Bernard Brodie, and the two men spent many hours talking. Kennan agreed with Brodie that the atomic bomb did not, in the traditional sense, even qualify as a weapon, but he was less hopeful than Brodie that the bomb could serve as an instrument of deterrence. Kennan feared that the continuing existence of nuclear weapons would, over time, no longer stimulate elegant and salutary ruminations like Brodie's. Instead, as Kennan later recalled, "I saw a realm of confusion and possibly horror looming up if this new military technology became a matter of competition. I came away from my time at the War College feeling that we must regard this discovery as a freak or aberration, and we must not let it get into our calculations and into our competition with the Soviets. If we embedded nuclear weaponry into the structure of our armed forces, we would continually have to plan for two contingencies: one in which nuclear weapons could, and might, be used; the other, in which they couldn't be used, so conventional weapons would have to make the difference. There would be a kind of permanent schizophrenia in our thinking about defense, and it would make it almost impossible for us to develop a coherent strategic concept."[9]

Quite simply, Kennan was not prepared to accept nuclear weapons as an integral feature of the modern military arsenal or a permanent part of the human condition. He was hoping that this "freak or aberration" would come to be seen as such, and that the attendant "confusion and horror" would somehow lead to its being throttled in the cradle.

In 1947 the rivalry between the United States and the Soviet Union was still driven by the political dynamics and military technology of the pre-nuclear era. The implication of the A-bomb for the future was a stimulating topic for discussion at the War College, but at the State Department there was more concern with the immediate task of rebuilding a Europe that had been devastated by the infantry divisions, the tank columns, and the heavy artillery of Hitler. Stalin commanded similar forces and thus posed a similar threat. It was to the task of meeting that threat that Kennan was soon assigned as the founding director of the State Department's newly created Policy Planning Staff.

The unit was set up largely because of growing anxiety about the Soviet

Union. During the war, General George Marshall had been among those who were willing to grant Stalin the benefit of the doubt and to believe that Soviet uncooperativeness "stemmed from the necessity of maintaining security."[10] Now, however, as secretary of state, Marshall, like so many others, was disillusioned and alarmed. He returned from a conference of foreign ministers in Moscow in late April 1947 convinced that the Soviets would be causing trouble in many ways and in many places, particularly Western Europe, for a long time to come.

So Kennan had long been warning. The issue of nuclear weaponry, still in its infancy and still exclusively in American hands, seemed incidental both to the Soviet threat and to the American response. On Marshall's first day back in Washington he summoned Kennan and asked him to establish and head the new office. Forrestal, still secretary of the navy but soon to become the nation's first secretary of defense, had been pushing Kennan for the job. Forrestal looked to Kennan as a personal advisor on Soviet affairs. Now Kennan would serve the same function in a more formal capacity for the secretary of state. As director of Policy Planning, with an office a conference room away from Marshall's, Kennan was uniquely positioned to provide intellectual guidance for the struggle ahead.

Without fully intending to do so, and in a way that he came later to regret, Kennan gave an added impetus to the growing tendency to see that struggle in military terms. In July 1947, an article appeared under the byline "X" in *Foreign Affairs*. It was the worst-kept secret of the foreign policy establishment that summer that the author was Kennan. He had sent a signed draft of the article to Forrestal; Arthur Krock of *The New York Times* saw it in Forrestal's office and recognized the anonymous version when it later appeared in print, so the identity of Mr. X soon became known. In rewriting the Long Telegram, Kennan sharpened its more militant points and blunted the cautionary ones. He inserted one sentence, with one word in particular, that would reverberate through American policy in the coming decades, and through the rest of his life: "It is clear that the main element of any United States policy toward the Soviet Union must be that of a long-term, patient but firm and vigilant containment of Russian expansive tendencies."

Kennan had undertaken the article, and the Long Telegram on which it was based, largely to counteract the tendency of others to oversimplify the Soviet threat. Yet he soon came to feel that his own idea of containment lent itself to dangerous oversimplification. He had second thoughts about his contribution to the intellectual arsenal of the postwar era much as a number of the nuclear physicists developed something close to remorse, or at least ambivalence, about their participation in the Manhattan Project. Kennan later insisted that he had meant neither that the means of Soviet expansion would necessarily be military nor that the means of Western containment should be military; rather, in both cases, the arena of competition should be primarily political, and one of the principal means of containing the Soviet Union should be the industrial and economic rebuilding of Europe.*

For just that reason, Kennan wanted Nitze, who had recently turned forty, to be his deputy on the Policy Planning Staff. Nitze was then working on economic affairs for the State Department as deputy director of the Office of International Trade Policy. He had taken that unexalted post after the war rather then accepting an attractive invitation to return to Wall Street in partnership with the tycoon John Hay Whitney. Kennan felt that Nitze's knowledge of international economics would be useful in what became the Marshall Plan.

But Under Secretary of State Acheson, who had so disparaged Nitze's alarm about the Stalin speech of a year earlier, now blocked his appointment as deputy director of Policy Planning. During the war, when Nitze had been with the Foreign Economic Administration, he had clashed several times with the State Department, which tried from time to time to secure diplomatic and military cooperation with other countries by offering them economic inducements. For example, when the United States wanted basing rights in Iceland, the State Department asked Nitze to designate Icelandic fish exports as strategic raw material for the war effort. Nitze refused, and believed that Acheson bore a grudge against him: "Dean thought I was a Wall Street operator, not the kind of deep thinker he wanted."

Also in 1947, largely because of his prominent role in the Strategic Bombing Survey, Nitze was mentioned as a possible candidate to be the nation's first secretary of the air force. But he lost out—for reasons of partisan politics, he believed. In those days he was a registered Republican, and the Truman White House decided to give the post to a Democrat, Stuart Symington, who had been serving as assistant secretary of war for aviation.[12]

The Super

In March 1949, George Kennan toured Germany, a country in which he had once lived and for which he had great affection. While Nitze's own visit to Germany in the 1930s had given him a glimpse into the evil of totalitarianism, Kennan's provided him with a vivid appreciation of the horror of all-

---

*Like almost every other aspect of the Cold War and its origins, Kennan's role has been the object of intense scrutiny and debate. Some scholars and commentators have argued that he engaged in a certain amount of revisionism with regard to his own thinking. They have contended that he protested too much and that he was a more witting contributor to the militant mentality of the postwar years than he has acknowledged in his memoirs and other writings.[11]

out war. Germany was still grotesquely scarred by Allied bombing. Kennan wrote in his notes from "poor old Hamburg":

> Here, for the first time, I felt an unshakable conviction that no momentary military advantage—even if such could have been calculated to exist—could have justified this stupendous, careless destruction of civilian life and of material values, built up laboriously by human hands over the course of centuries for purposes having nothing to do with war. Least of all could it have been justified by the screaming *non sequitur*: "They did it to us."

These sentiments, which implicitly repudiated the doctrine of nuclear retaliation, could hardly have been a more dramatic contrast to Nitze's ruminations on the wreckage of Hiroshima and Nagasaki. In his memoirs, Kennan added, "These were thoughts that were to pursue me into the trials and problems of future years."[13]

There seemed to be, in the late 1940s, an opportunity for American self-restraint. Even as the United States was perfecting and stockpiling atomic bombs, some American scientists believed it possible to develop a much more powerful weapon, based on a different principle of physics—the fusion of hydrogen atoms rather than the fission of uranium or plutonium atoms. The need for a so-called Super was less compelling as long as the United States alone had the absolute weapon. But all that changed suddenly in August 1949, five months after Kennan's visit to Germany. The Soviets set off their own fission explosion. American aircraft detected radioactivity from the blast. U.S. intelligence officials were stunned and embarrassed; they had believed the Soviets were at least two years away from having an atomic device.

For Americans, the intellectual and political challenge of living with the Bomb became much more complicated. Communism was an actual evil. It was oppressing and killing people every day. Moreover, Communism was an alien evil; it was over there, half a globe away. Nuclear weapons were a potential evil, and until now, one over which Americans had had proprietary control. It was true that American A-bombs had killed many thousands of Japanese, but they were casualties of a war in which the United States felt itself to be in the right. Even when nuclear weaponry was still in its infancy, Americans could look ahead and see that the Bomb might turn out to be the greatest evil of all, especially if it ever ended up in the wrong hands. In August 1949, with the test of "Joe 1," it came into the wrong hands.

The months that followed the first Soviet A-bomb explosion were also a turning point in the careers of George Kennan and Paul Nitze, and in the relationship between them. Kennan had greater doubts than ever about the wisdom of hostility toward the Soviet Union. "My message," he recalled, "was: 'It is a horrible regime in Moscow, but they know their limitations;

Stalin is a realist. We can deal with the Soviets.' That message was rejected by Washington the way a human body rejects a transplant.''[14]

In addition to resisting the development of the hydrogen bomb, Kennan recommended that as a first step toward nuclear disarmament, the United States should renounce its doctrine of keeping open the option of initiating use of the A-bomb. On the critical issue of whether to proceed with research and development of the H-bomb, Kennan had the support of J. Robert Oppenheimer, a consultant to the Policy Planning Staff, as well as other scientists who were then working on atomic weapons.

Oppenheimer's arguments against the Super in some respects anticipated some of those that would be used against SDI in the eighties. It would not work; it would divert resources from more promising and necessary military programs; and even if it did work, the Soviets would surely acquire one of their own, with the result of a new and dangerous dimension of the arms race. Oppenheimer argued the converse, too: if the United States showed restraint and resisted the temptation to develop the H-bomb, the Soviets would not try to build it either. At the root of his position was a moral conviction: the H-bomb, because it would be more destructive than the A-bomb, was an even worse instrument of genocide.

Oppenheimer's principal scientific adversary was Edward Teller, who thirty years later helped plant the idea of SDI in the mind of Ronald Reagan by offering arguments similar to those that he used in the late forties and early fifties on behalf of the H-bomb.

Oppenheimer and Teller were at opposite ends of the ideological spectrum, and some of the differences between them were rooted in their backgrounds. Oppenheimer's political awakening had come in the 1930s as he observed Communists opposing Nazism in Germany and fascism in Italy and Spain; he was on the fringes of the American left before the war and inclined to take a more tolerant view of the Soviet Union afterward. He saw the principal postwar threat as the power of the atom that he had been so instrumental in unleashing.

Teller, by contrast, was born and raised in Hungary, whose huge neighbor, Russia, was an enemy during World War I. As a child, he had witnessed the brief but brutal reign of a home-grown Hungarian Communist tyranny in 1919. Teller came to America in 1935, but some of his relatives remained behind and suffered under the Stalinist puppet regime that was imposed on Hungary after World War II. While Oppenheimer, Szilard, and other physicists were eager to close up shop at Los Alamos and return to teaching and pure research, Teller felt that the work of the Manhattan Project had just begun. There had merely been a shift in focus from one set of enemies, Germany and Japan, to another, Russia and the Communist world—and from one objective, the A-bomb, to another, more powerful weapon, the Super.

Teller had a strong proprietary interest in the H-bomb, since he had been one of the first to conceive of a fusion explosion and had pushed the idea hard when his colleagues and superiors chose to concentrate instead on the development of a fission weapon. After the Soviets exploded their own atomic device, Teller redoubled his effort to promote a thermonuclear weapon that could be hundreds of times more powerful. He saw the Super as a way of trumping Joe 1 much as SDI would later be a way of trumping the Soviet Strategic Rocket Forces.

Teller was a man of ferocious tenacity, overwhelming persuasive skills, and immense knowledge. He was the ultimate technological enthusiast. During the debate over the H-bomb in late 1949, Teller made one of his frequent visits to Washington. He sat Nitze down in front of a blackboard and, in a few hours, explained to him two alternative methods that he believed would succeed in setting off a thermonuclear explosion.

Both men set aside the issue of whether the Super would be good or bad for humanity. They concentrated on the question: Would it work? Contrary to what Oppenheimer was telling the Policy Planning Staff, Teller was sure that the answer was yes. Nitze prided himself on his ability to "take a brief"; and as he saw it, this was the ideal briefing, from an expert who confined himself to his field of expertise.

Nitze once described the attributes necessary for sound political judgment as a combination of "a truly humanistic background with a sense for relevant facts and an intense care for the significant details." On this occasion, Teller provided what Nitze considered the significant details. "Teller was a great expositor of a chain of ideas," he recalled. Oppenheimer, by contrast, "had gone beyond being a scientist to waging a peculiar battle. He justified his position by improper presentation of scientific facts. He was queering the science to sell a political idea, and on politics Oppenheimer was no better than any other citizen. In fact, some of his ideas were for the birds. On the questions of physics and engineering, Teller had him beaten hands down, because he concentrated on the issue of doable technology."[15]

The merits of the purely scientific dispute between Oppenheimer and Teller were less clearly in Teller's favor than Nitze believed at the time, or than he recalled thirty-seven years later. The ideas with which Teller dazzled Nitze on the blackboard were not so impressive to his fellow scientists; he had not in fact proved that the H-bomb was "doable" at all. The most perplexing question of physics and engineering at that time was how to use a small nuclear fission reaction to generate enough heat to trigger a large-scale thermonuclear fusion of hydrogen atoms. In late 1949, regardless of what he was able to persuade Nitze was possible, Teller and the other scientists working on the project were almost a year and a half away from establishing that the technology of the Super was indeed "doable."

As with so many other disputes over whether to proceed with new weapon systems, there were respectable scientists and plausible-sounding scientific arguments to support conflicting positions. Laymen gravitated toward those experts who supported their political predispositions. In that respect, too, the debate over the Super foreshadowed the debate over SDI. Teller's message corresponded with Nitze's belief that within certain limits, man could control his destiny; that problems, such as those of fission triggers for fusion bombs, could be solved; and that the United States had better stay at least one jump ahead of the Soviet Union.

Kennan, meanwhile, was on Oppenheimer's side in the controversy over the Super, also for essentially ethical reasons: Here was a technology that confronted mankind with the prospect of devastation far worse than what had been visited on Hiroshima and Nagasaki, not to mention ''poor old Hamburg.'' Kennan's view of the Soviet personality influenced him deeply in opposing the Super. He saw the men in the Kremlin as paranoid and insecure, and he believed that an American H-bomb would only make them more so, and therefore all the more dangerous.

Kennan's prescribed treatment for Soviet paranoia was for the United States to exercise restraint in hopes that the Soviet Union would follow suit. This growing predisposition toward disarmament-by-example soon put him at odds with Dean Acheson, who had now replaced the ailing George Marshall as secretary of state.

Meanwhile, Nitze had been accumulating experience, confidence, and standing. As an economic advisor to the State Department, he had been an effective and hard-working advocate of the Marshall Plan. A Democratic Administration succeeded in winning the support of a Congress controlled by the other party, largely by wooing Senator Arthur Vandenberg, a prominent Republican, into carrying the banner of bipartisanship and thus helping overcome the resistance of his conservative, isolationist colleagues. ''I lost fifteen pounds during the course of that battle,'' Nitze later recalled.[16] It was a battle on behalf of Atlanticism—the proposition that the United States had special obligations with regard to Western Europe—and it was one that he would fight for the rest of his career.

In May and June 1949, Nitze was at Acheson's side in a slogging negotiation with Stalin's foreign minister, Andrei Vyshinsky, during a conference in Paris. Nitze advised the new secretary of state on the complex and politically sensitive question of currency as it related to the future of two divided nations, Germany and Austria. This experience gave Nitze an early taste of dealing directly with Soviet officials (he was struck, as he often would be again, by their competence, intelligence, and tactical skill), and it gave Acheson a chance to revise his opinion of Nitze at a time when he was growing restless with Kennan. In the summer of 1949, Acheson appointed Nitze to the job from which he had blocked him two years before—deputy director of Policy Planning.

Acheson now considered Kennan too much of an ivory-tower intellectual and moralist to cope with a world in which things were suddenly going badly. Not only did the Soviet Union explode its own atomic bomb in August 1949, abruptly ending the American monopoly, but in a single week in early October the Soviets dramatized their determination to keep Germany divided by creating the German Democratic Republic and Mao Zedong's Communist forces completed their conquest of the Chinese mainland. The loss of China was one of the first losses, and certainly the biggest loss, of a Third World country to what then seemed the monolithic enemy camp.

In the wake of the first Soviet bomb test and Chiang Kai-shek's rout from the Chinese mainland, Acheson asked Kennan and Nitze each to spend a weekend pondering the significance of these events and, in Nitze's words, "the long-range future of our requirements in the nuclear-defense field." When they reassembled the following Monday, all three men had put their thoughts in writing.

Acheson and Nitze found that their views were almost identical. "Both of us," said Nitze, "had come to the conclusion that over time, the Soviets would persist in developing nuclear weapons and the technology associated with them. The gap between the two sides would get narrower and narrower, and, accordingly, any benefit we could derive from our nuclear weapons would diminish. Therefore the United States had two requirements: We had been totally improvident in the way we had demobilized after the war, so we must restore the balance."[17]

Kennan's weekend ruminations had resulted in a paper that struck a quite different theme: the "corrupting" influence of America's reliance on nuclear weapons now that the Soviet Union had them too. He had concluded that weapons of mass destruction could serve no constructive military or political purpose and that the only sensible course was to subject them to international control.[18]

Nitze found Kennan's weekend paper brilliantly written but profoundly wrong: "an oversimplification of considerable proportions; it was the basis in thought for self-deterrence in the name of mutual deterrence." Nitze believed that what mattered about the A-bomb was not whether it should exist but that it did exist, now in Soviet hands as well as American; therefore the United States had to make sure that its atomic arsenal, like the rest of its military forces, was sufficient to deter and, if necessary, defeat the U.S.S.R. As for the H-bomb, the question was not whether it should exist but that it *could* exist. As the unpleasant surprise of the Soviet A-bomb demonstrated, while many in the United States were, like Kennan, considering high-minded unilateral steps toward nuclear disarmament, the Soviet Union was on a crash program of nuclear armament. Therefore, the United States must have the Super if it was technologically possible.

Acheson was at first less certain, but he moved toward Nitze's side of the argument. "How can you persuade a paranoid adversary to disarm by example?'' he asked. He felt that the way to look at the U.S.S.R. was through the prism of ideology, not psychology: ''The threat to Western Europe seemed to me singularly like that which Islam had posed centuries before, with its combination of ideological zeal and fighting power.''[19] Acheson recommended to Truman that the United States proceed with the Super, and Truman agreed.

But the President, too, felt torn between the imperatives of having the weapon and of never using it. In an impromptu remark recorded by one of his aides on the day he gave the go-ahead for the H-bomb, Truman said: ''We have got to have it if only for bargaining purposes with the Russians.''[20] That comment suggested that Truman was the first of an unbroken series of Presidents, including Ronald Reagan more than thirty years later, who almost instinctively groped for ways to justify the ultimate instruments of war as part of a larger strategy for peace, a strategy that went beyond deterrence to embrace at least the idea of accommodation with the U.S.S.R.

Like so many American military systems that would follow, including SDI, the hydrogen bomb came into existence for a combination of reasons: first, because it was there, it could be done; second, because anything the United States *could* do the Soviets undoubtedly *would* do, and therefore it was something the United States *should* do; and third (last and usually least), because it might give the United States bargaining leverage in diplomatic efforts to avoid war and curb the military competition. The final reason has been a uniquely American afterthought: The distasteful decision to go forward with these weapons becomes somewhat more palatable, to Presidents and public alike, if couched in terms not of war or even of deterrence but of the active search for political and military stability.

In collaboration with other scientists, especially Stanislaw Ulam, Teller eventually solved the problem of how to trigger a fusion explosion, a breakthrough that Oppenheimer acknowledged was ''technically so sweet that you could not argue.'' The United States set off a thermonuclear device at Eniwetok Atoll in the Marshall Islands on November 1, 1952. It had a yield of over ten megatons, or the equivalent of ten million tons of TNT, nearly a thousand times as powerful as the A-bomb that had devastated Hiroshima. The Soviet Union followed with a test of its own in August 1953, but the design was primitive and the resulting blast was only a fraction of the American one. Neither of these huge and cumbersome mechanisms could be loaded easily into the bombers then in service. Not until March 1954 did the United States set off a real bomb at Bikini Atoll in the Pacific. The first true Soviet H-bomb test came in late 1955.

Kennan had clearly seen the danger of the arms race. He had urged that the United States call it off before it began. Nitze, by contrast, foresaw the arms race and accepted its inevitability, urging that the United States make sure that it stay ahead, or at least not fall behind. On the central issue that divided them in late 1949—whether the United States should build the H-bomb—Nitze established himself, in the eyes of the secretary of state and the President, as a hard-headed realist. He replaced Kennan not just as director of Policy Planning but as a man of the hour.

Kennan soon went on an extended fact-finding tour of Latin America, then left the government to settle, on the invitation of Oppenheimer, at the Institute for Advanced Study at Princeton. "On leaving the service," Kennan recalled, "I was psychically healthy; I would go on with my life. But I regarded myself as defeated. Paul never accepted the premise that I have always started from, and that is that there is no defense against nuclear weapons, therefore once both sides had them, there was no use for them. Paul regarded the atomic bomb as the decisive weapon, whether used or not used, since it could provide the basis for nuclear blackmail. I did not believe, and never have believed, in the reality of nuclear blackmail. These people—and Paul was one of them—would have their way. I didn't expect any good to come of it."[21]

CHAPTER 2

The Cartesian Pessimist

Paul Nitze took over the directorship of the Policy Planning Staff on January 1, 1950, the first day of a new decade that seemed destined to be a time of troubles. China was lost; so was the American monopoly of the Bomb. The Cold War was on; so was the search for scapegoats and spies. The junior senator from Wisconsin, Joseph McCarthy, was on the rise, and the Truman Administration, especially the State Department, was on the defensive. Alger Hiss—a prominent department official and friend of Dean Acheson's who had been accused of membership in an underground Communist organization in the thirties—was convicted of perjury on January 21 and sentenced to five years in prison.

February brought even more bad news. The British arrested for espionage Klaus Fuchs, a scientist who had worked on the Manhattan Project and had been passing American atomic secrets to the Soviets; Stalin and Mao Zedong signed a treaty that seemed to confirm the monolithic nature of international Communism; Joseph McCarthy delivered a speech in Wheeling, West Virginia, accusing the Truman Administration of harboring Communists.

For many reasons, the secretary of state felt a strong impulse to prove that on the central issue of meeting the Soviet challenge, the Administration he served and the department he headed were prepared to take tough measures in dealing with an aggressive, perfidious, and now nuclear-armed Soviet Union. Nitze was an important agent of that impulse. He had been among those who recommended an interagency study of the Soviet challenge. When Harry Truman directed that the State and Defense departments review "our objectives in peace and war . . . in the light of the probable fission bomb capability and possible thermonuclear bomb capability of the Soviet Union," Nitze led the effort.

For two months in early 1950, February and March, he chaired a State-Defense committee that reviewed documents, interviewed experts, and drafted a report. In early April, the document went to Truman by way of the National Security Council and was designated NSC 68. It contained a stark diagnosis of the nation's strategic ills, and it prescribed strong medicine: Peace must now be waged in much the same way that war had been waged in the past—by amassing and deploying military power. Never before had America maintained a large and expensive defense establishment in peacetime. It must do so now.

Dean Acheson wrote in his memoirs, *Present at the Creation,* that the purpose of NSC 68 was "to so bludgeon the mass mind of 'top government' that not only could the President make a decision but that the decision could be carried out." Like the campaign on behalf of the Marshall Plan, the preparation of NSC 68 was an occasion for a gathering of some of the citizen-statesmen who had, as the title of Acheson's memoirs suggested, helped create the postwar world order. Robert Lovett, who had served as an assistant secretary of war in the Truman Administration and was now a banker in New York, flew to Washington to assist Nitze by giving a pep talk to the committee that was preparing NSC 68: "We are now in a war worse than we have ever experienced. It is not a cold war. It is a hot war. The only difference is that death comes more slowly and in a different fashion."

Nitze himself told the group to "hit it hard." One of his favorite phrases was "getting from here to there."* Whatever the destination, Nitze sought to lay out the path in a series of logical steps. In doing so, he often relied heavily, both in his own thinking and in the way he tried to persuade others, on a vivid warning about another path, the one that would lead to disaster if the nation did not follow his advice. He spoke of a "logic chain": If A occurs, then B will occur, then C will follow as night follows day. A might be something bad, B something worse, and C a catastrophe. Once he had established where the logic chain led, Nitze asked himself: What was the "billboard effect"? What was the headline, the lead paragraph, on a necessarily complicated presentation? The result, in the case of NSC 68, was a highly classified manifesto that was intended to grab its few readers by the scruff of the neck and shake them, so that they would then go out and rouse the nation.[1]

NSC 68 portrayed the Soviet Union in a far more dismaying light than had Kennan's Long Telegram. Kennan had emphasized the neurotic, paranoid, fundamentally defensive roots of Soviet conduct; NSC 68 stressed the offensive nature of the threat. Kennan denied that the Soviet Union had a "schematic" plan for conquest. NSC 68 took a very different view:

> The Kremlin is inescapably militant . . . because it possesses, and is possessed by, a worldwide revolutionary movement, because it is the inheritor of Russian imperialism, and because it is a totalitarian dictatorship. . . . [It] requires a dynamic extension of authority and the ultimate elimination of any effective opposition. . . . [The United States]

Getting from Here to There: Papers on National Security was the title Nitze chose for an unpublished collection of his writings.

is the principal enemy whose integrity and vitality must be subverted or destroyed. . . . if the Kremlin is to achieve its fundamental design.

The author of the Long Telegram had seen the challenge as long-term and essentially political; NSC 68 depicted it as near-term and potentially military. Kennan had written, "Gauged against [the] Western World as a whole, [the] Soviets are still by far the weaker force"; that assessment had been widely shared, as had the assumption that the Soviet Union would not start a war except by miscalculation. Nitze and his colleagues disagreed. They saw the West as disarming itself in the face of a Bear still armed to the teeth; the West, if not in Spenglerian decline, then was at least in a foolhardy rush to put the last war behind it without thinking enough about the next war. If adverse trends continued, they concluded, the Soviet Union would soon be able to attack the West—and might very well be inclined to do so.

NSC 68 was an early example of what came to be known as threat inflation. Briefers from the Air Force and the still-infant Central Intelligence Agency told Nitze and his committee in early 1950 that the Soviets could have ten or twenty atomic bombs later that year, one hundred by 1953, and two hundred by 1955. There were estimates that roughly twenty bombs could inflict a knockout blow, putting the United States out of a war. The Joint Chiefs of Staff submitted a paper to Nitze's group warning of "a new type of Pearl Harbor attack of infinitely greater magnitude than that of 1941." These projections were little more than guesses, and they turned out to be much too high. The men who made them were worried about the consequences—for themselves and for their country—of guessing too low.

Almost as important as the weapons themselves were the means of "delivering" them. The authors of NSC 68 and many of the intelligence experts who advised them were concerned that, now that the Soviets had the atomic bomb, by hook or by crook the Kremlin would find some way of getting it to its targets, even if they had to put it aboard a tramp steamer and sneak it into an American harbor (a possibility that was seriously considered).

In 1950, the pride of the Soviet air force was a bomber called the Tupolev-4, a copy of the B-29 that had dropped the A-bombs on Japan in 1945. The Tu-4 could indeed reach the United States, but only on a one-way suicide mission. By 1954, the Soviets would add to their fleet the Tu-16, but this plane too lacked true intercontinental range. Yet on the advice of the Air Force, the authors of NSC 68 concluded that the Soviet Union already had aircraft of sufficient range to reach the United States and that by mid-1954, it would be able to drop a hundred bombs on the United States, enough to "strike swiftly and with stealth" and "seriously damage this country." Therefore, NSC 68 concluded, 1954 would be "the year of maximum danger."

Even before Stalin was in a position to unleash his bombers against the United States, NSC 68 warned, he would soften up the eventual targets of his aggression by waging subtler forms of warfare: "It also fits the Kremlin's design that where, with impunity, we can be insulted and made to suffer indignity the opportunity should not be missed." The Soviet Union would, in other words, do everything it could to foster the impression of the West in disarray and decline, therefore unable to resist future exertions of Soviet power. Part of the reason for the military buildup recommended in NSC 68 was to counter the perception of an imbalance in political will—to correct the impression that somehow the Soviets were serious in a way that the West was not.

George Kennan, now an outsider occasionally advising the government, was appalled by NSC 68. He considered it symptomatic of the panic then sweeping the country—and of the pitfalls of Nitze's highly quantitative approach to the Soviet threat. "Paul was in one sense like a child," recalled Kennan. "He was willing to believe only what he could see before him. He felt comfortable with something only if it could be statistically expressed. He loved anything that could be reduced to numbers. He was mesmerized by them. He was not content until he could reduce a problem to numbers. He'd have a pad before him, and when he wrote down the numbers, it was with such passion and intensity that his pen would sometimes drive right through the paper. Of course, the numbers were predicated on a total theoretical hostility that had to be assumed to give these figures meaning. He had no feeling for the intangibles—values, intentions. When there was talk of intentions, as opposed to capabilities, he would say, 'How can you measure intentions? We can't be bothered to get into psychology; we have to face the Russians as competitors, militarily. That's where I come in; that's where I'm in my element.' He accepted the characteristic assumptions of the Pentagon about the Soviet Union; he was enamored of Pentagon phraseology, which was stiff, meaningless, without nuance or political sensitivity."[2]

Kennan criticized Nitze for not paying more attention to the question of what the Soviet leaders actually wanted, and for not considering the possibility of what they might do in that light. In response, Nitze argued a variation of Winston Churchill's famous characterization of Russia as a riddle wrapped in a mystery inside an enigma: Even if less hostile Soviet intentions could at any time be accurately divined, they could also, on short notice, change. It was capacity to use force that Nitze felt could be both measured and treated as a constant. Soviet intentions were, or could at any moment be, not unknowable but the worst imaginable. That was why the bomb that Stalin exploded in the wastes of Central Asia in 1949 was seen as a greater threat to world peace than the ones Truman had dropped on two Japanese cities four years earlier, and it was why the Soviets' relatively primitive bombers were seen as an imminent threat to the United States in 1950.

Lurking in the background of these judgments was the premise that the Soviet Union was capable of acts of recklessness and aggressiveness that the

United States would find difficult to contemplate, certainly difficult to reciprocate, and therefore difficult to deter. The Soviet Union would not shrink
from inflicting nuclear destruction on others or on its own people if its
leaders concluded that such a horror was necessary. This was the most important respect in which the United States was vulnerable, and in which it
lagged "behind" the U.S.S.R. In some ways it was the most obvious; in
others, the most easily and frequently omitted from analysis and discourse.
It was the Spenglerian X-factor, the nonmathematical element in the equation that drove the sums more than the pure mechanics of addition.

NSC 68 posited that if it ever came to a showdown in which nuclear
weapons would be decisive, or in which an advantage would accrue to the
side that used them first, the Soviet Union was the kind of country that
would resort to nuclear attack; the United States was not. Therefore the
United States must not rely too much on its own nuclear weaponry for
deterrence. Even if the United States could maintain its nuclear superiority,
it might not be able to dissuade the Soviet Union from committing aggression. After all, the American monopoly in nuclear weapons had not stopped
Stalin from carrying out a Communist coup in Czechoslovakia in 1948 or
from blockading Berlin in 1949.

Nitze favored a nuclear buildup, but his principal recommendation was a
massive buildup in conventional—i.e., non-nuclear—forces. There was, at
the heart of NSC 68, a recognition of the dirty little secret of nuclear weapons: They were so cheap, so cost-efficient, offering so much bang for the
buck, that Western politicians, particularly in times of economic stringency
or a postwar rush to demobilize, would be tempted to substitute them for
large standing armies. NSC 68 was an appeal to resist that temptation.

While NSC 68 was one of the most famous interagency memos ever written, and a lasting source of great pride to Nitze, it did not succeed in pushing
Harry Truman into quick acceptance of its economically and politically bur-
densome recommendations. The President received the report with appre-
ciative words, but he put it aside. Not until after Communist North Korean
troops poured across the 38th parallel, invading South Korea, in the summer
of 1950 did NSC 68 become national policy. Only with an actual war to
fight against a Communist aggressor were the U.S. government and public
willing to follow Nitze's advice and spend the kind of money he urged,
concentrating on conventional armaments with the nuclear threat in the
background.

Nitze was less surprised than many by the outbreak of the Korean war. In
the spring of 1950, he had met with Alexander Sachs, a Wall Street economist who had played an important part in the early days of the Manhattan
Project, stimulating political and financial support for the physicists who
went on to develop the A-bomb. Sachs brought Nitze a study arguing that
the Soviets believed that the "correlation of forces" had shifted in their

favor and that Stalin was therefore likely to prompt an attack on South Korea in the near future.[3] The assumption then and for years afterward was that Moscow had ordered the invasion. In fact, the prime mover was actually Kim Il Sung—rather than being pushed by Stalin, he dragged Stalin along with him.* But in one respect, the Korean War did underscore the validity of part of Nitze's message in NSC 68: Regardless of who had pushed or pulled whom, a cabal of Communist leaders had obviously not been deterred by American nuclear weapons from committing aggression.

In December 1950, a group of distinguished private citizens, a number of them former government officials, established the Committee on the Present Danger. They appealed for a new resolve "to prevent a 'Korea' in Western Europe." Publicly echoing NSC 68, the committee pressed for a strengthening of America's ability to fight a conventional war and a lessening of reliance on nuclear deterrence. The principal founder of the group was Tracy Voorhees, who had resigned as under secretary of the army in protest over the cost-cutting policies of the secretary of defense, Louis Johnson.† Nitze was a friend of Voorhees and fully supportive of the main objective of the Committee on the Present Danger.[5]

One of Nitze's last projects as director of Policy Planning was NSC 141, yet another recommendation of a major, costly expansion of U.S. conventional capabilities. This report, which became known as "the legacy paper," was written as an urgent piece of parting advice from the Truman Administration to the incoming Eisenhower Administration. It warned that unless America rearmed massively, the threat of a direct Soviet attack on the United States would reach "critical proportions" by 1954, which NSC 68 had predicted would be the "year of maximum danger."

Sidelined

Paul Nitze admired Dwight Eisenhower as a wartime military leader and as the postwar chairman of the Joint Chiefs of Staff. But in 1952, when Eisen-

---

*Dictating his memoirs in retirement in the 1960s, the Soviet leader Nikita Khrushchev described in some detail how Kim came to Moscow in late 1949 to persuade Stalin that an invasion would touch off an uprising in the South. Stalin "had his doubts" but "didn't try" to talk Kim out of the plan.[4]

†Johnson took the place of James Forrestal, who had been a mentor to both Nitze and Kennan. In 1949 Forrestal had gone into a psychological decline and finally committed suicide by throwing himself from a sixteenth-floor window of the Bethesda Naval Hospital. He was a victim of paranoia and depression, but that clinical disorder was almost certainly exacerbated by his conspiratorial view of the world, particularly the obsession with the global Bolshevik menace that he and Nitze had spent so much time discussing a few years earlier. In his last days, Forrestal was convinced that Communists and Soviet agents were out to get him.

hower became the Republican candidate for President, Nitze saw him as cynically and unfairly blaming the Democrats for the Berlin crisis of 1948–49 and the Korean War, as failing to stand up to Joseph McCarthy, especially when McCarthy attacked George Marshall, and as lending his prestige to the accusation that the Truman Administration was ''soft on Communism.''

Nitze's own Republican affiliation was a vestige of his pedigree and of the Wall Street past that he had shed in the late thirties. Now he felt he belonged to the elite of Roosevelt and Truman foreign-policy advisors, not to the clamoring horde of critics and would-be usurpers who clustered around Eisenhower's banner in 1952. Nitze switched his registration from Republican to Democrat, not so much to vote for Adlai Stevenson as to vote against Eisenhower.

Nonetheless, when Eisenhower won, Nitze deeply wanted to remain in government, preferably as head of the Policy Planning Staff. He loved the job. More than three decades later, Nitze said that between 1950 and the beginning of the Eisenhower Administration he had held ''the best job in the world, far better than most executive jobs, which involve a lot of distractions and allow only restricted time on substance.''

For a while after Eisenhower's inauguration, Nitze was in limbo, waiting to see what his fate would be. As in later years, the Policy Planning Staff often served as a speechwriting shop for high-level pronouncements on foreign policy. Nitze had a hand in preparing the ''Chance for Peace'' speech that Eisenhower delivered to great acclaim at a convention of the American Society of Newspaper Editors on April 16, 1953. The speech was remarkably conciliatory. It noted that the cost of a single bomber would pay for thirty brick schoolhouses; it spoke of humanity ''hanging from a cross of iron'' and called for ''a peace that is true and total'' throughout the world.

This was hardly the message Nitze had been emphasizing since NSC 68. But Joseph Stalin had died a few weeks earlier, and it was hoped that the leaders in the Kremlin would be receptive to an American rhetorical initiative. Besides, as Nitze later explained the speech, ''a President must be seen as committed to peace, especially when the nation has had a recent taste of war, as we had during Korea. There's a fine balance to be struck there, if the public is going to stay behind the leadership and its policies. I tried to help Eisenhower in that regard.''

Nitze hoped that these and other services would earn him a permanent reappointment. He was a frequent visitor to the White House, where a retainer once mistakenly ushered him into the Eisenhowers' private quarters. Nitze found himself face to face with the President in his underwear. ''Once you've seen a man in his BVDs,'' Nitze later chuckled, ''the awe recedes.''

However, the new secretary of state, John Foster Dulles, refused to let Nitze stay at the State Department. The two men had known each other for some time. As a Wall Street lawyer, Dulles had done work for Dillon, Read.

As a prominent Republican when bipartisanship was the watchword of American foreign policy, Dulles had accompanied the American delegation to the Paris conference with Stalin's foreign minister, Andrei Vyshinsky, in 1949. Nitze later learned that Dulles boasted of having kept Acheson and Nitze from selling out to the Communists. Almost no charge stung Nitze more, then or later.

In recalling his youth for the Air Force oral history project in 1977, Nitze said that, while studying Latin at Hotchkiss, "I thought Cicero was an absolutely worthless character, and I still think him to have been worthless, pusillanimous—like John Foster Dulles. I loathed him."[6] Nitze's main accusation against Dulles was that he was a "shyster lawyer" who subordinated principle and, on occasion, the national interest to the political interests of his "client," Eisenhower.

Dulles gave a number of explanations for refusing to let Nitze stay on at the State Department in 1953: Policy Planning was doing valuable work, he said, but not in the field of diplomacy; grand strategy was a function that should be run out of the White House, not the State Department. Nitze concluded that the real reason was simpler: He was an Acheson man, a protégé of someone who had been pilloried by the powerful right wing of the Republican Party for defending Alger Hiss, for allegedly harboring Communist spies in the State Department, and for presiding over the "loss" of China. "Ike had campaigned against Acheson's foreign policy," Nitze recalled. The new vice-president, Richard Nixon, had denounced Acheson as "red dean of the cowardly college of containment." Therefore, "Dulles wasn't about to keep me on."[7]

By way of consolation, Dulles suggested finding Nitze a place in the Pentagon. The new secretary of defense, Charles Wilson, asked Nitze to serve as his special assistant and liaison with the White House. This was to be an interim assignment until the more important post of assistant secretary of defense for international security affairs (ISA) came open. ISA was to become the Pentagon's own "little State Department." It was heavily involved in the management of overseas alliances, particularly NATO; it ran military sales and grant aid, which were booming in the fifties; and it represented the Pentagon at meetings of various interagency committees. ISA's task was to make sure that decisions about the procurement of weapons and the deployment of troops were made with an eye to the big picture of geopolitics. Heading that office would have been an excellent post for Nitze, and perhaps a stepping stone to an even better one.

But once again domestic politics intervened. The tumult of that time was the result not just of controversy over foreign policy or the Soviet threat or the supposed infiltration of the American government by enemy agents. McCarthyism was in large part a socioeconomic phenomenon; it represented a middle-class, Middle American backlash against the moneyed, well-born, well-schooled East Coast caste that was seen to be in charge of U.S. foreign policy. Acheson was a symbol, and Nitze was a part, of a suspected conspiracy between the Red Menace and America's bluebloods. Colonel Robert McCormick's *Chicago Tribune* had denounced Acheson in 1949 as a "striped-pants snob" who "betrays true Americanism to serve as a lackey of Wall Street bankers, British lords, and Communistic radicals from New York."

In the early fifties, the journalistic voice of that view in the nation's capital was the *Washington Times-Herald*. On June 13, 1953, the paper carried an article by Willard Edwards, a Washington-based *Tribune* correspondent with close ties to Senator McCarthy, revealing that Nitze was "the latest Truman-Acheson lieutenant contemplated for retention in a powerful position under the Eisenhower Administration."

The article appeared two days before Nitze was to report for duty at the Pentagon. Senator Robert Taft of Ohio and a number of other conservative Republicans notified Vice-President Nixon that they objected to Nitze's appointment. Within a week Secretary Wilson told Nitze that "congressional opposition" had developed against him and that the White House was not prepared to back him.

Nitze set up shop at the School for Advanced International Studies (SAIS), a think tank that became a Washington-based graduate school of the Johns Hopkins University in Baltimore. He had founded SAIS during the war with Christian Herter, a prominent Republican who was married to Phyllis Nitze's cousin. SAIS and its fund-raising arm, the Foreign Service Educational Foundation, became Nitze's refuge when he was forced out of government, much as the Institute for Advanced Study in Princeton had taken in George Kennan three years earlier.

In his growing restlessness, Nitze made a brief and unsuccessful foray into politics, testing the waters to run for the Senate in Maryland. He kissed babies, gave speeches at firehouses, courted the state's power brokers and contributors. Finally he received a call from the local Democratic leader, who wanted to know whether Phyllis Nitze would be interested in running for office. Her mother, Ruth Pratt, had served as a Republican congresswoman from New York from 1929 to 1933. "He made no reference to me," recalled Nitze in a humorous, self-deprecating tone. But, he added somberly, he also felt that he had been "cast into outer darkness."

Thus, 1954—which Nitze had predicted would be the year of maximum danger in America's competition with the Soviet Union—turned out instead to be a high point of McCarthyism and a low point in Nitze's own career.

He watched with growing anger and dismay as the Eisenhower Administration summarily rejected NSC 141, "the legacy paper," and turned its back on NSC 68. As soon as the Korean War ended, the Administration and the Republican leadership of the Congress vowed to "cut the fat" out of the defense budget. Nuclear weapons seemed to offer a way of buying national defense on the cheap. In January 1954 Dulles gave a speech at the Council on Foreign Relations in New York proclaiming the doctrine of massive retaliation: Deterrence of Communist aggression would depend "primarily upon a great capacity to retaliate, instantly, by means and at places of our choosing."

Nitze was in the audience, and he was fuming. Afterward he and a number of others gathered for drinks and exchanged reactions. As Nitze recalled his own: "It seemed almost inconceivable that at the very moment when the loss of our atomic monopoly, which had long been foreseen as a probability, was becoming an actuality, Mr. Dulles should announce in blatant and offensive terms what he claimed was a new doctrine. . . . It was not a step forward; it was a step backward—a step back dictated not by new strategic considerations but by domestic political and budgetary considerations."

NSC 68 and virtually all of Nitze's later contributions to the strategic debate stressed the need for costly buildups. Being a superpower capable of defending not just itself but the rest of the free world was an expensive proposition. Reliance on nuclear weapons because of their cost-effectiveness "was a potentially disastrous and immoral kind of nuclear strategy." It represented "a dereliction from common sense."[8] When the Soviet Union had its own ability to inflict massive destruction, such a threat would hang over the United States, canceling out the American nuclear deterrent and leaving the Soviets free to exploit their advantages in geography and conventional weaponry around the periphery of the U.S.S.R., in Europe and Asia. Nitze believed that the new Administration, in its excessive enthusiasm for brandishing the nuclear stick, suffered, as he said, from "an apparent reluctance to face the simple but unpleasant fact that the atomic bomb works both ways."[9]

All the more reason, therefore, for a buildup in conventional forces of the sort that had occurred during the Korean War. As he put it at the time, "If it is said, as it sometimes has been, that we cannot afford another war like Korea, the answer is that such a war is the *only* kind which we or anyone else *can* afford. Only a madman would attempt to avoid it by plunging into the unspeakable disaster of a World War."

In a letter written on July 1, 1954, to his friend the syndicated columnist Joseph Alsop, Nitze elaborated on his misgivings about massive retaliation and another idea that was in fashion among the hawks of the time—massive preemption, or preventive war. For two and a half single-spaced typewritten pages, Nitze ran through his reasons for questioning the assumptions of military planners who believed that it would be possible for the United States to deliver a knockout blow against the U.S.S.R.:

I distrust experts who are unable to explain to laymen the essential chain of their reasoning. I have found few strategic bombing people who can give any reasonable analysis of the link between a given level of physical destruction and the economic, military, political, and psychological results expected to flow from that level. In the long run when one questions them, their beliefs rest more on faith than on analysis.

Then he came to "the last point, the point of conscience":

> I for one do believe that moral distinctions are possible, although extremely difficult, but there is something more to our quarrel with the Kremlin than just we or they, that leadership in the world today does involve a sense of responsibility for more than just oneself, and that without such confidence neither I, nor most others whom I respect, would be able to devote themselves self-sacrificingly to the immense tasks which any foreseeable circumstances are likely to put before us. . . .
>
> As you know, I generally felt the last administration [Truman's] was doing too little too late. The trouble is this administration [Eisenhower's] is doing less and less beyond issuing empty and misleading statements. The problems are certainly going to be harder in the future than they ever have been in the past. I do think it makes at least some difference whether we have some leadership or none. I do not believe leadership consists in advocating a course impracticable by any constitutional standards, dubious as to its outcome if it were practicable, and offensive to all morality, just because it appears neat, bold, and decisive one way or another and all other courses are uncertain, difficult, expensive, and complex.

This passage contained the nub of an important theme in Nitze's thinking then and later. In its "quarrel" with the Soviet Union, the United States had morality and conscience on its side. Conversely, the Soviet Union had amorality and lack of conscience on its side. For just that reason, American leaders must not let themselves be drawn into a situation in which nuclear weapons, which were offensive to morality and conscience, might be decisive in the resolution of the quarrel.

By the mid-fifties, there was almost universal agreement among strategic theorists outside the government that Dulles's doctrine of massive retaliation was, as Nitze had been saying since he first heard it enunciated, inadequate if not dangerous, foolish if not wicked. There were different schools of thought on campuses and in think tanks about what a prudent and effective U.S. policy should be. One school, which was centered at universities on the East Coast, held that, rather than being "massive," the degree of retaliation threatened must be in some way commensurate with the level of aggression it was meant to deter. A number of younger academics developed that idea, but one in particular created a stir.

In 1957, Henry Kissinger, a young lecturer in the government department at Harvard, published *Nuclear Weapons and Foreign Policy.* The book, which helped launch Kissinger's spectacular career, grew out of a series of meetings—a "study group"—held under the auspices of the Council on Foreign Relations. Nitze was a member of the study group. Participants in some of the meetings recalled that Nitze bridled visibly at Kissinger's already pronounced flair for the authoritative assertion. As Nitze himself later put it, "Henry managed to convey that no one had thought intelligently about nuclear weapons and foreign policy until he came along to do so himself." Nitze, who had been doing a good deal of such thinking himself for over a decade, was now fifty; Kissinger was thirty-four.

In his book Kissinger argued that Dulles's famous threat, first articulated on the premises of the Council, was simply not credible. The Soviets had too many ways of nibbling the United States to death, and as time went on, they would have too many weapons with which to counterretaliate if the United States ever did attack massively, or to hold the American strategic arsenal in a paralytic trance, like a cobra staring down a rabbit. What was needed, Kissinger argued, was a more subtle and flexible doctrine, a threat to make less-than-all-out use of nuclear weapons in response to less-than-all-out Soviet aggression. Such a doctrine would be more credible and therefore more effective as the basis for deterrence: The United States should threaten to fight a limited nuclear war, not to unleash Armageddon.

For all the hardheadedness of *Nuclear Weapons and Foreign Policy,* for all its author's apparent willingness to think about the unthinkable and to propound what was then and subsequently described as a doctrine of "nuclear war-fighting," Kissinger's real concern seemed to be largely with the political imagery of nuclear weapons, with the impressions they created in the minds of America's enemies and allies alike. He took seriously the interplay of perceptions and calculations of relative nuclear strength as nations maneuvered for advantage against each other; but he did not waste much intellectual energy trying to answer those questions that Bernard Brodie had said over a decade before no longer mattered: Who will win a real war? and What will winning actually mean? Almost whenever the prospect of actual use, as opposed to the threat of use, arose in *Nuclear Weapons and Foreign Policy,* it was couched in terms like "dilemma," "quandary," "paradox," and "ambiguity."

These were words and concepts that repelled Paul Nitze. He panned the book in *The Reporter,* complaining that Kissinger was having a "field day" with the abstract aspects of the issue while giving short shrift to "facts" and "logic." Neither then nor later did Kissinger have much patience with what he sometimes called the "awful numbers" of nuclear-weapons policy.

For Nitze, the numbers were anything but awful; they were vital. He took Kissinger to task for mistakes about the mathematics of calculating the increase in blast and heat effects of a nuclear explosion. Many years afterward Nitze was still arguing that such errors proved that Kissinger's whole thesis was "disconnected from just the elemental facts of nuclear warfare. None of it made any sense."[10] At the time of the review, Kissinger—whose self-esteem and temper fully matched Nitze's—threatened to sue for libel. Instead, he started work on a lengthy rebuttal, but never completed it.

Strength in Numbers

On November 7, 1985, President Reagan presided over a ceremony in the East Room of the White House at which he awarded the Presidential Medal of Freedom to Paul Nitze and Albert and Roberta Wohlstetter. Nitze's wife, Phyllis, who was suffering from acute emphysema, was in a wheelchair in the front row of the large audience. The President was acknowledging a debt to three progenitors of his Administration's strategic nuclear-weapons policy.

Nitze had known the Wohlstetters since the fifties. Like a number of other seminal thinkers of the nuclear age, including Bernard Brodie, Albert Wohlstetter had been on the staff of the RAND Corporation, a think tank in Santa Monica, California, that was devoted to research and development (hence its name). Its principal client was the Air Force.

Wohlstetter was a mathematical logician, a certified master of a discipline that Nitze valued highly. Mathematics and logic—and their offshoot, the new methodology of systems analysis—told him, and he did much to convince Nitze, that the bombers of the Strategic Air Command (SAC) might be sitting ducks for a preemptive Soviet attack. Wohlstetter's wife, Roberta, a social scientist and historian, wrote a detailed study of Pearl Harbor, not just as an important episode from history but as a cautionary tale of strategic vulnerability. Albert Wohlstetter believed that, like the capital ships of the U.S. Navy in December 1941, the bombers of the U.S. Air Force were clustered on a few bases, unprotected and insufficiently alert. He concluded that Soviet bombers, sneaking past American early-warning radars near the Arctic Circle or coming by a different route, could destroy 90 percent of the American bombers on their runways and in their hangars, crippling the means of the United States to carry out retaliation of any kind, massive or otherwise.

Picking up on these warnings, commentators at the time said that the United States suffered from a "bomber gap." The phrase was misleading.

During their annual May Day parade in 1955, the Soviets displayed a new, turboprop bomber, the Tu-95, code-named the Bear by NATO. The following year came the all-jet Mya-4 (the Bison). But by then the United States had already begun producing the B-52, a superior aircraft in every respect. American intelligence forecast an eventual force of five hundred Bears and Bisons. In fact, there would never be more than two hundred. In 1956, there were 340 American intercontinental bombers and another 1,300 intermediate-range B-47s, either based within striking distance of the U.S.S.R. or capable of reaching Soviet targets with midair refueling.

There was indeed a bomber gap, but it greatly favored the United States. Wohlstetter, however, was concerned primarily not about which side had more bombers, or better ones; rather, he was concerned with the damage that the Soviets could do if their inferior and less numerous bombers caught SAC sleeping. He was talking about what might more accurately be called a "bomber alertness gap." If the Soviet Union struck first and knocked out the American retaliatory force, American numerical and qualitative superiority would not matter, except to underscore the magnitude of the loss the United States would have suffered.

In part because the Soviet Union was on the losing side of the real bomber gap, the Kremlin leaders pressed all the harder to develop what quickly became by far the most important weapons of the nuclear age, ballistic missiles. The Soviets' Pobeda (Victory) rocket preceded the American Redstone by about four years.

Concerns about the Soviet missile program were simmering in 1957 when President Eisenhower established a blue-ribbon commission, headed by Rowan Gaither, the chairman of the board of RAND, to study the requirements for civil defense, especially for a nationwide system of bomb shelters. Although Wohlstetter was not on the Gaither Committee, its report drew heavily from a classified study on strategic vulnerability that he had supervised for RAND, updating his earlier studies on the danger that the Soviet Union would hurl its bombers against SAC. Looking ahead to the day when Soviet bombers would be replaced by intercontinental missiles, he warned that a bolt-from-the-blue attack would be able to knock out virtually all American air bases.

One of the principal figures on the Gaither panel was William C. Foster, who had been deputy secretary of defense in the early 1950s. Foster knew and admired Nitze's work on NSC 68, so he asked him for help in drafting the final version of the committee's report. Completed under the title "Deterrence and Survival in the Nuclear Age," the document went well beyond the original charter of the civil-defense issue. It concluded that American deterrence and survival were both in jeopardy.

The impact of the report had as much to do with its timing as its contents.

A month before it was submitted to the White House, the Soviet Union launched the world's first artificial satellite, *Sputnik* ("fellow traveler" or "companion"). This event came as a shock comparable to the first Soviet A-bomb test in 1949, which had given such impetus to NSC 68. The Gaither Report followed a pattern that had been established with NSC 68. In each case the Soviet Union had confronted the United States with an unpleasant surprise—the Soviet A-bomb test in 1949, *Sputnik* in 1957—and in response, a panel of presidential advisors erected a superstructure of pessimistic guess-work (known, appropriately, as "estimates") about how many additional weapons the enemy would soon have, and what means he might have of dropping them on American targets.

The booster rocket that lofted *Sputnik* into orbit was a close relative of the Semyorka, or No. 7, ICBM that the Soviets had successfully tested in August. The Gaither Committee concluded, on the advice of experts from the CIA and the Pentagon, that the U.S.S.R. would have a dozen operational ICBMs within a year, while it would take the United States two or three years to catch up. If the Soviets launched an ICBM attack, they would catch three-quarters of SAC's B-52s on the ground. A few who heard briefings based on these reports were so horrified that they advocated a preventive American attack on the Soviet Union while there was still time, although neither Nitze nor the committee advocated any such thing.[11]

The United States, however, had by no means been standing still in the development of long-range missiles. The Atlas, a large, cumbersome ICBM, was roughly the equivalent of Khrushchev's Semyorka, and the Air Force was well along in developing a more sophisticated successor, the Titan. Meanwhile the Navy was working on the Polaris missile, which could be launched from virtually invulnerable submarines. American scientists and technicians were making rapid strides not only in propulsion but in guidance technology and the design of missile warheads, or re-entry vehicles (RVs). The quality and variety of weapons on American drawing boards, test ranges, and launching pads greatly exceeded those of the Soviet arsenal. Nor was there any concrete reason to conclude, as the Gaither Report did, that the Soviets were ahead in quantity.

Once again, as with NSC 68 seven years before, the constant underlying American analysis of the Soviets' quantifiable capacity was an assumption of their malevolent intent. In the language of the Gaither Report, which Nitze drafted, Khrushchev's Semyorka was an instrument for a "disarming counterforce attack," while America's Atlas and Titan ICBMs, as well as its Thor and Jupiter intermediate-range land-based missiles, were "our deterrent power." ("Counterforce" refers to attacks against the key forces of the other side, such as bomber bases and missile launch sites.)

Like those of NSC 68, the recommendations of the Gaither Committee were understood to be as expensive as its findings were alarming: $10 billion in extra appropriations, and $30 billion over five years for fallout shelters alone; the nation's ICBM program should be greatly accelerated and expanded by 1959, the new "year of maximum danger."

Eisenhower, however, was not receptive. While he had yet to make the phrase famous, he was already wary of the military-industrial complex, of which the Gaither Committee represented an inner circle. The committee felt that *Sputnik* underscored the validity and urgency of its recommendations, but Eisenhower believed that public fears should be calmed, not stirred up.

It was a curious, even paradoxical clash: The professional soldier turned statesman was concerned with keeping the costs of military programs under control. He believed that national security depended on much more than military preparedness; overall security was a matter of maintaining prosperity, which could be jeopardized by expensive crash programs. The relative cheapness of nuclear weapons as the principal instruments—and of massive retaliation as the doctrine—of national policy drove him toward a reliance on what would later be called inherent or existential deterrence. In these instincts and preferences, he was at loggerheads with a group of advisors-turned-critics that included a number of captains of industry and, in Nitze, a former investment banker. Yet they seemed to be telling him: Costs be damned; spend whatever it takes to prepare for the worst case imaginable.

The Gaither Report was, implicitly, a harsh repudiation of the Republicans' stewardship of national security. Congressional elections were coming in the fall of 1958, and the President did not want to provide political ammunition to the Democrats. Some people associated with the committee, like Nitze, were Democrats. Many of them, including Nitze, wanted the report's recommendations to be implemented, and they considered implementation more likely if the report were released. Eisenhower refused. The report had been commissioned for him, not for the public. To his great annoyance, portions were leaked to the press anyway in December, a month when Senator Lyndon Johnson of Texas and others found it particularly convenient to invoke memories of Pearl Harbor.

Johnson already had his eye on the presidency. So did John Kennedy of Massachusetts. He, too, saw political pay dirt in the territory that had been scouted by the Gaither Report. Drawing on material prepared by Wohlstetter, Kennedy gave a speech on August 14, 1958, charging that Eisenhower's defense policies had cost the United States vital time, "the years the locusts have eaten."[12] As a result, he said, there loomed on the horizon a period in which America would lag behind the Soviet Union in its missile capabilities: 1960–64 would be "the most critical years of the gap." When 1960 arrived, the Democrats were pounding away at that last word. Their party platform claimed that "our military position today is measured in terms of gaps— missile gap, space gap, limited-war gap." The charge helped Kennedy defeat Richard Nixon in 1960.

In Dwight Eisenhower's last State of the Union address, on January 12, 1961, he voiced his frustration:

> Every dollar uselessly spent on military mechanisms decreases our total strength and, therefore, our security. We must not return to the "crash-program" psychology of the past when each new feint by the Communists was responded to in panic. The "bomber gap" of several years ago was always a fiction, and the "missile gap" shows every sign of being the same.

The passage sounded very much like a thinly veiled rebuttal to the Gaither Committee, which had been established supposedly to help Eisenhower but had ended up providing a powerful issue for the Democrats to attack him from the right.

Present at Another Creation

The Gaither Report helped bring the nation to an awareness that, even before he had grown used to the idea of living in the nuclear age, man was now living in the missile age. In little more than a decade, a handful of weapons had become a stockpile; kilotons had become megatons. But what most altered the psychology of the times was that the absolute weapon now had a means of "delivery" that was lightninglike and virtually impossible to defend against. The memory of Pearl Harbor no longer seemed to do justice to the fear that lay behind the cool rationalism of thinkers like Nitze and the Wohlstetters. The image of squadrons of bombers lumbering over the Arctic Circle with frightened and fallible young men in their cockpits somehow seemed quaint and manageable compared to the specter of a barrage of inanimate but precisely guided metal cones hurtling through space toward targets in the United States.

Like the prospect of being hanged in a fortnight, that nightmare wonderfully concentrated the minds of American planners and strategists not just on imperatives for U.S. military programs but on opportunities for diplomacy as well. They began laying the conceptual foundations for negotiations that might limit the numbers of weapons with which the Soviet Union could carry out a preemptive attack. This was the enterprise of nuclear arms control.

"I believed in arms control but not disarmament," Nitze recalled, looking back on his presence at the creation of both. While the distinction has been blurred, there is an important difference between the two. Arms control means the regulation of the military dimension of the Soviet-American competition. The goal is much the same as the goal of deterrence itself: *stability*, that strange safety in which weapons of vast destructiveness help keep the peace. Arms control is a refinement of, and supplement to, deterrence. It is the steady, deliberate quest for measures that decrease the danger that these weapons might go off by accident or because itchy fingers twitch on hair triggers during a political crisis. Arms control has the connotation of accepting nuclear weapons as a fact of life.

Disarmament, by contrast, seeks not just to set rules of the road for the arms race but to slow it down and if possible reverse it. The goal of disarmament is not just the reduction of the dangers that certain kinds of weapons pose but the reduction of the weapons themselves. Its ultimate goal is the ultimate reduction, to zero. If arms control seeks to promote a state of strategic nuclear stability, disarmament seeks a state of grace or innocence. Arms control has tended to be the concept favored by the pragmatists, the operators, the implementers—the Paul Nitzes—while disarmament has often been the plaything of cynical propagandists, as well as the stuff of which sincere idealists dream.

Over the years, there has been a tendency to treat arms control as an immediate opportunity and disarmament as a compatible but much longer-term objective. In the late forties and early fifties, the United States and the Soviet Union both, at various times and in various forms, espoused the goal of disarmament, but they did so as part of their contest for propaganda advantage rather than in any meaningful attempt to conduct genuine negotiations. Neither the United States nor the Soviet Union wanted to appear insensitive to the horror it was threatening to unleash on the world in the name of deterrence. There was always a strong incentive for each side to accompany its warnings of nuclear retaliation and boasts about its nuclear prowess and willpower with declarations of its eagerness to rid the earth of nuclear weapons and with proposals about how to do so. Proposals on both sides were designed primarily with an eye to public opinion.

Certainly that is how Nitze saw the exercise, and he was personally involved. Late in the Eisenhower Administration, he was an advisor to the American delegation at a round of negotiations in Geneva, first of five nations, then of ten, eventually of eighteen. Nikita Khrushchev scored points in the early rounds of the Geneva talks by proposing "general and complete disarmament." Nitze recalled "the frustration of being beaten over our heads" with that slogan. "We faced a terrible propaganda defeat." But then the United States recovered, countering with its own proposal for "total and comprehensive disarmament" to be achieved in phases. The phases were designed to accommodate the differing political interests of various American allies and also to give the package as a whole a look of seriousness. It worked. "We reversed our propaganda losses," said Nitze, "although none of this bore any relationship to reality."[13]

In the background of the public posturing for propaganda advantage of the late fifties, there was a parallel effort to advance a much more modest, practical, and technical process that would bear a very real relationship to reality. This was arms control. In that effort Nitze was not only involved but committed to the possibility of success.

NSC 68 had warned that ambitious disarmament plans were all but futile "unless and until the Kremlin design has been frustrated to a point at which a genuine and drastic change in Soviet policies has taken place." A year later, in 1951, Nitze helped prepare a paper for the National Security Council on the U.S. position at a United Nations meeting in Paris. Nitze argued that the Cold War made comprehensive disarmament impossible: "The high existing level of armaments is both a symptom of the conflict between the fundamental purpose of the United States and the Kremlin design as described in NSC 68 and also an independent cause of the present acute state of international tensions." Insofar as the military competition was a consequence of the basic rivalry, it neither should nor could be limited as long as the rivalry was unabated. But insofar as the arms race was a cause of tension, limitation was perhaps possible and certainly desirable. The paper set forth concrete proposals for ceilings on how much any country could spend on defense as a percentage of its gross national product; it also proposed separate, lower, and equal subceilings for the United States and the Soviet Union on defense spending and number of men under arms.

Nitze's purpose, he later recalled, was to recommend an American position for the conference that "accorded with our principles and made sense conceptually." He was still a long way from making proposals that might actually lead to agreements, overcoming the stumbling blocks of negotiability (Will the other side agree?) and verification (Can we tell if the other side cheats?): "I knew perfectly well that the Soviets would never buy the idea; nor, even if they did, would we have any way of getting a true account of how much they were spending or how many men they were keeping under arms." But he was already looking for a way of "working the problem" of arms control, and he was coaxing his government away from proposals that were purely propagandistic.[14]

A year after the Gaither Report, in 1958, Eisenhower and Khrushchev sent delegations to Geneva for yet another set of talks. The conference was close to a fiasco. Ten nations were represented. The American delegation was huge, with more than a hundred members drawn from across the political spectrum and with only the vaguest of instructions. Propaganda was still uppermost in the minds of the two governments. Not much was agreed on except the purpose of the exercise—though that in itself was a significant advance in the art of the possible. The stated objective was, for a change, not general and complete disarmament, or total and phased disarmament. Rather, it was an agreement on "measures to safeguard against surprise attack"—that is, to mitigate the problem of strategic vulnerability. A prominent figure on the bloated American delegation was Albert Wohlstetter.

While the conference produced little before it went into open-ended recess, the process of preparing for it had yielded a consensus among American experts: The greatest challenge to peace was the danger of a bolt-from-the-blue, disarming nuclear first strike, and therefore the principal aim of arms control should be to diminish, and if possible eliminate, that danger. That meant discouraging the development of weapons that could carry out a surprise attack while encouraging ones that could survive such an attack.

According to this view, which was articulated most forcefully by Wohlstetter and Thomas Schelling, a strategist at Harvard, nuclear weapons were indeed a permanent part of the modern condition; deterrence was, as Wohlstetter put it, "not automatic." Deterrence was, however, possible—it could be nurtured, sustained, and strengthened with a mixture of diplomacy and unilateral defense policies that, in Schelling's phrase, "explicitly identif[ied] arms control with reciprocally reduced strategic-force vulnerability."

Wohlstetter was preparing a sanitized version of his classified RAND studies on vulnerability. It was published, in January 1959, as a highly influential article in *Foreign Affairs* under the title "The Delicate Balance of Terror." A draft was made available to the American delegation to the Surprise Attack Conference. Deterrence should not, wrote Wohlstetter, be confused "with matching or exceeding the enemy's ability to strike first": rather, it depended on discouraging either side from seeking such an ability. But, given what was recognized as the impossibility of comprehensive defense, the mutual vulnerability of populations would remain.[15]

Nitze agreed. In 1959 he wrote an essay proposing what he called "an alternative nuclear policy as a base for negotiation."[16] He still strongly favored bomb shelters, but he acknowledged that popular resistance made a nationwide civil defense program unrealistic: "We had therefore better make up our mind to start working out right now the policies which would be prudent in a missile world in which we have no real protection for our civilian population." Such policies, he continued, should "at all cost deter the surprise-attack end of the spectrum."

Nitze explained that he would have been prepared to support a ban on all nuclear weapons if it were not for the problem of numerically superior Soviet conventional forces amassed on the borders of nations that looked to the United States for protection. Nuclear weapons would have to continue to serve as the great equalizers. But they should not be megabombs, the huge blunt instruments of massive retaliation. Nitze called for "a ban on the testing of all but the very smallest weapons" and "a ban on the use of nuclear weapons except in self-defense and within and over one's own territory." If, for example, Iran were attacked by Soviet forces, the Iranian government could use "nuclear weapons suitable for short-range tactical defense" against the invaders. Giving such weapons to Teheran "could make invasion of Iran, even by a large number of Russian divisions, a very dubious and hazardous operation."

Nitze then added a caveat: "In peacetime one would wish to see firm United States or United Nations control over the warheads for such weapons."

This was the germ of an extremely controversial idea that he developed in a speech in April 1960 at the National Strategy Seminar, a meeting of academics, policymakers, and strategists under the auspices of the Stanford Research Institute in Asilomar, California. As Nitze worked himself toward breathtaking new proposals for arms control, he engaged in tough talk about the Soviet challenge and the required American response, echoing the more pessimistic, hortatory themes of the past and anticipating some of the future. He rehearsed his longstanding objection to the idea of pure deterrence, as first advanced by Brodie:

> I fear that one nation, which devotes itself intelligently and persistently to the problem of how to win a war through a rational military strategy geared to a consistent political aim, may well develop a strategic doctrine, tactics, training, and deployments that will give it a decisive advantage against the side that devotes itself solely to deterrence of war through military means that cannot be adapted to any sensible military strategy if deterrence fails. . . . The early German successes in World War II were not based on any radical technological superiority. Their blitzkrieg successes were based more on doctrine, training, tactics, and initiative than on technical superiority of equipment.

Bomber gaps and missile gaps mattered if there was also a gap in seriousness of purpose, discipline, hardheadedness, and national will. He warned, yet again, that the United States faced a period of maximum danger during the next three or four years, a "period within which the U.S.S.R. would have the best chance of executing a counterforce disarming attack"—a nuclear blitzkrieg. Once again, he regretted the American people's refusal to support civil defense: "People just don't want to burrow into the ground on the off-chance that they will be enabled to survive long enough to participate in the immense job of recreating a nation from piles of nuclear rubble."

Then Nitze endorsed and refined the goal for arms control that had emerged from the Surprise Attack Conference:

> If either side, or both sides, have a strong first-strike counterforce capability but a weak second-strike retaliatory capability, the important

thing is who strikes first. Under such circumstances, any serious situation of tension, making it appear possible that one side might strike, will lead the other to try to get in a preemptive strike. If, on the other hand, both sides have inadequate first-strike counterforce capabilities but have strong second-strike capabilities, there will be little or no advantage in initiating a central war. In the latter case, a situation of relative stability should result.

Nearly a decade before the French word for reduction in tensions was incorporated into American discourse on Soviet-American relations, Nitze stressed that "a substantial measure of political détente" was an important political component of strategic nuclear stability.

He had recently returned from the Geneva talks on disarmament, where, he said, "it appeared that each side was jockeying to squeeze the maximum propaganda advantage out of its extreme position before going on to discuss more limited agreements. I would not assert that useful limited agreements are impossible." Proceeding from that cautious double negative, Nitze went on to make a new proposal: what he called a "tacit working agreement" between the superpowers for "reciprocal action based on a common interest in mitigating the dangers of a hazardous and unstable nuclear relationship." He urged a buildup on both sides of "secure, purely retaliatory systems" that posed little threat of a first strike and, at the same time, the scrapping of "fixed-based vulnerable systems" that might tempt the other side to strike first. He spoke approvingly of the Polaris submarine missile program and a mobile Minuteman ICBM, which was conceived in part as an answer to the threat of a Soviet preemptive strike: It could be launched on a moment's notice, before Soviet warheads arrived—hence its name.*

But the question remained of how to convince the Soviet Union that the American arsenal was as benign—as "purely retaliatory"—as the United States would claim. At that time each side had only a very limited recognized ability to monitor military developments on the other and thus independently to verify its adversary's compliance with agreements. The technology of spy satellites was still in its infancy, and flights by American U-2 spy planes over Soviet territory were still secret.

Recognizing that the Kremlin would never merely accept declarations out of Washington about the composition of American nuclear forces and the circumstances under which they might be used, Nitze made a huge leap. He proposed "that we multilateralize the command of our retaliatory systems by making SAC a NATO command, and that we inform the United Nations

---

*Minuteman was originally designed as a single-warhead ICBM that would move around on railroad cars, a forerunner of the small, mobile, single-warhead ICBM, or "Midgetman," that Nitze and others advocated in the eighties.

that NATO will turn over ultimate power of decision on the use of these systems to the General Assembly.'' The UN could order nuclear retaliation only against some nation that had ''initiated the use of nuclear weapons other than on or over its own territory in self-defense against military agression''—the same permissible exception Nitze had spelled out in 1959.

He anticipated objections and attached qualifications to what he called ''the great idea—or, if you will, the grand fallacy.'' The United States and its allies would continue to have responsibility for ''manning, maintaining, and improving'' the nuclear forces under UN command, and, ''in order to guard against the increased danger of local aggression, we and our allies would have to support a substantial increase in forces appropriate for limited war''—i.e., an expensive buildup in conventional forces.

Even in those days of 1960, before Charles de Gaulle challenged the supreme authority of the United States over NATO and before the influx of newly independent Third World countries made the UN General Assembly an often unfriendly and unruly place for the United States, Nitze's scheme was seen as highly dubious, and it was so denounced by other participants at Asilomar. ''Nobody at the conference thought I was anything but crazy,'' he later recalled somewhat ruefully. ''You can think things out rationally, but unless you make it ring politically in the group you're trying to work with, it's no good. What that speech taught me is you've got to stay in the world of the possible.''[17]

The episode left a lingering impression that here was a rather peculiar and unpredictable sort of hard-liner. He cast the Soviets in the darkest possible light; he talked about the danger of nuclear war in the coolest, sometimes most chilling terms; yet when he applied his formidable capacity for rigorous thinking to the problem of arms control, it led him to consider radical ideas, including ones for ambitious—and controversial—international agreements.

CHAPTER 3

The New Frontier

Early in 1960 Paul Nitze supported Hubert Humphrey for President. The two men had been friends for years, and Humphrey had a record with which Nitze could identify. He had stood up against the left wing of the Democratic party, supported the Marshall Plan, and consistently voted for Pentagon budgets. He was also an early advocate of arms control. In May Humphrey withdrew from the Democratic field after losing to John Kennedy in the West Virginia primary. Nitze then joined Kennedy's "academic advisory group," an assemblage of intellectuals put together largely to help the young senator compete for the nomination against better-known, more experienced liberals, notably Adlai Stevenson. In the position papers that Nitze wrote for Kennedy, he was the Nitze of the Gaither Report, not of the Asilomar speech; he stressed the threat of the Soviet ICBM buildup and the challenge to American unilateral defenses, not the opportunities for arms control.

After the election Nitze had hopes for a high post in the new Administration, and he felt encouraged by the President-elect. As Nitze recalled it, Kennedy offered him a choice between national security advisor and deputy secretary of defense. Nitze said he preferred the Pentagon job.[1] He might have gotten it if the secretary of defense had been Robert Lovett, with whom Nitze worked during the Marshall Plan and NSC 68. Lovett, however, declined the post and recommended the bright, hard-driving young president of the Ford Motor Company, Robert McNamara.

Instead of being given the job of McNamara's deputy, Nitze found himself on a short list of candidates. The other principal contender was Roswell Gilpatric, a lawyer who had been a classmate of Nitze's at Hotchkiss and who had served in the Pentagon during the Truman Administration. McNamara was looking for an all-purpose, adaptable number-two who would enable McNamara to devote himself to big thoughts and big plans. He chose Gilpatric. By Nitze's own account, McNamara "thought I was too tough, too opinionated, too difficult to get along with." What was needed in the job of deputy secretary was "somebody who would smooth the rough edges of McNamara's decisiveness."[2]

When Nitze learned that he had been passed over for a job he thought he had been promised, he phoned Kennedy to see if the original alternative, directorship of the National Security Council staff, was still open. It was not, and Kennedy never returned the call. He had already chosen McGeorge Bundy, the young and highly able dean of the faculty of arts and sciences at Harvard. A number of Kennedy's advisors, especially his brother Robert, were wary of Nitze's hawkishness and his forceful personality. Robert Kennedy later asserted that "the President didn't like Paul Nitze really at the end. . . . [Nitze] had made a good number of enemies. There were those who had worked with him who didn't feel he had the personality to carry the job, although he is supposed to be a very bright person."

Nitze finally joined the Defense Department as assistant secretary for international security affairs (ISA), settling for what was no better than his third choice—the same post he had almost received early in the Eisenhower Administration, only to be blackballed then by right-wing senators.

This time he had no difficulty, and sailed through his confirmation hearings. He had a strong supporter in Senator Henry Jackson, Democrat of Washington. Nitze and Jackson had known each other for some years. Jackson's principal foreign-policy aide, Dorothy Fosdick (daughter of the theologian and writer Harry Emerson Fosdick), had worked for Nitze on the Policy Planning Staff in the Truman Administration. Jackson was, Nitze said, "my kind of Democrat—clear-headed, tough-minded, liberal in the best tradition of the party but not in the least naive about the hard issues" of defense and foreign policy.

The New Frontier was crowded with Cambridge intellectuals and hard-charging industrialists with big ideas, big staffs, and big offices. Before Nitze assumed his duties at the Pentagon, Jackson gave him a spare suite next to his own on Capitol Hill. The two men spent hours discussing the Soviet military and political challenge, and when Nitze came before the Senate Armed Services Committee, Jackson delivered an encomium that eased the nominee's way past any potential opposition.

Jackson's praise notwithstanding, Nitze was regarded with suspicion by a number of his uniformed colleagues at the Pentagon, particularly the commander of the Strategic Air Command, General Curtis LeMay. In LeMay's view, the Strategic Bombing Survey at the end of World War II had disparaged American air power by questioning the "war decisiveness" of the bombing attacks on Japan. More recently, Nitze had vociferously opposed John Foster Dulles's doctrine of massive retaliation, which was central to the mission of the Air Force, and questioned the alertness, therefore the value, of the Strategic Air Command itself.

During a visit to SAC headquarters in Omaha, Nebraska, Nitze told LeMay and a number of other generals of his concern that the sheer destructive power of nuclear weapons made them useless. He said that the Air Force should worry about the collateral effect of what he called "your big, ground-burst and very dirty bombs." (A nuclear explosion at ground level kicks up a maximum of dirt and radioactive debris, which is then carried by the winds over a wide area; also, some nuclear devices, by their design, generate more radioactivity than others and are therefore said to be "dirty.") If these bombs were used against targets in the Soviet Union, asked Nitze, what would the fallout be on nearby American allies such as Korea, Japan, and Norway?

LeMay was furious. He believed that the doctrine of massive retaliation required weapons of uninhibited size and force. He could easily imagine meddlesome, weak-kneed congressmen raising the kinds of questions that he was hearing from Nitze and depriving the Air Force of the funds it needed. He also felt that Nitze was, at least indirectly, advocating nuclear disarmament. In fact, Nitze was urging smaller, more accurate, "cleaner" weapons that would be less self-deterring and therefore more usable in a conflict. But LeMay remained wary of Nitze, complaining about him frequently to conservative members of the Senate Armed Services Committee and calling him a "disarmer."*

In fact, Nitze continued to feel, as he had throughout the fifties, that "disarmament was an exercise in pure propaganda." Like its predecessors, the Kennedy Administration was still paying lip service to the grandiose goals at the Eighteen-Nation Disarmament Committee in Geneva. Those in Washington who dared to think small about what might be achieved in the near term and in the real world used a phrase in meetings and memos that was as revealing as it was cumbersome: "Separable First-Stage Disarmament Agreement." This mouthful was intended to make sure that no one forgot the ultimate objective of eliminating weapons from the face of the earth.

The Kennedy Administration achieved practical and lasting progress in only one area: the negotiation of a ban against the atmospheric testing of nuclear weapons—and that was largely because of widespread public concern over the radioactive contamination of the environment. Nitze participated in the Pentagon's preparations for those talks. In the spring and early summer of 1963, he sat in on skull sessions in which officials of the State and Defense departments tried to coach the Joint Chiefs of Staff to support the test ban in their testimony before the Senate. General LeMay was particularly hostile to the whole exercise. "General," Nitze would remonstrate, "please stay as much as possible within the facts, and try not to extrapolate too much from those facts." In the end, the Chiefs gave their grudging,

---

*In May 1961, *Newsweek* carried a long article about resentment among the top military leaders against the "woolly-headed" civilian intellectuals and "Whiz Kids" whom Kennedy and Robert McNamara had brought into office. The article quoted an unnamed general as saying, "This fellow Paul Nitze is one of our greatest headaches. He wants to throw the A-bombs out and fight with bayonets. That's what all that limited-war talk is all about." Twenty-five years later, Nitze remembered the article in detail, and that quotation almost verbatim. He was certain that the anonymous general was LeMay.[4]

qualified support to the Limited Test Ban Treaty, which banned testing everywhere but underground.[5]

Important as that agreement was, it did not go to the heart of the strategic nuclear rivalry. The Limited Test Ban was possible in large measure because both sides had already mastered the art of detonating thermonuclear explosions. Testing in the atmosphere was no longer vital to the conduct of the arms race. The superpowers were now devoting themselves to the steady accumulation of warheads and the improvement in the speed, accuracy, and stealth with which they could be hurled at their targets.

The Lesson of Cuba

Almost as soon as President Kennedy had moved into the White House, his top advisors began to express doubts about the existence of a missile gap. Robert McNamara, who now had access to secret intelligence data about Soviet programs, became convinced early on that the threat had indeed been greatly inflated. Within a month of the inauguration, he commented to a small group of reporters that there was no missile gap. McGeorge Bundy wrote a memo on March 13, 1961, saying, "The phrase 'missile gap' is now a genuinely misleading one, and I think the President can safely say so." Besides, noted Bundy, "no one has ever supposed that a naked count of missiles was in and of itself a sufficient basis for national security."

By November 8, Kennedy himself was willing to say in a press conference that "based on our present assessments and our intelligence, we . . . would not trade places with anyone in the world," and concluded that the military power of the United States was "second to none"—a phrase that would remain politically useful for American statesmen in the age of détente, since it had a ring of confidence while it implied the possibility of equality with another power. A few days later, McNamara said, "I believe we have nuclear power several times that of the Soviet Union."[6] On November 27, *The New York Times* editorialized: "The 'missile gap' like the 'bomber gap' before it is now being consigned to the limbo of synthetic issues, where it has always belonged."*

---

*The main mission of Francis Gary Powers, when his U-2 was shot down the previous year, had been to photograph Soviet missile sites near Plesetsk in northern Russia. There was still much debate within the government over how many ICBMs the Soviets had actually deployed. The estimates offered by the different services reflected their worst fears and their hopes for their own funding. The Air Force, which had to worry about a Soviet attack on SAC and wanted a vigorous American ICBM program, estimated that there were 300 intercontinental land-based Soviet missiles deployed. The Navy guessed 10. The CIA and State Department split the difference at 150. American spy satellites later confirmed that the low estimates were closer to the truth.

Nitze, who had been in the forefront of those heralding the existence of the missile gap in the late 1950s, was now both slower and less categorical than his colleagues to admit that there was no such thing. Unlike McGeorge Bundy, Nitze believed that "the naked count of missiles in and of itself" was an extremely important measure of national security. "Paul felt strongly that national will was very much a function of military capacity," recalled Bundy. "For him, the relationship between force and political pressure was a continuum: If I've got one more H-bomb than you do, I can put pressure on you."[7] That disagreement was basic to the great strategic debate of the nuclear era.

In September, Nitze had lunch with the Soviet ambassador to Washington, Mikhail Menshikov, and stressed the seriousness with which the United States regarded the Soviet program to develop ballistic missiles.[8] Three months later, Nitze gave a speech to the Institute for Strategic Studies in London acknowledging that the United States, along with its NATO allies, still enjoyed "a definite nuclear superiority" over the Soviet Union. However, he continued, the United States must maintain its overall advantage, for "we believe this superiority, particularly when viewed from the Soviet side, to be strategically important in the equations of deterrence and strategy."

There was particular urgency to the task of deterrence in those days. The existence of West Berlin, a capitalist, democratic enclave in the midst of the East German satellite state, was a major irritant to Nikita Khrushchev, just as it had been to Joseph Stalin before him. Unlike Stalin, however, Khrushchev had nuclear-armed ballistic missiles, and he rattled them in his various efforts to force the West into accepting a curtailment of access to the city. His foreign minister, Andrei Gromyko, warned that if shots were fired between American GIs and Soviet troops over Berlin, "modern military technology" would assure that the flames of war "would inevitably spread to the continent of America."

This threat seemed to confirm one of Nitze's worst fears: that the Soviet Union would eventually be able to use its intercontinental nuclear weapons to keep the American arsenal at bay while the Warsaw Pact made full use of advantages in geography and the regional balance of conventional forces to prevail in a political showdown.

At ISA, Nitze worked closely with ambassadors and generals representing America's allies to formulate military contingency plans for Berlin. The exercise had a number of lasting consequences for him. One was that, despite some frustrations and disagreements along the way, he was generally impressed with the European officials who were his counterparts in those consultations. They, moreover, were impressed with him. Nitze was already clearly identified as a dedicated Atlanticist. He had been intimately involved in the European recovery and the founding of NATO. His role in the response of the Kennedy Administration to the Berlin crisis further solidified his reputation as a friend of Europe and a supporter of transatlantic solidarity.

The contingency planning during the episode produced one particularly sobering and telling moment, although it remained a secret for some years afterward. Henry Rowen, a former analyst at RAND who worked for Nitze in the Pentagon, led a small task force that put together a plan for a preemptive air strike against a number of critical Soviet facilities, including bomber fields and missile launchers. The plan was highly detailed, pinpointing targets and stipulating the course, altitude, and evasive tactics that nuclear-armed U.S. warplanes should use in attacking. It drew on earlier studies that had been conducted at RAND. Rowen and others believed that the plan could be executed with high confidence of success.

Nitze was adamantly opposed. It was one thing for RAND or the Defense Department to rehearse scenarios or play war games between red and blue teams. But this was no game. The plan was intended as an option that the President might actually exercise in a world of facts. Facts could be unpredictable, and they could be unfriendly. Nitze was a believer in the soldier's adage "The map is not the territory." The recommended attack might succeed perfectly in destroying the few Soviet ICBMs that were then in existence, but the designers of the plan were less certain about the far more numerous short- and medium-range nuclear weapons that the Soviets also possessed. What if the Kremlin reacted by launching them at Western Europe, killing tens of millions of people? That possibility alone made the idea totally repugnant to Nitze, and he joined in quashing it.

The same operational pessimism that made Nitze so concerned about the danger of a Soviet sneak attack on the United States also made him cautious in the extreme about any thought of America's initiating the use of its own nuclear weapons against the Soviet Union. Even if an American preemptive attack could be carried out with conventional arms, it would risk provoking the Soviets to fire off their nuclear weapons ("use 'em or lose 'em"). The result would be a nuclear conflict. No one could know for sure in advance how "limited" the conflict would be or whether the resulting levels of damage would be "acceptable."

Whatever his disagreement with Bernard Brodie's notions about the inherent unusability and self-deterring nature of nuclear weapons, Nitze's own behavior in a long moment of real crisis in 1961 tended to confirm the truth of what Brodie had implied fifteen years before: "Planning" a nuclear war was almost a contradiction in terms. The consequences were too uncertain—especially tolerable consequences. That uncertainty made nuclear weapons all but useless except for purposes of threatening retaliation and posing intolerable consequences for the enemy if he attacked. Just as Brodie said, nuclear weapons were useless except for deterrence. At least, so it seemed during that particular showdown.

However, then and later, Nitze preferred to stress another lesson: The Berlin episode served primarily to remind him—and, he hoped, the nation—of how perilous it was to permit the Soviet Union to possess military advantages in any potentially critical category of weaponry and in any location where the West had vital interests.

In Berlin, the Soviets were trying to bully the West from a position of conventional strength near their own borders. In 1962, when Khrushchev tried to station SS-4 and SS-5 intermediate-range missiles in Cuba, the positions were reversed: The United States had geography on its side as well as naval supremacy in the Caribbean. In addition, the United States had overwhelming strategic nuclear superiority. It was that combination of advantages, Nitze believed, that allowed Kennedy to prevail over Khrushchev, forcing the withdrawal of the missiles.

Nitze was a member of the ad hoc executive committee ("ExComm") of the National Security Council, a panel of officials who advised President Kennedy during the Cuban missile crisis. From the first day, Nitze saw the Soviet action as a military threat, significantly affecting the strategic balance and exacerbating the problem of American vulnerability that he had been worrying about for years. He believed that the presence of missiles in Cuba meant that the warning time of an attack on some Strategic Air Command bases would be two or three minutes: The Soviet Union would have a pistol at America's head. Therefore, the United States must mount an immediate political and military response before Khrushchev's missiles were fully installed. Nitze initially favored an air strike to remove the Soviet missile bases by force. (Unlike Henry Rowen's first-strike plan during the Berlin crisis, this would have been a conventional attack on Soviet facilities that were not yet operational and that were far from the Soviet Union itself.)

George Ball—who had known Nitze since the days of the Strategic Bombing Survey and was now serving as under secretary of state—recalled Nitze as one of three "hawks" on the ExComm. The other two were Maxwell Taylor, the chairman of the Joint Chiefs of Staff, and Douglas Dillon, secretary of the treasury and former chairman of the board of Dillon, Read—the firm for which Nitze had worked in the thirties. "The hawks demonstrated increasing ferocity and more unity as time wore on," said Ball. "Paul Nitze was leading the charge of the hawks. I didn't believe the President would consent to an air strike on the missile bases in Cuba, but I was scared to death that Nitze, Dillon, and Taylor would wear the President down."

Robert McNamara opposed direct military action at that stage. He saw the stationing of the Soviet missiles near the United States as essentially a political challenge, requiring a political response, something more forceful than a démarche but posing less risk of escalation than an attack. He had in mind a naval blockade or a quarantine, which he hoped would in turn lead to the removal of the offensive forces.

Nitze and U. Alexis Johnson of the State Department worked out a "time-phased scenario": If a naval quarantine did not force the Soviets to fold, the United States would follow up with an air strike; if that did not work, there would be an invasion of the island. "Our theory," recalled Nitze, "was to use the minimum amount of force necessary to get the job done—but to be sure to get it done." This meant that Nitze was more ready than McNamara to resort to violent force. Along with Dillon and Taylor, he expressed confidence that there would be no Soviet military response to an American strike, since the United States had massive superiority in strategic nuclear weapons. He believed that the United States held strong enough cards to up the ante if necessary.

During critical meetings of the ExComm, on Saturday, October 27, the American leadership considered how to respond to a message from Moscow in which Khrushchev hardened the terms for a solution to the crisis. He wanted a compromise that would cover his retreat. In exchange for his pulling the Soviet missiles out of Cuba, the United States must "evacuate its analogous weapons from Turkey"—fifteen intermediate-range Jupiter ballistic missiles stationed within striking distance of Soviet territory, under the aegis of NATO. The Jupiters were due for retirement anyway, and President Kennedy was tempted by this formula; he was looking for a way that would help his Soviet adversary save face as the two of them backed away from the brink of war. Nitze spoke up repeatedly against the trade, calling it "absolutely anathema . . . as a matter of prestige and politics." He warned that allowing Khrushchev to shoehorn the Turkish Jupiters into the deal would raise the question of "whether we're going to denuclearize NATO," and he urged Kennedy to tell the Kremlin "that we're prepared only to discuss *Cuba* at this time." As an assistant secretary of defense, Nitze was, in bureaucratic terms, one of the junior members of the group, but his tone in the meetings was that of a stern elder, stiffening the backbone of the young President. Kennedy at one point lamented the complexity and riskiness of the process, noting in particular the danger that the Soviets might be able to string out the negotiations while they finished work on the missile sites in Cuba. Nitze's reply was almost a rebuke: "That looks like a rationalization of our own confusion. I think you've got to take a firmer line than that." Robert Kennedy later noted that Nitze's performance had displeased and "frustrated" the President; Nitze was "rather a harsh figure . . . the President wasn't very fond of him."

In the end, Khrushchev backed down without formal diplomatic or public assurances from the United States that the removal of the Turkish missiles would be part of the deal. However, the President's brother Robert Kennedy reportedly gave the new Soviet ambassador in Washington, Anatoly Dobrynin, private assurances that those missiles would shortly be withdrawn. That arrangement led Michael Mandelbaum, a scholar of nuclear policy, to comment that the resolution of the crisis amounted to the first Soviet-American arms-control agreement in history, and a precedent for the efforts of Ronald Reagan and Mikhail Gorbachev a quarter of a century later to negotiate a pact on the elimination of intermediate-range missiles—successors to the Soviet SS-4s and -5s and the American Jupiters.[9]

Nitze was willing to climb the ladder of escalation as high as necessary to end the crisis on terms favorable to the United States. There was, for him, a crucial difference between Cuba and Berlin. It helped, of course, that while Berlin was an enclave surrounded by the Soviet empire, Cuba was a red island in an American sea. But beyond considerations of geography and logistics, America's ability to engage in brinkmanship over Cuba, he believed, was a direct result of its strategic nuclear superiority. That superiority gave the decision-makers in Washington confidence that Khrushchev would not reciprocate with his own toughest available option—firing the missiles. Moreover, the United States would not need to resort to the use of nuclear weapons in order to take out the sites. The job could be done with conventional arms.

A number of others involved, notably McNamara and Bundy, saw the matter differently. They believed that, whatever the American advantage in strategic firepower, the brink of war was too dangerous a place to be, the ladder of escalation too dangerous to climb. Even from a position of great inferiority, the Soviet Union could still hurt the United States horribly. McNamara and Bundy attributed the resolution of the crisis to factors of geography and conventional forces, not to American strategic nuclear superiority.

Cuba was the closest that history came to providing a test case in the disagreement—personalized between Kennan and Nitze and writ large between the liberal and conservative schools of nuclear strategy—over the validity of concern about nuclear blackmail.*

At the conclusion of the episode, one of the chief Soviet negotiators, Vasily Kuznetsov, said to his American counterpart, John McCloy, "You Americans will never be able to do this to us again."[11] Nitze and others believed that Kuznetsov was referring to the strategic nuclear balance, there-

---

*On the twentieth anniversary of the crisis, in 1982, McNamara, Bundy, and four other members of the Kennedy Administration collaborated in a retrospective essay about the crisis and argued that Cuba's proximity to the United States and the U.S. Navy's domination of the Caribbean counted for a great deal, while America's capacity for intercontinental overkill counted for little. Nitze pronounced himself "furious" with the article. The authors' conclusion, he said, was "totally wrong, totally at odds with the facts of the case."[10]

by confirming Nitze's own view that the American strategic advantage had indeed mattered crucially in the thinking of the Kremlin during the crisis. Kuznetsov seemed also to be putting the American leadership on notice that the U.S.S.R. was determined to catch up with the United States once and for all: America's overwhelming advantage in nuclear weaponry during the fifties and sixties would prove as temporary as America's monopoly of the A-bomb had been in the forties.

Ambushed

In 1963, Roswell Gilpatric let it be known that he would soon retire as deputy secretary of defense. Paul Nitze believed that he was in line for that job. So did many others in the Pentagon, who congratulated Nitze on the impending promotion that they saw as a foregone conclusion. Robert Kennedy, however, remained wary of Nitze's hard-driving style and hard-edged views, and Robert McNamara decided on the mild-mannered Cyrus Vance instead. He had already, with a view to Vance's becoming an alternative to Nitze, promoted Vance from general counsel of the Pentagon to secretary of the army to train him for the job of deputy secretary of defense.

Meanwhile, the post of secretary of the navy opened up suddenly, and President Kennedy and McNamara decided to put Nitze there. Nitze was dismayed. The position of a service secretary was, he felt, out of the mainstream of what he considered real national-security policy. He complained directly to the President that the move from ISA to the navy would be seen as a demotion. Kennedy dismissed that objection with a laugh, but promised Nitze that if he took the job he would be rewarded with a more obvious promotion within a year.[12]

Nitze's confirmation hearings before the Senate Committee on Armed Services in November should have been almost *pro forma*. He had appeared before the same committee at the beginning of the Administration without much sharp questioning. Now he was changing jobs within the Defense Department in the middle of an Administration; the control of the Senate, and therefore of the committee, was firmly in the hands of the President's party. But this time he was ambushed by the right wing.

A young freshman Republican congressman from Illinois, Donald Rumsfeld, was looking for an issue to attract attention and establish his conservative credentials. The best way to attack the Kennedy Administration for being soft on defense was to expose one of its Pentagon appointees as a fuzzy-headed liberal who had toyed with dangerously naïve ideas of nuclear disarmament. Rumsfeld alerted his Senate colleagues to what looked like a deliciously frightful skeleton in Nitze's closet. It was the record of a conference that Nitze had attended in Cleveland, Ohio, in 1958.

The National Council of Churches had sponsored the conference, and John Foster Dulles gave the keynote speech. One of his aides (the State Department legal advisor, Ernest Gross, who was also an officer of the National Council of Churches) persuaded Nitze to chair one of the sessions, which produced a report titled "The Power Struggle and Security in a Nuclear-Space Age." Proceeding from the premise that "Christians have a loyalty which transcends the Nation," the report criticized the Eisenhower Administration for dragging its feet in pursuit of "the goal of universal disarmament" and urged greater reliance on the United Nations and more intense, sincere negotiation with the Soviet Union.

Nitze had argued in vain against many of the points that carried the day. Nonetheless, the record of that meeting was dredged up five years later as part of a campaign to block Nitze's confirmation as secretary of the navy. Richard Russell, the chairman of the Armed Services Committee, interrogated Nitze about the conference, wondering whether he supported the idea that Americans could "resolve all our differences by a policy of appeasement." Nitze produced a batch of letters from others who had been in Cleveland, supporting his disclaimer of responsibility for the views adopted in the report.*

Russell then moved on to a document Nitze had more trouble disavowing: the speech that he had given in Asilomar, California, in April 1960. The committee—primarily Russell and Strom Thurmond of South Carolina— savaged him for having raised the possibility of SAC being made a NATO command and of the authority for the use of nuclear weapons being placed in the hands of the United Nations.

Nitze explained to the committee that his purpose at Asilomar had been not to advance a serious proposal but "to shock people into a realization of what the requirements of our security were, and what unpalatable alternatives we might have to face if we did not do things, many of which we subsequently have done, to improve our defense posture." He flatly and repeatedly denied that he had "advocated" making SAC a NATO command and giving authority for the use of nuclear weapons to the UN. He stressed to the senators that in the speech itself, he had warned that such a proposal might be "the grand fallacy." That phrase, which in the original had seemed an almost decorative bit of irony, now became his escape clause.

In his effort to fend off the attack, Nitze made much of his involvement

---

*Rumsfeld, who served as ambassador to NATO, White House chief of staff, and secretary of defense in the 1970s, subsequently apologized to Nitze for his role in this episode.[13]

in NSC 68 and the Gaither Report, citing them as truer reflections of the position he had championed over the years. But the senators seemed only dimly familiar with those documents, which had not been declassified, and they kept coming back to the Asilomar speech. Thurmond accused Nitze of "lack of candor and forthrightness" in his answers and demanded, in the midst of the hearing, that he be sworn under oath—a stunning insult, since it implied that otherwise Nitze would lie about his past views.

Henry Jackson intervened during a particularly testy exchange over Asilomar to say that the author of that speech "is not Paul Nitze, the one I know. . . . I can say to the committee that he has always taken a hard, tough position in dealing with the enemies of this country."

Two weeks later Kennedy was assassinated in Dallas. The new President, Lyndon Johnson, who had the benefit of a honeymoon with the Congress, telephoned Russell and persuaded him to bring the nomination to a vote. It passed over opposition not only from Thurmond but from Barry Goldwater of Arizona. Another conservative Republican, John Tower of Texas, announced that as a Navy veteran and reservist, he could not support a nominee with Nitze's views.

The experience left a lasting scar on Nitze. Twenty-three years and two months later, on January 16, 1987, the Senate passed a resolution hailing Nitze on his eightieth birthday. One of his first reactions on hearing the news was to ask, with a thin smile, "That's nice. Who voted 'nay'?"

In fact, the resolution passed without dissent. By then, only Thurmond was still in the Senate. Goldwater had just retired. Tower had stepped down two years earlier. At the time of Nitze's eightieth birthday, Tower was the chairman of a presidential commission investigating the Iran-Contra scandal. He had also served, along with Nitze, as one of the Reagan Administration's arms control negotiators.

CHAPTER 4

Missiles That Kill Missiles

Paul Nitze's ordeal before the Senate Armed Services Committee took place on November 7, 1963. That same day the Soviet government was celebrating the anniversary of the Russian Revolution with the customary military parade through Red Square. Toward the end of his testimony, Nitze's principal tormentor, Strom Thurmond, held up a copy of that afternoon's *Washington Daily News* with an article filed earlier that day from Moscow, and read aloud the opening paragraph: "The Soviet Union today unveiled the vaunted antimissile missile [that] Premier Khrushchev once said could hit a fly in the sky. A squadron of three silver painted rockets, fitted with huge fins at midfuselage and tail, was hauled through Red Square on open trucks." Thurmond then asked a question that, both in tone and in context, was clearly intended as yet another challenge to Nitze: "Have you had occasion to give any attention to the importance of the antimissile missile, and what is your opinion of this weapon?"

Nitze at first dodged, saying that while he had discussed the issue with Defense Secretary McNamara, "it has not been within my sphere." But Thurmond pressed for an answer.

"My feeling," Nitze said, "is that . . . the development of [antimissile systems] should be prosecuted with all urgency, and I believe it is being prosecuted with all urgency."

"Thank you, Mr. Nitze," replied Thurmond. "Mr. Chairman, that is all the questions I have."

It was perhaps appropriate that the inquisition should end on the subject of antimissile defenses. This was in fact an issue to which Nitze had given a great deal of thought, an issue that already loomed large in the strategic debate. He and other U.S. defense planners had been pondering measures to counter the threat of ballistic missile warheads for some years. Unlike enemy bombers, Soviet rockets could not be adequately tracked on traditional radars, shot down with antiaircraft guns, or intercepted with jet fighters. One countermeasure was to keep a portion of the American intercontinental bomber fleet in the air at all times so that it could not be caught on the ground by a missile attack. Another was a program known by the initials ABM, for antiballistic missiles.

The idea of ABM had been around since the early days of the nuclear age, much favored by those left of center in the great debate over international security. J. Robert Oppenheimer, in his moral and intellectual repugnance at the image of two scorpions in a bottle, had urged finding a way to make defense, rather than offense, the basis for the nuclear peace. Oppenheimer frequently voiced the hope that the same scientists who had brought the A- and H-bombs into existence might find a technological way of undoing what they had done. In the early fifties, the Air Force sponsored Project Charles, a study of large-scale continental defenses against Soviet attack, in effect as an alternative to the threat of massive retaliation. One physicist who took part said that his involvement in Project Charles was atonement for the sin of his earlier work on the Manhattan Project.[1]

Since the mid-fifties, the U.S. military had been working on a variety of ABM projects. The resulting system worked in two steps: A powerful, long-distance radar would see an enemy warhead coming; then, guided by another radar, a nuclear-tipped interceptor missile would rise to meet the target and destroy it high above the earth. The different programs varied in scope. One was to protect large expanses of territory ("area defense"). Another was confined to defending specific sites that might be targets of a sneak attack, such as airfields or missile launching platforms. This was called "point defense."

In the view of its proponents, a highly effective area defense would ease the burden on offensive forces as the main instruments of deterrence. Area defense mitigated the need for the threat of retaliation. The closer a side came to having a totally effective area defense, the less it would need offensive forces at all. Point defense, by contrast, meant defending ICBM launchers, command-and-control bunkers, and other key "points" in the nation's network for waging nuclear war. Just the opposite of area defense, point defense would sharpen the threat of retaliation by assuring that American ICBMs would survive a Soviet attack in order to retaliate.

The Gaither Report called for an accelerated and expanded ABM program as part of the American response to the missile gap. The defense secretary of the time, Neil McElroy, wanted to proceed toward operational deployment of the Army's point defense system. The Air Force felt that the money Congress allocated to nuclear deterrence was better spent on offensive programs, such as the new Minuteman ICBM.

But Minuteman alone was not a fully satisfactory answer. The day might come when U.S. missiles would be vulnerable to preemptive attack. American strategists did not want to be forced to adopt a policy of shooting first and asking questions later—known as "launch on warning." Hair-trigger retaliation was too dangerous and insufficiently credible to assure the nuclear peace. It was dangerous because a war might start by accident (the classic example: a flock of migrating geese in northern Canada is mistaken by

American radar for a cluster of Soviet warheads, and the missiles fly); and credibility suffered because allies and enemies alike might doubt that an American President could act decisively when he had so little time. If he acted precipitously, Armageddon might ensue; if he was paralyzed, America might be defeated without firing a shot.

Partly as a hedge against the dilemma of relying on the increasingly problematic doctrine of instant retaliation, the Eisenhower Administration determined that ABM research and development should continue. Perhaps, with propitious discoveries in physics, engineering, and information processing, point defense might eventually be feasible and desirable as a way of assuring the survival of those American ICBMs that were not fired right away, thus enabling the United States to "ride out" a Soviet attack with enough weapons to shoot back in a purposeful manner. That possibility, in turn, would make the American threat of retaliation more credible and enhance deterrence.

The Soviets, meanwhile, plunged ahead with their own program. An important assignment of the American U-2 spy planes was to overfly and photograph the ABM experiments near the village of Sary-Shagan on the shore of Lake Balkhash in Central Asia. The work there was proceeding apace. At a congress of the Communist party in October 1961, the defense minister, Rodion Malinovsky, announced proudly, "The problem of destroying enemy missiles in flight has been successfully resolved," and a few months later came a classic Khrushchevian boast: The Soviet Union could now "hit a fly" in space. On the day of Nitze's grueling congressional testimony in 1963, what was believed to be the flyswatter itself appeared in the military parade on Red Square.

The Kremlin's nuclear-armed antimissile missile, code-named by NATO Galosh, was huge—considerably bigger then the American Minuteman ICBM it was meant to destroy. Therein lay an illustration of the dilemma, if not the fallacy, of strategic defense in the nuclear age: Thermonuclear weapons are relatively cheap, and ballistic missiles are so cost-effective as a means of delivering those weapons to their targets, that, just as Galosh was clunkier than Minuteman, so defense would perhaps always be at a disadvantage against offense. Galosh, to be sure, was a primitive ABM, while Minuteman was a relatively advanced ICBM. But the contrast between them was still a paradigm of the larger problem. As Galosh gave way to more capable antimissile defenses, all the American ICBM program had to do in response was to increase the multiplicity and sophistication of the offensive threat.

While Malinovsky's claim to have resolved the problem of destroying a few enemy missiles in flight might have been literally true, and Khrushchev's typical exaggeration about hitting a fly might have been figuratively so, their words were essentially empty. The "solution" actually posed a new problem: Strategic defense would provoke cheaper offensive countermeasures.

American strategists, including Nitze, had long been concerned that the attempt to defend against rockets would rapidly approach the point of diminishing returns. Even back in 1946, when such weapons were still in their infancy, Nitze wrote in the Strategic Bombing Survey report: "It would be rash . . . to predict an increase in the effectiveness of defensive control sufficient to insure that not a single enemy plane or guided missile will be able to penetrate." Thirteen years later, in 1959, Nitze could see that the American ABM program might turn out to be a mug's game: "No one believes that anything approaching a complete defense against nuclear missiles is possible. It is neither prudent to count on shooting most of them down in the air, nor to count on taking most of them out of their launching platforms before they take off."[2]

There was in that passage, and in much else that was said and written in those days, a mixture of revelation and resignation. From the outset of the American ABM program, there was resistance from the White House, Congress, and the American scientific community. In all quarters experts doubted that ABM would fulfill even the limited mission of point defense, let alone area or population defense. They had little hope that defense would ever replace offense as a basis for nuclear peace. Nor was that conclusion simply a matter of assessing what was feasible, given the technology of the time. Rather, it was, in the minds of many, an article of faith. The enormous destructiveness of offensive weapons and their low cost made them all but impossible to defend against.

The Hydra and the Heavy

By 1961, when Nitze arrived in the Pentagon, a consensus was forming that the most promising response to Soviet ABMs was not a comparable American defensive program but an offsetting means of proliferating American offenses, so that there would be too many flies for Khrushchev and Malinovsky to swat: Individual American missiles would carry warheads that would come in swarms, overwhelming Galosh and its successor systems.

The first multiple-warhead carrier to be developed by the United States was a naval weapon, the Polaris A-3, a submarine-launched ballistic missile (SLBM) that became operational during Nitze's first year as secretary of the navy. The Polaris was outfitted with a system called Claw: Warheads separated from the rocket after launch; their trajectory back to the earth's surface was determined by a single guidance system. They were multiple, but *not* independently targetable, re-entry vehicles—MRVs, not MIRVs.

Over time, the scientists and technicians learned how to endow the Hydra with a self-propelled maneuvering "bus" equipped with a sophisticated electronic brain, so that each warhead could be aimed at a separate target with greater accuracy as the system was perfected. In 1964 the Pentagon began pushing to develop a MIRV system for the Poseidon submarine missile and the Minuteman ICBM. Both systems were successfully tested from Cape Canaveral three years later, toward the end of the Johnson Administration.

MIRVs not only took advantage of American technological advances but were—like nuclear weaponry itself—highly cost-effective. In that respect they initially had a strong appeal to Secretary of Defense McNamara in his effort to contain the size and cost of the American defense program. He was resisting the deployment of ABMs, staving off Air Force requests for a new manned bomber to replace the B-52, and straining to hold the Minuteman ICBM program to a thousand launchers (LeMay and the Air Force wanted between two thousand and ten thousand launchers). MIRVs, it appeared, might help economize in all three areas: They were the most effective way of countering the Soviet ABM program and therefore an attractive alternative to American ABMs; they made ICBMs all the more preferable to manned bombers as the centerpiece of the American deterrent, obviating the need for an expensive new bomber; and they could triple the number of targets covered by Minuteman, obviating the need for more launchers.

But MIRVs also illustrated the problem of how an American innovation could come back to haunt the innovators. As with the technology of the Bomb itself, the American monopoly on MIRVs was bound to be temporary. Once the Soviets closed the gap in MIRV capability, they would, almost automatically, have an advantage in the number of MIRVs they had deployed on ICBMs.

It was natural that the United States and the Soviet Union developed very different nuclear arsenals. Russia had always been a land power whose military greatly valued artillery; the United States was, since its birth, a maritime nation and by the middle of this century had acquired prowess as an air power. Those basic differences in military tradition were reflected in the composition of the two sides' nuclear arsenals: The Soviets gave priority to land-based ballistic missiles, the artillery of the nuclear age, while the United States diversified its strategic forces on land, at sea, and in the air.

Partly because of their reliance on land-based missiles, and because their missiles tended to be behemoths that made up in lifting power what they initially lacked in sophisticated, miniaturized propulsion, guidance, and explosives, the Soviets developed over the years a preference for, and therefore a preponderance of, one kind of nuclear weapon: very large ICBMs. The Soviets established a considerable lead in the ability to heft pure bulk. Four days before the Gaither Committee presented its report in November 1957, the Soviets launched *Sputnik II*, with a payload of a thousand pounds, more than five times that of *Sputnik I* and many times larger than anything the

United States would lift into orbit for years. Coupled with an eventual ability to MIRV its rockets, that Soviet lifting power would eventually spell serious trouble for the United States.

At the annual military parade in Moscow on November 7, 1967—three years after Galosh had made its debut—the military attachés from the Western embassies assembled on bleachers in Red Square were aghast to see a huge offensive rocket roll past. It was nearly twice as long as Minuteman. Its single warhead was estimated to be in the 25-megaton range, more than twenty times that of Minuteman. Western intelligence agencies designated this behemoth the SS-9 (the prefix stands for "surface-to-surface").

Later, American intelligence observed the Soviets testing the SS-9 with a primitive, Claw-like forerunner of MIRVs. The "triplet" of dummy warheads fell too far apart to suggest they were meant to wipe out one city but too close together to destroy three. The targeting pattern, or "footprint," suggested instead, at least to some analysts, that the SS-9 was learning to stamp out one of the Minuteman fields spread out over many square miles in North Dakota, South Dakota, Montana, Missouri, and Wyoming. As the Soviets mastered the art of adding accurate warheads to the giant SS-9 and its successors, Soviet warheads might eventually become so accurate and powerful that they could destroy even underground American silos that were "hardened" with reinforced concrete, and they would become so numerous that they could overwhelm American ABMs.

Sheer numbers of Soviet weapons alone, along with the adverse ratio of Soviet warheads to American ICBM silos, did not by themselves make a surprise attack plausible. The Soviets would also have to achieve a high degree of coordination. All their warheads would have to detonate on their targets within minutes of each other in order not to allow the United States time to react and launch a devastating retaliation.

But, in Nitze's "logic chain"—his concern that if the Soviets possessed Capability A, they would be able to act on Intention B, and that could result in Catastrophe C for the West—the first-strike scenario could not be totally discounted. And as long as there was even a remote possibility of the worst happening, Nitze came to believe, prudence required preparing for precisely that possibility.

The Talks Begin

The arms race had its own logic: Semyorka and its successors stimulated American offensive countermeasures like Poseidon and Minuteman, along with "force multipliers," Claw and MIRV, as well as defensive countermeasures like the American ABM; now those same American programs were stimulating Soviet defenses like Galosh and the first of the Soviet "heavy" ICBMs, the SS-9, with its potential for carrying many more multiple warheads than the smaller American ICBMs.

Paul Nitze's boss at the Pentagon, Robert McNamara, saw clearly the problem of what he called "the action-reaction phenomenon." He was particularly worried that the interaction between offenses and defenses could work to the detriment of American security and undermine the stability of the superpower relationship. He argued that it was in the interest of each superpower not only to have an invulnerable retaliatory force of its own, but for its adversary to have the same thing: The United States was better off if the Kremlin was confident of its ability to survive an American attack and then retaliate; otherwise, the Soviet missile force was likely to go off half-cocked in a crisis.

While ABMs might seem desirable insofar as they made one's own offensive missiles less vulnerable to a first strike by the enemy, they were undesirable insofar as they made that same enemy fear that the purpose of the defensive system was to protect against a second, retaliatory strike. Such a defense would seem ominous because it might be intended to work in tandem with a first-strike offense. The dividing line between the two functions of ABM—one benign and "stabilizing," the other threatening and "destabilizing"—was extremely hard to draw, especially to the mutual satisfaction of both parties. Therefore, it might be better to ban, or at least hold to an absolute minimum, strategic defenses, and base deterrence on the combination of two bedrock conditions: vulnerability of populations and invulnerability of retaliatory forces.

McNamara saw not only the military danger of an offense-defense vicious circle but a diplomatic opportunity as well. By exercising restraint in its own deployment of strategic defenses, the United States might be able to induce the Soviet Union to join in negotiations toward an agreement that would diminish the danger of war and limit—perhaps even eventually lower—the levels of offensive weaponry on both sides.

In his last days at ISA before moving over to the Navy, Paul Nitze composed a lengthy set of guidelines for a new initiative. He collaborated with his naval aide at ISA, Captain Elmo Zumwalt. Theirs was to be a mutual admiration society of long standing: Nitze frequently referred to Zumwalt as "my kind of military man," and Zumwalt, who went on to be chief of naval operations in the seventies, considered Nitze "the Winston Churchill of today."[3] The two men frequently flew by helicopter out to Nitze's farm in Maryland for the weekend, and for a time Zumwalt and his family lived in the guest house there.

Many of their conversations in the fall of 1963 were on the interrelation between strategic nuclear offenses and defenses. They concluded that, even if it were feasible, the complete elimination of nuclear weapons would be undesirable. As Nitze later recalled, "We'd be better off with each side having a certain number of nuclear weapons, around five hundred each. That would be better than none at all." A small, "minimum deterrence" arsenal would serve to maintain peace between the superpowers and as a hedge against nuclear-armed third powers.[4]

Nitze and Zumwalt wrote a 43-page paper entitled "Considerations Involved in a Separable First-Stage Disarmament Agreement." Nitze did much of his share of the work in an all-out three-day stint, scribbling on a yellow legal pad while flat on his back at a military hospital, where he was recovering from a hernia operation. Shortly after finishing the paper, he passed it along to his successor at ISA, William Bundy. The brother of McGeorge and the son-in-law of Dean Acheson, William Bundy had been Nitze's deputy at ISA early in the Administration. Nitze urged that Bundy use the paper he had written with Zumwalt as a "frame of reference" in interagency discussions. The letter ended, somewhat sardonically, "Welcome to the world of arms control." But it also contained a heartfelt credo: "The entire disarmament effort would have collapsed long ago [were it not] that control and reduction of armaments can benefit both sides."

The Nitze-Zumwalt paper urged that the United States buckle down in pursuit of a new agreement based on two achievable objectives: First, the goal of an agreement on offensive arms should be "to reduce the size, weight, and likelihood of success of a Soviet strike against the U.S. or its allies" by exercising "control over superweapons" such as ICBMs, since they were the instruments of a first strike; second, offensive arms control would be possible only if there were "measures prohibiting the deployment of ABM systems."

Three years later, McNamara was pushing a similar proposal on Lyndon Johnson. The idea of forgoing antimissile defenses ran very much against the grain of traditional American thinking, particularly that of the military. In October 1966, over the objections of the Joint Chiefs of Staff, McNamara persuaded the President that a population defense was impossible and a point defense unnecessary; that the less expensive, more sensible way to counter Soviet defense was with additional offense; and that the prospect of an American defense should be used as leverage, or a bargaining chip, in arms control. McNamara urged that "we make every possible effort to negotiate an agreement with the Soviets which will prohibit deployment of defenses by either side and will limit offensive forces as well."[5] On January 21, 1967, Johnson wrote to the Soviet premier, Aleksei Kosygin, proposing negotiations on "the possibilities of reaching an understanding between us which would curb the strategic arms race." An ABM race, he warned, would impose "on both sides colossal costs without substantially enhancing the security of our own peoples or contributing to the prospects for a stable peace in the world."

Kosygin's initial response was not encouraging. At a press conference in London in early February he argued that defensive measures were more sensible and humane than weapons of mass destruction. But he reluctantly agreed to pursue the matter in diplomatic channels.

Four months later Kosygin was visiting the United Nations in New York, and from June 23 to 25, 1967, he and Johnson met each other halfway between New York and Washington, in Glassboro, New Jersey. The President and McNamara continued their efforts to impress upon the skeptical Soviet premier the logic of mutual vulnerability. "Mr. Prime Minister," said McNamara, "deployment of a Soviet ABM system will lead to an escalation of the arms race. That's not good for either one of us." Kosygin grew agitated. His face turned red and he pounded on the table: "Defense is moral; offense is immoral!"

Returning to New York after the meeting, Kosygin gave another press conference. "The antimissile system is not a weapon of aggression, of attack," he said. "It is a weapon of protection."

The allure of strategic defense was just as strong among American politicians. Governor George Romney of Michigan, who was then thought to be the front-runner for the Republican presidential nomination, vowed that he would make an issue of the ABM in the '68 campaign. Senator Strom Thurmond and Congressman Melvin Laird, the chairman of the Republicans' Congressional Policy Committee, made clear that they were going to use the ABM issue to challenge the Administration's strategic policies.

In June 1967, just before the Glassboro summit, the Chinese detonated their first hydrogen bomb. That event stirred additional calls for deployment of an American ABM. But it also provided the basis for a compromise between McNamara and the pro-ABM forces in Congress: As the United States moved into negotiations with the Soviets, it might deploy a system for defending itself not against the much-advertised danger of an all-out Soviet blow but against the incipient threat from China, an attack by some third party, or even a missile launched by accident.

The problem with this kind of so-called "thin" defense was that it would still require a nationwide system of radars to spot incoming missiles from any direction. The Soviet Union was sure to regard that feature of the system as the groundwork for a "thick" defense, a comprehensive system of interceptors to protect the entire country. For just that reason, McNamara had misgivings about the Chinese rationale for the ABM, even though he recognized that it might mollify domestic critics on the right and buy time for— and enhance American leverage in—negotiations with the Soviets on mutual restraints.

In July of the eventful year 1967, Cyrus Vance resigned as deputy secretary of defense because of a back ailment. This time Nitze succeeded in getting the number two post that he had wanted at the outset of the Kennedy

Administration. Nitze had recently turned sixty, an age when many men are thinking about retirement. Alice Roosevelt Longworth, a grande dame of Washington, remarked to him, ''Now that you have had your sixtieth birthday, you can tell everyone you are pushing seventy.'' The comment, Nitze recalled, ''gave me a shock.''

As deputy secretary, Nitze was back in the center of policymaking on strategy and arms control. He participated in the drafting of a landmark speech that McNamara delivered in San Francisco on September 18 to the editors and publishers of United Press International. It was a peculiar piece of argumentation that began as a forceful denial of the utility of strategic defenses:

> While we have substantially improved our technology in the field [of ABMs], it is important to understand that none of the systems at the present or foreseeable state of the art would provide an impenetrable shield over the United States. Were such a shield possible, we would certainly want it—and we would certainly build it. . . . But what many commentators on this issue overlook is that any such system can rather obviously be defeated by an enemy simply sending more offensive warheads, or dummy warheads, than there are defensive missiles capable of disposing of them.
>
> And this is the whole crux of the nuclear action-reaction phenomenon.

It was also to be the crux of the argument against strategic defenses two decades later.

Many in McNamara's audience reasonably expected him to announce that the Johnson Administration had decided against ABM deployment. Instead, he made a hairpin turn and unveiled President Johnson's politically motivated decision to proceed with a ''Chinese-oriented'' ABM program. This was a sop to the pro-ABM lobby on Capitol Hill which was putting such pressure on Johnson as well as an inducement to the Soviets to accept the U.S. proposal for negotiations that would prohibit ABM deployment and limit offensive weaponry. McNamara's lack of enthusiasm for the ABM decision showed, and he concluded with a warning: ''There is a kind of mad momentum intrinsic to the development of all new nuclear weaponry. If a weapons system works and works well, there is a strong pressure from many directions to procure and deploy the weapons out of all proportion to the prudent level required.''

It was the speech of a man riven by doubts about the wisdom of the policy he was supposed to be justifying. Those doubts grew. By 1968, in addition to his reservations about ABMs, McNamara was more skeptical than ever about the American MIRV program, which was moving into its testing phase. He believed that MIRVs should be subjected to the same sort of negotiated freeze as ABMs—and for much the same reason: "MIRV potentially is even more destabilizing than the ABM. It means very large numbers of separately targetable warheads and could arouse concern on the other side that the adversary is seeking a first-strike capability." In other words, McNamara was concerned that the Soviets, viewing the U.S. ABM and MIRV programs together, would fear an American first strike against the U.S.S.R. As for the danger of a Soviet first strike against the U.S., McNamara reported to Congress in February 1968 that it was "extremely unlikely" that Moscow would choose to build "a large Soviet ICBM force with a substantial hard-target-kill capacity."[6]

Nitze dissented on both counts. He believed that McNamara was worrying too much about American programs and too little about Soviet ones. Nitze had never taken seriously the idea of an American attack against the U.S.S.R., nor did he believe that the Soviets took such a possibility seriously; yet he took very seriously indeed the danger of a Soviet first strike, and he felt McNamara was entirely too sanguine about the Soviet ICBM buildup.

By early 1968 these disagreements were largely academic. Lyndon Johnson had already announced that McNamara would be moving from the Pentagon across the Potomac River to serve as president of the World Bank. The reason was the war in Vietnam. McNamara was convinced that the war had become a losing proposition and should be called off. Complaining that his secretary of defense had "gone dovish on me," Johnson replaced McNamara with Clark Clifford, who had been one of Truman's closest aides and who was now a prominent Washington lawyer and Democratic Party activist.

Arriving at the Pentagon to take up his new post, Clifford found himself "fortunate enough to have in place an extremely able deputy in Paul Nitze. I was all the more impressed by his sense of duty, for I could tell that he was exceedingly put out at having been passed over for the job that now fell to me."[7]

The Vietnam Distraction

From late 1963, when he reluctantly became secretary of the navy, until mid-1967, when he became deputy secretary of defense, Paul Nitze was deprived of a central role on the issues he cared about most—nuclear-weapons policy and grand strategy. But his tenure in the Navy Department also spared him much of the trauma that other policymakers, more directly involved with Vietnam, experienced during those four years. The chain of command for the conduct of the war went from the Joint Chiefs of Staff directly, via the secretary of defense, to the President, bypassing the service secretaries.

Not that the war was either out of sight or out of mind for Nitze. As a senior official of the Defense Department, he visited Southeast Asia, wrote reports about what he observed there, attended meetings on what to do, gave speeches in support of Administration policy, and engaged in countless arguments with colleagues and countrymen. The issue of the war was all-pervasive and all-preoccupying.

That, in Nitze's view, was just the problem. From his perspective as a back-bencher, he eventually became convinced that the Vietnam War was preventing the United States from concentrating on what he considered the primary challenge—the strategic nuclear threat posed by the Soviet Union. What should have been a peripheral entanglement was polarizing and paralyzing the nation, diverting American attention, depleting American resources, and sapping American resolve.

Nitze joined the inner circle of policymakers on Vietnam only late in the losing game, after he became deputy secretary. He frequently met on Thursday afternoons at the State Department with a group of senior officials who called themselves the "nongroup," because the existence of the committee was never formally acknowledged and it produced no minutes or reports.* The agenda was open to any aspect of the war in Vietnam. Nitze argued against continued American bombing of North Vietnam. He saw this particular ladder of escalation leading nowhere. Within the Pentagon, Nitze was part of an inner circle, seen elsewhere in the government as a cabal, that was determined to stop the bombing and start serious talks with the Vietnamese Communists.

The two other principal members of the cabal were the new secretary of defense, Clark Clifford—who had now, in Johnson's phrase, "gone dovish" himself—and Paul Warnke, who held Nitze's old portfolio as assistant secretary for international security affairs. Like Clifford, Vance, and so many other mandarins of the defense and foreign policy establishment, Warnke was an attorney. He had been a law partner of Dean Acheson's, and over the years he had heard Acheson praise Nitze many times. He had also listened to Nitze boast about how he had "toughened up Dean" on the Soviet threat during the Truman Administration. Nitze had supported Warnke for the ISA job. "The two Pauls," as they were often called, knew each other socially; they and their wives frequently dined together. And at the time,

---

*The "nongroup" met in the office of Nitze's State Department counterpart, Nicholas Katzenbach. They were joined by the President's national security advisor, Walt W. Rostow, who took McGeorge Bundy's place; Richard Helms, the director of Central Intelligence; Earle Wheeler, the chairman of the Joint Chiefs; and William Bundy, by then assistant secretary of state for East Asia.

they saw largely eye to eye on the war and the importance of ending it. In the last days of the Administration, Nitze gave Warnke a photo of himself, signed, "To my co-conspirator, with affection and regards."

Later Clifford and Warnke, now in law practice with each other, went public with their advocacy of a Vietnam peace settlement on terms that Nitze found imprudent if not dishonorable. Nitze depicted himself as having been the lone champion of a steady course toward an exit from the tunnel, and he complained about the erraticism of Clifford and Warnke. "Once McNamara got driven out and Clifford came in," Nitze recalled, "I devoted myself for at least a month to trying to persuade Clark that his hawkish handling of the situation was totally absurd." But Clifford went too far: "He suddenly flipped from being an extreme hawk to being an absolute incontinent cut-and-runner." When asked about Clifford during an oral history interview in 1981, Nitze said, "I was his deputy, and I have lived with Clark when he was the great hawk of all time, and I have lived with him when he was the great dove of all time. Frankly, out of lack of respect for him, I do not want to comment."

By then, other disagreements between Nitze and Clifford, as well as between the two Pauls, had magnified those they had once had about Vietnam. However, Warnke acknowledged that there had indeed been at least one significant dispute even during their days together in the Pentagon: Both men felt that the Vietnam War was disastrous for the United States; but Warnke saw it as a disaster in its own right, while Nitze was concerned—exclusively and excessively in Warnke's view—with its implications for the Soviet-American rivalry. Nitze, said Warnke, "was driven by one idea above all others: that the Soviets would make monkeys out of us—they would exploit our overinvolvement in Southeast Asia and take advantage of us elsewhere, particularly in the strategic nuclear competition."

Nitze confirmed that the essence of his misgiving about Vietnam was a concern that the war was "taking our eye off the ball," distracting the United States from "the overall strategic problem . . . the degree to which our position vis-à-vis the U.S.S.R. was weakening, and the degree to which support for our position in Europe and elsewhere had declined."

In one of their last meetings together in the Pentagon before the Johnson Administration left office, Nitze delivered a table-thumping lecture to Warnke and another colleague, Leslie Gelb, on the message that he most wanted to impress on his countrymen. "It's a we/they world," he said. "It's us against the Soviets. Either we get them first, or they get us first." Warnke was visibly appalled, wincing and shaking his head—and Nitze was just as visibly upset by Warnke's reaction.[8]

An Acronym Is Born

Precisely because Secretary of Defense Clark Clifford was so preoccupied with conducting and, if possible, ending the war in Vietnam, Paul Nitze, as the deputy secretary, had all the more authority and influence in his own area of principal concern—countering the Soviet military buildup and seeking a way to blunt that challenge through arms control.

Clifford delegated to Nitze the task of getting the Johnson Administration ready for talks with the Soviets. Nitze presided over an enterprise that was virtually without precedent: the systematic preparation of proposals that were designed to produce agreements that would limit the arsenals of the two sides rather than merely score propaganda points. He and the secretary of the air force, Harold Brown, persuaded the Joint Chiefs of Staff to look more seriously into the military consequences of arms control proposals. The chairman of the Joint Chiefs, Earle Wheeler, chose Lieutenant General Royal Allison of the Air Force to represent the interests of the uniformed military, while within ISA, Paul Warnke appointed Morton Halperin, a young academic who had worked with Thomas Schelling at Harvard on the early theory of arms control, to organize an ad hoc committee that would prepare a negotiating position for the United States.

Halperin remembered sensing during this period the beginnings of tension between Nitze and Warnke: "Over time, there developed a problem between the two Pauls: Nitze didn't think Warnke took the details and military nitty-gritty seriously enough; he felt Warnke was too interested in arms control for its own sake."

A central and contentious issue was what to do about MIRVs. Robert McNamara had been looking for a way to limit MIRVs when he left office. In 1968 Halperin and others designed a proposal that would include a delay in the beginning of American MIRV testing as a way to probe Soviet interest in a MIRV ban. Nitze passed the proposal along to Clifford, but with his recommendation that the idea not be pursued. He felt that American moratoriums, supposedly temporary and conditional, ran the risk of becoming permanent. He believed they also undermined negotiating leverage with the Soviets. Clifford accepted Nitze's advice. Later in the year, at an appearance before the National Press Club on September 5, the secretary of defense explained, "We have proceeded [with MIRV testing] on the basis that a position of substantial strength is essential and is the position from which we can negotiate agreements." Largely because of Nitze, the United States would, in the forthcoming talks with the Soviets, seek limits on ABMs but not on MIRVs.

Those members of the Johnson Administration who were most enthusiastic about arms control felt that blocking ABM was the sine qua non of nuclear diplomacy. Nitze's own position was more qualified. "For Paul," recalled Harold Brown, "it wasn't a question of whether ABMs were good or bad in some absolute sense; they were just another element in his analysis."[9]

Nitze was not a true believer in zero defense any more than he was a believer in total elimination of offensive weapons. A reduced and completely defenseless force of weapons might be more vulnerable to preemption than a larger force. Therefore Nitze was willing to entertain the idea of some form of point defense, as long as a way could be found to make the defense "cost-effective at the margins." This was a phrase that cropped up repeatedly in conversations Nitze had in the Pentagon and with his old friend Albert Wohlstetter. "Cost-effective" alone meant simply that it must be no more expensive to erect the defensive shield than to deploy offensive spears. The additional phrase, "at the margins," meant that the defensive system must continue to be cost-effective once it was in place and the other side began trying to hedge against it by adding warheads. Nitze recalled: "Wohlstetter and I puzzled and argued for hours over the cost of an interceptor 'slice' [an incremental addition to the whole defensive system] versus a warhead 'slice' [an incremental addition to the array of offensive countermeasures]. As long as it was cheaper to MIRV existing systems than to add interceptors, an ABM system would not meet the criterion of cost-effective at the margins. Wohlstetter felt that at some point, with some breakthrough, it would become cheaper to add interceptors. I was not persuaded. But it was also a question of what level of leakage was tolerable."[10]

Even if a few Soviet warheads "leaked" through a shield and fell onto American cities, the defense would have failed disastrously. But a small leakage that allowed a few warheads to get through not onto population centers but onto American ICBM silos in relatively remote, sparsely populated parts of the country, might be tolerable, as long as enough of the American ICBMs were successfully protected so that they could carry out the retaliatory attack.

Nitze continued to believe that pursuit of area, or population, defense was futile and dangerous, but he was eventually sympathetic to the idea of ABMs as a way of protecting Minuteman from a Soviet first strike. Already in 1968 he was against banning ABMs altogether. Rather, he wanted to see them limited at a level where they would, in the jargon, "enhance deterrence" by "assuring the survivability" of American missiles; the most stable form of deterrence might require a "mix" of offense and defense, with the proportions to be the principal item on the agenda of the proposed negotiations with the Soviets. During discussions at the Pentagon, Harold Brown and Morton Halperin, who were less worried about the vulnerability of Minuteman than Nitze was, pressed for maximum limitation if not an outright prohibition on

ABMs, while Nitze leaned toward the view that the clusters of Minuteman launchers should have batteries of ABM interceptors to defend them.

Meanwhile, however, there were new questions about congressional support for the ABM program. One of the many consequences of the war in Vietnam was to sour the Congress on defense programs in general, including the ABM. Having earlier been under pressure from Capitol Hill to deploy the system, the Administration now found itself fighting off congressional efforts to postpone deployment. With Clifford and Nitze lobbying hard, the Senate defeated an anti-ABM resolution in late June 1968. Four days later— a year and a half after Johnson's original proposal and a full year after Glassboro—the Soviets formally committed themselves to negotiations on strategic forces. It was probably, as the Russians like to say, not accidental that their agreement came just after ABM survived another onslaught by its Senate opponents. Certainly Nitze believed the timing was significant. In his view, the American bargaining chip, in the form of a program to develop and deploy strategic defenses, was now on the table, and the talks could begin.

Soviet and American diplomats maneuvered through the summer. The Central Intelligence Agency was looking for a convenient heading under which to file the sudden inundation of material on the subject. Separable First Stage Disarmament Agreement, or SFSDA, would just not do. Robert Martin, an official of the Bureau of Politico-Military Affairs at the State Department suggested SALT, for Strategic Arms Limitation Talks. His immediate superiors did not like the term—they found it too cute, as did the Arms Control and Disarmament Agency. But the CIA liked the coinage, and in one of its earliest skirmishes with State and ACDA over SALT, fought the issue up to a high-level interagency committee and won. An acronym was born. Halperin's ad hoc planning group, which reported to Nitze, became known as "the SALT Committee."[11]

On August 21 an announcement was to be made in the two capitals that Johnson would visit the Soviet Union in October for a summit in Leningrad and the opening of the negotiations. Paul Nitze almost certainly would have played a vital role in those talks. However, the night before, the Soviet Union and its Warsaw Pact allies invaded Czechoslovakia, crushing the reformist regime of Alexander Dubček. With Johnson a lame duck and the Kremlin leaders now denounced as international villains, the United States had no choice but to cancel the scheduled announcement and the summit. Even before the talks had formally begun, SALT was already a victim of "linkage," the idea that progress in arms control should be held hostage to acceptable Soviet behavior in other areas.

The Democrats, divided and demoralized, moved toward defeat in the presidential election in the fall of 1968. Hanging in the air was one of the more tantalizing what-might-have-beens of modern history. Had the Soviets not invaded Czechoslovakia and had the summit taken place as planned, SALT might have begun a year earlier than it did, in a Democratic Administration. Coming off of that diplomatic success with the Soviets rather than wallowing in the depths of a foreign-policy catastrophe in Southeast Asia, Johnson's vice-president and would-be successor, Hubert Humphrey, might have won the closely contested '68 election. He might also have given a high post in his Administration to an old friend and supporter, Paul Nitze.

CHAPTER 5

The Parity Perplex

During his tempestuous appearance before the Senate Armed Services Committee in November 1963, Paul Nitze had affirmed that he was "a strong believer in the importance of maintaining superiority over the Communist bloc in every element of our military power." Through most of the Johnson Administration, Nitze and others involved in arms control were still operating on the premise that an agreement with the Soviet Union would somehow incorporate, and thereby protect, American strategic superiority. That is what the stock phrase used in memos about SALT during the Johnson Administration—a "freeze at current levels"—meant in practice.

But by the end of the Administration, when the talks were supposed to begin, a freeze meant a smaller margin of superiority than had been the case earlier. Nitze had seen the numbers attached to "every element of our military power" change dramatically. The heavy SS-9 was just the most vivid proof that the Soviets were pouring resources into their Strategic Rocket Forces in order to achieve what became known as strategic nuclear parity.

Like so much of the theory and terminology of the nuclear age, parity was an American concept, borrowed from agricultural economics. It comes from the same Latin root as "peer" and "par," and it has the connotation of equality among competitors. Parity is something to which each competitor is entitled—and which is guaranteed as part of an overarching order. These connotations were supposed to carry over into the realm of the strategic nuclear competition. Parity came to be seen as a necessary condition for stability; the absence of parity would lead to instability, disorder, and the danger of war. Because neither superpower would tolerate the achievement and maintenance of superiority by the other, it was hoped that there would be a physical principle, like a law of hydrology or thermodynamics, pushing the two sides toward parity and keeping them there once they achieved equilibrium.

Yet unless it was clearly defined and strictly regulated, parity could also be a highly unstable state. Neither side was ever going to feel that its adversary was fully entitled to parity, or that it would use that status to benevolent ends—or, for that matter, that it would be satisfied with mere parity. Neither would ever entirely believe that its own forces were sufficient to deter the other. Each would indulge a temptation to improve around the edges of its position, cultivating something that might be called parity plus, while at the same time nurturing a suspicion that the other side was bent on doing the same thing, only to more sinister ends. There was also sure to be debate over how broad the band of parity was—how sensitive overall parity was to marginal advantages favoring one side or the other.

This troublesome, ambiguous concept of parity was to be both the starting point and the end point of SALT; the objective of the negotiations was to produce agreements that would increase the stability of the relationship, but all the time staying within the confines of parity. That meant accepting the premise that parity was more desirable than the alternative of constant jockeying for superiority. That was a difficult premise to accept if one believed, as Paul Nitze did, that the Soviet Union would, by its very nature, abuse the privileges of its status as a superpower and seek relative advantage.

In other words, to the extent that they could get away with it, the Soviets would "cheat" on parity. Arms control was an attempt to make it harder for them to do that. It was the diplomatic mechanism for defining and regulating parity and for helping America to answer the old question, How much is enough? Finding a finite, affordable answer was difficult for the United States in a competition with adversaries who seemed to be conducting their end of the rivalry on the principle that more is better, most is best.

Robert McNamara, his colleagues, and his successors developed various concepts and doctrines so that the United States might live securely with lower levels of nuclear weaponry at a time when the Soviets were greatly expanding their forces. The United States did not want to have to match the Soviets weapon for weapon, megaton for megaton. That sensible and moderate objective fostered some bloodthirsty-sounding terminology. The McNamara doctrine of "assured destruction" held that if the United States had the capacity to kill between a fifth and a third of the Soviet population, and to destroy between half and three-quarters of Soviet industrial capacity, that was enough to deter the U.S.S.R. from attacking the U.S., no matter how much destructive capability of their own the Soviets had. These figures, while gruesome, were also arbitrary. They were selected in large measure because they corresponded, very approximately, to American calculations of the point of diminishing returns: More American weapons would only marginally increase the United States's ability to inflict damage on the U.S.S.R. Therefore the United States could reach a certain level of armament and call it enough.

Far more controversial was another doctrine that came to be known, sardonically, as "mutual assured destruction" (MAD). McNamara argued that it was in the interest of the United States for the Soviets, too, to have a capacity for carrying out a retaliatory strike that would assuredly destroy the United States. Conversely, it was not in the American interest for the Soviet

Union to fear that the United States might be able to carry out a first strike and get away with it. A Soviet Union that felt itself vulnerable to an American first strike would be more likely to try to attempt a first strike of its own in a crisis. The idea of mutual assured destruction was nothing more than a refinement of Oppenheimer's strange stability and Wohlstetter's delicate balance of terror. MAD, in short, was an attempt to cope with an inescapable reality, and arms control was an attempt to codify MAD.

There was logic here—logic that Paul Nitze could understand, support, and help apply. But there was also trouble. Parity was an American euphemism for the loss of American superiority. As such, it remained for a long time a dirty word to many American ears, a synonym for defeatism. The Republican platform adopted at the convention that nominated Barry Goldwater in 1964 asserted that the Democrats had "adopted policies which will lead to a potentially fatal parity of power with Communism instead of continued military superiority for the United States." A Goldwater Administration would "maintain a superior, not merely equal, military capability as long as the Communist drive for world domination continues." Goldwater himself wrote: "In my judgment, McNamara should have been punished for his pursuit of a policy calculated to produce parity with the Russians as a satisfactory replacement for our earlier superiority."

If Robert McNamara was the principal villain in the eyes of the right, Paul Nitze was his chief accomplice. One of Goldwater's leading proponents and pamphleteers, Phyllis Schlafly, co-authored (with Chester Ward) a paperback book in 1964 called *The Gravediggers*. The title referred to Khrushchev's famous boast "We will bury you," and the book denounced the East Coast foreign policy establishment: "These men are not Communists. They are card-carrying liberals. They will not commit the crime. They will merely dig the grave. These gravediggers move in and out of the highest levels of our Government."

An entire chapter of the booklet was devoted to exposing "the Nitze Axis." The attack was reminiscent of the campaign against Nitze in the McCormick press ten years before and of Curtis LeMay's denunciations during the Kennedy Administration: Nitze was an accommodationist "New York investment banker" who fell for the "wildest notions of the most radical world-government pacifist disarmers." He was guilty of an "emotional monomania against weapons of massive megatonnage." His Asilomar speech of 1960 had been the "Disarmament Manifesto of President Kennedy's New Frontier and of President Johnson's Great Society." He had led a clique that took over the Pentagon, ravaged American defenses, and followed "a pattern of unilateral disarmament." As much as its namesake, Nitze was supposedly responsible for "the McNamara Gap."[1]

In 1964 extremism like Schlafly's contributed to Goldwater's crushing defeat. Lyndon Johnson capitalized on the widespread concern that Goldwater was a trigger-happy anti-Communist who might get the United States into a nuclear war. It was one of the few moments in American politics when advocacy of the hard line in Soviet-American relations proved a political liability. But even as Johnson fended off Goldwater's challenge from the right, he was careful not to concede that he was willing to settle for strategic nuclear parity with the Soviet Union.

"For the past four years," said Johnson in a message to Congress on January 18, 1965, "the focus of our national effort has been upon assuming an indisputable margin of superiority for our defenses." LBJ, after all, had made his own early move into the realm of presidential politics in the late 1950s as one of the first senators to exploit the Gaither Report and the missile-gap issue. Charges of a "McNamara gap" stung Johnson, and they stung Nitze as well.

In 1968, the Republican Party succeeded where it had failed four years earlier. It put the Democrats on the defensive by denouncing them for making "not retention of American superiority, but parity with the Soviet Union . . . the controlling doctrine in many critical areas." The Soviets had virtually pulled even with the United States in numbers of deployed ICBMs (although there were still many more American bombs and warheads). The Republican candidate that year, Richard Nixon, attacked his Democratic opponent, Hubert Humphrey, by using the same politically supercharged word that John Kennedy had so successfully wielded against Nixon himself in 1960: the Democrats, said Nixon in 1968, had permitted the development of a "gravely serious security gap."

It was not a gap in any particular weapon system, such as bombers or missiles, that Nixon had in mind. He was making a point more sophisticated, and harder to disprove with raw numbers, than the missile-gap issue that Kennedy had used against the Republicans in 1960. What Nixon was talking about, as he went on to explain, was not really a "gap" at all but a misplaced confidence that America could be safe in a world where the Soviet Union had caught up with the United States in overall nuclear strength.

"This parity concept," said Nixon in a campaign statement on October 24, 1968, "means superiority for potential enemies." There was an assumption here, widely and persistently held but rarely acknowledged so succinctly, that as long as Soviet behavior, actual and potential, was driven by the software of a totalitarian, expansionist ideology, the United States had better have an offsetting advantage in the hardware of deterrence.

But the Soviets, quite simply, would settle for nothing less than parity. In its Russian translation *(paritet),* it was an almost sacred term. It meant a Soviet gain eagerly sought and, once achieved, jealously guarded. Not only did the Soviets have the technological ability and production capacity to field nuclear forces as potent as those of the United States, but their political system made possible a degree of stringency, discipline, and militarization that the American Congress and public would never be willing to match. Therefore, an all-out, tit-for-tat arms race might at best be a no-win proposition for the United States. At worst it might be a losing one.

For that reason, once in office, Richard Nixon was as quick to renounce the quest for superiority as John Kennedy had been to repudiate the missile gap. Four months after his inauguration, at a press conference on April 18, 1969, Nixon recalled that at the time of the Cuban missile crisis, the United States had enjoyed a superiority of "at least four to one and maybe five to one, over the Soviet Union in terms of overall nuclear capability. Now we don't have that today. That gap has been closed. We shall never have it again because it will not be necessary for us. Sufficiency . . . is all that is necessary." He might have said: Sufficiency is all that is possible.

Also in April 1969, proclaiming an "era of negotiations" in a speech to the North Atlantic Council, President Nixon made clear that if this new doctrine of sufficiency was to enhance Western security, it had to be coupled with nuclear diplomacy:

> We must recognize that [arms-control agreements with the U.S.S.R.] would imply a military relationship far different from the one that existed when NATO was founded. Let's put it in plain words. The West does not today have the massive nuclear predominance that it once had, and any sort of broad-based arms agreement with the Soviets would codify the present balance.

Moreover, now that the Soviets had caught up with the United States, they finally had an incentive to deal. As Nitze later remarked, before the late sixties "the Russians were not about to enter into negotiations because they thought their position was not close enough to parity and they wouldn't negotiate on any basis other than parity."[2]

It was hard then, and would become harder still, for experts on the American side to agree among themselves what parity was or should be. Even harder was for two sovereign and adversary states to agree with each other. SALT was born of the recognition that, sooner or later, the Soviet Union would catch up with the United States in strategic nuclear strength. But SALT was beset from its inception by ambivalence among Americans over whether a mutually accepted, mutually regulated equality between the superpowers could somehow be made compatible with the goals of stability and safety.

Paul Nitze was the personification of that ambivalence.

Prudent Defense

The change of administrations at the beginning of 1969 left Paul Nitze once again without a job. He returned with little enthusiasm to his old office at the Johns Hopkins School of Advanced International Studies on Massachusetts Avenue. For years he had been driven home in a government limousine. Now, at the end of his first lonely day back at work as a private citizen, he discovered he had forgotten where he had parked his car. He spent a long time searching for it. The quest became more than an inconvenience—it acquired the dimensions of an existential crisis. Finally he found the car and he drove home, where he made himself a stiff drink, and told his wife, Phyllis, that it was "tough to be back in the wilderness."

While waiting for an opportunity to return to government, Nitze found an activity that would advance a cause he strongly believed in. Richard Nixon had decided against trying to erect an ABM system comprehensive enough to defend the American population. Shortly after coming into office, he said, "Although every instinct motivates me to provide the American people with complete protection against a major nuclear attack, it is not now within our power to do so. . . . And it might look to an opponent like the prelude to an offensive strategy threatening the Soviet deterrent."

This did not, however, mean a complete halt to the ABM program. Nixon announced that he would proceed with a system that would protect Minuteman silos. This limited system would be designed so that it would not appear to be the basis for a territorial defense that would provoke offensive countermeasures by the Soviet Union. The new American leadership would also pick up where the old one had left off in the pursuit of an arms-control agreement which limited offenses and defenses together.

It was clear both to Nixon, newly arrived in the White House, and to Nitze, now back in private life, that if the United States was going to use limitations on ABMs as an incentive to get the Soviets to limit their ICBMs, first there had to be an American ABM program; otherwise, the U.S. would lack leverage in the negotiations. The process of arms control was based in large measure on the idea of strategic defense as a bargaining chip to achieve limits on strategic offense.

The ABM program had the support of Nitze's erstwhile attackers on the Armed Services Committee, Strom Thurmond and Richard Russell, as well as his principal defender and close friend, Henry Jackson. But many Democrats in Congress wanted to put ABM on hold and proceed with SALT. They had the backing of a large and well-financed cluster of liberal organizations made up of scientists and public figures who favored a moratorium on ABMs until SALT was given a chance to head off a new round of competition.

The New York publisher Cass Canfield raised money to lobby against Senate approval of the system. The result was a roster of experts that read like a Who's Who of the liberal defense intelligentsia, people like Jerome Wiesner, who had been John Kennedy's science advisor and was now provost of the Massachusetts Institute of Technology, and the Nobel Prize–winning nuclear physicist Hans Bethe. Their arguments against the ABM could be reduced to two propositions: The system would be ineffective in the event of an attack, and it would stimulate a surge in the arms race.

Nitze considered Hans Bethe "a great pal," but on the ABM, he was contemptuous of what he regarded as Bethe's fuzzy-mindedness and susceptibility to fashion. Ever since he had seen Oppenheimer argue so passionately, and in Nitze's view, fallaciously, against the hydrogen bomb in the late 1940s, Nitze had been wary of great scientists pronouncing judgment on matters of politics, diplomacy, and military strategy. He was not prepared to accept the technological case against ABM, the flat assertion that it would not work on any scale that would serve U.S. interests; Bethe and the others were prejudging scientific and engineering issues that were still unresolved. As for the strategic argument, there, too, the anti-ABM forces were, Nitze believed, "driven by prejudice rather than analysis." Like Oppenheimer on the H-bomb, the big-name scientists were making what Nitze called "'should' judgments" rather than "'could' judgments"; they were speaking, and thinking, not as scientists at all but as all-too-fallible laymen.

To his ears, the arguments being advanced by the ABM opponents smacked of disarmament-by-example of the sort that he believed Robert Oppenheimer and George Kennan had favored in the debate over the H-bomb: "The whole anti-ABM crowd was caught up in a perfectly asinine line of thought—the sort of half-baked thinking that had gotten us into trouble before and would so do again."[3]

Another veteran of the H-bomb decision, Dean Acheson, agreed. He and Nitze enlisted Albert Wohlstetter, who was now at the University of Chicago, to mount a countercampaign in support of the ABM. They called themselves the Committee to Maintain a Prudent Defense Policy. To do what Nitze called the "necessary nitty-gritty of drafting papers to combat the arrant nonsense, the inaccuracies and logical tripe being perpetrated by the other side," the committee enlisted three young men, all protégés of Wohlstetter: Peter Wilson and Paul Wolfowitz, who had been students of Wohlstetter's at the University of Chicago, and Richard Perle, who had studied at the University of California, Los Angeles, and Princeton. Acheson called them "our Three Musketeers," and they then brought in their own d'Artagnan, Edward Luttwak, a young Rumanian-born economist, strategic analyst, military historian, and expert on armored warfare.

As Nitze recalled proudly, "With these fellows and only fifteen thousand dollars, half of which came out of my own pocket, we ran circles around Cass Canfield, his millions, and all his big-name experts."

Richard Perle had been a friend of the Wohlstetters' daughter Joan at Hollywood High School when Albert Wohlstetter was at RAND. Perle later said that until he fell under Wohlstetter's influence, he had been a fairly traditional sixties liberal on foreign-policy and nuclear-weapons issues. But impromptu seminars around Wohlstetter's swimming pool converted him to the views that brought him to work for Wohlstetter, Acheson, and Nitze in 1969: The United States must look first to its own offensive and defensive arsenals, assuring its ability to survive and retaliate against Soviet attack and cope with the danger of Soviet blackmail.

Perle was then twenty-eight, thirty-four years younger than Nitze. Perle gave the impression of having less use than Nitze did for the technical side of the strategic debate. He understood the numbers and could use them effectively, but more for tactical and forensic purposes, less because he believed in their meaning or value the way Nitze did. For Nitze the Spenglerian X-factor was just that—one factor, to be taken into account, along with other, more objective ones, in the calculus of strategic thinking. For Perle, the quality of the enemy—the essential wickedness, deceitfulness, and aggressiveness of the Soviet Union—was far more important than any quantities that could be measured, weighed, counted, or brought into balance: The Soviets were thoroughly bad actors on the world stage, with whom it was disreputable and dangerous for the United States to deal other than as antagonists. In that sense, his was a more purely ideological view.

Perle's personal style was deceptively mild. There was an almost cherubic roundness and softness to his face. The anomaly in these features was his eyes—dark, brooding, intense, and deeply recessed in cavelike shadows. For this reason, his sobriquet in later years was the Prince of Darkness. But he was not in the least Mephistophelean in manner. Even in argument, he frequently smiled and rarely raised his voice. His baritone could be smooth and soothing. His personality did not have the hard, sharp edges that Nitze's did. Both men were virtuoso debaters; both relished intellectual combat. But Perle seemed often to be improvising brilliantly, while Nitze was weighing every word. Perle preferred to work on a broad and impressionistic canvas, basing his case at the outset on assertions of principle, then working backward to specifics. Nitze's discourse was more scientific, more linear. He had a point-by-point, building-block approach; he started with the facts, then painstakingly established the logical interconnections among them, and eventually moved to broader conclusions. He gave the impression that there was a blackboard and a flipchart at hand.

Despite all the differences between them, for a while Nitze seemed to be developing a long-term mentor-protégé relationship with Perle. "He was brighter than hell, scrappy and dedicated,'' Nitze said. All three qualities proved useful as the Committee to Maintain a Prudent Defense Policy battled through the summer for the ABM program and helped the Administration win a narrow victory in the Senate.[4]

Channels

The battle over the ABM whetted Paul Nitze's eagerness to return to government service and clearly established him as an ally of the new Administration. A powerful official in the White House was willing to sponsor him—Henry Kissinger, the new presidential national security advisor. In his memoirs, Kissinger explains why he felt that Nitze, a Democrat, should have a place in a Republican Administration:

> One of our nation's most distinguished public servants and ablest theorists on national defense . . . [Nitze] had studied issues of national security all of his adult life; he had been one of the small group of dedicated and thoughtful men and women whose bipartisan support and occasional criticism had enabled American foreign policy to steer a steady course in the postwar period. He and I had had occasional disagreements, as is inevitable among serious men, but I had, and continue to have, the highest regard for him.[5]

On Kissinger's recommendation, President Nixon was prepared to appoint Nitze U.S. ambassador to West Germany. But the nomination ran afoul of J. William Fulbright, the chairman of the Senate Foreign Relations Committee, who held a grudge against Nitze from arguments about the war in Vietnam a year earlier.* Intercession by Clark Clifford and Paul Warnke on Nitze's behalf eventually traced the opposition to Barry Goldwater, at the other end of the ideological spectrum from Fulbright. Because of the lingering memory of Nitze's association with the National Council of Churches in 1958 and his Asilomar speech in 1960, said Fulbright, "Goldwater still thinks Nitze is one of those one-worlders." By then, Nixon had already turned to Kenneth Rush for the appointment to Bonn. A suggestion by Sec-

---

*In early 1968, Fulbright had conducted hearings into the Gulf of Tonkin incident of 1964, in which North Vietnamese patrol boats fired on American naval vessels, providing Lyndon Johnson with a pretext for a major escalation of the war. Fulbright had trouble getting a senior Pentagon official to testify. McNamara was then at the World Bank, and his successor, Clark Clifford, had no intention of stepping into the lions' den. Nitze, then deputy secretary, was served up to the committee. Almost inevitably, he became the target of antiwar senators' anger and frustration. There were disputes over the classification of intelligence intercepts from the time of the incident, and Nitze antagonized Fulbright.

retary of State William Rogers that Nitze be made ambassador to Tokyo ran aground for similar reasons.

It was only after these disappointments that Nitze was offered the job of representing Secretary of Defense Melvin Laird on the first SALT delegation, which was to begin work in the fall.

Partly because the domestic political struggle over the ABM had made him uncertain how strong a hand the U.S. would have in negotiations, the new President had moved slowly at first on the diplomatic front. He circled the idea of SALT cautiously, almost mistrustfully, before deciding whether and how to make it his own. When he moved, it was largely in secret. Hoping that SALT would encourage Soviet cooperation in other areas, Nixon and Kissinger initiated SALT I in a series of meetings with Ambassador Anatoly Dobrynin, the Soviet envoy in Washington with whom officials of the Johnson Administration had also been trying to get the talks started.

Thus SALT was born in the so-called back channel, a series of confidential tête-à-têtes between a Soviet official with a direct line to the Kremlin and a senior American policymaker who had the ear of the President and the authority to speak for him. Nixon and Kissinger knew that a large amount of slogging business would have to be done in formal negotiations; but that process would inevitably be cumbersome, and progress would be slow. Each delegation would contain representatives of the different agencies and interest groups that were vying with each other back home. The bureaucratic politics, even the personal rivalries, of the two capitals would be played out in microcosm at the talks as they migrated between Helsinki and Vienna. Nixon and Kissinger proceeded from the outset on the assumption that at critical moments, bold, quick decisions could be made within the U.S. government—and breakthroughs achieved with the other side—only if they were able to resort to a kind of superdiplomacy that bypassed the bureaucracy in Washington as well as the negotiating team in the field.

While Nitze was offered a job in the front channel, he later described how he also was promised access to the back channel. He went to the White House to discuss SALT with Nixon and Kissinger. He had little reason to harbor fondness for either man. Almost twenty years before, Nixon had joined in the savage attacks on Nitze's friend Dean Acheson; as vice-president, Nixon had acceded in the withdrawal of the offer of a Pentagon job that Nitze had been promised early in the Eisenhower Administration; then Nixon had gone on staunchly to defend the Dulles defense policies that Nitze found so objectionable.

As for the Harvard academic who was now at Nixon's right hand, Nitze's relations with Kissinger had been tense since they had encountered each other a dozen years before in the Council on Foreign Relations study group that helped inspire *Nuclear Weapons and Foreign Policy*. Kissinger had supported the idea of sending Nitze to Bonn, but, as both men knew, that was an ocean away from where Nitze most wanted to be: at the center of the action, in a high, policymaking position in the U.S. government in Washington.

As Nitze recalled the conversation at the White House, Nixon got down to business by saying: "You know, Paul, I don't have any confidence in Bill Rogers [the secretary of state]. I don't think he knows anything about arms control and dealing with the Russians. What I want you to do is report to me if anyone is about to sell the store." Nixon asked Nitze to establish his own back channel directly to the Oval Office by way of Kissinger: "You can communicate with Henry, and he'll communicate with me."

Nitze found all this, as he put it later, "offensively conspiratorial," in marked contrast to the collegiality that had prevailed in the Truman, Kennedy, and Johnson administrations.

"Mr. President," he recalled saying to Nixon, "that isn't the way the system works."

As Nitze remembered Nixon's reply: "God damn it, I've told you what the channel of communication is, and if anything comes up, I want you to use it."

Nitze's initiation as a full-time arms-control negotiator left him with some foreboding. Like so many others in his career, this job was a consolation prize. He was not even to be head of the SALT delegation. That post went to Gerard Smith, another of the distinguished Washington lawyers who gravitated to senior positions in the foreign-policy and national-security apparatus. He had been one of Nitze's successors as director of the Policy Planning Staff in the Eisenhower Administration. Smith was also to be director of the Arms Control and Disarmament Agency, the entity that had been created by statute in 1961 to make sure that the quest for regulation of the arms race had an institutional advocate in the executive branch.

While Nitze had personal respect for Smith, he did not consider him his superior in any but the most strictly bureaucratic sense.

Nitze was all the more determined to have a strong, trustworthy team working with him in his new assignment. He asked Richard Perle to join him when he went over to the Pentagon in the fall. However, during his summer's work in the ABM battle, Perle had found a new mentor in Senator Henry Jackson, who offered him a job on the staff of a subcommittee on national security and international operations. Rather than going to Europe to work as a negotiator with Nitze, Perle went to Capitol Hill, where he could remain first a watchdog, then a critic, and ultimately the single most effective opponent of the enterprise of which Nitze was now a part.[6]

Fearful Asymmetries

Even in the best of times, Washington is the scene of vigorous infighting over arms control. An adage of bureaucrats has it that "where you stand depends on where you sit." There are almost always as many different positions on arms-control issues as there are seats of power. The military services want to protect American weapons programs and press for arms-control measures that will slow down and ensure some degree of predictability in Soviet programs; the State Department seeks to advance negotiations (hence Nixon's suspicion that Rogers would favor agreement for its own sake); the vested interest of the Arms Control and Disarmament Agency has usually been apparent in its name; the CIA fights for provisions that will make it easier to verify Soviet compliance with treaties and fears that its experts will be forced, in congressional testimony on verification, to reveal the agency's secrets about how it monitors Soviet programs; the National Security Council staff is in the business of imposing harmony or at least brokering compromises among the often conflicting preferences of the other agencies; Congress, meanwhile, is constantly kibitzing; so too are the NATO allies, who have felt caught, both politically and geographically, between the superpowers and who understand that the weapons systems under negotiation are intended, in extremis, to fly over, if not land on, their heads. Finally, some of the most influential players are also the least predictable, because they can come from almost any part of the ideological spectrum: These are the Pentagon civilians, the political appointees who advise the secretary of defense on arms control.

The early months of SALT in 1969 and 1970 were not the best of times. Not only was the enterprise just getting under way; not only had the new Administration yet to sort out its objectives and assemble its final team, but there was a war on. As had been apparent during the ABM debate in the Senate, passions over Vietnam hindered rational deliberation on virtually all national-security issues, regardless of whether they had anything to do with thwarting the enemy in the jungles of Southeast Asia. No agency of the government—State, Defense, ACDA, or the NSC—had a clear idea what it wanted out of SALT. Not surprisingly, the infighting over SALT was especially intense and chaotic.

However, a few individual American officials knew exactly what they wanted, and Nitze was one of them. Having worked as an outsider in the summer of 1969 to make sure that the United States went into the negotiations with its ABM program moving forward, Nitze concentrated as an insider on the other half of the arms-control equation: the Soviet ballistic missile program that he felt must be constrained in exchange for limitations on ABMs.

Soon after joining the Nixon Administration, Nitze recalled, he was shown a report prepared by the intelligence community on long-range Soviet strategy in arms control. The document, he said, "made the outright judgment that the Soviets were interested only in parity, and that once they had attained parity, they would be satisfied and would stop. They would understand there was no point in their trying to achieve a position of superiority." This was a view with which Nitze had quarreled during the Johnson Administration, and he continued to do so now.

Nitze designed a diplomatic version of a war game, with a "red team" of American experts playing the part not of Warsaw Pact military commanders but of Soviet negotiators in SALT. The exercise convinced Nitze that "the Russians would look upon SALT as another forum for competition with the United States, and that it was their duty to try to achieve the best results for the U.S.S.R. and the worst results for the U.S."[7]

The red-team approach was indicative of Nitze's thinking throughout his career about the military and diplomatic challenge of dealing with the Soviets. If, as they surely did, the Soviets set up a "blue team" to anticipate what the United States would do in the negotiations, they would no doubt reach a conclusion that was the mirror image of Nitze's: The Americans would seek an outcome that inflicted maximum "damage" on the Soviet military (i.e., forced reductions in large, MIRVed ICBMs) while requiring minimum adjustment by the United States. What Nitze saw as a sinister Soviet game plan could also be interpreted as a natural, even understandable resistance to a certain didacticism in the American concept of arms control. The United States was trying to force the Soviet Union to restructure its deterrent according to American standards and preferences.

Nitze made no apologies for his view, then or later. Soviet ICBMs were dangerous, he believed, not only because of their inherent capabilities but also because they were Soviet. The Kremlin's relative advantage in ICBMs had long been troublesome and would become much more so. As the United States learned to live with the problematic notion of parity, it had also to cope with the problem that, within the context of parity, there were bound to be "asymmetries," categories of weapons in which one side would have advantages over the others. The most important asymmetry favoring the U.S.S.R. was in ICBMs. Land-based ballistic missile warheads have a number of attributes that make them especially threatening to their enemies: They are fast, accurate, and highly destructive; and since they are based on land, they can be on high alert, quickly responsive to an order from the political authorities to launch an attack.

Throughout the 1970s, an important companion to the concept of parity was that of "offsetting asymmetries," a technician's concept given currency by Henry Kissinger in his effort to downplay the relative Soviet advantage in ICBMs. The asymmetry, or disparity, in ICBM warheads favoring the Soviet Union was believed to be offset by the United States's quantitative and qualitative advantages in other types of weaponry, such as intercontinental bombers, submarine-launched ballistic missiles (SLBMs), and, later, cruise missiles, jet-powered (''air-breathing'') drones. Each of these weapon systems had certain advantages over ICBMs: Bombers can be more readily controlled; cruise missiles are suitable for penetrating enemy air defenses, as well as for precise, selective strikes of the sort envisioned in scenarios for ''limited war''; SLBMs are less vulnerable to preemption because the submarines in which they are carried are far harder for the enemy to target than fixed silos on land. For some years, the prevailing view in the United States was that the Soviet advantage in land-based ballistic missiles did not translate into militarily usable or politically meaningful supremacy.

Nitze came to worry that America's supposedly compensatory lead in bombers and SLBMs was cold comfort, because those were weapons suitable only to a second, retaliatory strike. Bombs and cruise missiles were too slow to carry out a sneak attack, and SLBMs were too imprecise to destroy enemy ICBM silos. Only ICBM warheads qualified, in the jargon, as ''prompt hard-target killers''—weapons that could, by the mid-seventies, quickly destroy the hardened, underground missile silos of the other side. In the games of chicken that superpowers played, or were presumed prepared to play, it was hard-target killers that counted most.

Nitze was fond of quoting an observation by Clausewitz: Napoleon may have been a military genius, but he also had more men and firepower in the battles he won, while he was in a numerically inferior position in those he lost, including, notably, Waterloo. ''I think anybody who deals with [matters relating to the superpower nuclear competition],'' said Nitze, ''has to be aware of the relative physical force capabilities on both sides as well as the political-psychological climate.''[8] It was an article of faith, or of fatalism, in the prenuclear era that, in Voltaire's words, ''God is always on the side of the heaviest battalions.'' Nitze believed that a very powerful devil was now on the side of the heaviest missiles. As long as the U.S.S.R. could threaten American ICBM silos with preemptive attack and the United States could not do the same in reverse, there would be a critical asymmetry in vulnerabilities between the superpowers.

This was to become the most contentious strategic issue of the next decade and the basis of fears in the late seventies about the ''window of vulnerability.'' With the prospect of the Soviet Union piling up an excess of prompt hard-target kill capability, the day might come when the Kremlin could blind American command-and-control facilities, wipe out the United States's entire force of one thousand ICBM silos, and destroy any bombers not already in the air and any submarines that had not yet put to sea. With the loss of its ICBMs, the United States would be deprived of its ability to attack the most valuable Soviet military targets. Those American bombers and submarines that escaped initial destruction would be able to strike back only in helter-skelter vengeance against Soviet cities. Yet the Soviets would still have enough weapons left over for a second attack on American cities if the United States attempted such a retaliation. Hence the United States and its allies might be forced to surrender.

There were a number of links in this logic chain that other strategists found weak. The premise of a Soviet first strike against American ICBMs rested on assumptions that were doubtful enough when taken separately and all the more so in combination. These were assumptions about what the Kremlin would believe it could do—and what it would believe the United States would *not* do in response. The Strategic Rocket Forces would have to achieve not only total surprise but near-perfect accuracy. That would mean launching its own ICBMs for the first time over the North Pole. Those doomsday trajectories would be influenced by gravitational and other forces different from the ones that could be measured when the Soviets calibrated the guidance systems of their missiles in west-to-east test shots into the Kamchatka Peninsula at the easternmost end of Siberia or into the Pacific Ocean. The Kremlin would also have to be confident that the United States would not retaliate with its surviving SLBMs and bombers—or that the U.S.S.R. would be able to absorb an American blow and then counterretaliate with its own ICBMs that had been held in reserve for just such a contingency.*

Would any imaginable Soviet leadership indulge in such a grotesque gamble with the lives of its own people and those of the rest of the planet? The answer, if not yes, was, to Nitze, at least maybe. On this point, virtually nothing had changed since NSC 68: Whether "the year of maximum danger" was predicted to be 1954 or 1974 or 1984 or 1994, he saw the Soviet Union as the one superpower that might actually start a nuclear war; therefore, it was especially imprudent to grant it, in SALT, the theoretical capacity to do so.

In 1969, as a recently appointed, middle-level member of the Nixon Ad-

---

*According to widely accepted estimates in the 1980s, Soviet ICBMs might, theoretically, be able to destroy about 97 percent of America's ICBM warheads in a flawless first strike. However, Soviet ICBMs and SLBMs together could destroy only about 40 percent of *all* U.S. strategic warheads (those on ICBMs, SLBMs, and strategic bombers). On the other hand, U.S. ICBMs could destroy only about half of the Soviet ICBM force, while U.S. ICBMs and SLBMs together could destroy about half of the total Soviet strategic warhead inventory. Thus, there was indeed a wide "asymmetry of vulnerability" favoring the U.S.S.R. if the comparison was limited to ICBMs. Hardliners tended to concentrate on ICBMs (a) because they were supposedly first-strike weapons and (b) because they were the category in which the enemy was ahead. But the asymmetry favored the United States, albeit more narrowly, if the comparison was broadened to include the other two "legs" of the strategic triad.

ministration, Paul Nitze fought a losing battle on behalf of what amounted to rollback strategy for the negotiations. He believed that SALT must not just, in President Nixon's phrase, "codify the balance" in overall military strength; it must rectify a looming imbalance in ICBMs.

The Administration was divided over whether in SALT to seek deep reductions in or merely a freeze on launchers for ballistic missiles, especially Soviet ICBMs. Nitze fought hard for reductions. In a series of meetings in Washington before the talks began, and in numerous cables back home once they were under way, he focused on one key piece of data about the Soviet Strategic Rocket Forces, one of the "facts" that he was always looking for in his effort to work a problem: an objective measurement of the huge Soviet capacity to hurl its warheads at American targets. This index of strategic power became known as ballistic missile throw-weight, the total weight of what can be carried by a missile over a particular range. Throw-weight was the power to heft the weight of the business end of the rocket; it included the armaments along with the hardware necessary to get them to their targets back on earth from the apogee of a ballistic trajectory, once they had been "boosted" to that height by the launch vehicle and after the other stages of the missile had fallen away.

Nitze was in the forefront of those who gave currency to the term and concept of throw-weight. It appealed to his lifelong desire to quantify the threat, to put calipers to the rubble. Throw-weight was the bottom line in the calculations of Nitze as Cartesian pessimist, Exhibit A in the worst-case scenarios about a Soviet attack. Of all the many ways to gauge strategic nuclear power, missile throw-weight represented the single largest advantage that the Soviet Union had over the United States. The Soviets got their throw-weight primarily from their large ICBM launchers. The more throw-weight the U.S.S.R. had, the greater the danger of a nuclear blitz of the sort conjured up in the nightmares of the Gaither Report and the various Wohlstetter studies for RAND—and the greater the challenge to arms control.

Nitze pressed hard for instructions to seek, and to hold firm in seeking, a reversal of the buildup in Soviet ballistic missile throw-weight. His way, as he put it, of "getting a handle" on the problem of throw-weight was for the United States to insist on reductions in the U.S.S.R.'s arsenal of "modern large ballistic missiles," the so-called "heavies" that then went under the designation SS-9.

He had to contend with disagreement from a number of quarters, including General Royal Allison, the Air Force officer who had worked with him during the Johnson Administration to get the Joint Chiefs of Staff "on board" SALT when it was launched. Allison now represented the Chiefs on the SALT delegation. He felt that throw-weight was too crude a measure of strategic nuclear capability and too difficult to monitor, and that besides, American technological superiority—particularly the accuracy of American

MIRVs—would compensate for Soviet brute strength. Without highly accurate MIRVs of their own, the Soviets' advantage in throw-weight was not militarily useful to them and therefore not militarily threatening to the United States. Accuracy, in short, was a more realistic measure than throw-weight of "hard-target kill capability," and by that measure the United States had less to fear.

That more relaxed view of throw-weight prevailed in the short term, not least because, once the negotiations got under way, the Soviets adamantly refused to consider reductions in their heavy missile force. But Soviet stonewalling confirmed Nitze's suspicion that the real "red team" was indeed up to no good in SALT. As he later explained:

> From the very beginning there was a question as to how the Soviet side would approach the talks. [The majority] opinion was that the Soviets shared our view that in such bilateral negotiations between the two major nuclear powers, neither side could expect the other to settle for less than parity . . . that it was in everyone's interest to arrive at agreements which would reduce the instabilities of the past and thus enhance security on both sides.
>
> A minority on the U.S. side, particularly those who had, over the years, studied Soviet theory and practice, had a different view. They believed that the Soviet side would look at the talks primarily from their own political viewpoint, would seek to optimize Soviet gains through the talks, and would use tactics similar to those they had used on important issues in the past. I shared the hopes of the majority but also the skepticism of the minority. . . .
>
> At the very first session at Helsinki, it became clear that the skeptics had a strong case. It soon became evident that the Soviet side had worked out a highly one-sided theory and was prepared to use a wide range of tactics to achieve its goal.

Nitze spent many hours in Helsinki instructing both his American colleagues and his Soviet counterparts on "the distinction between a zero-sum game, in which one side's gains are equal to the other side's losses, and a non-zero-sum game, in which both sides can either win or lose." Even later in the seventies, when laying the groundwork for his opposition to SALT II, he maintained that a "non-zero-sum approach" was "essential to negotiating sound agreements." His basic complaint with the Soviet Union was that while the United States was seeking a draw, the Kremlin leaders were still playing to win. Winning would mean emerging from SALT with their advantage in ballistic missile throw-weight and their monopoly in heavy ICBMs intact.[9]

The Hydra Survives

Paul Nitze was the Nixon Administration's Cassandra on the critical and divisive issue of throw-weight. But on another, related and equally fateful issue he shared the prevailing view and had less reason for pride in his prescience. This was the problem of MIRVs.

What made throw-weight threatening was precisely that it could be used to *throw* a multiplicity of warheads at American targets. Therefore, it might have followed logically from Nitze's own advocacy of throw-weight reductions that the goal of SALT should also be a ban on MIRVs. Even though the United States was ahead in the development of technology for dispensing multiple warheads from a postboost vehicle, or "bus," launched into space, the Soviets were virtually certain to catch up sooner or later; and when they did, large-throw-weight MIRVs would enhance their advantage, since they had more and larger rockets with which to launch more and larger warheads. The SS-9 would give way to a MIRVed successor, the SS-18, each with as many as ten independently targetable warheads.

For just that reason, Robert McNamara had hoped that the twin problems of MIRVs and ABMs could be nipped in the bud together; he believed that arms control required an intimate linkage between strategic offense and strategic defense. Morton Halperin—like Nitze, a veteran of the Johnson Pentagon now serving the Nixon Administration—resurrected the idea of suspending tests of MIRVs to see if the Soviets were interested in a ban on MIRVs in SALT I. Halperin had the support of Gerard Smith, head of the SALT delegation and director of ACDA.

Nitze opposed a moratorium on MIRV testing, just as he had when the idea first arose during the Johnson Administration. He still believed that if the United States held back, it would only make it easier for the Soviets to catch up; it would be a mistake to go into a new negotiation proposing to ban a system in which American technological prowess gave the United States a head start. Henry Kissinger and President Nixon had much the same view. Kissinger was convinced that the Soviets would never agree to stop their MIRV program until they had caught up with the United States.

Secretary of Defense Melvin Laird, Secretary of the Air Force Harold Brown, and the Joint Chiefs of Staff were all increasingly interested in multiple warheads for a reason similar to the one that originally made MIRVs enticing to McNamara: As "force multipliers," they were highly cost-efficient. A single rocket could carry a number of warheads and "cover" a number of targets. That was an especially attractive feature as America looked for a way to counter the Soviet offensive buildup in an era of congressional resistance to defense spending. So MIRVs were politically appealing, and it was questionable whether Congress would agree to suspend the program even if the Administration had wanted to do so.

Nor was there any evidence that the Soviets would have accepted measures that would have truly stopped the MIRV race. It had, after all, already begun, and the United States was ahead. The Soviets were probably committed to catching up. For all these reasons, an effective MIRV ban may never have stood a chance even if the United States had seriously proposed one.

Nonetheless, William Hyland, who was a close associate of Kissinger's at the time, calls the conclusion on the American side that a MIRV ban was not in the U.S. interest "the key decision in the entire history of SALT . . . that changed strategic relations, and changed them to the detriment of American security." Eventually Kissinger, too, publicly voiced regret: "I would say in retrospect that I wish I had thought through the implications of a MIRVed world more thoughtfully in 1969 and 1970 than I did."[10]

For Nitze, the links of a logic chain were present, but he did not put them together. The obvious relationship between MIRVs and throw-weight—the virtual inevitability that a Soviet advantage in throw-weight would become a Soviet advantage in MIRVs—might have led him to seek a MIRV ban. Instead, it led him to fear Soviet throw-weight all the more, to try all the harder to reduce Soviet throw-weight in SALT, and to feel all the more disappointment when SALT failed, in his view, to "get a handle" on the problem.

CHAPTER 6

Exotics

When it became clear that SALT would not adequately address his concern with the problem of Soviet throw-weight and the fearful asymmetries in the offensive competition, Paul Nitze appeared to some of his colleagues often to be trying hard to contain his discouragement and anger. They noticed that he spent more time than usual on horseback riding and music. In Helsinki, he had a grand piano in his hotel suite. Gerard Smith lived nearby. Listening to Nitze practicing in the evening, Smith had the impression that he was taking out his frustrations on the instrument, perfecting his technique and seeking consolation in the orderly beauty of the Bach partitas.[1]

On the job during the day, Nitze shifted his attention from strategic offense to another problem that could be worked more to his satisfaction. This was in the realm of strategic defense. His objective was to prohibit either side from developing territorial defenses that would provoke offensive counter-measures by the other side. He did not wish to ban defenses entirely. Just as he had during the Johnson Administration, he still wanted to permit the use of a limited American ABM system to protect the U.S. Minuteman force from attack—a hedge against the vulnerability in which he deeply believed. But even that limited mission for an ABM system had to be sanctioned by a treaty. A pact with the other superpower was necessary to ensure that the Soviets did not go too far in their own defensive program, but also because of public and congressional resistance in the United States to strategic defenses in any form, be it a nationwide network of bomb shelters or an antimissile system: "If the negotiations failed, we still were not going to have an ABM program, because the Senate wasn't going to give it to us."[2] Nitze felt that the only way to get an ABM system of any scale was to make it part of a larger arms-control framework.*

By virtually all accounts, Nitze was the most dogged American negotiator

---

*In the SALT I treaty as signed in 1972, each side was allowed an ABM installation at one ICBM site and one near its capital city. Two years later, the parties agreed to cut back to one site per side. The United States had chosen to defend only a field of Minuteman launchers at Grand Forks Air Force Base in North Dakota, but even that facility was soon mothballed, since it was deemed not to be a cost-effective way of assuring the survival of the ICBMs it was supposed to protect.

on a number of ABM issues.[3] He was also, by his own lights, successful. Unlike the SALT I interim agreement on offensive weapons, which ended by merely freezing launchers, the SALT I treaty limiting ABMs was a document in which he felt pride of authorship.

During the spring of 1971, more than halfway through SALT I, John Rhinelander, a lawyer on the U.S. delegation, began to draft treaty language. He raised a question that occasioned much intense deliberation back in Washington: whether—and if so, exactly how—the treaty should limit what were then called "future systems" or "exotics." The missile-killing devices of the time were interceptor rockets launched from fixed sites on the ground, with nuclear warheads that exploded near incoming warheads. However, scientists and military planners could already imagine various ways in which lasers or charged-particle beams might be fired at enemy missiles from the ground or even from space.

If such systems were to be constrained, the treaty could limit just deployment, or development and testing as well. The problem with limiting only deployment was that permissible work in the laboratories and particularly tests of space-based devices might yield a nationwide system which could be deployed on relatively short notice. This would be a so-called "breakout" that would violate the agreement and upset the strategic balance. Guarding against the breakout of a new enemy weapon system was a concern of military planners and arms-control specialists alike. What if Soviet scientists came up with the basis for a new super antiweapon? That concern was reason enough for restricting development and testing of space-based exotic ABMs, insofar as compliance with such restrictions could be monitored and verified. But it was also reason for an American R&D program as a hedge against some Soviet breakthrough that the United States would then need to match or counter.

To complicate the matter further, the U.S. military was already conducting secret experiments with ground-based lasers. The Joint Chiefs of Staff insisted that this program be exempt from any ban. Therefore, in August 1971, responding to the language for the treaty that the delegation had submitted in July, the White House sent the delegation new instructions, based on a presidential directive, about how to deal with the question of future ABMs. "The agreement," said the cable from Washington, "should contain a provision whereby neither party shall develop, produce, test, or deploy: (a) sea-based, air-based, space-based, or mobile land-based ABM launchers, ABM missiles, or ABM radars; (b) ABM components other than ABM interceptor missiles, ABM launchers, or ABM radars to perform the functions of these components."

In that one sentence, authorized by Richard Nixon in 1971, the United States government was declaring its conviction that a program like Ronald

Reagan's Strategic Defense Initiative of 1983–88 should be prohibited by the ABM treaty. The reason for the prohibition was embedded in the logic of the treaty itself: A mobile ABM system—particularly a large-scale, exotic, space-based one like SDI—would raise the specter of nationwide defense, which was anathema to prevailing wisdom about how to maintain stability and keep the peace.

However, fixed-site, land-based exotic ABMs, of the sort the Pentagon was then interested in, were seen as offering the promise of geographically restricted, therefore not necessarily destabilizing, point defense. To protect both the U.S. laser program and the secrecy then surrounding it, the presidential directive enjoined the negotiators in Geneva not to get too specific about various technologies: "In presenting this position, the delegation should not invite a detailed negotiation or discussion of future ABM systems. Our objective is to reach agreement on the broad principle that the agreement should not be interpreted in such a way that either side could circumvent its provisions through future ABM systems or components."

If there was a lack of precision in the final negotiating record and even in the treaty itself, it was, at least in part, the result of an American decision to conceal an American program. Smith and his colleagues were to press the Soviets for a deliberately imprecise provision that would permit the development and testing, and prohibit only the deployment, of fixed, land-based exotic ABMs such as those with which the American military was already experimenting. But the delegation should seek just as vigorously to prohibit the development and testing, as well as the deployment, of space-based and other mobile exotics.

A critical exchange took place in late August between Alexander Shchukin, a septuagenarian specialist in radio wave theory who represented the Academy of Sciences, and Harold Brown, who had served with Nitze in the Johnson Administration Pentagon and was now the "public" representative on SALT. "Would it be possible," Shchukin asked on August 24, "for the U.S. to clarify its understanding of the notion of 'development' and of practical application of limitations at this stage?"

The SALT I negotiating record shows that three days later, after checking his answer with his superiors, Brown replied: "By 'development' we have in mind that stage in the evolution of a weapon system which follows research (in research we include the activities of conceptual design and laboratory testing) and which precedes full-scale testing. The development stage, though often overlapping with research, is usually associated with the construction and testing of one or more prototypes of the weapon system or its major components. In our view, it is entirely logical and practical to prohibit the development—in this sense—of those systems whose testing and deployment are prohibited."

Without, of course, knowing that he was doing so, Brown was laying down a marker that fifteen years later would be troublesome to advocates of SDI and helpful to critics of the program.

In a matter of weeks in the fall of 1971 the negotiators secured Soviet agreement to the essence of Article V of the treaty, which eventually stated: "Each Party undertakes not to develop, test, or deploy ABM systems or components which are sea-based, air-based, space-based, or mobile land-based." Fixed land-based systems were covered in a separate paragraph, which remained in dispute for some months. Article II eventually defined an ABM system to be "a system to counter strategic ballistic missiles or their elements in flight trajectory, currently consisting of [ABM interceptor missiles, launchers, and radars]."

The phrase "currently consisting of" was inserted at the suggestion of Raymond Garthoff, the executive secretary of the American delegation. It was a classic case of how heavy a burden semantics must sometimes bear in the rarefied art of treaty drafting. The Americans were looking for an open-ended, all-inclusive definition of ABMs. Without the adverb "currently," the treaty might have been interpreted as applying only to systems then in existence. With the insertion, Garthoff was underscoring that the treaty covered *all* systems, those that then (i.e., "currently") consisted of old-fashioned devices but also future ones. He repeatedly emphasized that point in 1971 to his Soviet counterpart.[4]

The American negotiators subsequently obtained Soviet agreement that the deployment of fixed, land-based exotics would be banned. In the process they worked out an "agreed statement," one of a number of such footnotes to the treaty that were initialed by the heads of delegation and transmitted to the Senate as part of the treaty. This was Agreed Statement D:

> . . . the Parties agree that in the event ABM systems based on other physical principles and including components capable of substituting for ABM interceptor missiles, ABM launchers, or ABM radars are created in the future, specific limitations on such systems and their components would be subject to discussion . . . and agreement.

In other words, if R&D and testing at ABM test ranges were to yield breakthroughs in the permitted area of fixed land-based exotic ABMs, there would have to be a new negotiation and a new agreement before there could be any deployment of such systems. But it was both the intent and the understanding of the American negotiators that development and testing of any mobile systems, including space-based ones, were still banned by Article V.

The phrase "systems based on other physical principles" was coined by Nitze as a catch-all term that would apply to future systems based on technologies not in use in 1971, including ones so exotic they were then not even a gleam in scientists' eyes. The Joint Chiefs were still extremely protective of the secrecy of their laser program. For months the American negotiators could not even mention lasers as an example of the "exotics" that might be developed and tested from fixed ground-based sites. Partly for that reason, there was persistent wrangling with the Soviets. The Soviet representatives professed puzzlement over how a treaty could ban "things that do not exist." In making this point, they were probably buying time while seeking their own instructions from Moscow. They were also trying to smoke out details of the American laser program, which was being shielded by the proposed language. The Soviets alternately played dumb and turned aggressive in their questions. Over time, however, it became clear that they understood perfectly well what the Americans had in mind. Moreover, the Soviet Union wanted to develop a fixed-site facility to test large lasers of its own near Sary-Shagan in Central Asia.

Nitze and his colleagues were deeply involved in many rounds of verbal shadowboxing over this issue with a number of the Soviet negotiators, including Victor Karpov, who remained a fixture on the Soviet side of the arms-control bargaining table until well into the second Reagan Administration. The Soviets continued to grumble about "outlawing things that don't exist." But in less than a month, on September 8, 1971, they put forward a new formulation for an article on mobile systems that amounted to acceptance of the American position. On September 13, Karpov noted that the new Soviet draft "took into account the wishes of the U.S. side." Two days later, on September 15, Karpov seemed to acknowledge in another statement, which became part of the classified negotiating record, that he understood what was being banned—the development and testing, as well as deployment, of "any type of present *or future* components" of ABM systems—and that his government agreed to such a ban.

Even at the time, it was clear that a lot was riding on the resolution of the problem of future systems. In SALT I, the United States sought a permanent set of rules to regulate the interaction between offensive and defensive competitions. The goal of the negotiations was an ABM treaty of unlimited duration. Nitze was a strong advocate of such treaties; he felt that agreements that expired after a specified period of time were conducive to surges in the arms race, especially on the Soviet side, since the Kremlin would plan new weapons for deployment after the expiration of the agreement. An ABM treaty of unlimited duration had to cope with what has always been a dilemma of arms control: Technology moves forward, leaving arms control behind; scientists are forever coming up with weapons, or antiweapons, more sophisticated and capable than those that diplomats have in mind as they haggle over treaty language. Scientific breakthroughs—the development of new devices—translate into military breakouts—the deployment of new weapons that upset strategic stability.

With the provisions in SALT I on exotic ABMs the ground was laid for one of the most important and divisive debates about SDI in the 1980s: how, and indeed whether, the testing of such a system would be limited by the ABM treaty. Had the superpowers agreed in the early seventies to limit only those ABM systems that were based on technologies existing at that time, the fruits of their labor would have become meaningless as soon as physicists and engineers perfected new missile-killing technologies. Those new systems would be more effective than the old ones, yet they would automatically be exempt from the testing restrictions of the agreement. Furthermore, the testing of a space-based exotic system might be little short of deployment. In that case the barrier that the treaty was supposed to provide against breakout would have all but collapsed.

The theoreticians of deterrence and arms control, including Paul Nitze, had always been concerned about the consequences of unfettered defense, no matter what the technology or "physical principle" at hand. Nitze's conclusion back in 1959 that it was "neither prudent to count on shooting most [enemy missiles] down in the air, nor to count on taking most of them out of their launching platforms before they take off" was based not simply on an assessment of what was feasible with the technology of the time.[5] Rather, it was a premonition of a fact of life in the nuclear age: The quest for a comprehensive defense can be a losing proposition, undermining the security of each side and the stability of the relationship between them.

What might have seemed an abstract and abstruse matter in 1971–72 had deep roots at the core of the strategic covenant between the United States and the Soviet Union. It also had enduring implications for the future of the nuclear peace. As technology advanced, the issue of exotic systems would inevitably become more troublesome. The passages in the SALT I negotiating record and final treaty in which Smith, Nitze, Brown, Rhinelander, Garthoff, Shchukin, Karpov, and others tried to head off that trouble turned out, fifteen years later, to be the source of a fierce and drawn-out battle over SDI, a battle fought on three fronts: within the Reagan Administration, between the Administration and the U.S. Senate, and between the superpowers themselves.

Radars

One of Paul Nitze's specialties on the American delegation during SALT I was defining when a radar should be a permissible part of the nation's early-warning system (a boon to deterrence) and when it should be regarded as an impermissible step toward building a nationwide ABM system of the sort the treaty was meant to preclude (a detriment to deterrence).

Originally in SALT I, the Joint Chiefs of Staff had wanted to limit ABM interceptors but let radar tracking systems virtually run free. Nitze disagreed. Interceptors, he argued, were relatively easy to build, deploy, move about, and hide. Radars were not. Yet radars were a vital part—the eyes and ears—of any ABM system. Therefore, said Nitze, it was especially important that they be limited: "If you had already built the radars, you could break out rapidly and have a great big system."[6]

Eventually, Nitze prevailed both within his own government and, over time, in the negotiations with the Soviets as well. Smith later wrote that Nitze's "argumentation and persistence resulted in more, and more precise, controls over radar than had been generally expected by the delegation or by Washington agencies."[7]

Nitze concentrated his arguments on Alexander Shchukin, whose other counterpart, Harold Brown, divided his time between the negotiations and his responsibilities as the president of the California Institute of Technology. During Brown's absences, Nitze was responsible for the "Shchukin account." Nitze and Shchukin were the oldest members of their respective delegations. They considered themselves, and each other, Renaissance men; they shared an interest in European literature; they spoke in French about art and classical music; and they each felt that they had more license than other senior delegates to engage in private talks. As a result, they opened a kind of side channel within the front channel.

When the negotiations reached a sticking point on some excruciatingly technical questions about radars, Shchukin invited Nitze to get together over lunch with their wives and listen to some records he had just acquired. The elaborate meal went largely uneaten, the records unplayed, and the two couples soon went outdoors for a stroll. With their wives trailing farther and farther behind, Shchukin and Nitze fell into intense conversation. "Here we are," said Shchukin, gesturing theatrically at their bucolic surroundings. "No one can hear us. How would we solve this problem if it depended on just the two of us?"

Some of the answers he and Nitze worked out became part of the basis of the eventual treaty. On other points, they were overruled by their governments. The episode had an importance beyond the matters then at hand. It firmly established, in Nitze's own mind at least, a lesson for the future. When formal negotiations reached a deadlock, it sometimes helped for a senior American, literally or figuratively, to take a walk in the woods with his Soviet counterpart.

As a scientist, Shchukin was receptive to Nitze's recurring efforts to get beyond polemics and posturing—to objectify, even quantify, the issues that divided them, thereby perhaps making them easier to resolve. On the tricky and critical issue of radars, Nitze and his staff developed a complex formula for a new index called power-aperture product, calculated by multiplying the mean emitted power in watts of a radar by the antenna area in square meters (''watt-meters-squared''). The resulting huge figure would measure the capability of radars and define a threshold for those radars that would be permitted under a treaty. This addition to the jargon of arms control was the object of heavy sighs, eye-rolling, and jokes even among the cognoscenti on the American side. Shchukin expressed doubt about whether it was reasonable to expect the leaders of the Soviet Union to comprehend power-aperture product.

Nitze persisted with colleagues and Shchukin alike. For him, power-aperture product served a purpose comparable to that of throw-weight with ballistic missiles: It reduced one aspect of the military competition to a single, albeit mind-boggling, number. It was a way, as he put it, of making arms control ''a blackboard rather than a sandbox exercise.''

At the eleventh hour of SALT I, the Nixon Administration was impatient to move to final agreement and instructed the delegation in Geneva to accept the Soviet position on the size of radars that would be permitted under the treaty. The Kremlin was holding out for a high threshold on permissible radars. Nitze felt that American capitulation on this point would be unjustified. Latitude of the sort the Soviets were seeking might constitute a loophole, permitting them later to violate the treaty's prohibition on area defense. He also felt that capitulation was premature and unnecessary, since he was sure that Shchukin understood the merits of his proposed solution and sensed that Shchukin could, if given time, carry the day with his home office. Nitze persuaded his own superiors to hold out for a few days; the Soviets, he predicted, would accept the American position.

So they did. As a result, Nitze's index of power-aperture product, and his eventual preference for the limit on permitted radars (3×10^6, or 3 million watt-meters-squared), became an esoteric part of the legacy of SALT I and an important precedent for the future. Moreover, without Nitze's persistence on this issue, it would have been easier and more tempting for the Soviets to play fast and loose with their anti-aircraft facilities, giving some of them anti-missile capability as well. The resulting furor might well have rendered the ABM treaty a dead letter years before the Reagan Administration took office in 1981.

Snubbed

The broad outlines of the 1972 SALT I accords had been established before the negotiations began. Indeed, they were established back in the Johnson Administration: a treaty limiting ABMs, an agreement freezing ballistic mis-

sile launchers, and an allowance for MIRVs—then an American advantage—
to run free.

The first venture in strategic arms control took two and a half years of
negotiation, partly because of the perennial difficulty of defining "strategic." That word is generally understood to mean weapons with which one
country can reach the territory of its potential enemy and negotiating partner. ICBMs and intercontinental-range bombers definitely qualify; so do
SLBMs, since the submarines that launch them can prowl close enough to
the other nation's shores to strike deep inland.

But the Soviets also considered "strategic" America's intermediate-range
nuclear forces based in and around Europe, since those weapons, too, could
reach Soviet territory. Soviet negotiators liked to point out that they cared
where a weapon landed, not where it took off. Therefore, in SALT I they
pressed to take account of American "forward-based systems" around the
U.S.S.R. Moscow also demanded "compensation" for the independent nuclear arsenals of two American allies, Britain and France. The United States
successfully resisted on both counts. In effect, the issues were deferred to a
future negotiation.

The Soviets created further delay and difficulty in SALT I when they tried
to separate the issues of offense and defense. They sought an early agreement
that would limit only ABMs (the system in which the United States had a
technological advantage) while leaving wide open the offensive lane of the
arms race (where the U.S.S.R. was moving ahead in the number and size
of its ICBMs). In the course of years of negotiation and extensive rethinking
of their own interests and objectives, the Soviets had come a very long way
since 1967, when Prime Minister Kosygin had argued, in his meeting with
Johnson and McNamara at Glassboro, that limiting defense was immoral
and that arms control should be confined to offensive arms. Resorting frequently to his back channel with Anatoly Dobrynin, Henry Kissinger impressed upon the Kremlin that the linkage between offense and defense was
mandatory and that a defense-only deal was unacceptable.

As the negotiations moved toward their climax and a summit meeting
between Nixon and Leonid Brezhnev in May 1972, Kissinger excluded the
delegation all the more. In April, Paul Nitze, Gerard Smith, and Royal
Allison were recalled to Washington and told by Secretary of State William
Rogers about a secret Kissinger mission to Moscow in which the subject of
SALT "had come up." That was a considerable understatement. Kissinger
and Brezhnev had negotiated some key provisions on the treatment of
SLBMs.

At the Nixon-Brezhnev summit in May, Nitze, Smith, Allison, Garthoff,
and a few of the others were flown in from Helsinki just long enough to
discover how totally Kissinger had taken over the bargaining during the final

scramble for an agreement. When he landed in Moscow, Nitze was left stranded in the airport VIP lounge. The car assigned to him had a driver who spoke no English. Arriving late at Spaso House for a banquet, he was stopped at the gate and detained by American security guards. A Soviet foreign ministry official recognized and rescued him, ushering him from the American compound to the Kremlin for the treaty-signing ceremony.

The next morning, over breakfast, Kissinger's aide William Hyland briefed Nitze and Allison on the rather frantic last-minute action they had been missing. Hyland had a droll sense of slapstick and the absurd, but Nitze was not amused. He used Hyland's anecdotes as ammunition for his own more sarcastic and cautionary tales about how not to negotiate with the Soviets. On the airplane back to Helsinki to close up shop, Nitze drafted a mock memorandum titled "The Last Twenty Minutes of a Negotiation Are the Most Important"—a favorite Soviet saying. It set forth guidelines that the Soviets might have used to dominate the end of the negotiations.

The whole experience tended to confirm Nitze's apprehension—shared over the years by other, more adamant critics of arms control—that among the asymmetries favoring the Soviet Union was one in sheer negotiating skill and tactical hardheadedness. He tended to make that charge particularly with regard to negotiations from which he and the Geneva team had been excluded. Nitze felt that in the rush to agreement, Kissinger had acquiesced in a number of provisions in SALT I that were ambiguous or disadvantageous to the United States, or both.*

During the Senate hearings on the SALT I accords, Nitze was in the uncomfortable position of having to defend the agreement, including some of those provisions concerning the limitations on strategic offense about which he had growing reservations. On June 20, 1972, he was subjected to a particularly stiff inquisition by his old friend Senator Henry Jackson, whose sharp questions had been prepared by Nitze's former protégé Richard Perle.

At the time of the approval of the SALT I interim agreement on offenses, Jackson sponsored a resolution requiring that any future strategic-arms agreement must "not limit the U.S. to levels of intercontinental strategic forces inferior to the limits provided for the Soviet Union." That convoluted phrasing translated simply enough: A powerful senator was registering his

---

*Of particular concern was the failure to reach either a precise definition of the heavy ICBMs that the Soviets were allowed to keep or a specified limit on the size of the "light" ICBMs they could add to their arsenal. "Heavies" were the largest bearers of throw-weight. Not only were the Soviets going to be allowed a monopoly in heavies, but they would, it appeared, be permitted to proceed with the deployment of a new ICBM that—while smaller than the heavy SS-9 or its MIRVed successor, the SS-18—would still be much larger than anything on the American side. When it came into service, the new Soviet ICBM, which was designated the SS-19, was armed with six warheads, so it considerably increased the number of hard-target killers facing the United States.

disapproval of the SALT I freeze on offensive forces, since it left the Soviets with more ICBM launchers, and he was putting the executive branch on notice that the next negotiation, SALT II, would presumably have to limit launchers at equal levels. In numerous speeches at the time, Jackson made clear that as long as he had anything to say about how his amendment was interpreted, he would insist that throw-weight, too, be subject to equal ceilings. Given the asymmetry in the two sides' reliance on ICBMs, that would mean deep reductions in Soviet throw-weight.

While Jackson believed that SALT I had not gone far enough in limiting Soviet ICBMs, he felt it went too far in limiting the American ABM program. For him, ABMs represented a technological advantage for the United States and a potentially useful line of defense against a Soviet first strike. Jackson unsuccessfully tried to attach another amendment, which called on the United States to abrogate the treaty if the Soviets deployed ICBMs that threatened the American deterrent, even if those ICBMs were permitted under the terms of the interim agreement on offenses.

Jackson was the leading senator who expressed concern about the ban in the ABM treaty on future defensive systems, but he was not the only one. Strom Thurmond also worried that the treaty "prevents us from developing new kinds of systems to protect our population. The most promising type appears to be the laser type, based on entirely new principles. Yet we forgo forever the ability to protect our people." Senator James Buckley, a conservative Republican from New York, opposed the treaty on the ground that "it would have the effect . . . of prohibiting the development and testing of a laser-type system based in space. . . . The technological possibility has been formally excluded by this agreement."

Thus, when it voted overwhelmingly to give the SALT I treaty the force of law, the Senate did so on the clear understanding that it was ratifying a prohibition on the development and testing, as well as the deployment, of space-based, exotic ABMs, while keeping open the right to continue research.

Even some hard-liners who were deeply skeptical of arms control and who felt that comprehensive defense was scientifically feasible reluctantly supported ratification of the treaty on the grounds that the nation could not afford more than an ABM research program. One of these was Edward Teller:

[T]he ABM treaty which is up for ratification does not introduce an essential change in the existing situation. It merely recognizes political realities. We must make a choice if we indeed care for the safety of the American people. We might decide to spend a minimum of an additional $100 billion for defense in the next five years, and thus build a full-scale antimissile defense system. No great gift of prophecy is needed to know that this will not happen. The only alternative is to ratify the treaty.[8]

Walking Out

As the Nixon Administration prepared for SALT II in the fall of 1972, there was clearly trouble ahead from Henry Jackson and other congressional conservatives. President Nixon hoped to head off that trouble by taking a broom to the Arms Control and Disarmament Agency and the negotiating delegation, sweeping away those individuals whom Jackson saw as having been too soft during SALT I. A number of officials involved in SALT I resigned under pressure, were fired, or were reassigned.

Richard Perle was intensely active in the background, spreading criticism of what he called the "knee-jerk arms-controlitis" of the old team and picking a new one. Perle had a collaborator on Kissinger's staff at the NSC, John Lehman. With Jackson and Perle pushing from the outside and Lehman from the inside, the Nixon White House assented in cutting the ACDA budget by a third, its staff by a quarter. Gerard Smith was replaced as chief SALT negotiator by U. Alexis Johnson, a career diplomat who had worked with Nitze during the Cuban missile crisis; Smith's other portfolio, as director of ACDA, was given to Fred Iklé, a strategist from RAND, whom Perle helped persuade to take the job. Eventually Lehman moved over to serve as Iklé's deputy at ACDA. Another close associate of Perle's who ended up at ACDA was Paul Wolfowitz, his former partner in the pro-ABM Committee to Maintain a Prudent Defense Policy in 1969.

Having resisted the quest for reductions in ballistic missile throw-weight and questioned the vulnerability of Minuteman, General Allison, too, was a marked man. The Chiefs had their own candidate to replace him, but so did Jackson and Perle; they hand-picked an Army officer, Edward Rowny, whom they knew personally, to represent their own, as well as the Chiefs', interests in SALT II.

Nitze was one of the few to survive the Jackson purge of SALT in 1972–73. He retained Jackson's respect and support, largely because he had fought the good, if losing, fight for more stringent controls on Soviet heavies and throw-weight in SALT I. That fight, however, continued.

When Leonid Brezhnev visited the United States in June 1973, the Watergate scandal was growing. Nixon's presidency was slowly collapsing around him, and his foreign policy was widely seen as a saving grace. Henry Kissinger became secretary of state in August. He was determined to run SALT II his way. From Nitze's standpoint, that meant too much eagerness for an agreement and too little determination to constrain Soviet ICBMs and throw-weight.

Ralph Earle, a lawyer whom Warnke had brought into the Pentagon and who had worked closely with Nitze over the years, was now serving as a consultant to the Defense Department. He proposed making Nitze a ''czar'' for arms control. Melvin Laird's successor as secretary of defense, Elliot Richardson, considered Nitze ''the best single person in the Administration in the analysis of strategic issues and the formulation of negotiating positions.'' Richardson wanted to broaden Nitze's portfolio by making him, in addition to the Pentagon's delegate in Geneva, also its representative on the interagency committee in Washington that wrote the delegation's instructions.[9]

That plan came to naught when Richardson suddenly moved over to the Justice Department as attorney general. He was replaced as secretary of defense by James Schlesinger, another former RAND analyst who had been in the forefront of strategists concerned about the consequences of the Soviet ICBM buildup. His nickname in the Nixon Administration that winter and spring was ''Mr. Throw-Weight.'' From his new office in the Pentagon, and in close coordination with Henry Jackson's office on Capitol Hill, Schlesinger urged Kissinger to seek throw-weight reductions in SALT II. In this effort Schlesinger had vigorous support both from Nitze in Geneva and from Nitze's former aide Elmo Zumwalt, now chief of naval operations.

Largely in response to this prodding, Kissinger tried and failed to get the Soviets to join in what he called a ''conceptual breakthrough'' on the desirability of equal ceilings on ''MIRVed throw-weight'' (the total throw-weight of ballistic missiles capable of carrying MIRVs). Schlesinger felt Kissinger gave up too easily, and so did Nitze.[10]

In March 1974, Schlesinger tried to bring Nitze back into the Pentagon as assistant secretary for international security affairs, the job he had held in the Kennedy Administration, more than a decade before. Once again, however, Nitze's lingering reputation as a soft-liner came back to haunt him. His Asilomar speech of 1960 and his fleeting, unwanted, and contentious appearance at the Cleveland conference of 1958 had never been entirely forgotten or forgiven. During a meeting on SALT at the Pentagon, one of Nitze's successors as deputy secretary of defense, William Clements, teased him by saying, ''Of course Paul would argue that position. He's for the Russians.'' Nitze's face grew red, and he demanded an apology on the spot.

When the possibility arose of Nitze's returning from Geneva to the Pentagon, Senate conservatives like Barry Goldwater and John Tower grumbled ominously. Goldwater let it be known that if Nitze's nomination went forward, he might reconsider whether he would support the President in the event of a Watergate trial in the Senate. It was as though the senator were saying that the appointment of Paul Nitze to a third-echelon position in the Department of Defense would be an impeachable offense by the President.[11] One of the epithets that reverberated through the halls of Congress was "McNamara–Whiz Kid recycle," which was doubly ironic, given the hard line Nitze was taking within the Administration and his age at the time, sixty-seven.*

Nitze's life in Geneva was turning unbearable. He often arrived at his office in the morning sputtering over the latest headlines about Nixon and Watergate. "Did you see what that crook has done now?" he would ask of his staff. There was little for him to do but attend tedious receptions, engage in sterile exchanges with the Soviets, practice the piano, and brood over the disasters that he saw ahead.

In April and May, he spent six weeks drafting a letter to the President that set forth his views on the "objectives and constraints" of arms control. The objectives were to reduce the risk of war, to attain roughly equivalent forces, and to enhance "crisis stability" (i.e., reduce the temptation of a first strike). Nitze concluded, as he later put it, that "Kissinger and Nixon were determined to get an agreement come hell or high water."[12] With a third Nixon-Brezhnev summit scheduled for June 1974 in Moscow, Nitze feared that once again Kissinger would shoulder the negotiators aside in a burst of activity in the back channel, just as he had done in 1972, and that Nixon would sign a SALT II treaty that worsened the problem of ICBM asymmetries left over from SALT I.

To many of Nitze's colleagues in Geneva this fear seemed greatly exaggerated, not least because the two sides were still far from agreement. Nitze, Schlesinger, Jackson and others had applied a great deal of pressure to redress the imbalance in MIRVed throw-weight. They had succeeded in setting a standard for success in the negotiations that would be extremely difficult to meet any time soon.

Back in Washington, Admiral Zumwalt persuaded his colleagues on the Joint Chiefs of Staff formally to endorse Nitze's letter in a memorandum of their own to Schlesinger. Even though Schlesinger agreed with many of the points, he never relayed the letter to the President. If a Pentagon view was going to be presented to the Oval Office, it was going to be that of Schles-

---

*At that time, Phyllis Schlafly and Chester Ward, the co-authors of the anti-Nitze tract *The Gravediggers* in 1964, were collaborating on a new, much longer diatribe. The principal villain of this 846-page book was identified in its title, *Kissinger on the Couch*, but Paul "Hilken" Nitze had almost as prominent and diabolical a role. Nitze's real middle name was Henry; Paul Hilken was the uncle who had committed treason on behalf of Germany during World War I. Nitze, Schlafly and Ward implied, was hardly less traitorous: They accused him of originating, with McNamara, the "it's-safer-to-be-weak-than-strong" concept of parity and of aspiring "to replace Kissinger as Unilateral Disarmer-in-Chief of the United States."

inger himself. He saw it as Nitze's job to represent the Pentagon in Geneva, not at the White House.[13]

At the end of May, Nitze's frustrations boiled over, and he decided to quit. He wrote a second letter to Nixon, this one of resignation. Concerned about Nitze's considerable prestige in Europe and at home, Kissinger hoped to minimize the embarrassment by sitting on the resignation until after the summit. Schlesinger, too, tried to dissuade Nitze from resigning, because he thought it would make a bad situation worse to have a senior official leaving in a huff just as the beleaguered President was about to sit down with Brezhnev.

But Nitze was determined. On June 14, less than two weeks before Nixon flew to Moscow for the summit, Nitze sent yet another letter to the President: "My request of May 28th to resign not having been accepted, I now feel compelled unilaterally to terminate my appointment effective today." Simultaneously he released a statement to the press:

> It was almost 29 years ago that I supervised the on-site investigation of the effects of the atomic weapons dropped on Hiroshima and Nagasaki. Since that time much of my thought and endeavor has been directed to the twin goals of preserving the general security of the United States while lowering the risks of nuclear war.
>
> For the last five years I have devoted all my energies to supporting the objectives of negotiating SALT agreements which would be balanced and which would enhance the security of the United States, and also of the Soviet Union, by maintaining crisis stability and providing the basis for lessening the strategic arms competition between them. Under the circumstances existing at the present time, however, I see little prospect of negotiating measures which will enhance movement toward those objectives.
>
> Arms control policy is integral to the national security and foreign policy of this nation, and they, in turn, are closely intertwined with domestic affairs. In my view it would be illusory to attempt to ignore or wish away the depressing reality of the traumatic events now unfolding in our nation's capital and of the implications of those events in the international arena.
>
> Until the Office of the Presidency has been restored to its principal function of upholding the Constitution and taking care of the fair execution of the laws, and thus be able to function effectively at home and abroad, I see no real prospect of reversing certain unfortunate trends in the evolving situation. Time is now of the essence in establishing the precondition for such a regeneration.
>
> In the meantime, it is essential that the orderly process of government

continue. It is the genius of the United States form of government that it has the flexibility to compensate for individual deficiencies. All those who are continuing to maintain the orderly process of government despite the tensions between their loyalty to higher authority and their loyalty to their oath of office have my full sympathy and admiration. I regret that tension has now become too great for me to continue in office with them. As a private citizen I shall support them to the best of my ability.

Nitze included this last paragraph at the urging of Ralph Earle, who was now on the SALT delegation in Geneva, in order to tone the letter down and keep it from being read as an exhortation for everyone in the Administration to resign. Two weeks later, Zumwalt, whose tour of duty on the Joint Chiefs was coming to an end anyway, departed with much fanfare, blasting Kissinger's conduct of SALT II. In his memoirs Zumwalt called Nitze's press release "my favorite SALT document."

A few days later, on July 2, Nitze appeared before the House Armed Services Subcommittee on Arms Control for an angry swan song. He criticized Kissinger for giving up on the "conceptual breakthrough" of equality in MIRVed throw-weight. Nitze cited the work of his friend Albert Wohlstetter in support of the warning that "the United States has for many years underestimated future Soviet offensive deployments." The Soviet Union, he said, was well on its way to achieving usable strategic superiority over the United States, and too many in the American government were burying their heads in the sand.

These accusations on the eve of the summit contributed to an air of embattlement when Nixon and Kissinger arrived in Moscow. At a press conference during the summit, Kissinger was barraged with questions about the charges being made back in Washington. In his response, he said: "One of the questions we have to ask ourselves as a country is: What in the name of God *is* strategic superiority? What is the significance of it, politically, militarily, operationally, at these levels of numbers? What do you *do* with it?"

In his memoirs, Kissinger tried to explain what he called his "cri de coeur." While he, like others, "had been haunted by the loss of our strategic superiority for twenty years," he was also

> beginning to despair of the rote tendency to measure the strategic balance by numbers of delivery vehicles in a period when the numbers of warheads on both sides were much more worrisome and when any analysis showed that no building program could avoid casualties likely to paralyze statesmen and frighten peoples toward pacifism. Whatever we did, it would be impossible to recapture the overwhelming superiority that we had enjoyed until the early 1960s and it was sheer escapism to yearn for a past that technology proscribed.[14]

Kissinger did not see America's loss of primacy as necessarily entailing military or even political vulnerability. He also questioned whether one particular military advantage, in MIRVed throw-weight, conferred significant political advantage to the Soviet Union in a regional crisis.

Paul Nitze, who personified the "rote tendency to measure the strategic balance by numbers of delivery vehicles," was driven to fury by Kissinger's skepticism about the ultimate meaning of charts, graphs, and calipers, as well as by his domination of both the policy process and public attention. On November 24, 1974, Nitze was attending a reception in New York after the wedding of a Harvard classmate of his son William. At the punch bowl Nitze struck up a casual conversation with a young lawyer. The stranger innocently asked Nitze if he knew Henry Kissinger, whose diplomatic high-wire act was, as usual, in the headlines, invoking astonishment and admiration around the world. Nitze's considerable charm and enjoyment of the occasion instantly evaporated.

"That man is a traitor to his country," he said, almost spitting out the words. He turned on his heel and walked away.

Years later, he cited his resignation from the SALT II delegation to refute the charge that he cared more about having an official position than about principle or the substance of policy. There were indeed limits to his desire to be an insider, and his objection to Nixon and Kissinger's approach to SALT carried him well past those limits. But he was not in the least happy now to be an outsider again.

CHAPTER 7

Fatal Flaws

Almost exactly five years elapsed between Paul Nitze's resignation from the Nixon Administration and the signing of the SALT II treaty by President Jimmy Carter and Leonid Brezhnev in June 1979. A number of times during that period the diplomatic enterprise was severely buffeted by American domestic politics. In every case, the politician applying the most effective pressure was Henry Jackson; the key person on Jackson's staff was Richard Perle; and one of their principal allies outside the government was Paul Nitze.

After Richard Nixon was forced from office, the new President, Gerald Ford, was eager to keep arms control alive but to do so in a way that met the condition of "not unequal" aggregates that Jackson had imposed after SALT I. Ford met with Brezhnev at Vladivostok in November 1974, and they agreed on a framework for SALT II that set an equal ceiling of 2,400 total offensive strategic nuclear launchers (ICBM silos, SLBM tubes, and intercontinental bombers) and a subceiling of 1,320 on MIRVed ballistic missile launchers (land- and sea-based). One reason the Soviets entered the Vladivostok accord was that the new, equal ceiling and subceiling of SALT II were high enough to leave intact the weapons they most cared about, and to continue full-tilt their program of MIRVing their ICBMs. Other Soviet concessions, too, came at a price: The United States had to give up its pursuit of a cutback in Soviet heavy missiles, which now numbered 308 and were on their way to being armed with as many as ten warheads each. Therefore, the problem of MIRVed ballistic missile throw-weight loomed larger than ever. As Nitze put it a short time later, "It is difficult to see how the [Vladivostok] accord reduces, in a meaningful way, the U.S. strategic defense problem posed by the new family of Soviet missiles and bombers which are now completing test and evaluation and whose large-scale deployment is now beginning." The United States, he warned, would soon have only half, or even a third, as much ICBM throw-weight as the U.S.S.R.[1]

The second major intrusion of American domestic politics into SALT II came early in 1976. Ronald Reagan was running hard for the Republican nomination, charging Ford, Nixon, and Henry Kissinger with having presided over the "neglect" of American defenses.*

In January 1976, Kissinger flew to Moscow to attempt a breakthrough at the highest level and on short order. It was the first month of an election year; détente, SALT, and Kissinger himself were being attacked by candidates in both parties—particularly by Reagan but also by Jimmy Carter. Kissinger struck a tentative deal; but back in Washington, a number of presidential advisors opposed him.

Two of the principal figures were Donald Rumsfeld, who had helped instigate the opposition to Nitze's nomination as secretary of the navy in 1963 and who was now secretary of defense, and General Edward Rowny, the Joint Chiefs of Staff representative on the SALT II delegation, who was serving as Jackson's and Perle's man in Geneva, alerting them to American "giveaways" at the talks. Others were Fred Iklé and John Lehman, the two Jackson-Perle allies who had been running the Arms Control and Disarmament Agency since the post–SALT I purge. ACDA, for the first time in its fifteen-year history, was now aligned with the Pentagon against the State Department in support of the hard line on arms control. Rumsfeld and Iklé made the case to Ford that the compromise Kissinger had arranged with the Kremlin demanded too little of the Soviets, too much of the United States, and was susceptible to charges of a sellout from Reagan and the right. At the urging of the Pentagon, the National Security Council met while Kissinger was in Moscow and in effect vetoed the deal that Kissinger thought was at hand.

For years afterward, some participants were haunted by another of those what-might-have-been questions: They wondered whether Ford had made a fatal mistake when he let Rumsfeld, Iklé, and Lehman seize the initiative. Had he overruled the Pentagon and ACDA, backed Kissinger, and pressed ahead to sign a SALT II deal in the summer or fall of 1976, he might have beaten Reagan handily for the nomination and gone on to defeat Carter in the fall. Carter's national security advisor, Zbigniew Brzezinski, told William Hyland after the election that the Carter campaign's greatest fear was the announcement of a Ford-Brezhnev SALT agreement on the eve of the election.[2]

---

*The accusation was far from fair. Throw-weight apart, the United States was in fact well on its way to increasing the number of critical Soviet targets it could attack from 1,700 in 1970 to 7,000 before the end of the decade. In the same period, the Air Force deployed 550 Minuteman ICBMs with three warheads each, converted its sea-based missile force to nearly 500 new Poseidon missiles, each with 10 to 14 warheads, replacing the older, single-warhead Polaris missile. The longer-range, more accurate Trident submarine missile was under development, and construction of the first Trident-class submarine began in 1975. The B-52 bomber fleet was modernized with new avionics and engines, and it was equipped with short-range attack missiles, and the supersonic B-1 bomber was under development. Air-launched cruise missiles were being developed and tested.

Team Player

The same month when Henry Kissinger was in Moscow trying to achieve a breakthrough in SALT II—January 1976—Paul Nitze published a widely noted article warning that the emerging treaty might worsen America's strategic predicament. The piece, titled "Assuring Strategic Stability in the Era of Détente," appeared in *Foreign Affairs,* the journal of the Council on Foreign Relations, where Nitze's and Kissinger's tumultuous association had begun twenty years before.* "Unfortunately," Nitze concluded,

> and to the profound regret of one who has participated both in the SALT negotiations and in a series of earlier U.S. decisions designed to stabilize the nuclear balance—I believe that . . . there is every prospect that under the terms of the SALT agreements the Soviet Union will continue to pursue a nuclear superiority that is not merely quantitative but designed to produce a theoretical war-winning capability. Further, there is a major risk that, if such a condition were achieved, the Soviet Union would adjust its policies and actions in ways that would undermine the present détente situation, with results that could only resurrect the danger of nuclear confrontation or, alternatively, increase the prospect of Soviet expansion through other means of pressure.

The article contained a footnote: "To see how top officials viewed American nuclear power even in the period of American monopoly, one can now consult the recently declassified text of the NSC 68 policy paper dated in the spring of 1950." In the Winter 1976–77 issue of *Foreign Policy,* published by the Carnegie Endowment for International Peace, Nitze wrote another article with a similar thesis and a more pungent title: "Deterring Our Deterrent." His concern, which he had nurtured since his dispute with Bernard Brodie in the 1940s—that deterrence would become a one-way proposition, working against the United States—was now more acute than ever. And SALT II, he believed, was partly to blame.

Nitze's *Foreign Affairs* article made much use of a mathematical model projecting what would happen if the superpowers got into a slugging match against each other's military targets. The model was illustrated by two charts that represented the growing advantage that the Soviet Union held over the United States in ballistic-missile throw-weight. These charts were based on

---

*The editor of the journal, and of Nitze's article, was his onetime deputy and eventual successor in ISA at the Pentagon, William Bundy.

data assembled and analyzed by Thomas K. ("T.K.") Jones, a young engineer who had been one of Nitze's technical advisors during his tenure on
the SALT delegation. Jones believed that a nuclear war could be won or
lost, depending on which side had the most powerful weapons—and which
had taken the most sensible precautions. Much, in his view, would depend
on civil defense.*

Since leaving Nitze's staff in Geneva, Jones had been working for the
Boeing Corporation, a powerful corporate constituent in Senator Jackson's
home state, Washington. There he ran a study simulating the effects of nuclear blasts on bomb shelters. As with other aspects of nuclear strategy, such
as offensive weapons like ICBMs and active defenses like ABMs, the question of whether passive defenses like bomb shelters contribute to the overall
stability of deterrence could be answered differently depending on whether
one was speaking of American or Soviet programs. Even as they were ru-
minating on the benefits of American civil defense as a way of shoring up
deterrence and demonstrating American will, Nitze and Jones were concerned about what they saw through the looking glass: Soviet civil defense
also signified national will, but of a particularly ominous if not warlike kind.

The Soviet shelter program seemed to fit into the sinister pattern of an
emerging first-strike capability: Soviet ICBMs could attack American Minuteman silos; Soviet air defenses and the ABM system around Moscow could
blunt any retaliation that ensued; and the damage of the American counter-
blow would be further limited because a disciplined populace had been
shielded underground. Thanks to Soviet civil defense, the plausibility of a
first strike would increase; therefore, so would the vulnerability of the United
States, if not to an actual attack, then at least to intimidation in a political
crisis.

The twin threats of the growing Soviet offensive forces and population
defense were very much on Nitze's mind when he was given a visitor's pass
to return to government service. In June 1976, President Ford's new Director
of Central Intelligence, George Bush, created a kind of visiting committee
of outsiders to carry out an exercise in "competitive analysis." This meant
offering a critique of, and alternative to, the CIA's assessment of Soviet
capabilities and intentions. The exercise, known as Team B, was Bush's
attempt to help the Administration fend off the challenge from the right,
particularly from Ronald Reagan, who was doing well in the Republican
primaries and piling up delegates to the party's nominating convention later

---

*As a Pentagon official during the Reagan Administration in 1981, Jones created an uproar when
he ventured the opinion in a newspaper interview that the United States could not only survive an
all-out nuclear war but could regain its prewar gross national product in a few years, if only
everyone built backyard bomb shelters: "If there are enough shovels to go around, everybody's
going to make it. It's the dirt that does it."

that summer. It was also an effort to blunt the criticisms—and, if possible, garner the support—of influential, hawkish private citizens, of whom Nitze was a prime example.

The impetus for Team B came from the President's Foreign Intelligence Advisory Board (PFIAB). The scientist on the board was Edward Teller. George Shultz, the former secretary of the treasury, was another member. In its growing misgivings about the prevailing views of the CIA, the PFIAB was greatly influenced by Albert Wohlstetter, who contended that the American intelligence community had been persistently underestimating the Soviet nuclear threat.

A professor of Russian history at Harvard, Richard Pipes, was recruited to chair Team B. He had come to the attention of the PFIAB largely because Henry Jackson and his assistants, Dorothy Fosdick and Richard Perle, admired Pipes's sharp critique of the Nixon-Ford-Kissinger policies. Among the people Pipes chose for Team B were Nitze, Paul Wolfowitz, and Daniel Graham, a general who had retired early in 1976 as director of the Pentagon's Defense Intelligence Agency.

Team B went far beyond its charter of estimating Soviet intentions and capabilities; it ended up prescribing what amounted to a crash program of American buildup. In that respect particularly, it was reminiscent of the Gaither Committee: a Republican Administration sought the advice of outsiders, who concluded that the first team—the government insiders whom they were being invited to second-guess—had let down the side, underestimating the enemy and allowing the American guard to slip.

There was a cyclical aspect to the American perception of the Soviet threat. Nitze had been part of the earlier cycles as well. In NSC 68 he had sought to inject a kind of therapeutic pessimism into the postwar view of the Soviet Union; the Gaither Report did much the same in the wake of *Sputnik;* the CIA overestimated Soviet strength in the late 1950s and thus contributed to the panic about the missile gap. Chastened by that experience, the agency then scaled back its projections during the late sixties. Now along came Team B, pushing again from the right, trying to persuade the Administration of the day, Ford's, to make policy on the basis of the worst case.

Graham later said that one of the principal pieces of evidence supporting Team B's alarm was "the discovery of a very important civil defense effort [in the U.S.S.R.]—very strong and unmistakable evidence that a big effort is on to protect people, industry and store food."[3]

Nitze's membership on Team B coincided with his participation in the founding of another organization. On Thanksgiving Day, 1975, Eugene Rostow, a former under secretary of state in the Johnson Administration and dean of the Yale Law School, wrote a letter to Nitze and a number of others proposing that like-minded private citizens should band together to alert the nation to the growing Soviet threat. In March 1976, Rostow and Nitze met for lunch with Elmo Zumwalt, Nitze's former Pentagon aide in the Johnson Administration and his ally against Kissinger in the Nixon Administration; Richard Allen, who had been shouldered aside by Kissinger as Nixon's national security advisor in 1969; and Max Kampelman, a prominent lawyer and active Democrat. A close aide to Hubert Humphrey in Minnesota and later in Washington, Kampelman had fought hard against the left wing of the Democratic Party in the 1940s and had been deeply alienated by what he regarded as the takeover of the party in 1972 by soft-headed liberals under the banner of George McGovern.*

The lunch served as "an organizing meeting" for what they at first called an "emergency committee." Later, the group decided to name itself after the Committee on the Present Danger of the early fifties, which had publicly urged the Truman Administration to adopt recommendations for a military buildup similar to those that Nitze secretly urged in NSC 68. But the founders of the new committee had another, much more recent model in mind. As Kampelman noted, "The intellectual basis for the Committee grew out of the work of the now-famous Team B."[4]

The Pond House

The Team B intelligence review and the formation of the Committee on the Present Danger took place during the summer, fall, and early winter of 1976. During the same period, Paul Nitze, now approaching his seventieth birthday, contemplated the possibility of returning to government service—of moving from Team B to Team A.

Throughout the year would-be members of a new Democratic administration had been gravitating toward presidential candidates of their choice. For example, Cyrus Vance, who had preceded Nitze as deputy secretary of defense in the Johnson Administration, supported his old friend Sargent Shriver, whom he had known from their days together as students at Yale. Nitze, however, was an early backer of a dark horse. During a lively discussion with his children at his farm one weekend early in the campaign, Nitze recalled, "they all started ganging up on me, saying, 'We need a younger President, someone closer to our generation.' " Nitze asked whom they

---

*Kampelman, a devout Jew, had been a conscientious objector on religious grounds during World War II. He was exempted from combat but not from hardship. He volunteered as a human guinea pig in experiments on human starvation at the University of Minnesota. As an aide to Humphrey in the Senate, Kampelman helped draft a bill that would have made membership in the Communist party a crime, and he supported the Communist Control Act of 1954. In the 1960s, he was a hawk on the Vietnam War.

liked. They were interested in Jimmy Carter. Nitze sent Carter some of his speeches and a financial contribution. Later, he encountered Carter at a reception, and the two men fell into conversation. Carter told Nitze he had read the materials. He not only praised them but said he often quoted from them in his own speeches on the stump.

Carter possessed a number of qualities that appealed to Nitze, including an engineer's love of precision, detail, and logic in argument. "He had a respect for and a command of facts," Nitze recalled, "and I always admire that." Carter was determined to become President almost by sheer force of will. That, too, impressed Nitze. Also, Carter was making much in his campaign of sharp criticisms aimed at the man who had dominated American foreign policy for the past few years—Henry Kissinger.

In one respect, however, Nitze and Carter were very different. Even when he was outside the government, Nitze was still the ultimate Washington insider, while Carter, even as he was preparing to take over the Oval Office, was the ultimate outsider. He ran for President as such. Watergate had given Washington a bad name; the Vietnam War had done much the same thing to the foreign-policy establishment. Carter rarely missed a chance to remind voters that his roots lay far from the banks of the Potomac and the meeting rooms of the Council on Foreign Relations.

Once he was assured of the nomination, Carter sought ways to demonstrate that he was master of the Democratic house. One means to that end was a series of "seminars" on major policy issues which he held at his home in Plains, Georgia. These were designed to acquaint him not only with the issues he would confront if elected but with prospective candidates for service in a Carter Administration. If stalwarts of the old guard were going to be accepted in the new regime, they were going to have to undergo a rite of passage by undertaking a pilgrimage to Plains.

On July 26, one of these seminars and group job interviews was held on defense policy. In addition to Nitze, there were three of his former colleagues from the McNamara Pentagon: Cyrus Vance, Harold Brown, and Paul Warnke. The up-and-coming generation of defense intellectuals was represented by two young lawyers, James Woolsey, who had worked for Nitze on SALT, and Walter Slocombe; Lynn Davis, a political scientist at Columbia University; and Barry Blechman, head of the defense analysis staff at the Brookings Institution.

During the long bus ride to Plains from the Atlanta airport, Nitze was charming and voluble. As a gentleman farmer who raised a variety of livestock and crops on his estate in Maryland, he knew more about agriculture than any of the others, and he delivered a learned commentary on the fields they passed, explaining soil condition and climate. But those pleasantries gave way to a sharp exchange between Nitze and his seatmate Harold Brown over whether the strategic-arms relationship between the United States and the Soviet Union could be characterized as parity. Nitze later recalled thinking that Brown "took much too optimistic a line."[5]

On arrival in Plains, the visitors met with Carter and some of his campaign staff in the Pond House, so called because the candidate had built it for his mother next to a dredged pond. The encounter was a critical point in Nitze's star-crossed career. He overplayed the role of stern elder. He sat in a straight-backed chair, looming over Carter, who was in an easy chair. Pulling T. K. Jones's charts and graphs out of a briefcase, Nitze began to talk. There was an intensity to his presentation that seemed discordant with the relaxed setting. He was convinced, he said, that the Soviet Union was beefing up its civil defense at a rate and in a manner that left only one conclusion: Not only would Soviet offensive forces soon be able to attack and destroy the U.S.'s ICBMs, but with a nationwide network of underground shelters, the Soviets would increase their confidence that they could survive a retaliatory strike from American SLBMs. The American doctrine of nuclear deterrence was all but bankrupt, and the U.S.S.R. might feel free to use its conventional strength against American allies in Europe. He was presenting Carter with a view of the world and of the imminent threat from the Soviet Union that the future President could see would leave his Administration with no choice but to adopt an extremely expensive defense policy, including a major program of civil defense. Twenty-six years and five Presidents later, Nitze was relying on both the logic chain and the billboard effect of NSC 68 all over again.

The episode cost Nitze any chance of a senior job in the Administration. Carter later recalled his reaction to the performance. "Nitze was typically know-it-all," he said. "He was arrogant and inflexible. His own ideas were sacred to him. He didn't seem to listen to others, and he had a doomsday approach."

Only Woolsey congratulated Nitze on his lecture. The others were awkwardly subdued. Vance commented softly to Warnke and Brown that Nitze had "blotted his copybook" by "browbeating" and "haranguing" Carter. Even at the Atlanta airport, as the group disbanded, Nitze was discoursing passionately, karate-chopping the air for emphasis, possessed by the urgency of his message and oblivious of the impression he had made.

His fellow pilgrims to Plains—Vance, Brown, Warnke, Woolsey, Slocombe, Davis, and Blechman—all received important posts. Nitze alone did not. Vance suggested him for high jobs on several occasions. So did Richard Holbrooke, the campaign's foreign-policy coordinator; as editor of *Foreign Policy,* he helped Nitze with his article "Deterring Our Deterrent." When Nitze's name came up, Carter would assume the same glacial politeness with which he had listened to the lecture in the Pond House. He commented to Vance at one point, "I don't think that man has the breadth or balance we need."

Harold Brown—who got the job of secretary of defense—considered bringing Nitze back into the Pentagon, but he felt that Nitze was too senior for an assistant secretaryship, such as his old post at ISA.

Even as Nitze was being blackballed, he was also being used. Carter asked him to give him his thoughts on arms control. Nitze wrote a five-page paper compressing and refining his main points from the *Foreign Affairs* article and personally dropped it off at the home of one of Carter's foreign-policy advisors, Anthony Lake, one Sunday morning in September.[6] Except for an acknowledgment of receipt, that was the last Nitze heard about the paper from the Carter camp.* Lake, then thirty-seven, went on to become director of State Department Policy Planning, the job Nitze had so relished nearly three decades before.

During the campaign and after the election in November, Carter's aides put out the word that he was receiving advice from across the spectrum, "from Paul Nitze to Paul Warnke." Without a position of his own, Nitze nevertheless tried in vain to get Ralph Earle the chairmanship of the SALT negotiating team and T. K. Jones a Pentagon job. He failed. He also made a number of other attempts to impress on Carter some of his strongly held views, including one that had a ring of better-late-than-never: "de-MIRVing," or moving toward deterrence based on one-warhead ICBMs. Even though he had played a key role in the decision to proceed with MIRVs in the sixties and early seventies, Nitze was now an advocate of relying on large numbers of small, single-warhead, mobile ICBMs.

With an array of new programs already under way, the Carter Administration was not receptive to the idea of yet another weapon system. Moreover, it was a well-established tenet of arms-control orthodoxy that since it was harder to keep track of mobile ICBMs, agreements that permitted—to say nothing of encouraged—mobility would be harder to verify.

As it became more obvious that he was being passed over and his advice waved aside, Nitze expressed deep bitterness to a number of old friends who he felt were on his side. Others could sense his embitterment. Vance looked back on the Pond House session as "the start of real mutual souring" between Carter and Nitze and "a terrible blow to Paul, because there was every reason to think it was his last chance for a senior position." Vance was saddened by what he saw happening in his friend. He was also apprehensive: "There was a chip on Paul's shoulder, and a new shrillness in discussion."[7]

---

*Nearly six years later, on February 23, 1982, Carter, as former President, received a visit in Plains from the Finnish ambassador to Washington, Jaakko Iloniemi. Carter said he had been going through his archives and found Nitze's paper. He expressed regret that he had not paid more attention to it at the time. Iloniemi passed this message on to Nitze, by then an official in the Reagan Administration.

Chairman, Policy Studies

After nearly a year of preparation, the Committee on the Present Danger was formally launched at a press conference on November 11, 1976—two days after Jimmy Carter's election. The list of members was a roster of people who would serve Ronald Reagan when he replaced Carter four years later. Reagan himself was a member of the founding board of directors of the committee, and he drew repeatedly from the writings of his fellow members in the radio broadcasts he made in 1978 and '79, particularly those of Pipes on the nature of the Soviet Union and of Rostow on the perilous deficiencies of SALT II.

Nitze's title on the masthead of the Committee of the Present Danger was "Chairman, Policy Studies." He worked out of a spacious suite at the System Planning Corporation, a defense contracting firm in Arlington, Virginia. His office overlooking the Potomac was like a shadow Pentagon, with Nitze as the shadow secretary of defense. He worked away on papers and speeches for the committee, gave briefings for the press, prepared for appearances before congressional committees, and arranged seminars of mostly like-minded experts.

Participants in these sessions were often astonished at how much inside information Nitze had from the Pentagon and, later, from the SALT II negotiations in Geneva. The old channel between Rowny, who remained the Joint Chiefs' representative for SALT, and Richard Perle remained very much intact, and Nitze was sometimes cut in on the flow of information.

Among the influential private citizens on whom Nitze concentrated his powers of persuasion was Henry Kissinger. A mutual friend, Joseph Alsop, had, with some difficulty, arranged a partial and, as it turned out, temporary reconciliation between them. Kissinger listened attentively to Nitze's detailed presentation, shaking his head in dismay over the charts and graphs illustrating the asymmetries in throw-weight and hard-target kill capability. He pronounced himself to be largely convinced and said he shared Nitze's alarm over the policies of the Carter Administration, even though the arguments Nitze was making were almost identical to those that Kissinger had rejected a few years before. As Nitze noted wryly during this brief détente between them, his relationship with Kissinger "has had its ups and downs. At the moment it is up, because neither of us is in the government."[8]

Nitze's attacks on the policies of the new Administration became highly personal when President Carter nominated Paul Warnke to be both director of ACDA and chief SALT negotiator. Initially, Nitze said he meant only to oppose the idea that Warnke should wear both hats. But his opposition quickly became less modulated. At the hearings on the nomination in February, Nitze recalled that he and Warnke had disagreed during the Johnson Administration on the question of whether to move forward with an American ABM. Warnke had favored a moratorium. "I can assure you," Nitze told the senators, "that if Mr. Warnke's advice unilaterally to refrain from starting an ABM deployment program had been followed, we could not possibly have succeeded in obtaining a prudent ABM treaty."

In 1975, Warnke had written an article in *Foreign Policy* called "Apes on a Treadmill."[9] He treated the Soviet-American nuclear competition as a case of monkey-see, monkey-do. He expressed doubt about whether asymmetries in the nuclear balance truly mattered. Warnke's recommendation had been, as in the case of the ABM, unilateral American restraint: "We can be the first off the treadmill. That's the only victory the arms race has to offer." In other comments, quoted back to him during his confirmation, he had said, "The numbers game is not worth playing" and that it was "a mindless exercise."

Warnke had also made fun of those who advocated civil defense for Americans and feared civil defense programs in the U.S.S.R. When, in the course of a congressional hearing, Warnke was asked about the Soviet Union's presumed determination to disperse and shelter a significant portion of its leadership and population so that it would survive a nuclear war, he replied that since his own residence was close to the District of Columbia, he personally stood little chance of surviving the war and therefore was not going to worry about the outcome elsewhere.

For Nitze, with a bomb shelter at his farm in the countryside, this seeming flippancy was infuriating. He called these and other views of Warnke's "demonstrably unsound" and "asinine"—a "screwball, arbitrary, fictitious kind of viewpoint that is not going to help the security of this country."

Finally Senator Thomas McIntyre asked, "Are you saying that you impugn [Warnke's] character as an American citizen?"

"If you force me to, I do," Nitze replied.

"That is very interesting. Do you think you are a better American than he is?"

"I really do."

Henry Jackson could see that Nitze was going too far, so he intervened to preserve Nitze's effectiveness as an opponent of Warnke's confirmation. In an attempt to return the proceedings to a higher plane and reinforce the credibility of a witness who had momentarily allowed himself to engage in character assassination, Jackson read into the record Nitze's curriculum vitae "so that we can have before us your distinguished record for the benefit of the committee," and he delivered a lengthy encomium ("He is a real professional; he is intellectually honest and a very courageous person; he has no axe to grind''). Then Jackson endorsed Nitze's opinion about Warnke's qualifications to guide the new Administration's search for a SALT II treaty.

Shortly after his attack on Warnke, Nitze flew to Colorado Springs, Colorado, for a conference at the United States Air Force Academy. The other participants could see he was deeply agitated, still in a combative mood. He was quick to tell anyone who asked that the nation was heading for disaster, that knaves and fools were taking over in Washington. The rough-and-tumble of the past few days had filled him with resentment against those colleagues of the past whom he associated with the folly of the present.

The after-dinner speaker at the banquet in Colorado was George Kennan. He was introduced extravagantly, even reverentially. Nitze's mood, already gloomy, discernibly worsened. Listening to the outpouring of praise for Kennan as one of the great wise men of his generation, Nitze's jaw was set even more firmly than usual; he began flexing his cheek muscles and clenching his fists. Finally he turned to one of his neighbors and unleashed a tirade not so much of criticism as of naked jealousy. He spoke softly, but his voice rasped with intensity and pent-up emotion:

For more than thirty years Kennan had been idolized; he had been the darling of the intellectuals. It apparently made people of almost all ideological stripes feel virtuous to praise Kennan's supposed virtues as a sage and a statesman, as someone who knew what the Russians were all about and how to deal with them. Well, Nitze was getting tired of it. Where had Kennan's way led? It had led into the current mess, into a world in which the United States was weak and almost willfully letting itself get weaker. Kennan's way had been tried; it was apparently going to be tried again by Carter, Warnke, Vance, Brown, and the rest. The contest, however, was not over. Nitze saw the right way, and sooner or later—he hoped not too late—the country would see it, too.

When it came time for his own remarks at the conference, Nitze was under control, speaking coolly, analytically, civilly, with an extended metaphor from chess. "You know," he said,

In chess it isn't necessary that your queen take any pieces. If she's in the right position, she can support and dominate many squares on the board. If the other player's queen is lost or bottled up, it can't cover those positions. In a way, it seems to me that the basic nuclear strategic relationship is comparable to the queen's role in the game of chess. If you've got the advantage in that position, you've got an advantage that you don't ever have to use but that sends its message out to a lot of different positions.

The Soviet Union, he believed, had stronger pieces in the form of MIRVed

ICBMs, advantage of position on the board, and, in the most sinister sense, a will to win.[10]

"No, No, No"

On March 9 the Senate confirmed Paul Warnke as director of ACDA by a vote of 70 to 29, but by the much narrower margin of 58 to 40 as chief SALT negotiator. Henry Jackson, Richard Perle, and Paul Nitze considered the latter vote a symbolic victory for their own position and a stern warning to the Administration, since it was less than the two-thirds majority that would be required to ratify the SALT II treaty Warnke must now try to negotiate.

The negotiations moved slowly, for the executive branch had to contend simultaneously with obstinate Soviets, increasingly assertive domestic critics, and divisions within its own ranks.* The principal disagreement was between Secretary of State Vance and Warnke on the one side and the President's national security advisor, Zbigniew Brzezinski, on the other. Brzezinski was a former professor at Harvard and Columbia. Nitze was in general mistrustful of academics in government (they tended to "follow the wrong logic chain," he often said). For his part, Brzezinski was disparaging of Nitze's caste—"the WASP/Eastern Seaboard/Ivy League/Wall Street/foreign affairs elite." Brzezinski may have aimed that MIRVed pejorative at his colleague Cyrus Vance, but it applied equally to Paul Nitze. Yet Brzezinski and Nitze had at least two things in common: a deeply embedded anti-Sovietism and an abiding sense of rivalry toward Henry Kissinger.

Brzezinski knew early on that the new Administration was acutely vulnerable to second-guessing from conservatives. An interagency group, chaired by the Pentagon, prepared a document that became known as Presidential Review Memorandum No. 10, or PRM-10, which recommended proceeding with new Trident submarine missiles, upgrading Minuteman ICBM warheads, building the MX, a ten-warhead successor to the Minuteman, and developing cruise missiles. These measures were all seen as correctives to the alleged "decade of neglect" (even though they were continuations of programs to which the Nixon and Ford administrations had been committed during that same infamous decade).

Nitze was not impressed. He had wanted the Administration to adopt a

---

*For an account of how the treaty was negotiated, see the author's *Endgame: The Inside Story of SALT II* (Harper & Row, 1979).

much more extensive—and expensive—program to upgrade the nation's de-fenses. "PRM-10," he said later, *"tried* to be another NSC 68."[11]

During the first year of the Carter presidency, members of the Committee on the Present Danger were invited to meet with the President as well as Defense Secretary Brown and National Security Advisor Brzezinski.* Vance and Warnke were kept out of sight—and, it was hoped, out of mind—at these sessions. But frequently these "stroking sessions," as they were some-times called, served only to exacerbate the tensions. Most dramatic was a meeting in August 1977 at the White House. Carter listened attentively while a delegation from the committee reviewed the evidence of a mammoth So-viet buildup and stressed the grave danger to the United States. Carter replied that American public opinion would not support the kind of budget-busting crash programs that the committee felt were necessary. As Carter spoke, Nitze began shaking his head, murmuring, "No, no, no."

"Paul," said the President, "would you please let me finish?"

It was an exaggerated version of the Pond House encounter between the two men of just over a year before, this time replayed in the White House, with Nitze no longer a potential insider but now an implacable outsider. There was a widespread assumption among his friends, former friends, and opponents that Nitze had reached that point in his career where there was nothing left for him to do but to murmur "No, no, no" from the sidelines and perhaps write his autobiography. In 1978 Barry Blechman, who had been with Nitze at the Pond House and was now on Warnke's staff at ACDA, asked him if he had started work on his memoirs. "Come on, Barry," Nitze replied. "I know why you want me to write my memoirs; you want to get me involved in something that will keep me out of influencing policy. Forget it."

The Precepts of the Apostle Paul

In the months that followed, Paul Nitze did indeed influence policy. Even though it was almost certain that he would, when the time came, oppose the ratification of SALT II, he still had considerable influence on the delibera-tions within the Carter Administration over what the treaty should try to accomplish.

---

*The only person associated with the Committee on the Present Danger at its inception who went on to receive a high post in the Carter Administration was James Schlesinger. His own reputation for hard-line views kept him from returning to the Pentagon under Carter; instead, he was made secretary of energy.

Since he was sure that SALT II would not redress the imbalance in ballistic-missile throw-weight—hence, would not sufficiently blunt the threat of Soviet MIRVed ICBMs—Nitze believed that the American deterrent would remain vulnerable to Soviet attack. It was in this context that the phrase "window of vulnerability" was coined by Pentagon analysts and put into circulation by Nitze and other critics of the treaty, then still a work in progress.

Nitze wanted to make sure that, at a minimum, the United States would be able to undertake measures that would diminish that vulnerability. One such measure was a so-called shell game, advocated by Harold Brown, whereby the United States would remove some or all of its own ICBMs from their stationary silos and base them instead in a system of multiple shelters so that the Soviet Union would never know exactly where the missiles were. Nitze became a leading advocate of this scheme. Cyrus Vance, Paul Warnke, and others opposed the idea, arguing that the problem of vulnerability was greatly exaggerated and that "protective/deceptive" basing plans made it more difficult to verify compliance with arms-control agreements.

In 1978, the White House overruled these objections and instructed Warnke to notify the Soviets that the United States reserved the right to play the shell game. Warnke dutifully raised the matter first with Ambassador Anatoly Dobrynin in Washington, then with the chief Soviet negotiator in Geneva, Vladimir Semyonov, a holdover from SALT I.

Shortly afterward, Semyonov was transferred to Bonn as ambassador, and Warnke resigned as chief negotiator, partly to avoid jeopardizing the treaty by provoking further controversy about himself. Both men were replaced by veterans—Semyonov by Victor Karpov and Warnke, in his chief negotiator's role, by Ralph Earle, who had been Nitze's choice for that job two years earlier.

The treaty was finally signed by Carter and Brezhnev at a summit meeting in Vienna in June 1979. The final version of SALT II contained some features that would serve to constrain ballistic missile throw-weight as well as the number of warheads that the Soviets could array against the United States. There was a separate subceiling on MIRVed ICBMs (820) and a freeze on the number of multiple warheads per type of ICBM (for example, ten per SS-18). But the treaty as a whole remained anathema to its critics.

Even with the shell game in and Warnke out, Nitze remained unmollified. Many of his friends and former colleagues from the Kennedy and Johnson administrations were astonished by the ferocity of his attacks not just on the substance of the pact but on the intelligence, competence, and character of the Americans negotiating it. In Geneva, his negotiating partner from SALT I, Alexander Shchukin, professed a personal sense of puzzlement and dismay. "What has become of my old friend Paul?" he asked. "Why is he saying these things?"

Ralph Earle was asking himself the same thing, and his answer was "Hell hath no fury like Paul Nitze spurned."

At the Carter-Brezhnev summit in June 1979, Earle, now chief negotiator, gave a background briefing to some reporters. He said that given two hours and a copy of the treaty, he could persuade any reasonable man to support ratification. Richard Strout of *The New Republic* asked whether Paul Nitze was a friend of Earle's and a reasonable man. Earle said, "Yes, on both counts." Then could he persuade Nitze to support the treaty? Earle said he thought he could. Strout wrote a column about the exchange.

When he returned to Washington to help in the uphill SALT-selling effort, Earle got a call from Nitze, who said, "Phyllis and I would like you to come down for the weekend. And bring a copy of the treaty." Earle drove to the Nitzes' farm in Maryland on Saturday, July 7. The Senate Foreign Relations Committee hearings were to begin the following Monday. The two men sat by the swimming pool and had a civilized argument, in which Nitze focused on his concern that the treaty was still ambiguous on the permissibility of a shell game to protect American ICBMs.

"Paul," said Earle as they were parting the next morning, "you're going to play a major role in the ratification hearings. It's going to be very important. Please, Paul, don't screw it up." Earle added that he had never entirely understood why Nitze was so opposed to the treaty.

Nitze smiled, but there was little humor in his expression: "Well, Ralph, what else would I have had to do these past couple of years?"

Nitze appeared before the Senate Foreign Relations Committee the following Thursday, July 12, 1979, along with General Edward Rowny, who had left the delegation on the eve of the treaty signing, then campaigned against its ratification. But it was Nitze's testimony that most impressed the senators and dominated the headlines. He criticized virtually every aspect of the treaty. SALT II, he said, "with all its fallacies and implausibilities, can only incapacitate our minds and wills." What he called his number one concern was the large number of Soviet MIRVed ICBMs permitted by the treaty.

In stressing the "asymmetries" in the "MIRVed ICBM balance," he reiterated a point from his thirty-year debate with Brodie, Kennan, and others. "It is likely that if deterrence fails," he said, Soviet land-based warheads "would be the key element in an initial strike. . . . This exchange could well determine the military outcome of the war. . . . I should doubt that the Soviet Union would cold-bloodedly choose to launch a nuclear attack on the U.S. homeland. Irrespective of the probability, I would not rule out the possibility." That possibility—however remote, however much the worst case—must figure in strategies for peace as well as war.

Nor was it just this treaty he objected to. His writings for the Committee on the Present Danger during this period, particularly an article titled "Is SALT II a Fair Deal for the United States?," were filled with reminders of his discomfiture over the loss of American strategic nuclear superiority: "To have the advantage at the utmost level of violence helps at every lesser level. In the Korean War, the Berlin blockade, and the Cuban missile crisis, the U.S. had the strategic edge because of our superiority at the strategic nuclear level. That edge has slipped away." And the slippage, he feared, would continue. In his testimony against the treaty, he warned, "It is almost certain that if SALT II is ratified as signed at Vienna, SALT III will be less favorable to the United States and more favorable to the U.S.S.R. than SALT II."

He was asked repeatedly whether—despite all his objections, despite all the improvements he could imagine and would like to see—the United States would actually be worse off if SALT II were ratified. Conversely, would it be better off if the treaty were not ratified? In the absence of SALT II, might not the Soviets deploy even more ICBMs with more warheads? They were already bumping their heads against the subceiling of 820 MIRVed ICBMs, and without the SALT freeze on MIRVs at the number already tested on each type of missile, the Strategic Rocket Forces could easily increase the MIRV load on the SS-18 from the maximum of ten warheads permitted by the treaty to as many as forty, quadrupling the threat that heavy ICBMs posed to the United States.

It was precisely because of these constraints on Soviet forces that General David Jones, the chairman of the Joint Chiefs of Staff, endorsed the treaty, calling it "a modest but useful step" that would add a measure of "predictability" to future Soviet programs, thereby somewhat easing the American military's task of anticipating and countering those programs.

Nitze disagreed sharply, saying that the Chiefs' argument was "weak." The ceilings, subceilings, and MIRV limits were "so designed and so high that they put no effective limit" on the Soviet threat. The Strategic Rocket Forces were already at an optimum level with 820 MIRVed ICBMs. The freeze of ten warheads per SS-18 was, he said, "one of the most overplayed so-called assets of SALT II." As for talk of "predictability," the mere echo of that defense of SALT II ten years afterward made him angry: "If a man is under sentence to be hanged by the neck until dead—that's predictability. But is it necessarily beneficial? Does it do the condemned man any good? The Chiefs' twaddle about predictability was always unthinking."[12]

A number of pro–SALT II senators noted that while the Soviet Union was genuinely constrained by the treaty, the United States, for all intents and purposes, was not. There seemed to be virtually no American strategic program realistically in prospect that would be inhibited. In reply, Nitze focused on the ambiguity of the record of the negotiations and the text of the treaty with regard to the permissibility of a shell game as "the method of assuring the survivability of our ICBMs." To ratify the treaty without clarification of that point would be foolish. As part of his exhortation to resolve the issue, he told the committee: "In the conduct of foreign affairs and defense policy, we should adhere to the Apostle Paul's precept: 'Let all things be done decently and in order.' "

As the July 12 hearings approached a luncheon break, Claiborne Pell, Democrat of Rhode Island, asked him for a simple thumbs-up or thumbs-down on ratification. Nitze dodged, saying he was urging a package of amendments to rectify the treaty's shortcomings. Pell was not satisfied: "I understand, but if that does not happen, from the viewpoint of people thinking like you, would we be better off as a nation to reject the treaty as is or to ratify it?" Nitze suddenly, and uncharacteristically, took refuge in an almost bureaucratic answer: "I discussed that with the executive committee of the Committee on the Present Danger, and we decided that the time had not yet come to take a position on that." For the moment at least, he was reserving final judgment.

As with his attacks on Warnke's confirmation two and a half years earlier, Nitze's position hardened over time. The political climate turned sharply against SALT II, especially in the wake of the much-publicized "discovery" in September of a Soviet "combat brigade" in Cuba. In fact, the unit had been on the island for years, and its military significance was greatly exaggerated both by an Administration and its supporters in Congress who were on the defensive, looking for ways to prove their vigilance and toughness, and by a body of critics who were on the offensive, looking for ways to discredit what was left of détente.

In October 1979, Henry Jackson chaired hearings behind closed doors before a subcommittee of the Armed Services Committee. Richard Perle was the sole staff member present. He wrote Jackson's talking points, passed him slips of paper, often whispered in his ear, and took extensive notes on the testimony of various government witnesses. These supposedly confidential proceedings were repeatedly given an interpretation damaging to the Administration's case and leaked, often with tidbits of classified information, to anti-SALT journalists, especially the syndicated columnists Rowland Evans and Robert Novak.

When Nitze appeared before the Armed Services Committee in October, he went well beyond his earlier recommendation of amendments. Now he was calling for negotiation of a new treaty: "My view is that it would be advisable for the Senate to withhold its consent to the treaty and concurrently . . . ask the executive branch to go back to the negotiating table, even though that might take some considerable period of time, to work out a better agreement."

He wrote a lengthy paper for the Committee on the Present Danger that served as its definitive statement on SALT II. It was withering in its criticism and clear in its recommendation: ". . . In order to provide the preconditions necessary for an agreement that satisfies American interests, ratification of

SALT II should be withheld. The United States should first take appropriate steps to correct the problems I have mentioned, which would put it in a better position to negotiate a new and better SALT agreement.''

Yet the title of the paper rather oddly beat around the bush: "Considerations Bearing on the Merits of the SALT II Agreements as Signed at Vienna.'' For years afterward, Nitze cited the "carefully chosen words'' of that title as he engaged in revisionism about his own role. Without ever retracting the specifics of the case he had made, he denied that he had ever actually "opposed'' SALT II.

When members of his personal staff assembled his papers for possible publication, they wrote a brief introduction to "Considerations Bearing on the Merits . . . ,'' saying: "As director of policy studies for the Committee on the Present Danger, Nitze was an instrumental figure in the committee's lobbying efforts to defeat the SALT II treaty.'' In editing that passage, Nitze deleted the words "lobbying'' and "defeat'' and rewrote the passage to read: ''. . . Nitze was an instrumental figure in the committee's effort to assure Senate understanding of the SALT II treaty and its implications before deciding whether or not to vote for its ratification.''

In the fall of 1980, shortly after Ronald Reagan had defeated Jimmy Carter for the presidency, Nitze asked Ralph Earle: "Well, what are we Democrats going to do now that the Republicans have won the election?'' There was no ironic smile.

Earle said he was astonished that Nitze could pose such a question, given his role in the SALT II debate and the importance of his attacks against the treaty in Reagan's campaign. Nitze insisted that he had never actually come out against SALT II. He objected to the very phrase "SALT debate''; it had been a "dialogue.'' All he had wanted to do was contribute to the "discussion.'' In June 1985, speaking to an interviewer, he further refined his position in retrospect: "I never did say to the Senate that they should *not* ratify. I said you can make up your mind whether you want to ratify—that's your task. But you really ought to understand it. You ought to understand that *it limits the wrong things,*'' i.e., launchers rather than warheads and throwweight.[13]

Nitze's attempt to rewrite his own role in the drama of SALT II smacked of ambivalence if not regret. It was as though he realized his opposition to the treaty could not be adequately explained by the intellectual content of his complaints. Where you stand depends on where you sit, and when he sat on the sidelines—or at the witness table as a private citizen, commenting on the handiwork of an Administration that had snubbed him—he was all the more inclined to stand against what that Administration was doing.

Paul Warnke explained Nitze's behavior by quoting a twist on Lord Acton's famous maxim, coined by the Canadian statesman Lester Pearson: "Power corrupts, but the loss of power corrupts absolutely.''[14]

There was that in Nitze's opposition to SALT II, but there was more as well. His ego had been engaged, but so had his intellect. He had been driven by pique, but also by principle. Beyond a vendetta against Warnke and others, SALT II was part of the battle of ideas. The episode reflected a concern that went back to Nitze's Spenglerian broodings in the thirties and to the dark vision of NSC 68. The treaty aroused his lifelong worry about the basic flaccidity of the West. His commitment to arms control had always been conditional, and the conditions in which SALT II had come before the Senate were not, in his view, auspicious. He was afraid that ratification of the treaty would appear to vindicate the broader policies of the Carter Administration, policies that he equated with an excessive eagerness to sit down with the Soviets at the negotiating table and a lamentable reluctance to stand up to them in the military competition.

CHAPTER 8

Deep Cuts

Ronald Reagan's inauguration in January 1981 was the culmination of a long struggle by the right wing of the Republican party, stretching back to the defeats of Robert Taft for the nomination in 1952 and Barry Goldwater for the election in 1964. Reagan was the latest standard-bearer of a movement with a thirty-year grudge against the East Coast foreign-policy establishment, a movement that had, on at least three occasions, denounced and rebuffed Paul Nitze. In 1953 Senate conservatives and the McCormick press had joined forces to block his appointment to the Pentagon, driving him out of government. In 1963 Goldwater and others had opposed his nomination as secretary of the navy. In 1974 much the same constellation of senators had thwarted his attempt to break free of Secretary of State Henry Kissinger and work for Secretary of Defense James Schlesinger instead. That last setback had triggered Nitze's resignation from government and led to his long stretch in the wilderness. At the fringes of what was now the Reagan wing of the GOP, celebrating its triumph in 1980, were extremists for whom Nitze was the antithesis of everything Reagan represented.

But for all Reagan's strongly held views, he knew that whatever ideological and political shifts had brought him to power, the nation was still essentially centrist and highly diverse. In the transition of late 1980 and the early post-inaugural period of 1981, there was an attempt to reach out beyond the hard core of the Republican far right to a wider, more respectable pool of talent. However, the new Administration quickly turned out to be an awkward and fractious assemblage, particularly in the conduct of arms control. Paul Nitze's return to government service came about as a result of an early skirmish in the bureaucratic warfare that continued for the next eight years.*

The new secretary of defense, Caspar Weinberger, was a Californian and an old friend of Reagan's. At first, his appointment was reassuring to moderates. They remembered his reputation as "Cap the Knife," a determined cost-cutter, when he had served as director of the Office of Management and

---

*For an account of arms control in the first Reagan term, see the author's *Deadly Gambits: The Reagan Administration and the Stalemate in Nuclear Arms Control* (Knopf, 1984). This chapter draws extensively from that work.

Budget and secretary of health, education and welfare in the Nixon Administration. Some hoped that he would approach the Pentagon as the ultimate manifestation of federal overspending.

That was not to be. Weinberger quickly established himself as a dogged company lawyer. Whatever his priorities in the past, his clients now were the Department of Defense, with its institutional interest in generous spending, and the new President, with his conviction that the nation must reverse a "decade of neglect" in the development and deployment of new weapons systems.

Weinberger threw himself into the task of making the case—in public, in congressional testimony, at National Security Council meetings, and in private visits with his longtime associate in the Oval Office—for the largest possible defense budget and the most vigorous and extensive "strategic modernization" program ever. Weinberger had what one of his aides called a "Churchill complex." He was an Anglophile who, as secretary of defense, enjoyed visiting England and debating at the Oxford Union. He quoted Winston Churchill's wartime speeches with a verve that suggested not just admiration but emulation. He often talked as though he saw the West approaching its darkest, most difficult, yet potentially finest hour, a twilight struggle against a latter-day Axis that ran from Moscow to Havana to Hanoi.

At Weinberger's right hand was Richard Perle. He was Weinberger's one-man brain trust on all matters relating to arms control. Especially at its outset, this was an ideological Administration more than a partisan one, and Jackson Democrats were welcome. Perle was made assistant secretary of defense for international security policy. This was loosely the equivalent of the ISA job that Nitze had held in the Kennedy Administration.

On the Pentagon organization chart, Perle was subordinate to the under secretary of defense for policy. Nitze might have been given that position himself—and thus been Perle's boss—had it not been for lingering opposition from conservative Republican senators like Goldwater and John Tower. Instead, the under secretary's job went to Fred Iklé, who was no match for Perle in deftness and assertiveness. Perle had been instrumental in bringing Iklé to Washington to toughen U.S. arms-control policy in the early seventies, and Perle remained the kingpin now that the principal figures of that earlier episode were reassembling. Another of that group, John Lehman, who had been Perle's confederate on the NSC staff and Iklé's deputy at the Arms Control and Disarmament Agency during their anti-Kissinger maneuvers of early 1976, was the new secretary of the navy.

The first of Reagan's six national security advisors was Richard Allen, who had expected to serve in the same capacity at the beginning of the Nixon Administration, only to be shouldered aside by Henry Kissinger. Allen was looking for a way to offset the influence of Secretary of State Alexander Haig and his right-hand man, Lawrence Eagleburger, first head of the European bureau, later the under secretary of state for political affairs. Unlike Allen, Haig and Eagleburger had both thrived under Kissinger's patronage and tutelage. Allen was determined to prevent them now from restoring Kissinger's policies.

At the outset of the Administration, the intention had been to appoint Edward Rowny as director of ACDA—the agency that had been conceived as an institutional advocate of arms control but was now, along with the Pentagon, to serve as a counterweight to the State Department. But however much Rowny might be due a reward as the good soldier of the war against SALT, he was neither an impressive figure nor an effective bureaucratic infighter. He had a cumbersome, ham-fisted style of argument that often made even those who agreed with him wince. Allen worried that Rowny would not be able to stand up to Haig in the coming battles over arms control. For the directorship of ACDA, therefore, Allen turned instead to his colleague from the Committee on the Present Danger, Eugene Rostow.

Allen saw Rostow as having a knack for geopolitics and spokesmanship—"the big picture stuff, with drums rolling and flags snapping," as Allen once put it. A key part of Rostow's message was that the Soviet purpose in possessing nuclear weapons was "to serve as the ultimate engine of the process of nuclear blackmail—a process of expansion involving the use or the credible threat to use propaganda, terrorism, proxy war, subversion, or Soviet troops themselves under the sanction and protection of what they hope will be Soviet nuclear superiority."[1] Rostow eventually brought in Nitze as one of his closest advisors.

Having been deprived of the ACDA directorship, Rowny was made chief negotiator for strategic arms control. Political pressures from Congress made it impossible simply to let those negotiations lapse. Whatever the public disappointment with the record of the détente era, there was still strong support for arms control. No President, not even one as popular as Reagan, could afford to be seen as walking away from the negotiating table. Instead, Reagan attacked traditional arms control, as it were, from the left: Mere arms *control* was not good enough, he said; what was needed was disarmament, or at least major progress in that direction. The "L" in SALT stood for "limitation." He christened his own attempt to improve on SALT with the acronym START, for "Strategic Arms *Reduction* Talks."

The idea of dramatic reductions, or "deep cuts," in strategic nuclear arms was appealing not just to Reaganauts. It was on this issue that George Kennan made a brief but significant reappearance on the scene. On May 19, 1981, Kennan went to Washington to be awarded the Albert Einstein Peace Prize. The ceremony was well attended by the stalwarts of the pro-détente, pro–arms control community. Also present was Soviet ambassador Anatoly Dobrynin. His attendance at the lunch for Kennan was a reminder of the good old days of SALT and détente.

Kennan delivered a speech calling for "an immediate across-the-board reduction by 50 percent of the nuclear arsenals now being maintained by the two superpowers." The idea was widely dismissed as a pipe dream, even by many liberals who politely applauded the grand old man of Soviet-American relations and his latest expression of eloquent despair at the madness of the arms race. It was not, however, dismissed by Paul Nitze. Senator Alan Cranston, a Democrat of California who was a leading advocate of arms control, telephoned Nitze and asked his reaction to Kennan's proposal. Nitze replied that in principle, 50-percent cuts would serve the cause of stabilizing the competition as long as both sides agreed to eliminate the largest, most heavily MIRVed ICBMs first.[2] In practice, that meant deep cuts not just across the board but in large Soviet ICBMs, especially the heavy SS-18s.

As the Administration prepared to make a proposal in START, Nitze was in a peculiar and frustrating position. Even though he had for years been intimately involved in SALT and had led the charge in the campaign against SALT II, he was not initially given a direct role in the new Administration's attempt to improve on SALT. In that sense, he was still an outsider even though he was back on the inside.

Nonetheless, he served as a kind of in-house consultant on START, primarily through his close association with Rostow, in the formulation of the START proposal. He joined forces with Perle and other hard-liners in the Administration in pressing for deep cuts in ballistic missile warheads, which he called "the cutting, killing edge" of the Soviet arsenal, as well as ballistic missile throw-weight.

The proposal that Reagan eventually put forward in May 1982 would have required that the Soviet Union reduce by two-thirds both the number of its ICBM warheads and its aggregate throw-weight. There was to be virtually no tradeoff in the existing American arsenal for this huge Soviet concession. The United States would have to pay a price in the number of weapons it could deploy in the future, but it would not have to give up any of the programs in its strategic modernization program. It would be able to proceed with the development and deployment of the MX; the Trident II, or D-5, the new SLBM with hard-target-kill capability; two new bombers designed to penetrate Soviet air defenses, the B-1 and the Advanced-Technology Bomber (ATB), or Stealth, which would be nearly invisible to enemy radar; and a family of new cruise missiles.

Leonid Brezhnev and his comrades in the sluggish gerontocracy then ruling the Soviet Union were not about to agree to the President's overall formula, since it would require the U.S.S.R. to build down while allowing the United States to build up in certain categories; it would force a massive restructuring of Soviet missile forces yet place few constraints on American bombers and cruise missiles. Rowny's appointment as chief START negotiator provided further assurance that the negotiations would go nowhere. To reverse what was seen as the dishonorable tradition of seeking ''agreement for agreement's sake,'' he was to sit in Geneva out-frowning, out-waiting, out-stonewalling the Soviets. It was a role for which he was well suited and in which he seemed to take satisfaction.

"An Inveterate Problem-Solver"

There was another arms-control challenge that required immediate attention. This was the necessity of conducting separate negotiations on what became known as intermediate-range nuclear forces, or INF.

Under various initials, the issue had been around for decades. In the late fifties and early sixties the United States kept medium-range Thor and Jupiter missiles in Britain, Italy, and Turkey to offset roughly comparable Soviet missiles, SS-4s and SS-5s. The Eisenhower Administration considered a scheme for mounting missiles on trucks and deploying them on the Autobahns of West Germany. When Paul Nitze joined the Pentagon in 1961, he helped persuade the Kennedy Administration that ''having these missiles in trucks running around the roads—the interface with the public—was politically dangerous, and dangerous in itself.''

That idea was dropped for one that Nitze considered no better—the creation of a sea-based ''Multi-Lateral Force,'' or MLF, which would consist of a mixed-nationality NATO fleet of surface vessels armed with Polaris missiles. Nitze argued to Robert McNamara that it was ''outrageous to have an alliance in which the subsidiary partners could commit the major partner to war or to an escalation of war. . . . Clearly, we should not put ourselves in a position where the Europeans could fire off these nuclear weapons without our consent.'' McNamara, however, deferred to Secretary of State Dean Rusk, who favored the plan.[3]

There ensued a divisive and embarrassing squabble within the Alliance over command structure and American veto power, while the Soviets had a propaganda field day with the prospect of German fingers near nuclear triggers. The MLF died a slow, painful, but in the end unmourned death.

The American Thors and Jupiters were removed, in part because it was felt that America would still have sufficient nuclear firepower in Europe. But by the late seventies, the Soviets had ''modernized'' the clunky, obsolescent SS-4s and SS-5s by fielding a new generation of weapons, the extremely accurate SS-20, a mobile, triple-warhead ballistic missile.

In Nitze's chess analogy, just as the heavy SS-18 ICBM was seen to threaten strategic checkmate, the SS-20 was a way for the Soviets to dominate with intermediate-range bishops and knights the European squares on the board. The pawns of tanks, artillery, and infantry suddenly became more important. With the American nuclear arsenal supposedly "neutralized," the numerical superiority of the Warsaw Pact's conventional forces might now be the determining factor in a replay of the Berlin crisis.

In October 1977, Helmut Schmidt, chancellor of West Germany, delivered a speech in London in which he asked the United States to take on the task of "removing the disparities of military power in Europe." In the context both of the speech and of the times, this meant a new, Europe-oriented dimension of nuclear arms control or a new, Europe-based generation of American nuclear weaponry—or both. Over two years later, in December 1979, the foreign and defense ministers of NATO followed Schmidt's exhortation. They committed their governments to the so-called two-track decision. NATO would proceed toward deployment of 572 new intermediate-range American missiles in Europe to offset the SS-20s. These were to be a combination of two weapon systems: Five NATO members would accept batteries of Tomahawk ground-launched cruise missiles; West Germany, which already had 108 American Pershing I ballistic missiles, would permit the upgrading of those launchers to the Pershing II, which had more than twice the range and a much more accurate warhead, allowing it to threaten hardened targets well inside the U.S.S.R. At the same time, the United States, on behalf of its allies, would propose negotiations with the Soviets on a settlement: a scaled-back deployment of American "Euromissiles" in exchange for a reduction in SS-20s.

The Reagan Administration inherited the two-track decision. Left to their own inclinations, many of the new officials in Washington would have preferred to dump that legacy, along with SALT, onto the ash heap of history. Richard Perle scoffed openly at the idea of "paying billions of dollars for a mere 572 weapons—a hell of a price tag for a marginal military fix." He considered the December 1979 initiative to be "a lousy decision, if ever there was one." The government's resident Atlanticists, Alexander Haig and Lawrence Eagleburger, prevailed in arguing that the new Administration must preserve a degree of continuity with the past and accommodate the interests of the allies.

Eugene Rostow, the director of ACDA, wanted Nitze to be the chief negotiator for INF, but Nitze was reluctant. Like Perle, he had disapproved of the two-track decision. He considered the deployment track all too reminiscent of the Eisenhower Administration's idea of letting missiles roam the West German Autobahns and the ill-fated Multi-Lateral Force of the early sixties. Nonetheless, unlike Perle, Nitze felt it would be "disastrous to go back on that decision since it would appall the Europeans and confirm the impression that the United States can't be counted on for anything."

Haig and Eagleburger were against giving Nitze the chief negotiator's job. They remembered Nitze well and without affection from the late Nixon Administration, when, as White House chief of staff, Haig had to contend with what he regarded as Nitze's desertion from the SALT II delegation. Eagleburger warned that Nitze's misgivings about the December '79 decision and his "notorious hawkishness might scare off the allies." The State Department had its own candidate for the job: Maynard Glitman, a professional diplomat with experience in NATO affairs.[4]

"I insist on prevailing," Rostow told Haig and the White House. Nitze's appointment, he said, would be "the best possible signal to the Europeans and the Russians alike that we take these negotiations seriously."

Perle observed this episode with a sense of personal ambivalence and rising apprehension. He owed Nitze a great deal; Nitze had helped bring him to town, and they.had been through the war against SALT II together. But Nitze had for some time been the object of Perle's reservations and growing mistrust. His former mentor was, he said, "an inveterate problem-solver . . . result-oriented to a fault." Perle was suspicious of Nitze's penchant, in which Nitze himself took considerable pride, for "working the problem." Perle was afraid that once Nitze was assigned to negotiate an agreement, that was exactly what he would do.

Paul Warnke, long since back in law practice with Clark Clifford, used almost identical words to praise Nitze's appointment. Despite the scars he still bore from Nitze's attacks on him in 1977, Warnke told a number of friends that bringing Nitze into the government was "a stroke of genius, probably unintended. Now that he's back on the inside, Paul will get the job done—he'll get this Administration a deal whether it wants one or not."

Thus, Nitze came back into government at the age of seventy-four, after a hiatus of seven years, under inauspicious circumstances. He was given at best a third-level position. He was not even the Administration's senior arms-control negotiator; that distinction belonged to Rowny. The political and military stakes in INF seemed considerably less important than those in the primary enterprise, which was still strategic arms control. Nitze was hired largely as an ornament. The very existence of his portfolio was controversial; he had doubts about it himself. The conduct of any negotiations ran counter to the Administration's desire to defer arms control indefinitely while the United States built up its defenses. Powerful officials in the Pentagon felt that the Administration should not be negotiating INF at all, and powerful officials in the State Department felt that Nitze should not be the negotiator.

Moreover, Nitze's principal sponsors never established themselves in the new regime, and their influence was already diminishing rapidly. For the second time in his career, Richard Allen quickly washed out as presidential national security advisor, resigning in January 1982 after less than a year on the job. His replacement was a longtime Reagan associate from California, William Clark, a former judge with little knowledge of foreign policy and little affinity for Nitze's one remaining high-level patron, Eugene Rostow. Rostow overplayed the role of graybeard, earning a reputation among some of the President's associates for patronizing and badgering the White House. Clark fired Rostow as director of ACDA in early 1983, replacing him with Kenneth Adelman, a onetime protégé of Donald Rumsfeld's and a neoconservative newcomer to arms control with close ties to Richard Perle.

Nitze was left in a lonely position to do a thankless, if not hopeless, job. INF was the bastard child of SALT. Nitze was to be the caretaker of that bastard child in an Administration that was bent on disowning SALT itself.

The Zero Option

The first round in the protracted struggle over arms control in the Reagan Administration had concerned whether to proceed with INF negotiations at all. On that, Alexander Haig and Lawrence Eagleburger had won, and the negotiations went forward. The second round was over what proposal the United States should make at the outset of the negotiations. The State Department wanted to propose a settlement along the lines of what NATO had intended with the two-track decision: a reduced deployment of U.S. missiles in exchange for reductions in the SS-20s.

This time, however, Perle prevailed in forcing through the Zero Option: elimination of all Soviet INF missiles in exchange for cancellation of the NATO counterdeployments—no Tomahawks, no Pershing IIs, no SS-20s. "Absolute zero," as it was sometimes called, was to be a "global" solution to the problem of INF missiles. SS-20s in Asia should be eliminated along with those in Europe. The launchers were mobile. Therefore, those deployed east of the Urals, in Siberia and Central Asia, and presumably targeted against China, Japan, or South Korea, could be loaded onto the Trans-Siberian Railway and moved westward, within range of NATO. If the Asian SS-20s were "zeroed out," the United States would be easing the anxieties of its European and Pacific partners alike. Perle's original version of the Zero Option would also have applied to shorter-range Soviet ballistic missiles in Europe, the SS-12, SS-22, and SS-23, since these, too, were mobile and could, if deployed in Eastern Europe, threaten targets in Western Europe.

The simplicity and boldness of the basic scheme appealed to President Reagan: Here was *real* arms control—indeed, here was disarmament—which he could understand, with the onus on the Soviets to make amends for the offenses they had committed against peace and stability. It also had the advantage of seeming to give some of the noisier Europeans what they wanted. The West German Social Democrats had originally come up with the concept of the *Null-Lösung*, the "zero solution." Thus Perle was able, in a single catchy phrase, to appeal to European leftists and the conservative American President.

In 1981 there were no American INF missiles in Europe. The United States was offering to stay at zero if the Soviets would come down to zero. Unless and until the United States actually had missiles deployed to trade away against the SS-20s, the Zero Option was generally acknowledged to be non-negotiable; the Soviets would never accept it. But "negotiability" was, in the Reagan Administration, a dirty word from the lexicon of SALT and the bad old days when Americans were driven to imprudent and fatally flawed "agreements for agreement's sake." Besides, the real purpose of the INF negotiation was not to achieve an agreement before deployment of the American missiles. Rather, it was to make sure that the deployment proceeded on schedule.

Paul Nitze was never comfortable with the idea of the Zero Option as anything other than a "going-in position," an opening proposal that would in due course give way to compromise. After President Reagan sided with Perle against the State Department and formally proposed the Zero Option on November 18, 1981, Nitze was asked whether there was any chance the Soviets would accept it. His reply: "It's hard to conceive that they'd accept it fast. But that's not the appropriate criterion for judging the proposal. The appropriate criterion should be, and is, 'Is it a solid basis for continuing negotiations?' And the answer to that is yes." He spoke of the negotiations as a "dialectical process," hinting at an eventual synthesis in which the United States would scale back its INF deployment and the Soviets would scale down their SS-20 force, just as the NATO ministers had intended in 1979.

In their last conversation before Nitze left for Geneva to begin the talks, Perle warned him that he must be prepared to "tough it out for a long, long time," and that he must "resist the temptation of agreement for agreement's sake." On December 1, Perle testified in Washington before the same congressional body that had been the source of so much grief for Nitze over the years, the Senate Armed Services Committee. "We have gone to Geneva with a proposal we can defend, and defend it we will," Perle told the committee:

There has been speculation in the press that Paul Nitze has left for Geneva with a fallback position to be tabled in the event that the Soviets do not embrace the President's proposal. I can assure you that these reports are false. We have learned from bitter experience that nothing would so dash our hopes for the successful negotiation of our proposal as a briefcase full of positions to which we are ready to fall back.

To that statement Nitze had no objection. He agreed it was tactically unwise to hint at compromise before a negotiation had even begun. But Perle went on to read from the memoirs of Samuel Hoare, the British statesman whose reputation as an appeaser in the 1930s kept him out of the wartime cabinet of Winston Churchill. Perle quoted Hoare reflecting ruefully on Neville Chamberlain's meeting with Adolf Hitler in Munich in 1938:

> I had been caught up in the toils of a critical negotiation. The longer it went on and the more serious the issue became, the more anxious I grew to see it succeed. This is almost always the course of negotiations. As they proceed, the parties in them become increasingly obsessed with the need to prevent their final failure. If they are to continue, it is necessary to make concessions, and one concession almost invariably leads to another. The time comes when the question has to be faced: Is the substance being sacrificed to the negotiation, and is it not better to admit failure rather than to make further proposals and concessions? Throughout the Munich discussions I often asked myself whether the slide into surrender had not started.

This was strong stuff. In context, coming just as Nitze was about to be "caught up in the toils of a critical negotiation," Perle seemed to be putting the problem-solver on notice that INF was a problem he had better not try too hard to solve, for if he became the Administration's principal advocate for compromise in INF, he, like Jimmy Carter in SALT II, would be open to the charge of appeasement.

As the talks got under way, Nitze's requests for flexibility were frequently quashed. At one point, when yet another unwelcome order came in from Washington, Nitze pursed his lips, shook his head, and said, "Well, it's just one more hole we'll have to dig ourselves out of later on."

During extended consultations in Washington between negotiating rounds, Nitze became increasingly impatient and angry. He complained to Rostow of Perle's "obstructionism," and in one particularly acrimonious interagency meeting in January 1982, he blew up at Perle himself, accusing him of "talking rubbish," or raising "phony" problems, and of trying to "torpedo" the negotiations.

Nitze's relations with Alexander Haig and other officials of the State Department were little better. They frequently criticized him for "clientitis"— excessive concern for the sensitivities of the European allies. They felt that he overestimated the danger that European public opinion would rebel against the deployment of the American INF missiles. Haig and Eagleburger had initially opposed Nitze's entry into the Administration ostensibly on the grounds that he would arouse European anxieties. Now they criticized him for being too sensitive and deferential to the hand-wringing then going on in Bonn, Brussels, and London.

Nitze complained about being treated "like a lackey" around the corridors of the State Department; the secretary of state, he said, was surrounded by "poisonous" people. On a number of occasions he threatened to resign. At a meeting in Washington in May 1982, when Robert Dean, a deputy assistant secretary of state, thirty-five years Nitze's junior, icily refused Nitze's latest request for additional flexibility in his instructions, Nitze exploded. "I'm not going to work in these conditions," he said. William Clark, the national security advisor, had to calm him down.

The slights and slapdowns were bad enough, but Nitze's greatest frustration was his growing sense that he was part of a charade. Moscow, too, was fixated not on the pursuit of compromise but on a winner-take-all showdown over whether new American missiles, capable of reaching Soviet territory, were to be allowed onto European soil. Preventing the NATO deployments had become an imperative of Soviet policy. It had been one for some years and would remain one for years to come.

The emergence of the SS-20s in 1976–77 had been a high-water mark in a trend that had been building for more than a decade: the Soviet military's devotion to nuclear-armed ballistic missiles. But at that same time, a new trend appeared. The civilian leaders began to have doubts about whether more and more weapons like the SS-20 necessarily meant more security and power for the U.S.S.R. The Kremlin initiated a gradual shift in emphasis from nuclear to conventional weaponry as instruments of Soviet influence and intimidation, particularly in Europe.

In January 1977, Brezhnev had given a speech at a World War II commemorative celebration in Tula, a city south of Moscow. On that and subsequent occasions, the Soviet leader laid down what became known as "the Tula line": Nuclear superiority was "pointless"; it was "dangerous madness" for anyone even to think of victory in a nuclear war; all the Soviets needed was nuclear forces that were "sufficient" to hold those of the U.S. in check. "Sufficiency" was a word and a concept that had been commonplace among NATO strategists for decades. Soviet doctrine seemed finally to be catching up with Western conventional wisdom.

The same month as Brezhnev's Tula speech, Nikolai Ogarkov became chief of the Soviet General Staff. Marshal Ogarkov was a controversial choice among the top brass; he had been the chief military representative in SALT. The civilian leadership apparently picked him because he, too, believed in nuclear sufficiency, parity, and stalemate. He also favored Soviet-American agreements as a means of regulating the arms race. Ogarkov, however, was no dove. The money that might be saved by relying less on nuclear missiles he wanted to spend on advanced conventional weapons. He had no interest in seeing those rubles diverted to the beleaguered Soviet consumer economy.

There was in the Tula line both good news and bad news for the West. A recognition of the pointlessness of nuclear superiority was welcome, especially if it meant that the Soviet Union might be coaxed into retiring some of its most threatening nuclear weapons in exchange for the right American concessions. The bad news was that Moscow seemed bent on increasing its influence in Europe—and on using its huge conventional military strength to do so. Under the Tula line, the U.S.S.R. might rely less on nuclear weapons like the SS-20 to pressure the Europeans, but it could be expected to rely more than ever on tanks and howitzers. Ogarkov made clear that "the military-technical revolution" must benefit the ability of the Warsaw Pact to conduct an armored blitzkrieg through West Germany.

Moreover, in Moscow's thinking, the partial denuclearization of Soviet military strategy required the much more thorough denuclearization of the American military presence in Europe. Moscow might be more willing to bargain away some of its own missiles, but it was also more determined than ever not to sanction the stationing of new, land-based American nuclear weapons near the borders of the U.S.S.R.

Once the INF talks began in the late Carter and early Reagan administrations, the Soviets sought, by a combination of carrots and sticks, to induce the increasingly nervous West Europeans to reject, or at least postpone, the American deployments. The Soviets seemed genuinely concerned about the Pershing II ballistic missile. With a flight time of only a few minutes, that weapon, they said, might be used to destroy Soviet command-and-control facilities in the western regions of the U.S.S.R.

But beyond its military concerns, the Kremlin argued, sometimes explicitly, that the United States was not a legitimate power on the continent of Europe and therefore had no right to put its missiles there. By their adamant and "principled" refusal to accept even one American INF missile on European soil, the Soviets left themselves little choice but to withdraw from the negotiations if and when NATO went ahead with deployment.

Nitze could see that what might very well be his final appointment to government service was turning out to be not an exercise in problem-solving at all but a diversion, a smokescreen, so that others, notably Perle, could make sure that the problem of managing the military competition between the superpowers was *not* solved by arms control.

The Walk in the Woods

In the spring and summer of 1982, realizing that INF was going nowhere—and that nowhere was precisely where some of his colleagues back in Washington intended it to go—Nitze decided to set out on his own for a different destination. His partner was Yuli Kvitsinsky, the head of the Soviet INF team.

At forty-five, Kvitsinsky was a rising star of the diplomatic service. Not by coincidence, he was a specialist in German politics as well as arms control. The single most important and obvious goal of Soviet policy in INF was to induce the Federal Republic of Germany to miss the late-'83 deadline for beginning deployment of the American missiles, particularly the Pershing IIs, all 108 of which were to be based on West German soil. Kvitsinsky's background included service in the Soviet embassies in both East Berlin and Bonn.[5]

In private conversation with Kvitsinsky, Nitze took pains to recall in detail his experience negotiating privately and "off the record" with Alexander Shchukin during SALT I. That channel, he stressed, had proved highly productive, leading to some important breakthroughs in the ABM treaty and the summit meeting between Richard Nixon and Leonid Brezhnev in 1972. Nitze then led Kvitsinsky into a discussion of whether another summit, between Brezhnev and Ronald Reagan, might not be possible in the fall of 1982 if he and Kvitsinsky were to "put our heads together and explore ways to contribute to that possibility."

They met and talked on a number of occasions. The climactic session occurred on the rainy afternoon of July 16, 1982. Nitze and Kvitsinsky drove into the Jura Mountains outside the village of Saint-Cergue near the French border. There, on a wooded mountainside where Geneva-based diplomats often went to ski cross-country, the two men went for a long walk. Eventually they sat on a log and, sheltering their papers against the drizzle, put the finishing touches on what they called "a joint exploratory package for the consideration of both governments." It became known as the "walk in the woods" formula.

Each side would be allowed 75 INF launchers in Europe. For the Soviets, that meant 75 mobile launchers with one missile each for the triple-warhead SS-20—a two-thirds reduction from the number then deployed. For the United States, it meant 75 Tomahawk launchers, each armed with four cruise missiles. Thus, there would be a total of 300 American cruise missiles based on the territory of Western Europe to offset the 225 SS-20 warheads threatening NATO. Such an outcome would have strengthened the "coupling" of

American and West European defenses. It would have at least partially re-dressed the balance upset by the SS-20s, affirmed the right of the United States to put new missiles into NATO, and been consistent with the December '79 two-track decision.

The major concession for the United States would have been to restrict its part of the new equation to cruise missiles, canceling the deployment of its own ballistic INF missile, the Pershing II—although later, after consulting closely with the representative of the Joint Chiefs of Staff on his delegation, General William Burns, Nitze intended for the United States to reserve the right to deploy an improved version of the shorter-range Pershing I. The numerical advantage in American warheads was intended to help make up for the fact that cruise missiles were far slower than SS-20s and vulnerable to air defenses. At the same time, the Soviets' monopoly in ballistic missiles would allow them to claim, to themselves at least, that they had achieved "compensation" for the ballistic missiles in the independent British and French arsenals. A freeze on Asian SS-20s would have enabled the United States to assure China, Japan, and South Korea that European arms control was not being conducted at their expense.

By Nitze's estimation, the contents of this package were 80 percent his own and 20 percent Kvitsinsky's. Kvitsinsky made clear that he was nego-tiating on authority from Foreign Minister Andrei Gromyko. The principal Soviet interest in the deal was stopping the Pershing II program.

The walk-in-the-woods formula was what is called in diplomatic parlance a "nonpaper": it could easily be disavowed by higher authority. Nitze took the package home and, with the help of his closest ally, Eugene Rostow, tried to sell it first to the White House through national security advisor William Clark and to the new secretary of state, George Shultz, who had replaced the tantrum-prone Alexander Haig in June.

In refining the deal back in Washington, Nitze relied heavily for technical advice on James Timbie, a professional expert on the staff of the Arms Control and Disarmament Agency. Timbie was to be at Nitze's side, albeit in the shadows, throughout the Reagan years. He was a veteran of SALT, a career arms controller. He had been a highly respected junior staff officer during SALT I, then an aide to Paul Warnke during SALT II. Timbie had stayed on at ACDA under Rostow, despite the grumbling and mistrust of some Reaganauts. He was the agency's institutional memory on all the arms-control issues that kept coming up with the Soviets, and within the U.S. government.

The walk in the woods provoked another in a series of complex, fractious, and prolonged deliberations among the various agencies and offices involved in arms control. For Shultz, as the new man on the team, it was a bizarre initiation into the ways of the Administration. The government was bickering furiously at the highest levels over not just a proposal but a tentative agreement that came about as a result of what Shultz called "freelancing" by the negotiator.

Not until late August did the Administration focus on the substance of the walk-in-the-woods package as opposed to the unorthodox procedure that Nitze followed. The real trouble began when Richard Perle swung into action. At meeting after meeting, he blasted away at both the package and its principal author. At one encounter in the Situation Room of the White House on September 1, when Perle tried to force through a peremptory repudiation of the deal, one of Shultz's assistants protested, "Ambassador Nitze deserves more of a hearing than that." Perle snapped back, "Nitze doesn't deserve a damn thing."

Perle said he considered the walk in the woods "an act of intellectual and political cowardice." By accepting a limit on SS-20s in Asia, Nitze had given up the quest for a "global"—that is, U.S.S.R.-wide—solution to the problem of the SS-20s. By giving up the Pershing II, he had left the Soviets with a monopoly in modern INF ballistic missiles, just as SALT I and SALT II had left them with a monopoly of heavy ICBMs.

This last complaint was particularly effective. It allowed Perle to play on President Reagan's rudimentary understanding of nuclear weaponry. As part of his on-the-job education about the arsenal over which he had ultimate authority, Reagan had learned that cruise missiles, which were sometimes called "slow-flyers," were *good* (that is, instruments of retaliation, therefore of deterrence, therefore of stability), while ballistic missiles, which were called "fast-flyers," were *bad,* because they were instruments of a first strike.

The White House "tasked" the Joint Chiefs of Staff to study the question of whether, from a strictly military standpoint, the security of the United States and NATO would still be served by an INF deal that excluded the Pershing II. The Chiefs warned that there were risks in giving up the Pershing II, especially if cancellation of that particular program established the precedent that the United States would never, under any circumstances, be able to deploy long-range ballistic missiles in Europe. But the Chiefs also concluded that precisely because the Pershing II was a ballistic missile much feared by the Soviets, it was the principal source of leverage for the United States in the negotiations. The chairman, General John Vessey, and the Air Force chief of staff, Charles Gabriel, went one step further: They felt that while giving up the Pershing II was a large price to pay, it was a price worth paying for a major reduction of SS-20s in Europe and a limit on them in Asia. While the Chiefs' final report was carefully hedged and stopped short of a clear recommendation, it might have provided the basis for a presidential decision to proceed with the walk-in-the-woods formula.

However, the Chiefs' answer never reached the White House. Perle and

Weinberger intercepted it, squelched it, and sent in its place one of their own which unequivocally reiterated Perle's own denunciation of the deal.

At a National Security Council meeting on September 13, Nitze made the case directly to Reagan for giving up the Pershing II in exchange for what otherwise would have been a package made up mostly of Soviet concessions to the West. Reagan was unmoved. He repeated his feeling that it was unfair and dangerous to counter Soviet "fast-flyers" with American "slow-flyers." Besides, he still liked the straightforwardness and simplicity of the original Zero Option. Why, he asked, if the United States was willing to live without deployment of its new missiles in Europe, couldn't the Soviets live without their SS-20s?

Because, Nitze replied, there was a big difference between not deploying a weapons system still under development and removing one already perfected and in place. It was inconceivable that the Soviets would ever accept a proposal that required them to dismantle every last one of their most modern intermediate-range missiles in exchange for the United States tearing up nothing more than a piece of paper—the deployment decision of December 1979. That was simply asking, and hoping, for too much.

"Well, Paul," said the President, "you just tell the Soviets that you're working for one tough son-of-a-bitch."

With Reagan's wishes so starkly put, Shultz, too, opposed the sacrifice of the Pershing II. The White House promulgated a presidential directive that preserved the Zero Option as the Administration's preferred outcome in INF; conceding that a fallback might at some point be worth considering, the directive stipulated that any compromise that allowed the Soviets to keep some of their SS-20s must also permit the United States to deploy ballistic missiles of its own—i.e., the Pershing II.

That directive constituted the White House's repudiation of the walk in the woods—just what Perle had been looking for. It became the basis for Shultz's "talking points" in a meeting with Gromyko in New York on September 28 and for a statement that Nitze was instructed to make to Kvitsinsky the next day, when the talks resumed in Geneva. Not until that occasion did the Soviet rejection come. Kvitsinsky "implemented" a set of instructions similar to those under which Nitze was now operating. He had brought with him from Moscow a document cleared by the Politburo itself reaffirming the Kremlin's formal, front-channel position on INF: a freeze on Soviet deployments in exchange for cancellation of the NATO deployments. Kvitsinsky claimed that his bosses had given him a hard time for his part in the walk in the woods. He put Nitze on notice that if their back-channel dealings were to advance further, Nitze would have to be speaking for Secretary of State Shultz as well as for himself: "No more walks in the woods unless you're under instructions, too."

Nitze became increasingly alarmed that without an agreement of some kind, the deployment would proceed only at great expense to the solidarity of the alliance. So he was told repeatedly and with mounting urgency by a variety of Western Europeans, particularly West Germans. As a confirmed Atlanticist with a penchant for worst-case scenarios, Nitze believed what he heard and passed it along to Washington. At a meeting in Washington in January 1983, Nitze warned that unbending adherence to the Zero Option would blow up in the Administration's face. "Don't you know the house is burning down?" he asked. "Do you want to wait until it burns to the ground before you do anything?"

Perle adopted a solicitous tone: "Who's Paul been talking to over there? Whoever it is has really got the poor man in a state of despair." Even George Shultz's principal aide on European arms control, Richard Burt, remarked, "Nitze's utterly spooked; he's gone around the bend; he's panicking; he's falling apart."

However, in March, largely at Burt's behest, the Administration proposed what it called the "interim solution": The Zero Option remained the objective of the talks, but in the meantime, the United States would reduce the level of NATO deployments (although keeping Pershing IIs as part of the mix) in exchange for "global" reductions in SS-20s.

By now, the Soviets were hunkered down for the moment of truth at the end of the year. When Nitze gave Kvitsinsky a preview of the interim solution, the Soviet said that his government would "promptly and unambiguously" reject it; the Kremlin was not going to be party to any arms-control deal that "blessed" America's right to put missiles in Europe that threatened Soviet territory, particularly the "first-strike" Pershing II.

The Europeans were now clamoring for resurrection of the walk-in-the-woods deal. In the fall of 1983, Nitze tried to get White House approval for a last-minute American proposal that would have sacrificed the Pershing II. Even if the Soviets turned it down, the offer itself would, Nitze argued, "head off disaster" with European public opinion. "Sorry, Paul," said William Clark, "it's simply no go. The President's mind is made up." By now Shultz, too, had become convinced, as he said, that "the Pershings in some fashion are an essential part of our deployment package."

Back in Geneva in November, a few days before the first American missiles were due to arrive in Europe, Kvitsinsky proposed an eleventh-hour effort to break the impasse, saying that his government had instructed him to express to Nitze its willingness to consider a new compromise. On a Saturday morning, November 12, Nitze and Kvitsinsky went for another walk, this time in the botanical gardens across the street from the American mission. This outing became known as the "walk in the park"; it produced a variation on the original walk-in-the-woods formula that would have preserved the American right to deploy the Pershing IIs, but the numbers were skewed in a way that would in effect penalize the United States for exercising that right and, conversely, would provide an incentive for proceeding with a deployment package made up exclusively of cruise missiles—hence, a package that would be more acceptable to the Soviet Union.

Nitze's attempt to draw Kvitsinsky out with an American counter-proposal failed. When he reported on the exchange to the State Department, Richard Burt complained that Nitze was "still off there in the goddamn woods with Kvitsinsky, cooking up deals to kill the Pershing II."

On November 22 the West German Bundestag gave its final approval to the deployment of the Pershing IIs. The next day the American and Soviet negotiating teams were scheduled to hold a plenary meeting at the American mission. Nitze, as the host, invited Kvitsinsky to make an opening statement. Kvitsinsky read a paper saying that the Soviet side was discontinuing the negotiations and was not willing to discuss a date for their resumption.

Shortly afterward, at a press conference, Nitze tried to put the best face on the melancholy culmination of what had been the most difficult and discouraging assignment of his career. The Soviets, he noted, had not said they were pulling out of arms-control talks forever; he hoped they would be back. His face was drawn with exhaustion. His voice, hoarse from a lingering cold, lacked conviction.

While the American side of the story of the walk-in-the-woods eventually emerged, a mystery lingered over what had happened on the Soviet side—and, hypothetically, what might have happened if the Reagan Administration had quickly and unequivocally endorsed the package deal. There was never enough evidence to conclude with certainty that the Administration missed an opportunity to reach what would have been a very good agreement for the West, in both its political and its military consequences.* It was at least as plausible that the package would have still been repudiated in Moscow regardless of how Washington responded. So Nitze himself, in his own postmortem of the affair, came to believe.

Regardless of whether the walk-in-the-woods formula could have been

---

*However, one piece of evidence to that effect came on July 18, 1986—nearly four years after the walk in the woods—when former President Richard Nixon visited Moscow and called on a number of officials, including General Victor Starodubov, the General Staff's representative at the arms-control talks in Geneva. According to a memorandum that Nixon wrote for President Reagan on the meetings:

> On INF, Starodubov was particularly interested in whether the Nitze "walk in the woods" formula, which would have limited American deployments in Europe to cruise missiles, was viable. I pointed out . . . [that] I knew President Reagan had always insisted upon retaining some Pershings in the U.S. deployment if his zero-option proposal was not agreed to. Not unexpectedly, Starodubov made the point that an agreement which would exclude our Pershings might be much more attractive to the Soviets.

achieved, many Western defense experts, generals, and politicians believed that it would have better served American and allied interests than the Zero Option; and many of these same observers were privately nostalgic for the walk in the woods when a revised version of the Zero Option became the basis for the treaty that Reagan and Gorbachev signed at their summit meeting in December 1987. By permitting NATO to proceed with a deployment of cruise missiles, Nitze's scheme would have established that the United States did indeed have the right to put new missiles into Europe that could reach the territory of the U.S.S.R.; it would have reaffirmed the principle of "coupling."

Even Richard Perle acknowledged the merits of the plan. Once it was clear that there was no chance for the walk in the woods or any other compromise in INF, Perle began to speak more kindly of the idea. Nearly a year later, in congressional testimony in July 1983, he claimed that he and the rest of the Administration had been "prepared to consider [the walk in the woods] further," but that the idea came a cropper because "the Soviet Union categorically and emphatically rejected" it. Subsequently, in an example of revisionism every bit as extraordinary as Nitze's own claim that he had never opposed SALT II, Perle told Nitze privately that if the walk-in-the-woods deal in its original form had been accepted as a package, it would have been good for the United States and NATO. He told others that he had "never opposed" Nitze's initiative "on its merits."

Nitze himself would only say, with a thin smile, "It proves you can't keep a good idea down."

Perle had waited until it was too late to matter before he conceded the virtues of the plan that he had done so much to spike. He had never cared much for either the deployment or the arms-control half of the December 1979 INF decision. At stake on the Western side were only 572 warheads which, in Perle's view, cost too much money and caused too many political headaches. What Perle cared about was holding the line against compromise in strategic arms control. The big, numerous, U.S.-based weapons, the ones that really counted in the nuclear balance, were not on the table in INF. Nor were they affected by the pieces of soggy paper that Nitze and Kvitsinsky passed back and forth as they sat on the log in the woods.

To Perle's undisguised satisfaction, the collapse of the INF talks had led almost immediately to the suspension of START as well. Arms control went into limbo for the duration of the first Reagan term. For Perle, that was exactly where it belonged.

Nitze, too, was in limbo. He still had a title as a chief negotiator, but there was no longer a negotiation. Nor did his predictions of "disaster" in Europe come true now that the missiles had been deployed without an agreement. He had to put up with the smug I-told-you-so comments of Burt,

Perle, and others. As Nitze celebrated the Christmas holidays of 1983, followed in January by his seventy-seventh birthday, all he had to show for his boldest attempt ever at working the problem of arms control was an empty portfolio, the antagonism and mistrust of numerous powerful colleagues, and a repudiation—if not a reprimand—by his President.

PART TWO

Defense

CHAPTER 9

The Absolute Antiweapon

On May 30, 1985, Paul Nitze spoke at the commencement exercises of Johns Hopkins University's School of Advanced International Studies. Government officials frequently used such occasions to explain and promote government policies. For over two years, one of the most controversial policies of the Reagan Administration had been the Strategic Defense Initiative, which the President had unveiled in a nationally televised speech on March 23, 1983. Addressing the faculty and graduating students of SAIS, Nitze came as close as he could to endorsing SDI, putting the best possible face on a program about which the President cared passionately. He told his audience that Ronald Reagan's proclamation of the goal of comprehensive strategic defense was comparable to the Truman Administration's plan for the rebuilding of Europe. The Marshall Plan and the Strategic Defense Initiative, said Nitze, both illustrated what he called "a grand generality appropriate for this occasion. . . . The mere formulation of a goal can have immense and constructive consequences":

> [George Marshall] had set a goal, and someone had to see about fulfilling it. A few of us at the State Department were asked to develop a concrete and workable plan for his concept. We did so. As it turned out, the Marshall Plan proved to be a tremendous success story in the reconstructions of postwar Europe.
>
> So, as you move into the outside world, I encourage you to set lofty goals, even if you do not have a precise idea as to how to achieve them. You may well surprise yourselves by what you in fact manage to accomplish.

The goal of reconstructing the political and economic order of a war-torn continent, while controversial and expensive, had been feasible and desirable. It was what Harry Truman wanted; it was what George Marshall wanted; it was what Paul Nitze wanted as an official of Truman's Administration and Marshall's State Department. And to a remarkable extent, it was what they and others achieved.

SDI was an altogether more dubious proposition, and Nitze's attitude toward the program was quite different from what his attitude had been toward the Marshall Plan in 1947. He was neither a stranger to nor an enemy of the idea of strategic defense. Nitze had advocated bomb shelters for civilian populations since his visit to Hiroshima and Nagasaki in 1945; he had favored a limited ABM system to protect American ICBMs. But with SDI, Ronald Reagan had taken the idea of strategic defense much further. Rather than simply wanting to provide city dwellers with shelters where they could hide from enemy bombs, Reagan envisioned a system that would keep the bombs from ever arriving. Reagan believed that deterrence could be based on a system not just of protection but of foolproof prevention.

Niels Bohr, Robert Oppenheimer, Bernard Brodie, McGeorge Bundy, and others had been consoled by the idea that nuclear weapons might be inherently unusable. Now along came Ronald Reagan to suggest that they might be made unusable by a concerted effort to harness American technology to that task.

If what Reagan had called for in March 1983 could be achieved, it would have been as momentous a change in international politics as the creation of the Bomb itself. His was not merely a proposal to solve the main strategic problem that had preoccupied his predecessors—the supposed vulnerability of American forces to preemptive attack. It was nothing less than a way of altering the strategic landscape so drastically that the problem would cease to exist. The pursuit of this goal would deny the basic premise of the nuclear age up to that time—the unchallengeable superiority of offense. It would replace an acceptance of vulnerability with a guarantee of invulnerability and replace mutual assured destruction with what Reagan called "mutual assured survival."

The origins and development of SDI dramatically underscored the contrast between the President and his senior advisor on arms control. Nitze prided himself on his pragmatism, his love of rigor, his reliance on the facts, no matter how dry, mind-numbing, or discouraging. Reagan, on the other hand, seemed to see himself as possessed of an ability to transcend mere facts and plug into larger verities and possibilities. He was comfortable talking about hopes and fears. SDI was a hope to combat a fear. The key word in his Star Wars speech was "dream." He would repeat it many times. His attachment to SDI was the most vivid and enduring example of Reagan's proclivity for grand gestures of political imagination, and a refusal to let discouraging facts (or the absence of encouraging ones) get in the way.

Nitze was never comfortable with the dream. Moreover, despite what he told the SAIS graduates, he was not at all sure that the "mere formulation" of the goal of SDI would necessarily have "constructive consequences." He believed that the only way to solve problems was to advance toward a solution one logical step at a time. He was not willing to join in the leap of faith that Reagan invited with SDI. Intellectual standards similar to those that had led Nitze to resist Bernard Brodie's concept of the absolute weapon in the forties made him at least as skeptical of Ronald Reagan's vision of the absolute antiweapon in the eighties.

Such skepticism, however, could be fatal to the influence if not the career of the skeptic. In 1983, when Reagan so enthusiastically unveiled SDI, and in 1985, when Nitze so halfheartedly endorsed the program, Reagan was President of the United States; it was at his pleasure that Nitze served in government. There was no subject on which this President felt more sure of himself than SDI—and no subject on which he was more impatient with naysayers, especially those who worked for him. If Nitze was going to change the way in which the dream was brought down to earth, he was not only going to have to disagree with his President on SDI but to defy him—and to do so in a way that the President would not fully grasp. This would require not just the persistence of will and the powers of persuasion that Nitze had been exercising for a lifetime but also a degree of subtlety, discretion, and even deception, the last of which particularly did not come naturally to him.

In his personal effort to work the problem of SDI, Nitze was still relying on a logic chain, but the real billboard effect of what he was trying to do—which was ultimately to trade concessions on SDI for reductions in Soviet offensive forces—was hidden behind a false front of support for presidential policy.

"A Helluva Way to Run a Railroad"

At first, only one aspect of Ronald Reagan's favorite national-security program seemed to elude his control: He could not prevent the press from giving it what he considered an unsavory and prejudicial nickname. To his intense annoyance, the plan he announced on March 23, 1983, was almost immediately dubbed "Star Wars." The press was already drawing on a popular series of science-fiction movies in writing headlines over stories about Reagan's speeches. In one he had given to a gathering of evangelical Christians on March 8, just two weeks before, the President's rhetoric prompted commentators to compare him to a Jedi knight pitted in mythic combat against the "evil empire." On another occasion Reagan said, "The Force is with us." Now, in addition to "the Force" of democracy, he seemed to be announcing that the United States could have a light saber with which to disarm its heavy-breathing, dark-helmeted enemies.*

---

*For more on the background and consequences of Reagan's anti-Soviet rhetoric, see the author's

Reagan did not like the label "Star Wars" because opponents used it derisively to underscore their contention that the program was a kooky futuristic fantasy. Richard Perle, however, told a staff meeting at the Pentagon that he rather liked the designation. "Why not?" he said. "It's a good movie. Besides, the good guys won."

The State Department felt something more dignified was in order: Defense Against Ballistic Missiles, pronounced "DABUM." That acronym was rejected as sounding too much like a hair tonic. Eventually, Strategic Defense Initiative, or SDI, became the official name, but "Star Wars" stuck in the headlines. In a way it was fitting that this should be so, since, more than any other, SDI was a presidential initiative that gave truth and meaning to clichés about the President's own origins in Hollywood.

Reagan's approach to big issues often invited comparison to movies. That was not just because of his background as a screen actor. It was also because his years in studios had imbued him with ideas that kept resurfacing in the form of themes to bolster his policies. His speech announcing SDI was an eerie example of life imitating art. In 1940, the year Paul Nitze first came to Washington to work for the government, Ronald Reagan was on the other side of the continent starring in a Warner Bros. spy picture, *Murder in the Air.* He played Brass Bancroft, a double agent assigned to help protect a vital U.S. military secret, the "Inertia Projector," an airborne death-ray that could destroy enemy aircraft before they could bomb the United States. This "new superweapon," according to the film, "not only makes the United States invincible in war, but in so doing promises to become the greatest force for world peace ever discovered, which is the hope and prayer of all thinking people, regardless of race, creed, or government."

Twenty-six years later, in 1966, Alfred Hitchcock made an espionage thriller called *Torn Curtain.* In the film, the Pentagon is trying to develop a system of "antimissile missiles." But first the Americans must get their hands on a complex formula known only to an East German scientist. So a physicist with the all-American name Michael Armstrong, played by the all-American actor Paul Newman, pretends to defect to East Germany. He arrives in East Berlin and gives a press conference, at which he explains the purpose of his mission: "We will produce a defensive weapon that will make all offensive nuclear weapons obsolete, and thereby abolish the terror of nuclear warfare."

Reagan frequently referred to movies in his press conferences, interviews, and speeches. Some combination of those dramatic passages from *Murder*

The Russians and Reagan (Council on Foreign Relations/Vintage, 1984); also, on the origins and context of SDI, a sequel, written with Michael Mandelbaum, *Reagan and Gorbachev* (Council on Foreign Relations/Vintage, 1987).

in the Air and *Torn Curtain* may have been in the back of his mind when he came to the punch line of his Star Wars speech: "I call upon the scientific community in our country, those who gave us nuclear weapons . . . to give us the means of rendering these nuclear weapons impotent and obsolete." A number of his aides were struck by the similarity of the language.*

In any event, the idea for what became known as SDI had been germinating in the President's mind for some time. When Reagan's political horizons had begun to expand beyond the state of California, he naturally thought about the responsibilities of the Oval Office. As early as 1976, when he was challenging Gerald Ford for the Republican nomination, Reagan criticized deterrence, comparing the arrangement to two people with guns cocked at each other's head. In late July 1979, when he was beginning his campaign for President, he toured the headquarters of the North American Air Defense Command deep inside Cheyenne Mountain in Colorado. He asked the commander a simple question: What could the United States do if its radar spotted a Soviet missile coming? He got a simple answer: Nothing. The United States survived from day to day on the sufferance of the Soviet Union; the day that the Politburo decided otherwise, there was nothing the United States could do other than retaliate and incinerate millions of Russians. "Gee," he commented, "it's a helluva way to run a railroad, isn't it?"

At Reagan's behest, one of his advisors, Martin Anderson, wrote a memorandum in August 1979 arguing that a protective antimissile system "is probably fundamentally far more appealing to the American people than the questionable satisfaction of knowing that those who initiated an attack against us were also blown away." The memo also warned that it would be difficult for any President to sustain support for the kind of American offensive buildup that would be necessary to deprive the Soviets of the superiority they were believed to have acquired in the 1970s. That consideration, too, made a greater reliance on strategic defense seem attractive.

Left to his own devices, Reagan might have made an appeal for a comprehensive, impregnable shield part of his campaign for the presidency in 1980, but his advisors talked him out of it: It would be too controversial, they said; it would open him to the charge that he was reckless and would get the United States into a fearsome new arms race if not a nuclear war. Conservative Republicans remembered all too well how Barry Goldwater had allowed himself to be tarred with that brush in 1964. Nonetheless, the 1980 party platform—which also called for the re-establishment of military

---

*So was Paul Newman. He was active in liberal political causes, particularly arms control, and a vigorous opponent of SDI. He was both amused and appalled when, in October 1987, he learned of the way his lines in the film seem to have ended up in Reagan's speech.

and technological superiority over the Soviet Union—contained an appeal for "vigorous research and development of an effective antiballistic missile system."

Not that such a program was precluded by the SALT I antiballistic missile treaty. Quite the contrary, when Secretary of Defense Melvin Laird and Admiral Thomas Moorer, the chairman of the Joint Chiefs of Staff, testified on behalf of the ABM treaty in 1972, they made clear that they were conditioning their approval on continued funding for research into defensive technologies. But that program was definitely, in Pentagon parlance, "on the back burner"; it was seen largely as a hedge against whatever the Soviets might eventually do. Reagan wanted to move it to the front burner.

Once he was in office, Reagan became, if anything, even more uneasy with nuclear deterrence and more intrigued by the idea of strategic defense. In conversation with Edward Rowny, Reagan once asked whether there was some way to escape the absurdity and horror of the two sides holding guns to each other's head.

"You could put on a helmet," Rowny said, "but the scientists haven't developed one yet."

Reagan replied, "Well, that should be their challenge, and we should set them to this task."

It was a challenge that scientists had set themselves long before. Edward Teller had been promoting research on strategic defense since the fifties. In 1962, he had written a book, *The Legacy of Hiroshima,* saying, "It would be wonderful if we could shoot down approaching missiles before they could destroy a target in the United States." In 1969, he told an interviewer, "I cannot tell you how much more I would rather shoot at enemy missiles than to suffer attack and then have to shoot at people in return. I want to repeat— with all possible emphasis—that defense is better than retaliation."

However, Teller shared the concern of others, including Paul Nitze, that the quest for a comprehensive defense would prove both elusive and expensive, and that meanwhile an all-out Soviet defensive system would greatly complicate the task of American deterrence. That was why, in 1972, he reluctantly supported the ABM treaty.

By the early eighties, a group of scientists at the Lawrence Livermore National Laboratory near San Francisco had achieved potentially important progress in a program that had been going on for years under the name "Excalibur": a way to channel the energy from a thermonuclear explosion into X-ray laser beams that might be directed at individual targets, such as enemy missiles. Unlike traditional ABMs, which were themselves nuclear-armed missiles that rose to destroy enemy warheads in space or in the terminal stage of their descent, Excalibur and similar "directed energy" projects offered the promise of a new generation of weapons that would travel at the speed of light and that might, when fired from space, destroy enemy missiles at the beginning rather than the end of their journey toward American targets.

Teller had been the director of Livermore and still maintained close ties there. He had given Reagan a tour of the laboratory in 1967, when Reagan was governor. Now it looked as though Livermore might be on its way to making antimissile defense feasible. Between January and September 1982, Teller met on several occasions with Reagan and urged that he initiate a new Manhattan Project to develop strategic defenses.

Teller's enthusiasm for directed-energy weapons was shared by a number of conservative Republican senators who became known as the "Laser Lobby."* Another influential figure was Daniel Graham, the retired general who was a veteran of Team B, an advisor to Reagan in his '76 and '80 campaigns, and the moving force behind an organization called High Frontier which advocated space-based defenses. He had met with Reagan on a number of occasions in the late seventies to urge, in his words, a program that would eventually make it possible to "implement a basic change in U.S. grand strategy and make a 'technological end-run' on the Soviets."

There were differences among these groups over what sort of technology should be used and how a system should be based. Teller's Excalibur X-ray laser was supposed to be compact and light enough to be put aboard American submarines that would patrol near the Soviet coast; it would be "popped up"—or launched into space—on notification that a Soviet missile attack was about to begin. The Laser Lobby tended to favor larger, chemical lasers that would be placed on orbiting battle stations, while High Frontier promoted not lasers at all but space-based antimissile missiles.

President Reagan's science advisor early in the Administration was George Keyworth, a nuclear physicist from Los Alamos; Teller had recommended him for the White House job. In January 1983 Keyworth gave a lecture at Livermore hailing the "bomb-pumped X-ray laser" as "one of the most important programs that may seriously influence the nation's defense posture in the next decades." Inside the Administration he argued for an alternative system: ground-based lasers that would bounce their rays off mirrors in space.

The following month the idea of exotic defenses gathered momentum as a result of a meeting that the President held with the Joint Chiefs of Staff on February 11, 1983. The chairman of the Chiefs, General John Vessey, was concerned about the various setbacks to the Administration's strategic modernization program. The program to deploy the new, ten-warhead MX as a successor to Minuteman had been undergoing a Chinese water torture

---

*One of the leaders of this group, Senator Malcolm Wallop of Wyoming, had co-authored an article on strategic defense in the summer of 1979 and sent the draft to Reagan. In 1981, Wallop and Senator Harrison Schmidt of New Mexico co-sponsored legislation to fund the development of laser defenses.

of public and congressional opposition. Since the debate over the "shell game" during the Carter Administration, one Rube Goldberg scheme after another for protecting the MX had become the butt of jokes and editorial cartoons. The latest variation on the original shell game was known as "closely spaced basing," or "Densepack." By clustering MX launchers, the plan relied on the phenomenon of "fratricide"—enemy warheads blowing each other up—and therefore virtually invited saturation attack.

It was increasingly clear that the United States might have to give up on the idea of a mobile, transportable, or deceptive basing mode for the MX. Instead, when the new missile was finally deployed, it would be in stationary—and theoretically vulnerable—silos.* American first-strike weapons, heavily MIRVed ICBMs, would be at risk from a Soviet first strike. That was exactly the outcome that Nitze and others had opposed during the Carter Administration. Nitze had criticized SALT II largely because of what he considered its failure to ensure the right to proceed with the shell game. Now, in 1983, with the death of Densepack at the hands of editorial cartoonists, the Reagan Administration was about to exacerbate the problem of strategic vulnerability in the way that it deployed the MX.

During the Chiefs' meeting with the President, General Vessey stressed that he was deeply concerned about whether the United States could keep pace with the ongoing Soviet ICBM buildup. The United States, he said, needed a new "strategic vision." He did not enunciate a concrete or detailed proposal, but in the course of discussion, a number of participants agreed that perhaps the United States should see if there were some way to redefine deterrence on the basis of combined offense and defense. Amid the public debate over Densepack, a number of experts had already pointed out that the system would be more plausible if the clusters of MX launchers were protected by a new, improved ABM.

The Chiefs wondered whether the technology of ABMs might have improved sufficiently in the past decade to make it worthwhile, in Vessey's words, to "take another look" at the ABM question. The chief of naval operations, Admiral James Watkins, said that the United States had what he called a "moral imperative" to keep up the search for something better than mutual assured destruction. At that time, the American Catholic bishops were raising fundamental questions about the morality of deterrence.[1] Watkins himself was a devout Catholic. A Navy White Paper on deterrence, drafted at his behest, asked whether it would not be better to save lives than to avenge them. Reagan said that he, too, had been thinking a lot about the "immorality" of MAD. As Reagan later recalled this decisive moment:

At one of my regular meetings with the Chiefs of Staff, I brought up

---

*Silo deployment finally came late in 1986.

this subject about a defensive weapon . . . and I asked them, "Is it possible in our modern technology of today that it would be worthwhile to see if we could not develop a weapon that could perhaps take out, as they left their silos, those nuclear missiles?" . . . And when they did not look aghast at the idea and said yes, they believed that such a thing offered a possibility and should be researched, I said, "Go."[2]

The Chiefs presented the President with a range of options for bolstering deterrence. These included shifting emphasis from ICBMs to SLBMs and strengthening conventional forces. The President's clear preference, however, was for strategic defense.

Washington was locked that day in the grip of a huge blizzard. Subsequently, the meeting became known within the bureaucracy as "the Great Snow Job." What happened next was as different from the norms of governmental policymaking, especially where major departures in national security are concerned, as the phenomenon of spontaneous combustion is different from the workings of an internal combustion engine. No true decision was really made at all; nothing was "staffed out"; there were no interagency policy reviews or congressional hearings.

The President was scheduled to give a televised speech on March 23, 1983, primarily to rally support for the entire defense budget, particularly the beleaguered MX. It was what his aides and speechwriters referred to as "the standard threat speech." Pentagon officials who participated in the drafting expected it to generate newspaper headlines saying PRESIDENT STRESSES NEED FOR WEAPONS BUILDUP AND MX. When a draft came back from the White House, these officials noticed "[INSERT]," near the end, and they asked their contacts on the National Security Council staff what Reaganesque homily would be plugged in there. They were told that the insert would contain "something of substance." The speech was nicknamed "MX Plus"—"plus" because of its surprise ending that announced, in effect, that the MX was a mere stopgap in the realm of offense-dominant deterrence to buy the United States time to enter the brave new world of defense-dominant deterrence. The bombshell passage was extremely closely held. All the President told Teller was: "Edward, you're going to like it."[3]

The Joint Chiefs of Staff were shocked at the President's precipitate action—and embarrassed by their own part in encouraging him. They had only meant to suggest that research and development on strategic defense get more consideration and funding. Their chairman, General Vessey, recommended against the President's giving the speech. So did Secretary Shultz. Learning of the insert at the last moment, he denounced the plan as lunacy. Secretary Weinberger warned that it was "not something I can endorse at this time."

None of these objections did much to dim the appeal of SDI to Reagan.

SDI seemed to shore up the Administration's right and left flanks simultaneously. To those conservatives who worried primarily about the Soviet threat, the President could present the program as a way of disarming the Communist enemy. To liberals, he could offer not just a new, more humane basis for deterrence but a way of eliminating the danger of nuclear war.*

More than any other program in the area of foreign policy and national security, SDI bore Reagan's personal imprimatur. It was truly his initiative, and he took pride in the simplicity and straightforwardness of the plan. Two days after the speech, he told a group of reporters about its origin: "I've been having this idea, and it's been kicking around in my mind for some time here recently. And constantly I have thought about the fact that the nuclear missile seems to be one of the only major weapons systems in history that has never produced or brought about a defense against itself." On another occasion, he remarked, "It kind of amuses me that everybody is so sure that I must have heard about it, that I never thought of it myself. The truth is I did."[4]

The intensity of the President's commitment to his original vision was illustrated by an incident that occurred a year later, early in 1984. The National Security Council asked the State Department to prepare a paper on the elimination of nuclear arsenals. The department concluded that total nuclear disarmament was neither desirable nor possible: The nuclear genie was out of the bottle; nuclear weapons could not be uninvented; even if the superpowers sacrificed all their stockpiles on a huge bonfire, there would always be the danger that the Soviet Union might do what it knew how to do on short notice—make a new set of bombs with which to attack or intimidate the United States; besides, nuclear weapons were necessary for extended deterrence and for defense against a nuclear-armed "madman" in the Third World.

Secretary of State George Shultz sent a shortened version of the paper to the White House. It was not well received. The President complained that he had wanted support for his interest in the elimination of nuclear weapons, not a long list of reasons why it couldn't be done. The department prepared a new paper, this time pointing out the problems and the obstacles but concluding that the world might be a safer place without nuclear weapons

---

*Insofar as SDI made the President the nation's leading nuclear abolitionist, there was a point of some tension between him and the principal scientific advocates of the program. In the view of Edward Teller and a number of others, the most promising technology was the nuclear-pumped X-ray laser. Not only would this device entail setting off nuclear explosions in space on the day that the system had its baptism by fire, but it required repeated underground nuclear tests in the meantime. For the President, however, this seemed not to be a major problem. The "business end" of the system would be the X-ray lasers, not the blast that would generate them. Moreover, knowing of his desire for a system that was not only purely defensive but purely non-nuclear, his briefers stressed that there were alternative technologies worth exploring as well (kinetic kill vehicles, particle beams, etc.).

after all—as long as the United States had SDI on its side. It would do the Soviet Union no good suddenly to manufacture nuclear weapons—nor would it do Muammar Khaddafy any good to get his hands on an Islamic bomb and a missile to hurl it at the United States—if omniscient, omnipotent American battle stations high in the heavens were standing guard, ready to zap the offending launcher.

Reagan believed that if a leader dared to ask elementary questions, the most intractable problems could suddenly become amenable to solution; the leader's constituents might suddenly feel that there was hope, that he embodied that hope, and that they were fortunate that he was in charge. Bold, simple schemes worked well for him as political rhetoric. He preferred to say, in effect: Here's the problem (poverty, inflation, international terrorism, nuclear war); now here, in a simple declarative sentence, is the solution: Let's do it. If the United States is running a dangerously large budget deficit, why not simply outlaw it by adopting an amendment to the Constitution requiring a balanced budget? If Europe is in an uproar over the deployment of Soviet SS-20s and the prospective counterdeployment of American INF missiles, why not adopt the Zero Option? If the United States is threatened by Soviet ballistic missiles, why not simply develop a system to shoot them down before they can do any harm?

This approach appealed to Reagan's image of Uncle Sam as an enterprising, self-reliant fix-it man with more trust in his own common sense than in what the know-it-alls might say. He always enjoyed a story about an eccentric inventor who tinkers for years in his garage with a gadget the neighbors chuckle over—until it whirs and takes flight, changing the face of civilization.

Of all the speeches he gave as President, his one on Star Wars was the most similar to the ones he had given in the fifties and early sixties as a pitchman for General Electric, celebrating the limitless possibilities of what science and industry could do for the American consumer. Gary Wills, in his 1987 book *Reagan's America: Innocents at Home,* called the corporate phenomenon of which Reagan was a part in his GE days "creating a demand before supplying the demanded items."[5] SDI was the ultimate example of advertising an imaginary product.

But Will It Work?

At first, the Star Wars speech was greeted with bemusement bordering on incredulity, even scorn. As Gerold Yonas, chief scientist for the program, recalled later, "The President clearly caught many people by surprise by calling for these studies in his address. It would have been less disturbing had the studies been carried out quietly before the President made his specific program request in public.''[6]

Among those surprised were the top people at the State Department, the Arms Control and Disarmament Agency, and the Pentagon. Many who heard the President's speech understood the profound implications of what he was suggesting, but they assumed that Reagan himself did not understand. They waited for Press Secretary Larry Speakes to ''clarify'' this latest presidential statement, or for George Shultz to hurry to Capitol Hill to testify about what Reagan had really meant to say.

Only after the President had delivered the speech was there anything like a formal study of the idea sponsored by the executive branch, and that was by a panel of scientific experts headed by James Fletcher, a former administrator of the National Aeronautic and Space Administration.* Much like Team B in the seventies, the Fletcher panel was selected with a particular outcome in mind: The members leaned toward different technologies, but they had in common an enthusiasm for the idea of exotic, large-scale defenses. The panel recommended that the government back research on not just nuclear-driven X-ray lasers but beams of neutral particles and kinetic energy weapons—devices like ''rail guns'' that would fire guided projectiles, sometimes called ''smart rocks,'' as well as space-based ''rubber mirrors'' that would deflect lasers beamed from earth, compensating for the distortions of the atmosphere, so that they could intercept Soviet missiles.

The White House, however, quickly had to contend with a vast outpouring of expert opinion that it had not solicited. The ensuing debate in the broader scientific, engineering, and strategic communities yielded a large body of forcefully articulated skepticism about whether the President's objective was feasible in the foreseeable future at any price, let alone one that American taxpayers would be willing to pay. The case against SDI took shape well before the outlines of the program itself emerged. That was not surprising. After all, the idea of population defense had not sprung full-grown out of Reagan's forehead the day he gave the speech. Serious people had been thinking about the issue for decades. Nor was Reagan the first to foresee what futuristic technologies might be able to do. They had figured in the deliberations of Paul Nitze and the other negotiators of SALT I in the early 1970s when the ABM treaty addressed the prospect of ''systems based on other physical principles.''

Judgments about the feasibility of SDI depended on one's ability to imagine, first, a full-scale Soviet missile attack against the United States, then a layered American defensive system that would thwart the attack, then the

---

*Fletcher was later reappointed to that post in the shakeup of NASA after the explosion of the space shuttle *Challenger* on January 28, 1986.

countermeasures that the Soviets might use to neutralize the American defenses, and finally the counter-countermeasures that the U.S. would use to protect its defenses.

The trajectory of an ICBM proceeds in four stages. The "boost" phase lasts from the launch of the missile until, after exiting the atmosphere, the booster rockets have completed their burn and the missile reaches high enough speed to hurl its warhead-dispensing bus toward distant targets. In the post-boost phase, the bus maneuvers, dispensing its warheads as well as many much lighter decoys that can confuse and thwart a defensive system. During this and the longer mid-course phase that follows, the objects travel outside the atmosphere from one continent to another. Discrimination between real warheads and hundreds, possibly thousands, of light decoys is one of the main problems of the mid-course phase for a would-be defender. The fourth and final stage is the re-entry, or terminal, phase, when the warheads, each independently targeted, sometimes accompanied by heavier decoys, re-enter the atmosphere and crash down on silos, air bases, submarine pens, command-and-control bunkers, or cities.

For the purposes of a truly comprehensive defense, the boost phase is crucial, because the rockets have not yet released their multiple warheads. A single death ray or interceptor that "kills" a single ICBM could prevent as many as ten enemy warheads from ever reaching their targets. Boost-phase interception has been compared to sacking the quarterback before he can throw the ball, thus ruining the opponent's play before it can develop. Lasers were prominent candidates for this task, but some scientists favored space-based kinetic-kill vehicles ("smart rocks") instead. Whatever the technology, it was bound to be expensive. Many installations—certainly dozens, more likely hundreds, perhaps even thousands—would be required to destroy the entire Soviet missile force. Even the strongest partisans of strategic defense admitted that some way would have to be found to produce the relevant technologies far more cheaply than was currently possible.

Defenses designed to destroy missiles in their boost phase could not be based in the relative safety of the defender's territory. If they were, the attacker's weapons would already have reached the mid-course or perhaps even the re-entry phase by the time the defenses were activated. The most logical deployment for boost-phase defenses would be for them to orbit above the territory of the U.S.S.R. In that case, however, they would be easy targets for the Soviets. Instead of beginning its first strike with a launch of its ICBMs against targets in the United States, the Soviet Union could start by attacking SDI battle stations with antisatellite (ASAT) weapons, clearing the way for a barrage of missile warheads. Laser-equipped platforms might defend American cities, but what would defend the defenders?

Various schemes were conceived to answer that question. One was Teller's favorite, to "pop up" the space-based—and therefore most vulnerable—part of the system, firing it quickly into space just in time to be used. Another would be to equip the battle stations with their own defenses—i.e., anti-ASATs. Still another would be to predeploy these components in great numbers and use radar-invisible "stealth" technology to hide them in the void of space. None of these schemes, however, no matter how ingenious, seemed foolproof.

Aside from the problem of vulnerability, the whole system would rely on as-yet-unbuilt computers of unparalleled power, with software of vast complexity, to coordinate the main tasks of detecting the beginning of a Soviet attack, discriminating between real warheads and fakes, training lasers or projectiles on myriad, fast-moving targets, and verifying "kills"—all in a matter of seconds if not microseconds. The level of performance would have to be much higher and more certain than that of any untested system of far less complexity, and SDI could never be fully tested before it would have to work. If it did not work perfectly—if, for instance, it destroyed only 90 percent of the nuclear weapons that the Soviet Union fired at the United States in an attack using only 10 percent of its arsenal—the largest cities in North America could still lie in ruins half an hour after launch, with tens of millions of Americans dead or dying. SDI's proponents—and particularly its principal proponent, Ronald Reagan—had set a very high standard indeed for their brainchild: It had to be nearly perfect in order to discourage, rather than encourage, countermeasures by the enemy.

There was, in the opinion of some scientists, no useful precedent for what Reagan had proposed. In reply, supporters of SDI assembled a long list of they-said-it-couldn't-be-done stories: Thomas Edison had once said, "Fooling around with alternating current is just a waste of time"; Albert Einstein had written in 1932, "There is not the slightest indication that [nuclear energy] will ever be obtainable"; Admiral William Leahy, chief of staff to President Truman, had warned early in 1945, "The [atomic] bomb will never go off, and I speak as an expert in explosives"; and John Kennedy's vow to put a man on the moon had been greeted by a chorus of skepticism about whether the timetable was reasonable and whether the mission would be scientifically useful.

Opponents of SDI pointed out that the electric light bulb and the A-bomb itself simply sat there, waiting to be invented. They never took countermeasures against their would-be discoverers. Nor did the moon ever shoot back at the Apollo spacecraft. By contrast, the Soviet Union was not going to watch passively while the United States developed SDI; it would do everything in its power to thwart the program, by proliferating offenses to overwhelm American defenses, by teaching its offensive weapons tricks and giving them qualities that would make them harder to intercept, and by erecting defenses of its own.

In short, SDI, even as it was refined in the months and years after Reagan gave his speech, still failed to answer two basic questions, one technical and logical, the other theoretical and psychological. The technical question was the one that had led Robert McNamara to oppose ABMs in 1967: Defense provokes more offense which provokes more defense which provokes more offense—"the whole crux of the nuclear action-reaction phenomenon," the "mad momentum intrinsic to the development of all new nuclear weaponry," including *defensive* systems. The same concern had led Paul Nitze to help negotiate and argue for the ratification of the ABM treaty as an agreement of indefinite duration.

The psychological question was, Why would the other side see SDI as purely defensive? Why would the Soviet Union not see SDI as a shield that made the offensive spears in the American arsenal more threatening? What if the purpose of SDI were not, as advertised, to protect against a Soviet first strike but to fend off a Soviet second (i.e., retaliatory) strike, and thus enable the United States to strike first? The only answer, usually implicit but occasionally explicit, was a reiteration of the old American belief in a malevolence factor "favoring" the U.S.S.R. Just as many Americans had felt in the late 1940s that the Bomb would be an instrument for preserving the peace as long as the United States maintained its monopoly, so members of the Reagan Administration argued that SDI would serve the same benevolent purpose—as long as the Soviets did not develop such a program of their own.

The most forthright and persistent spokesman of this point of view was Secretary of Defense Caspar Weinberger. Over a period of years, in interviews, speeches, briefings, and articles, Weinberger made statements of stunning candor and crystalline succinctness about his attitude underlying not just SDI but the entire strategic relationship. Mr. Secretary, he was asked repeatedly, you say SDI offers us peace and stability; what if the Soviets were to develop SDI?

His answer: That would be a disaster.

Why? Isn't that inconsistent?

No.

Why?

Weinberger's response, often in so many words: Because they're aggressive and we're not.

On March 27, 1983, four days after Reagan's SDI speech, Weinberger said on NBC's "Meet the Press":

Bear in mind that we have had and did have a monopoly on nuclear weapons for some years and never used them. And that is, I think, widely known to the Soviets, that we would never launch a first strike. . . . The other reason why they have no need to worry [about SDI] is that they know perfectly well that we will never launch a first strike on the Soviet Union. And all of their attacks, and all of their preparations—I should say, and all of their acquisitions in the military field in the last few years—have been offensive in character.

Weinberger believed that American fears of a Soviet attack were well founded, while Soviet fears of an American first strike were nonsense. That conviction followed logically enough from the view that the U.S.S.R. was "ahead" in ruthlessness and malevolence. Weinberger was sure that the Soviets knew perfectly well that the West would never attack them, even as they went about making contingency plans to attack the West, should their interests ever so require. It was as though the Soviets should be expected to base policy or conduct diplomacy on the assumption of their own essentially criminal nature, recognizing the United States as a restraining influence.*

"The Greatest Sting Operation in History"

When the President first announced his determination to build a defensive system that would eventually eliminate the need for offensive weapons, Caspar Weinberger, like almost everyone else in the government, was not only surprised but skeptical. The secretary of defense had told an aide that "the whole thing sounds kind of far out"; it was probably "cooked up" in the White House; he worried that, both as a controversial concept and as a competing budget item, SDI would get in the way of the strategic modernization program—that is, the development and deployment of new offensive weapons. Only later did Weinberger climb aboard the SDI bandwagon. Once there, however, he became its most spirited passenger. Eventually he tried to take the reins and personally drive the program forward.

Robert McFarlane, by contrast, helped get the bandwagon rolling in the first place. Later he tried to slow it down, only to be thrown from the driver's seat.

---

*On other occasions Weinberger said or wrote:
• "I can't imagine a more destabilizing factor for the world than if the Soviets should acquire a thoroughly reliable defense against [ballistic] missiles before we do."
• "If they [the Soviets] should develop [large-scale strategic defenses] first . . . we would then be, and the world will be, in a terribly dangerous position, because we would know that our weapons were no longer of any use and they had a means to destroy [the United States retaliatory force]."
• "Imagine the world situation if they made a breakthrough, and we were the ones whose missiles had been rendered obsolete. The whole world would suddenly become vulnerable to Soviet political blackmail. . . . And I cannot imagine that the Soviets, if they had a monopoly position, would do anything other than try to blackmail the rest of the world."
• "In fact, the Soviet Union now spends ten times more than we do on all forms of strategic defense. We must recognize what this means—the Soviets are seeking a first-strike capability—and plan accordingly."[7]

At the time of the Star Wars speech, McFarlane was deputy assistant to the President for national security affairs. His immediate boss was William Clark, an old friend of Reagan's. Clark knew and cared little about SDI, except that it offered Reagan a chance to turn his back on the past and establish his own legacy. Clark was a former California judge and future secretary of the interior. His tenure as presidential national security advisor was brief and undistinguished; he knew little about nuclear strategy, diplomacy, or bureaucratic politics. On all three subjects, he relied heavily on McFarlane.

The son of a Texas congressman, "Bud" McFarlane had graduated from the Naval Academy, earned a master's degree from the Institute of International Studies in Geneva, served in the Marine Corps, fought in Vietnam, and retired after some twenty years as a much-decorated lieutenant colonel. In the Nixon Administration, he was assigned to the National Security Council staff and came under the powerful and lasting influence of Henry Kissinger. For years afterward, McFarlane, who was otherwise almost painfully shy and serious, given to weary sighs and long silences, would surprise and amuse his friends by slipping into an eerily convincing impersonation of Kissinger, complete with orotund baritone and German accent. Just as Kissinger's own bent for droll and disarming self-deprecation masked an immense and fragile ego, so McFarlane's bursts of irreverence seemed part of his emulative obsession with his former mentor. During the Carter years, McFarlane worked as a congressional aide for Nitze's one-time nemesis Senator John Tower of Texas and helped the Senate Armed Services Committee sharpen its objections to the SALT II treaty.

McFarlane joined the Reagan Administration as an aide to Secretary of State Alexander Haig, then went to work for Clark at the NSC. On a number of occasions during the knock-down, drag-out battles over INF and START in the first Reagan term, McFarlane discreetly but effectively made common cause with the State Department—first under Haig, then under George Shultz—against Weinberger and the Pentagon. He intitially opposed Nitze's walk-in-the-woods formula for INF, but that was, he explained, primarily because of the "private, unauthorized" nature of the venture; Nitze had "wandered off the reservation." The walk in the woods was an act of insubordination, offensive to McFarlane's sense of order and discipline.

More than anyone else in the President's entourage, McFarlane midwifed the birth of SDI. At the turning-point meeting with the Joint Chiefs of Staff in February 1983, when General Vessey spoke of the need for a new "strategic vision," it was McFarlane who turned the conversation toward the possibility of American strategic defense as an answer to the challenge of Soviet strategic offense.

SDI was, if nothing else, a way of shaking up the status quo. In McFarlane's view, four adverse developments required something drastic: (1)

the continuing Soviet offensive buildup; (2) the breakdown of arms control—both the erosion of the old SALT constraints and the unlikelihood that START would produce a new agreement; (3) the continuing domestic political opposition to the President's strategic modernization program, particularly the MX; and (4) the prospect of mobile ICBMs—particularly mobile Soviet ICBMs.

For years, many American strategists had been urging that the United States "go mobile." Mobility, they believed, was a partial solution to vulnerability: a missile launcher that could move around would be harder for the enemy to target. Nitze had long been an advocate of ICBM mobility. In the first Reagan term, he worked from within the government to encourage a campaign on behalf of a weapon that did not then exist—a mobile, single-warhead "Midgetman" ICBM—as a successor to the three-warhead Minuteman and alternative to the ten-warhead MX.

Midgetman was favored by a coalition of moderate Democrats in Congress, such as Senator Sam Nunn of Georgia and Representatives Albert Gore, Jr., of Tennessee and Les Aspin of Wisconsin. They worked behind the scenes to broker a number of compromises between the Reagan Administration and its congressional critics over the strategic modernization program and the U.S. negotiating position in START during 1983, before the collapse of negotiations late that year.

The development and eventual deployment of Midgetman was also among the recommendations of a presidential commission on the future of strategic forces. The panel was chaired by Brent Scowcroft, a retired Air Force lieutenant general who had worked closely with McFarlane on Kissinger's staff at the NSC in the seventies. Scowcroft had succeeded Kissinger as national security advisor to Gerald Ford. When Presidents run into domestic political trouble with their defense and foreign policies, they tend to turn to distinguished outsiders, veterans of earlier Administrations, to provide as much blessing as possible and as much mediation with the Congress as necessary.

In April 1983 the Scowcroft Commission released a report that was drafted largely by Nitze's former protégé James Woolsey, now an attorney in Washington. The document dealt severe blows to two sacred cows of the Administration—SDI and the urgency if not the existence of a "window of vulnerability."

The report concluded that no ABM technologies appeared to combine the necessary virtues of practicality, survivability, low cost, and technical effectiveness to justify proceeding beyond R&D. The report also endorsed the usefulness of the ABM treaty and cautioned against any steps that might violate it. Several key members of the commission were willing to grant that the match-up between Soviet ICBMs and U.S. missile silos was a discouraging and dangerous prospect—as long as it was viewed in isolation. If, however, American bombers and their bases were taken into account, the

United States could no longer be said to face strategic vulnerability. The disavowal of any notion of a near-term threat of a disarming strike, in addition to reflecting the judgment of the panel's members, was necessary to reinforce the logic of their recommendation to base the MX in fixed silos as a stopgap until Midgetman could be developed. If American silos were believed to be vulnerable to Soviet attack, it would make little sense to put MXs in them in the near and middle-term future.

In its conclusion that the danger of a preemptive Soviet attack was neither clear nor present, the Scowcroft Commission report was a forceful repudiation not only of the Reagan Administration as a whole but of Woolsey's mentor Paul Nitze in particular. More than almost anyone else, Nitze had given currency to the phrase and legitimacy to the notion of the window of vulnerability. In discussing that feature of the report, Nitze shrugged and commented stoically, "Some points are clearly still open to dispute, but the bottom line is that the Scowcroft Commission favors moving toward small, mobile, single-warhead ICBMs, and in that we are in total agreement."

McFarlane, however, did not share in that agreement. He supported Scowcroft, Woolsey, Nunn, Gore, Aspin, and others in their overall effort to forge a bipartisan consensus on defense and arms-control issues, but he was never sold on the virtues of mobile ICBMs. He feared that many of the same politicians, antinuclear activists, and environmentalists who had blocked various protective and deceptive basing schemes for the MX would band together to prevent Midgetman from ever roaming the highways or even the military reservations of the American heartland.

McFarlane was concerned that while the United States was debating whether to proceed with a Midgetman program, the Soviet Union would be busily developing and deploying just such a system of its own, which McFarlane jokingly referred to as "Midgetmansky." The U.S.S.R. had more territory in which to hide mobile ICBMs; and, unlike their American counterparts, Soviet generals did not need to accommodate the concerns of local politicians or worry about environmental impact statements. Indeed, the Soviet design bureaus and production plants were already turning out a whole family of mobile missiles for the Soviet Strategic Rocket Forces. These included the two-stage, intermediate-range, mobile SS-20, which had already created such problems for America's allies in Europe and Asia; the three-stage, intercontinental, mobile, and MIRVed SS-24 (roughly the equivalent of the MX); and "Midgetmansky" itself, the SS-25 (in effect, a longer-range, three-stage, single-warhead version of the SS-20).

Therefore, as McFarlane later put it, the United States needed some way to say to the Soviets, "Okay, you guys can go mobile with your ICBMs, including with MIRVed mobiles. We can't. But if you insist on going down that road, there are things we can do that will make you very sorry—things that will complicate your calculations, threaten the effectiveness of your missiles once they are in flight, and greatly drive up the cost of your end of the competition.'' McFarlane hoped that ''space-based, boost-phase defensive systems might provide an extra measure of protection against Soviet mobiles—a necessary corrective'' for a MIRVed, mobile world.

McFarlane recalled arguing that for a number of reasons—''the East-West political dynamic, congressional politics, trends in domestic thinking, and arms control strategy''—strategic defense was ''an initiative whose time had come.'' Perhaps with SDI suddenly in the vocabulary on the American side, the sterile dialogue of recent years could turn into a real negotiation, and that negotiation could lead to a good deal for the West: ''We can say to the Soviets, 'We see an imbalance. The traditional ways of dealing with the military problem [i.e., traditional arms control, such as SALT and START] haven't worked. We've tried to get you guys to come down [reduce your offensive forces], but you haven't been willing to do so. Now we see a way of defending against your offense. Now we have a way of restoring stability by our lights, using things in our area of advantage. We'd rather not do that, but you've got to join us in correcting unfavorable trends in deterrence.' ''

Thus, in McFarlane's mind, SDI was, at its inception, a step toward an agreement in which the program to develop and deploy defenses might be limited in exchange for reduction of Soviet offensive missiles. ''The arms-control potential'' of SDI, he said, ''was always at the center of my motives.''

That purpose of SDI was quite explicit when McFarlane later talked with other government officials about the President's speech and, in the guise of a ''senior official'' who was not supposed to be publicly identified, gave background interviews to small groups of reporters. He argued that a highly publicized, presidential push to develop space-based strategic defenses could turn out to be ''the greatest sting operation in history.'' McFarlane used that phrase on a number of occasions to assure skeptics, inside the government and out, that SDI was a way of recovering the negotiating leverage in arms control that the United States had lost as a result of congressional opposition to the MX.

However, McFarlane had to be careful talking about SDI in this way. In dealing with civilian officials of the Pentagon, he dared not even hint at using SDI to advance strategic arms control, since that was not a cause for which they had great sympathy. If they learned of his motivation, they would use it, as he once commented, to ''crucify'' him with the President. Very discreetly, he sounded out Scowcroft, who was deeply skeptical. The whole idea, said Scowcroft, was far too complex, both as a bureaucratic maneuver and as a negotiating ploy.

McFarlane also tried to persuade Robert McNamara—like Scowcroft, now a private citizen—that SDI might yet serve the cause of arms control. McNamara, too, was doubtful. The idea that the Soviets would reduce their offenses when they were confronted with the possibility of increased American defenses was, he said, ''flawed at its very core.'' The ''illogic'' of that position, McNamara continued, was all but acknowledged in Reagan's Star Wars speech, in the passage where the President said: ''I clearly recognize that defensive systems have limitations and raise certain problems and ambiguities. If paired with offensive systems they can be viewed as fostering an aggressive policy, and no one wants that.''

''I know,'' replied McFarlane. ''I wrote that section into the speech myself.'' But he still hoped that precisely because the prospect of the vicious circle was so ominous, the Soviets would move to head it off at the negotiating table. ''Our leverage,'' he said, ''derives from the Soviets' fear of our technology. They are afraid that their huge investment in offensive forces will be neutralized if we go ahead with this program. That gives us real purchase.''

The counterargument was that, quite the contrary, it was the Soviets who would ''neutralize'' the huge American investment in SDI simply by proliferating offenses to a level with which the United States could not possibly cope. Whatever the advantages of American technology, it would still be far cheaper, and easier, for the Soviets to crank up the offensive side of the offense-defense spiral by increasing existing weapons than for the United States to mount an entirely new, exceedingly expensive system.

Within the Administration itself there was doubt about whether even an unlimited investment would ever yield a foolproof defense. Six weeks after Reagan's speech, the Pentagon's chief scientist, Richard DeLauer, the under secretary of defense for research and engineering, noted that ''with unconstrained proliferation'' of Soviet warheads ''no defensive system will work.''

McFarlane was undaunted. He pointed out that the ''flip side'' of DeLauer's observation was that the Soviet Union might see it as in its interest to reduce its warheads as an inducement for the United States to accept limits on SDI. He was still trying to promote SDI for the leverage it gave the United States in arms control. Part of the reason for the incredulity he was encountering was that everyone knew McFarlane was just one of the scriptwriters in the drama then unfolding; he was neither the director nor the star of the show. It was interesting and perhaps reassuring for Scowcroft, McNamara, and others to learn that McFarlane had an ulterior motive for fostering SDI. But what about the man who delivered the lines, the President who took such pride in the idea of SDI being his own? Would Reagan agree to let his dream turn out to be merely the bait in an elaborate scam?

Among the many appeals of SDI for Reagan was one that ran entirely counter to McFarlane's hidden agenda: The program was attractive precisely because it seemed to have so little to do with negotiated arms-control agreements. The program gave the President, who had never cared much for arms control, a way of holding out the promise of a better world without reopening the dismal prospect of yet another interminable and ultimately frustrating negotiation with a perfidious adversary. American proposals were subject to the Soviets' saying *nyet*. Even if talks eventually produced agreements, there was the ever-present danger that the Soviets would cheat. However, in the President's conception of strategic defense, there would be no way for the Soviets to cheat, or at least no purpose in their doing so, since all their nuclear missiles—regardless of whether they were permitted by international agreement—would be rendered useless by SDI.

Reagan later offered to share defensive technology with the Soviets. According to some of his associates, the President wanted to preempt the objection that SDI was part of his broader anti-Soviet agenda. Later still, he amended his offer by saying that the United States would share not the exotic technology itself but the "benefits" of the program. The suggestion that battle stations made in the U.S.A. might someday protect the U.S.S.R. from its enemies was not likely to be comforting, enticing, or plausible to the Kremlin.

In the years that followed his speech, part of Reagan's refrain was, "We're not going to give anyone a veto over this thing." Yet arms control, whether as negotiation or as agreement, is by its nature subject to the veto of either party at any time. Much as the image of Battleship America, an ocean away from the turmoils of the Old World, had seemed an appealing justification for America's staying out of World War II, the notion of Battlestar America, safe beneath the protective shield of SDI, appealed to Reagan as a way of avoiding World War III. SDI, in its original and purest form, was a quintessentially isolationist idea, a throwback to an attitude that Paul Nitze, like so many others of his generation, had shared nearly half a century before when the clouds of disaster darkened across the Atlantic in the late 1930s.

The unilateralism, isolationism, and non-negotiability implicit in SDI worried the European allies from the outset. The United States might be safe beneath its warhead-resistant Astrodome, but Western Europe, Japan, Korea, and other allies would be all the more vulnerable to Soviet conventional forces and bombers. That concern was much on the mind of British Prime Minister Margaret Thatcher when she came to Washington for talks with Reagan in December 1984. She had recently met in London with Mikhail Gorbachev, then an up-and-coming member of the Soviet Politburo. Both in private and in public, Gorbachev had warned that SDI posed a major obstacle to arms control. Thatcher had been impressed both by the man, then already being touted as the likely successor to the ailing Konstantin Chernenko, and by his argument.

In a private session with President Reagan at Camp David on December 22, Thatcher spoke bluntly about Star Wars: The plan had profound technological defects; it would split the alliance; it made no strategic sense. She also made an appeal for preserving a legacy of the past, the SALT I antiballistic missile treaty of 1972. "The ABM treaty is of enormous value," she said. "It must not be cast aside." She warned that while she would support continued research on strategic defenses, the President had better not imply her approval of advanced development, not to mention deployment, or she would publicly repudiate the whole program.

The President was soothing. "Well, Margaret," he said, "research is what this is all about." He assured her that there was no intention to jettison or violate the ABM treaty: "We won't even know the result of our research for a long time."

That was just what Thatcher wanted to hear. She had brought with her the text of a public statement she intended to make after the session. It said she favored SDI research "as a matter of balance. The Soviet Union is already doing such research." However, it continued, "production and deployment . . . has to be a matter of negotiation because deployment is covered by treaty obligations." Those negotiations, she continued, "should aim to achieve security with reduced levels of offensive systems on both sides."

McFarlane, who was present at the meeting, welcomed the statement, since it endorsed SDI only insofar as the program was compatible with, and conducive to, arms control. McFarlane showed the paper to George Shultz, who also approved it.

When delivered publicly with Reagan's endorsement, Thatcher's statement was dubbed "The Treaty of Camp David" and cited by the State Department for years afterward as evidence of presidential circumspection. It was nothing of the kind. All Reagan's own subsequent statements and decisions made clear that he had not meant to confine SDI to the laboratory. Nor had he meant to deliver a ringing reaffirmation of the ABM treaty. He had simply wanted to tell Margaret Thatcher what she wanted to hear, to let her say what she wanted to say, and to cast SDI in the terms most acceptable to an important ally.

When Caspar Weinberger found out what had happened at Camp David, he was furious. He complained that Shultz and McFarlane not only had organized an "end run" around the Pentagon but had tried to "sandbag" the President.

In response to allied concerns that SDI was isolationist or would prove detrimental to the credibility of the American nuclear umbrella over Europe, the scope of the program was later said to be "global" (i.e., American battle stations in space would be able to shoot down shorter-range Soviet missiles aimed at European and Asian allies as well as ICBMs fired at the United States itself). This adjustment, like the invitation for the allies to partake in the development of the program, obscured the essence of what attracted Reagan to the plan: SDI was something the United States could do on its own; it required neither the consent nor the cooperation of any foreign power, friend or foe.

Even as it later evolved, SDI kept its hard core of subliminal unilateralism and deliberate, defiant non-negotiability. Those qualities seemed to be part of its beauty for Reagan, and they put McFarlane at a disadvantage as he continued to maintain for some years that when the right moment came to cut a deal, the President would, as McFarlane put it hopefully, be "willing to return to, and reaffirm, the concept of deterrence as we've known it, albeit at lower levels of ballistic missiles systems."

In September 1985, McFarlane was at a conference in Colorado Springs, Colorado, in the heart of Star Wars country. Colorado Springs was the home of the U.S. Space Command, which would be the headquarters for SDI if it was ever deployed. During a quiet moment between sessions, he was reminiscing with an old friend about his role in the inception of the program that had now taken on such a robust life of its own. He paused, heaved one of his characteristic sighs, and said, "I guess maybe I've created a Frankenstein monster, haven't I?"

In August 1986, he remarked, "Much as we may not like the program, it may give us leverage over the Kremlin in the short and medium term." But if SDI was going to be a con job, it was not only the Soviets who would have to be stung or tricked. So would the President himself.[8]

Juices Begin to Flow

When news of the President's Star Wars speech came across the wire service tickers in the U.S. arms-control mission in Geneva, Paul Nitze was slogging toward the unhappy ending of the INF negotiations. The transcript of the speech sat unread on his desk for several days. Neither he nor his American colleagues nor their Soviet counterparts paid much attention to the passage near the end of the speech in which the President seemed to engage in a flight of fancy about perfect defense. "The idea of not paying adequate attention to defense offends me as a strategist," he told the historian Gregg Herken in an interview six weeks after Reagan's speech. "But it seeems to me asinine to be talking about this until you have some clearer idea of where you might go."

Nitze was typical of sophisticates in the field of nuclear strategy: For a long time he simply did not take SDI seriously. Not until more than a year later—well after the Soviets had walked out of INF and indefinitely suspended START—did he pay close attention to SDI and its implications for arms control. He did so about the same time that the Soviets began to hint that they might be willing to reopen negotiations with the Reagan Administration, this time with the issue of strategic defense at the center of the table.

The delay on the Soviet side was partly a result of the Kremlin's traditional sluggishness in response to new moves by its adversary. During much of 1983, the Soviet leadership was literally incapacitated, for Chernenko's predecessor, Yuri Andropov, was dying. A few days after Reagan's Star Wars speech, Andropov released a statement saying that the President's plan would seem truly defensive only to "someone not conversant with these matters"; SDI was actually a "bid to disarm the Soviet Union in the face of the United States's nuclear threat." Andropov proposed a treaty that would ban the "militarization" of space.

But then Andropov and his colleagues quickly let the issue of strategic defense slip to the side. In diplomacy and propaganda alike, they returned to what for them was the more urgent task of blocking the deployment of the American Euromissiles at the end of 1983. When the U.S. missiles went in on schedule, and the Soviets walked out of the talks in Geneva, Andropov was said to be suffering from a severe "cold" that kept him out of sight. In fact, he was suffering from terminal kidney disease.

Shortly after Andropov died in February 1984, Chernenko delivered a speech which contained a carefully underscored hint that if the United States agreed to a variety of arms-controls steps, there could be not just a resumption of negotiations but a "real breakthrough" in the relationship. One of the proposed steps was a treaty on the demilitarization of space. On June 29, the Soviets publicly called on the United States to meet in Vienna in mid-September to negotiate such a treaty, including a ban on antisatellite (ASAT) weapons. Some forms of ASAT might have much in common with some forms of SDI, since the task of intercepting a satellite in orbit was similar to that of destroying a missile warhead at certain points in its trajectory. The Soviet proposal of an ASAT ban was an early attempt to nip SDI in the bud, and it was seen as such in Washington.

Largely at McFarlane's behest, the Reagan Administration promptly accepted the Soviet proposal for new talks but refused to concede in advance that the negotiations would necessarily lead to a treaty on weapons, or anti-weapons, in space. The agenda, said the White House, must be broadened to include ground-based offensive systems as well. Thus McFarlane sought to lay the ground for tradeoffs between offense and defense, between Soviet ICBMs and American SDI. He felt he had reason to hope that the sting operation was already beginning to work.

It was during this period that Paul Nitze finally began to focus his attention on SDI and to participate in policymaking. He had grown increasingly discouraged during the election year of 1984. His assignment in INF had come to nothing. Administration arms-control policy was in disarray. There seemed little prospect for progress in the second term. Nitze had talked to McFarlane about leaving the government in October, shortly before the election. McFarlane had urged him to stay. Nitze agreed, primarily because he was intrigued by the possibility of working a deal on offense and defense. It was that possibility, he later said, that made his "juices start to flow."

McFarlane wanted to bring him into the White House as an arms-control "czar." Nitze said he would accept only if the idea had the full support of Shultz. Arms control was a key area of foreign policy, and Nitze knew he must not appear to be in competition with the secretary of state. Perhaps sensing precisely that danger, Shultz told McFarlane that Nitze was "too valuable for me to lose." Rather than letting Nitze move to the White House, Shultz gave him a new post within the State Department. Nitze moved from an office on the fifth floor, in the area assigned to the Arms Control and Disarmament Agency, to one on the seventh floor, around the corner from Shultz's own office—an arrangement similar to the one Nitze had had with Dean Acheson thirty-five years before. Shultz was becoming increasingly impatient with Kenneth Adelman, the director of the Arms Control and Disarmament Agency, who was routinely siding with Richard Perle against the State Department. Nitze was given the new, loftier title of special advisor to the President and secretary of state on arms control matters. In elevating Nitze, Shultz was in effect both downgrading and bypassing Adelman.

In preparation for the Soviet-American meeting expected to take place in Vienna in mid-September, other State Department officials—in the European and political-military affairs bureaus—had dusted off old fallback proposals for the suspended Strategic Arms Reduction Talks and linked them with new proposals for a moratorium on ASAT tests and a vague arrangement for keeping SDI within the confines of the ABM treaty. Together, these would have been the elements of an interim, or temporary, agreement until a permanent pact could be worked out.

Nitze vigorously opposed this plan. "We've never gotten anything out of interim agreements or moratoriums," he said; agreements that expired invited both sides to prepare for breakout by developing and stockpiling weapons that were prohibited by the pact but would be allowed as soon as it ended. If there was to be a strategic offense-defense agreement, said Nitze, it should be of indefinite duration, like the SALT I ABM treaty.

Nitze did not approve of a moratorium on ASAT testing in 1984 any more than he had favored a moratorium on MIRV testing on the eve of SALT I. He believed that only if testing continued could the United States maintain its bargaining leverage. "Red-teaming" the prospective negotiation in his mind, Nitze could easily imagine how the Soviets, with their strong tendency to treat nuclear diplomacy as a zero-sum game, might turn a moratorium to their advantage. By merely pretending to negotiate in good faith but actually hunkering down for a long bout of stonewalling, the Kremlin could string out forever a supposedly temporary delay in the American ASAT program.

Nitze said that those promoting the State Department plan "have no idea how you negotiate. They're thinking just in terms of promoting the appearance of international comity. There's no hope of getting an agreement with this option as a going-in position. It's the way to disaster. The Soviets would give up nothing in exchange for the U.S.'s giving up quite a bit. And the Soviets will be asking for a lot more than the U.S. can or should give up.'"9

Nitze wanted to move toward a more ambitious, open-ended agreement, in which the Soviets would give up a great deal—i.e., large numbers of their MIRVed ICBMs—in exchange for constraints on SDI. He assembled for Shultz what he called "the theory of the case." It contained few specifics. Instead, it elaborated on "the concept of the interrelationship of offense and defense."

The document stressed continuity between the policies of the past and the ones Nitze was recommending for the future. The paper harked back to the beginnings of SALT I, when the Nixon Administration used the threat of a superior American ABM system to induce the Soviets to accept a freeze on the number of silos for their ICBMs. Nitze advised Shultz that it was important, once again, to "get both sides of the equation [offense and defense] going concurrently," and to "make sense out of" SDI (i.e., develop a strategically sound rationale for the program), rather than letting the Soviets make "propaganda hay."10

All this preparation came to naught in the short run. American foreign policymaking had often been impaired by presidential politics, and in the fall of 1984 the Soviets themselves did not help. They were stalling and squirming, perhaps because they were having trouble figuring out whether, and how, to deal with an Administration that was in the midst of a re-election campaign. The Kremlin spent an awkward month reformulating its own proposal so as to make it truly unacceptable, and finally let it lapse altogether.

In the end, no delegations went to Vienna in September 1984 to negotiate on the demilitarization of space or anything else. However, Reagan and Foreign Minister Andrei Gromyko did meet that month at the White House. Working from talking points prepared by McFarlane, Reagan told Gromyko that the United States would be willing to "consider" restraints on anti-satellite weapons if the arms control process as a whole were to be renewed. In the wake of that meeting and of Reagan's overwhelming re-election in early November, the Soviets decided finally to re-enter negotiations.

On November 22, Thanksgiving Day—almost exactly a year after the Soviet walkout from INF—there was a joint announcement in Moscow and Washington that Shultz and Gromyko would meet in Geneva in early January 1985.

Shultz began spending several hours a day studying the issues and the opportunities that lay ahead. His principal tutor in these sessions was Paul Nitze.

Meanwhile, it was increasingly apparent inside the Administration and out that Nitze was going to play a critical role in shaping policy on SDI. On November 14, 1984, Nitze was given an award for public service by the Georgetown Center for Ethics and Public Policy. Several colleagues from the past and present were invited to speak. Elmo Zumwalt was master of ceremonies, and President Reagan sent a message of congratulations.

Harold Brown used the occasion to question the wisdom of SDI and to suggest that of all the people then connected with government, Nitze was best qualified to analyze the strategic implications of the program.

The next speaker was Weinberger, who departed from his prepared remarks to rebut Brown: "I would have to say—with all due deference to my immediate predecessor—that I do believe the Strategic Defense Imperative [sic] is achievable; that it is well within our technology, scientific and inventive and productive genius, and skill. The pursuit of it, as the President wishes, is perhaps the most moral of all of the activities in which we can engage."

In his own remarks on that occasion, Nitze confined himself to personal reminiscences, steering clear of the dispute that had just broken out between the two secretaries of defense. During the banquet afterward, he was studiously noncommittal when Brown pressed him further on the issue of SDI. Later, however, proudly displaying the citation that had come with the award, Nitze pointed to one line: "Steeped in the Judeo-Christian moral heritage, he has never confused impossible dreams with attainable ends." Smiling broadly, he remarked, "I'll let that be my guide as I sort out all this good advice I'm getting from Harold and Cap."

During the Christmas holidays, Nitze gave up his usual skiing vacation in Aspen and worked furiously at the State Department. He talked at least once almost every day to Shultz, either in person or on the phone. Both men later commented that it was during this period that they developed a close collaboration.

The Concept

Paul Nitze liked to say that a fool was someone who defined a problem in such a way that it could not be solved. He sometimes added that a knave was someone who did so deliberately. In the protracted battle over SDI within the Reagan Administration, Nitze often felt surrounded by both fools and knaves. In December 1984, as he helped George Shultz prepare for the Geneva meeting with Gromyko, Nitze set about to define the problem of strategic defense in such a way that it could be solved diplomatically, with an arms-control agreement that enhanced strategic stability.

The Soviet Union was about to return to the bargaining table that it had left a year before. The obvious question that everyone asked was whether SDI was on the table as a bargaining chip. The Reagan Administration did not have a unified or coherent answer to that question. Having just been overwhelmingly re-elected, the President was starting his second term on a high note, full of confidence that his policies were working and had strong public support. It was no time for his subordinates to be suggesting that his most cherished single policy in the realm of national security should be a mere bargaining chip in a poker game that he was not even particularly eager to play. The surest way for an official to provoke a reprimand from the White House was to hint that SDI was negotiable. Whatever Robert McFarlane's own motives in helping draft the Star Wars speech, the fact remained that it was Ronald Reagan's initiative and Ronald Reagan's Administration, and his vision did not yet seem to allow for the possibility, in any sense, of trading away SDI. Therefore, whenever journalists asked government spokesmen, as they frequently did, if SDI was a bargaining chip, the answer, on the record, was an emphatic no.

Yet the real answer—in the minds of McFarlane, Shultz, and Nitze—was yes, although it was almost always elliptically phrased. Appearing on the CBS television program "Face the Nation" on November 25, 1984, McFarlane said, "There's no dearth of interest in identifying where compromise might result in an agreement that serves our interest militarily and makes matters more stable." State Department officials carefully noted that "a unilateral transition to an SDI world is not in the cards" and that the transition would have to be "bilaterally agreed and jointly managed." Those were code words for arms control and compromise.

On the eve of his January 1985 meeting in Geneva with Gromyko, Shultz said privately on a number of occasions that he was prepared to "signal" that SDI was "open for discussion" as long as Gromyko acknowledged that the Soviet superiority in ICBMs was also negotiable.

For his part, Nitze said that his greatest fear about SDI was that "we'll give it up and we won't get a goddamn thing for it." How, then, to make sure that the United States "got something" for SDI without explicitly putting it forward in an offer to trade? The answer that Nitze came up with was contained in four sentences totaling less than a hundred words:

> For the next ten years, we should seek a radical reduction in the number
> and power of existing and planned offensive and defensive nuclear arms,
> whether land-based, space-based, or otherwise. We should even now be
> looking forward to a period of transition, beginning possibly ten years
> from now, to effective non-nuclear defensive forces, including defenses
> against offensive nuclear arms. This period of transition should lead to

the eventual elimination of nuclear arms, both offensive and defensive. A nuclear-free world is an ultimate objective to which we, the Soviet Union, and all other nations can agree.

This came to be called the "strategic concept." It was part of Nitze's effort to make a silk purse out of the sow's ear of SDI. In it, Nitze was trying to skirt the pitfalls, while capitalizing on the opportunities, of the President's attachment to SDI. The strategic concept established a timetable that was, in Nitze's words, "front-loaded toward the doable"; it gave priority to the more realistic and useful aspects of the program while postponing the more dubious ones. The main purpose of the strategic concept was the stated goal for the immediate future and for ten years to come: "reduction in the number and power of existing and planned offensive and defensive nuclear arms, whether land-based, space-based, or otherwise." This was the only part of the strategic concept that addressed the here and now. A subsequent version of the statement sharpened the point, saying that the objective in the first ten years was "the stabilization of the relationship between offensive and defensive nuclear arms, whether on earth or in space." Parsed carefully, the first sentence of the strategic concept said that there should be not only a reduction in existing, land-based offensive nuclear arms (such as Soviet ICBMs) but also constraints on planned, space-based defensive arms (presumably such as those contemplated for SDI).

The strategic concept put Nitze on record as accepting the legitimacy of the President's dream of a nuclear-free, defense-only world. But Nitze had added a vital condition, implicit in the document and quite explicit in what he said about it later: "The elimination of nuclear weapons is not an impossible goal, assuming cooperation between the two principal powers."[11]

Nitze took the strategic concept from office to office in Foggy Bottom and across the Potomac to the Pentagon, tailoring his sales pitch to the different constituencies. At first, he expressed skepticism tinged with distaste about the whole exercise, calling the strategic concept itself a "gimmick," and, at best, "a way of imposing order on the chaos." But eventually, in the words of one of his associates, "Paul warmed to his own theology."

McFarlane, who saw clearly how the strategic concept served the purpose he wanted to accomplish with SDI, shepherded Nitze's four sentences through an interagency review so that the statement became Administration policy.

When Shultz met Andrei Gromyko in January 1985 in Geneva, the strategic concept was the centerpiece of his forty-five-minute opening statement. Gromyko, looking especially dour, seemed at first ready to dispense with the translation into Russian and rely on his passable English. But when Shultz came to the strategic concept, broadly hinting how SDI might relate to arms control, Gromyko leaned forward and became more attentive.

"That was an important and principled statement," the foreign minister said when Shultz had finished. "I want to hear the translation."

Gromyko and Shultz agreed fairly quickly that formal negotiations between the superpowers would resume in three areas, or forums. Two would be intermediate-range nuclear forces and strategic arms, the agendas of the INF talks and START suspended in late 1983. Defining the third forum was more difficult. The Americans wanted to designate the subject "defense and space." Gromyko objected to the word "defense" in any connection whatsoever with SDI. "Whatever you call them," said Gromyko, "these are all offensive systems." The preferred Soviet designation of the American program was a system of "space-strike arms." Gromyko called SDI a "sword of Damocles," and invited Shultz to climb a tower in Moscow to see "objectively" how the situation would look from there and why the Soviet Union felt threatened by SDI.

The secretary of state responded by suggesting that Gromyko join him at the top of a different tower, somewhere to the south and west, between the superpowers; from that vantage point, looking eastward, Shultz said, Gromyko would see a great many Soviet offensive weapons threatening the deterrent forces of the United States. Shultz pressed Gromyko to spell out exactly what the phrase "space-strike arms" meant and how it would be interpreted for purposes of an agreement.

There was an awkward silence on the Soviet side of the table. Gromyko's advisors clustered around their boss as he shuffled through his papers. He found what he was looking for and read from it carefully. The paper had apparently been drafted in Moscow and approved by the Politburo. It said that space-strike arms were systems in space designed to attack objects in space or on earth and systems on earth designed to attack objects in space. This was a rigged and one-sided definition, since the phrase "designed to" concerned the intention of a system rather than its capability. The Soviets had already deployed any number of weapons that were capable of attacking objects in space (for example, some of their ballistic missiles could be used against satellites). Yet as long as they disavowed such an intention, they could avoid having their own programs constrained by their definition of space-strike arms. By contrast, it was the avowed purpose of SDI to attack objects in space (i.e., Soviet missiles and warheads); therefore, anything associated with the program would be banned under the Soviet proposal.

"Your definition," said Shultz to Gromyko, "is inherently prejudicial and totally unacceptable. And surely you know it."*

---

*The Soviets had tried to use this tactic before in arms control. In the SALT I treaty, the phrase "tested in an ABM mode" was a compromise between the Soviet preference, which was to limit systems "designed to" be used in an ABM mode, and the American phrase, "capable of" being so used. In INF, the Soviets had tried to define an INF missile as one "intended to strike" targets

The exchange demonstrated once again the dynamic that had so often brought the superpowers together at such meetings—and kept them apart once they got there: The United States came looking for reductions, particularly in existing Soviet arsenals; the U.S.S.R. sought constraints on modernization, particularly in future American arsenals. The Soviets were concerned about SDI in its own right, but they were also worried about it as a manifestation of the American penchant for changing the rules of the competition by introducing high-tech innovations.

The Soviets gave up on getting the words "space-strike arms" into a joint communiqué that Shultz and Gromyko released at the end of the meeting; but on another drafting point, they were adamant and successful. They insisted that the communiqué make clear that they were agreeing to "new negotiations," not simply a resumption of the old INF talks and START, and that while they were to be divided into three forums, the issues would have to be resolved "in their interrelationship"; the objective of the negotiations would be to terminate the arms race on earth and prevent one in space.

There was much more at stake than wrangling over semantics. The Soviets, along with many Western experts observing the process from the outside, argued that the communiqué established clear linkage—and set the scene for eventual tradeoffs—between reductions in strategic offense and restrictions on strategic defense.

Spokesmen for the U.S. government retorted that the "interrelationship" mentioned in the communiqué did not necessarily mean limiting SDI. Quite the contrary, the stipulated interrelationship might in practice consist of reducing offenses even as defenses were steadily introduced (the hoped-for "cooperative transition" to an SDI world). Nor would the eventual erection of a space-based defensive system necessarily constitute an "arms race" in space at all. Rather, it would be the orderly, jointly regulated, and thoroughly salutary replacement of arms with antiarms as the new basis for world peace.

That was the official position of the Reagan Administration. It was not, however, Paul Nitze's view. He, like many of the Administration's critics—and like the Soviets themselves—believed that sooner or later, an agreement reducing nuclear weapons would have to be contingent on an agreement limiting SDI, just as limitations on offensive arms in SALT had required the ABM treaty. Indeed, perhaps all that would be required to limit SDI would be maintenance of the ABM treaty itself, although, necessarily, in an updated form.

---

in Europe, thus exempting, by their claim, their own mobile Asian systems and including American FB-111 bombers in the U.S., which were indeed "intended" to be moved to Europe in a crisis.

The Criteria

After the Geneva meeting between George Shultz and Andrei Gromyko, Paul Nitze and Robert McFarlane briefed the NATO allies, then flew home to Washington together from Paris. They spent much of the flight talking about what the Administration should say next about SDI. Even if American research and development produced a system that could be deployed, there would be a question of whether it *should* be deployed—that is, whether it would enhance the safety of the United States and the stability of the Soviet-American strategic relationship.

Officials of the Pentagon, both civilians and uniformed officers, had been concerned about that problem for some time. Frank Miller, a professional strategic expert on Weinberger's staff, had developed three standards that SDI would have to meet before it could be deployed. As Miller put it in testimony before a subcommittee of the House Committee on Foreign Affairs on July 26, 1984:

> If at some point in the future, the end of this decade, the beginning of the next, the Administration decided to come to the Congress to ask you to fund full-scale development and beginning deployment, that Administration would have to convince you, as well as itself, that such a system would be effective; that it would be cost-effective; and that it would be survivable. Whether a defense system can be developed with these three characteristics is what this entire research program is designed to find out.

In a speech in Los Angeles in January 1985, Admiral James Watkins, whose ruminations about the immorality of traditional deterrence had helped trigger the President's decision to announce SDI, cautioned that the program should go forward only if the system could be made "highly survivable" and "if it can be made more expensive for an attacker to add warheads than for a defender to increase defense capability." Watkins added, "The only way to determine if these requirements can be achieved is . . . through a concerted program of research and evaluation."[12]

Nitze had used variations of these same standards in the debate over ABMs in the sixties. He and Albert Wohlstetter had refined the concept of cost-effectiveness "at the margins" to deal with what he called "the issue of the incremental case": The driving consideration should be not how expensive it was to erect an effective defense but whether it would then be cheaper to keep it effective against whatever offensive countermeasures the enemy attempted.

Nitze adopted effectiveness, survivability, and cost-effectiveness at the margins as the three "criteria for success" in SDI and highlighted them in a speech before the Philadelphia World Affairs Council on February 20, 1985. Within days, commentators and defense experts were talking about "the Nitze criteria." Along with the strategic concept, the criteria had acquired the status of holy writ within much of the Administration. McFarlane saw that they were circulated to the bureaucracy as a presidential directive. References to them were woven into speeches and congressional testimony by government officials.

SDI enthusiasts denounced the adoption of these standards. "The Nitze criteria were put in to kill—not to enhance—the prospects for SDI," said Daniel Graham, the head of High Frontier.[13] By the same token, many SDI skeptics assumed that Nitze was on their side. They believed that he was deliberately setting criteria that the program could not possibly meet, thus reining it in and limiting the damage it might do to strategic stability and arms control. This was not the kind of credit Nitze wanted, since it jeopardized his position within the Administration. In public and at meetings with outsiders, Nitze denied that he had any idea whether SDI would ultimately pass the test he had set, and he criticized others for prejudging the issue. For example, on April 10 and 11, 1985, he and James Schlesinger, the former secretary of defense, encountered each other at a weekend seminar on arms control and national security. Reiterating the traditional view, Schlesinger contended that a cost-effective defense was by definition impossible. Nitze objected: "What is your evidence, Jim? How can you be so sure? Why can't you keep an open mind on this? My own mind is entirely open."

Another of Nitze's former colleagues now on the sidelines of policy, Henry Kissinger, was critical of the three criteria for much the same reason that Schlesinger seemed to endorse and welcome them: They served as a check on the program. That same month, April 1985, Kissinger said, "Paul's position kills defense. The criteria are not meetable. And if you put the transitional phase [of deploying defenses under the terms of the strategic concept] ten years into the future, Congress will kill it long before deployment. I'd like to move the transitional phase to the present." In other words, Kissinger was saying, SDI should be judged by criteria less stringent than Nitze's and deployed as soon as possible.[14]

A stunning role reversal was taking place. Henry Kissinger was maneuvering to the right of Nitze. Kissinger was now on the outside looking in, and Nitze was on the inside trying to work a deal. Sensing that Nitze was preparing the ground for an offense-defense tradeoff, Kissinger was staking out a position from which to accuse his old rival of being soft in arms control, selling short American advantages, and playing into the hands of the Soviets—all echoes of charges that Nitze had made against Kissinger in the seventies during SALT.

Meanwhile, similar opposition, from more predictable quarters, was building against Nitze within the Administration.

CHAPTER 10

Restraint

To be a true Reaganaut, one had to love SDI and hate SALT. By both standards, Paul Nitze failed. As a critic of U.S. policy outside the government in the mid-to-late seventies, he had fought ferociously against the SALT II treaty. But once he became a member of the Reagan Administration, he worked almost as tenaciously, although far less conspicuously, to continue American compliance with the terms of SALT II. The curiously durable agreement had its revenge—not only against a President who had campaigned on the charge that it was "fatally flawed" but also against a presidential advisor who had been its fiercest and most effective detractor only a few years before.

For Nitze, the United States had to keep the old arms-control "regime" in place long enough to reach a new agreement on strategic offenses that would replace—and, he hoped, greatly improve on—the inheritance of SALT. By contrast, Richard Perle wanted to force what he often called a "clean break" with SALT. That meant both the offensive agreements of SALT I and SALT II as well as the defensive agreement of the ABM treaty. Perle seemed to have three reasons for wanting to junk the agreements of the past. First, he believed that they were bad for American military security, primarily because they left the Soviets with too many first-strike weapons. Second, in his view, the entire enterprise of arms control had a lulling or soporific effect on the body politic of the West. Third, he feared that if left intact, the old agreements might stimulate the achievement, and form the basis, of new agreements that would be just as bad for American and Western interests as the old ones. Perle led the effort, largely against Nitze, to scrap all vestiges of SALT.

Early in the first Reagan term, Perle's long-time associate John Lehman, the secretary of the navy, publicly accused the Carter Administration of "illegally" abiding by the SALT I Interim Agreement on offensive weapons, which had technically expired in 1977. "I have no hesitation at all," said Lehman, "in recommending that we not comply with SALT I." Ronald Reagan was receptive to this advice, since he had campaigned against SALT for years. Richard Allen, Reagan's first national security advisor, William

Casey, the director of Central Intelligence, and Caspar Weinberger all tried a number of times to convince the President that SALT prevented the United States from going forward with necessary new weapon systems. Their views were opposed by three military men—Alexander Haig, General David Jones, chairman of the Joint Chiefs, and Admiral Bobby Ray Inman, then Casey's deputy at the CIA.

With considerable difficulty, Haig, Jones, and Inman managed to keep in place a policy of "not undercutting" SALT. This awkward euphemism for continued compliance was meant to obscure the logical contradiction between what Reagan, Nitze, and the others had said about SALT II in 1979 when they were in the opposition and what they did about the treaty now that they were in office. The Administration as a whole and Nitze in particular chose the "no undercut" policy for the simple reason that, just as its defenders had said during the debate over ratification in 1979, the terms of the agreement imposed more limits on Soviet forces than on American ones; SALT II was, as General Jones had said in his tepid endorsement two years before, a "modest but useful" step in advancing not just the cause of arms control but the security interests of the United States.

During the first Reagan term, there was good reason for American concern about the consequences of letting SALT lapse. By exceeding the SALT ceilings and subceilings, the Soviets could increase the number of warheads on their ballistic missiles on short notice, while there was little the United States could do in response. By some estimates, in the absence of the SALT II subceilings, the Soviet Union could quickly add to their Strategic Rocket Forces more than 200 ICBMs with some 1,100 warheads, more than 100 SLBMs with some 1,000 warheads, and 50 Bear bombers with at least 400 air-launched cruise missiles. In the absence of the SALT II freeze on the number of MIRVs per type of missile, the Soviets could, without a large-scale testing program or major changes in design, increase the MIRV load of the SS-18 heavy ICBM from ten to fourteen warheads per rocket. Over time, they could plausibly put as many as forty warheads on each SS-18.

All the while, because of a variety of political, technological, and budgetary constraints, the United States would probably be hard pressed to maintain the programs that it was planning anyway—and that it was permitted to have under SALT II.

Nonetheless, by the end of the first term of the Reagan Administration, the policy of continued compliance with SALT was becoming harder to sustain. START and the INF negotiations had collapsed, with no immediate prospect of their resumption, so it was harder to recommend that SALT should be kept in place just a little longer, as a stopgap until the Reagan Administration could produce an agreement of its own. The principal advocates of the "no undercut" policy were gone—Haig had been fired, Jones had retired, and Inman had resigned—while the principal opponents, notably Perle, were still in place.

Nor had the President grown any less disenchanted with the SALT legacy. Quite the contrary. "It was assumed the treaties would lead to a stable balance and, ultimately, to real reductions in strategic arms," said Reagan in his weekly Saturday radio address on July 13, 1985. "But the Soviet Union has never accepted any meaningful and verifiable reductions in offensive nuclear arms. None."

The argument against continued American compliance seemed to be considerably strengthened by indications that the Soviets were not abiding by the terms of SALT themselves; therefore, American compliance seemed—to those who opposed it, anyway—all the more unwise.

It was almost an article of faith in the Reagan Administration that the Soviet Union cheated on arms-control agreements. The facts, however, were more ambiguous. The Soviet record was one of chiseling at the margins, taking advantage of loopholes and imprecisions, rarely of outright violation.* In litigating the Reagan Administration's charge of Soviet "noncompliance" with SALT, a Philadelphia lawyer could spend a long and lucrative career representing the Kremlin. Soviet diplomats and military officers held their own against American accusations at the Standing Consultative Commission (SCC), the secrecy-shrouded deliberative body that was established as part of SALT to discuss, and if possible resolve, disputes over compliance.

In 1983, American reconnaissance satellites spotted a giant radar facility under construction at Abalakovo near the town of Krasnoyarsk in central Siberia. Unlike conventional radars common in the fifties and sixties, with their huge, mechanically steered dishes, this one was a "phased-array radar." Its flat faces were to be covered with thousands of individual elements, each emitting a tiny beam. By electronically coordinating these beams and reading the reflected signals, a phased-array radar could simultaneously detect and track large numbers of enemy warheads.

---

*Two examples:

The Soviets used codes in the electronic transmission of data from rockets during tests. SALT II did not forbid "encryption of telemetry" unless such activity "impeded" the other side's ability to monitor and verify compliance. The text of the treaty made it difficult to prove that the other side was "impeding" verification, as opposed to taking permissible measures to protect its legitimate military secrets.

SALT II permitted each side one "new type" of ICBM. The Soviets designated a MIRVed missile, roughly comparable to the American MX, as their one new type. This was labeled by the West the SS-24. Then they were discovered to be testing another, smaller, single-warhead missile, the SS-25, similar to the Midgetman that many Americans advocated. This was the "Midgetman-sky" that McFarlane feared would so complicate the strategic balance. Taking full advantage of the technical definition of a new type in SALT II, the Soviets claimed that the SS-25 was not a prohibited "second new type" but a permissible successor to an old one, the SS-13.

The principal purpose of the SALT I treaty was to strengthen deterrence based on the threat of retaliation while discouraging an offense-defense arms race. In its treatment of radars, the treaty sought to prevent either side from deploying an active "territorial"—i.e., nationwide—ABM defense. The pact did, however, allow each side to maintain "early warning" radars, so that it would have time to retaliate if it came under attack. The issue arose of how to distinguish between permissible early-warning radars and impermissible installations that might be, or later become, part of a territorial defense. The solution adopted was largely a matter of geographical location. Each side was allowed early-warning radars only "along the periphery of its national territory and oriented outward." That provision seemed to preclude radars that might be used, in conjunction with ABM interceptors, to mount a defense against an attack.

The facility under construction at Krasnoyarsk was about 750 kilometers from the nearest border, with Mongolia to the south, and it was pointing toward the Soviet Union's northeastern border, some 4,000 kilometers away.

The Soviets claimed officially that the radar, when it was finished, would be used not for tracking enemy warheads but for tracking space launches and satellites, a function permitted by the treaty. But it was misplaced for space tracking, and even critics of Administration charges on other compliance issues agreed that Krasnoyarsk was a violation. Starting at an SCC session in Geneva in the fall of 1983, the U.S. delegation charged that Krasnoyarsk was a clear-cut, potentially ominous violation of the ABM treaty.

On the first day of his own talks in Geneva with Andrei Gromyko in January 1985, George Shultz cited the Krasnoyarsk radar as an example of Soviet behavior that undermined arms control. Gromyko replied stonily, "The Soviet Union lives by its obligations." During a visit to the United States in March—cut short by Konstantin Chernenko's death and Mikhail Gorbachev's accession to the top job in the Kremlin—another Politburo member, Vladimir Shcherbitsky, gave Shultz a map, explaining the need for a space-tracking radar station in that part of Siberia. Moscow's representatives to the SCC in Geneva and its ambassador in Washington, Anatoly Dobrynin, during an arms-control conference in Atlanta, promised that American experts would be invited to inspect the radar when it was finished.*

Other Soviet officials, however, seemed defensive and embarrassed about Krasnoyarsk. They all but admitted that their government had been caught in a violation. One authoritative representative of the Academy of Sciences explained that if the radar had been built strictly in compliance with the

---

*Such a visit was arranged for U.S. congressional experts in September 1987, well before the completion of the facility.

ABM treaty, it would have been put in the remote tundra, where it would have been far more expensive to construct and maintain; therefore, he added sheepishly, "some of our people may have cut some corners."

During 1985, Soviet diplomats dropped broad hints that they were looking for a face-saving way to "remove the obstacle" of the Krasnoyarsk radar. In October, they proposed to stop construction on the project if the United States would halt its own upgrading of existing American radars at Thule in Greenland and Fylingdales Moor in Great Britain. These two sites had been part of the American early-warning system for years. Now the United States was replacing conventional, movable-dish radars with the much more capable phased-array type, and in the case of Fylingdales Moor the U.S. was erecting a new facility. The Reagan Administration maintained that this so-called "modernization" was entirely legal under SALT I.[1]

Regardless of questions about its own compliance with the ABM treaty, the Reagan Administration rejected the Soviet offer of a compromise on Krasnoyarsk, saying that the United States was not going to stop doing something it was entitled to do as a way of rewarding the U.S.S.R. for ceasing a clearly illegal activity.

Paul Nitze was dissatisfied with that response. He was almost unique in his knowledge of the background of this troublesome issue. As a negotiator of the ABM treaty, he had specialized in defining what radars would be permissible under the treaty. He had spent many hours with Alexander Shchukin during SALT I trying to head off exactly the sort of problem that Krasnoyarsk now posed. He was interested in exploring the possibility of a tradeoff—perhaps a different way of upgrading the American radar at Fylingdales in exchange for a halt in the construction of the new Soviet facility.

At a number of meetings, he criticized the rest of the government for "getting too dug-in without carefully analyzing the case." As so often in the past, he used the pursuit of the facts—what he called "the essential elements of information"—to reach a political and diplomatic destination. He had a long list of questions for the experts gathered around the table at interagency meetings: What was the relative military value to the United States if the Soviets stopped work at Krasnoyarsk in exchange for something less than a full-scale upgrade at Fylingdales? Wasn't Fylingdales too far from the United States to be of real use in a war? Wasn't the facility too far forward to discern the nature of an enemy attack? Would it "see" the launch before or after Soviet missiles dispensed their warheads? What was an American decision-maker going to do with the knowledge that ten thousand warheads were heading his way if he didn't know where they were supposed to land? If Fylingdales could provide "impact-point prediction" within a radius of only 120 miles or so, what good was that? How did the British feel about the issue? Would they be upset or relieved if the United States called off its upgrade?

These were leading questions, intended to raise the possibility that Fylingdales was of marginal value and set up what Nitze's critics would almost surely denounce as a dishonorable tradeoff.

Just as he had "worked the problem" of ABM radars with Shchukin fifteen years before, Nitze was prepared to do so again now. But the Administration was not willing to let him. McFarlane was siding with the Pentagon against him, and Shultz remained above the fray. Krasnoyarsk had too much symbolic significance; it was the "smoking gun" in the American case against Soviet cheating. Nitze's attempt to engineer a compromise on Krasnoyarsk failed within the United States government, just as his walk-in-the-woods scheme had failed during the first term.

Krasnoyarsk also figured importantly in the Pentagon's argument that the United States should cease its own "unilateral" compliance with the agreements. "Why should we be bound if the other side clearly is not?" asked Perle in numerous meetings. Sometimes military officers present would answer with a reiteration of the argument that General Jones had used with the President during the first term: Without SALT II to constrain them, the Soviets would rapidly and menacingly accumulate offensive weapons. A breakdown in the SALT regime would lead to a breakout on the Soviet side in the arms race.

Perle had for years contended that every Soviet warhead was a dagger pointed at the heart of America. Now he adopted quite a different point of view. It would make no difference if the SALT II limits went "out the window," he said. True, the Soviets would have the right and the ability quickly to add warheads. True, the Strategic Rocket Forces were already bumping up against the SALT II subceiling of 820 MIRVed ICBMs. True, the MIRVed SS-24 (the Soviet counterpart of the MX) might be ready to deploy sometime in 1985, with the single-warhead, mobile SS-25 ("Midgetmansky") coming along behind it. But, Perle insisted, the Soviets would have no interest in exceeding the SALT limits. They would be "resource-constrained" from doing so; and even if they did deploy more warheads than permitted by SALT II, it would not matter: "No one has shown me a convincing list of targets for those extra weapons. It would be a foolish investment for them. They've crossed a threshold of being able to attack and destroy our ICBMs, and a few thousand more won't make much difference."[2]

These and similar statements were a far cry from the claim Perle had made for years that the Soviets' huge advantage in ballistic missile throw-weight allowed them to proliferate additional warheads at relatively little expense. What was consistent was his distaste for arms control and his ingenuity in turning any situation to his advantage in the ongoing battle with the State Department.

• • •

A moment of truth for the Administration's "no undercut" policy was coming in late 1985. The SALT II treaty, had it been ratified, would have expired on December 31. Shortly before then, the U.S. Navy would be putting into service a new missile-firing Trident submarine, the U.S.S. *Alaska*. Unless the Navy simultaneously retired an older, Poseidon boat, the United States would have more MIRVed ballistic missiles in its arsenal than SALT II allowed. Completely aside from consideration of arms control, there were sound practical reasons to retire the Poseidon once the Trident put to sea. Keeping both boats in service would strain the budget and the pool of available manpower. Besides, the Poseidon was already nearing the end of its lifespan, and prolonging its service would require the very expensive process of "recoring"—replacing most of the atomic reactor that powered the boat. Another option—drydocking the Poseidon and holding it in reserve—was also expensive.

These were arguments that Paul Nitze, as a former secretary of the navy, could well understand and put to use in his dispute with the Pentagon. During much of 1985, he was one of the most vigorous advocates of maintaining the "no undercut" policy, or, as it was also called, "interim restraint"—a phrase intended to underscore the temporary and unilateral nature of the arrangement.

By whatever name, interim restraint had strong support in Congress, where many members lacked confidence in the intentions and competence of the Reagan Administration to produce an arms-control agreement of its own. The policy of interim restraint was also favored by the Joint Chiefs of Staff, for reasons similar to those that General Jones had argued in the past (SALT II constrained current Soviet forces and provided a degree of "predictability" for future ones). Robert McFarlane, too, felt that the military and political risks of violating the SALT limits far outweighed the benefits of doing so.

The principal opponents of interim restraint were Caspar Weinberger and Richard Perle. They had long been looking for a way to demonstrate that SALT was cramping U.S. military programs. They wanted to force an American breakout from SALT. The Trident deployment offered an opportunity to accomplish both these objectives.

Like so many other interagency wrangles over arms control, this one ended in a temporary truce and a half-a-loaf compromise in June 1985. The old Poseidon boat would be dismantled, so the United States would stay in compliance with SALT for the time being. But the Administration would also prepare for "proportionate and appropriate" American "responses" to Soviet violations. The plan itself became the object of intense bureaucratic warfare, with the Pentagon civilians pushing for additional submarine ballistic missiles or air-launched cruise missiles—anything that could be done quickly and that would punch through the treaty's subceilings.

Nitze pointed out that none of the more serious of the Soviet violations of SALT entailed going over the subceilings per se. Therefore, the United States should look for measures that would, in Nitze's words, "increase our capabilities but not violate the numerical limits in SALT." Meanwhile, he said, the United States should continue its policy of interim restraint.[3]

The tug-of-war between the Pentagon and the State Department continued well into 1986. By early April, Perle, Weinberger, and their bureaucratic allies, including two who had offices at the State Department building in Foggy Bottom—Edward Rowny, now a nominal but not very influential advisor to Shultz, and Kenneth Adelman, the director of ACDA—had forced the issue to the fore again. Another Trident boat, the U.S.S. *Nevada,* was about to begin sea trials, raising the question of whether to retire two more Poseidons in order to remain under the SALT II subceiling on MIRVed ballistic missile launchers. There was another issue as well. B-52s were being converted into carriers for air-launched cruise missiles (ALCMs). Bombers armed with cruise missiles counted against a separate SALT II subceiling on the aggregate of MIRVed ballistic missile launchers and ALCM carriers; later in the year, the 131st of these B-52 conversions would push the American arsenal over that subceiling unless the Air Force or the Navy took out of service some MIRV launchers either at sea or on land—presumably, additional Poseidon boats or the older, less accurate versions of Minuteman.

The Pentagon wanted the Administration to proceed unrestrained with the Trident and the B-52 ALCM programs, exceeding both SALT II subceilings—and to proclaim publicly in advance its intention to do so. Nitze retorted that if the Pentagon had its way, there would be a backlash in Congress against funding for the President's strategic modernization program and a surge of anti-American sentiment in Western Europe. The Soviets, he said, "would be filled with glee to see us do damage to our relations with our allies and the chances of support for our defense program."

The Joint Chiefs of Staff, now under the chairmanship of Admiral William Crowe, agreed with the State Department, but only passively. Unlike David Jones, who was a holdover from the Carter Administration, Crowe owed his job largely to Weinberger and was not eager to cross him, at least not so early in his tenure as chairman. That was apparent when the well-worn issue of what to do about the Poseidon submarines resurfaced at a National Security Council meeting on April 16. The meeting quickly degenerated into a technical disagreement over how many years of life the old boats had left in them. To strengthen the case for leaving the Poseidons in service after the new Tridents were launched, Weinberger put forward some data that the Navy itself found questionable.

"I'd be very much interested in the view of the military," remarked Shultz dryly. "I haven't had access to military advice."

"Just give me a call," snapped Weinberger, "and *I'll* give you military advice." The secretary of defense was making clear that he spoke for the entire Pentagon, including the Chiefs.

This exchange turned even testier when Weinberger accused the State Department of wanting to "reaffirm" the SALT I and SALT II treaties.

"I've never liked SALT and neither have you, Mr. President," said Weinberger.

"Never liked it at all," agreed Reagan.

Shultz had been distracted by an American bombing raid on Libya a few days before and had come to the meeting ill prepared to defend the department. Nitze spoke up to say that Weinberger was misrepresenting State's position. The department was not trying to reaffirm SALT at all, he said; it was simply recommending that the Administration stick to the policy it had laid down the previous June, reserving the right to undertake "proportionate and appropriate responses" to Soviet violations in due course; the President would be free to break with SALT whenever he wanted and whenever it made sense, but he should not do so now.

Nitze came out of the meeting fuming. He told a colleague he was "shocked and horrified by Weinberger's performance. He has reached new heights of misinformation and dishonest tactics. He fills me with desperation and frustration. He's no better than that other shyster lawyer, that dreadful man Dulles."

Nitze was almost as angry at Adelman, who was routinely siding with the Pentagon civilians. "That son of a bitch behaved unforgivably," Nitze said on returning to the State Department after the meeting. "He was just trying to curry favor where he thinks it will do him some good."

A short time later, Nitze warned the National Security Council staff that this time the President would have to decide clearly and firmly between the State and the Pentagon position. "You can't have a consensus on this one," he said.

Nonetheless, that was exactly what the NSC staff tried to produce—another in a long series of jury-rigged compromises. This time there was a short-term concession to the State Department and a more significant, but at first unpublicized, longer-term fulfillment of Weinberger and Perle's wishes: The Administration would proceed with the dismantlement of two Poseidon submarines. It would do so strictly for economic reasons, not in order to comply with SALT. Later in the year, the United States would finally go over the SALT II limits by deploying ALCM-armed B-52s in excess of what the treaty allowed.

Press leaks and public statements by officials at first concentrated on the Administration's "tentative decision" to retire the old submarines. The Soviet news agency, TASS, crowed over this latest indication that warmongers of the Administration could be pressured by progressive forces into reasonable behavior.

The decision was considered tentative because it was supposedly subject to consultation with the allies. It fell largely to Nitze to carry out those consultations. His role during INF had made him the most respected and trusted member of the Administration in the eyes of the Europeans. However, now, as so often before, he was a messenger bearing bad news about a policy with which he did not fully agree. The allies were clearly relieved by the first part of the decision, on dismantling the submarines. But, just as Nitze had predicted, they were dismayed by the unpublicized second part, that the United States would exceed SALT II later in the year with new ALCM bombers.

Nitze did his best to make his government's policy palatable. "If you go through careful and thorough analysis," he said in London, it would be clear that an American policy of open-ended compliance with SALT was "debilitating," because there would be no planning for future deployments that made military sense in their own right. Nor would continued compliance send the "right signals" to the Soviets in response to their violations, such as Krasnoyarsk. The recoring or drydocking of old Poseidons was uneconomical, so restraint was militarily justifiable in that case. Air-launched cruise missiles, he continued, were a different matter. They were weapons "with practical utility" because they could penetrate Soviet air defenses. Therefore, deploying ALCMs in excess of the SALT II limits made military and economic sense. Besides, doing so was a "reversible violation": It could be undone, either by taking ALCM-carrying B-52s out of service later or by retiring older, less accurate ballistic missiles (since ALCM carriers were covered along with MIRV launchers by a common SALT II subceiling).

Much as they respected the messenger, Nitze's Western European hosts considered his message pure casuistry, and they virtually said as much. Margaret Thatcher expressed directly to Nitze her acute displeasure with Administration policy, then sent a letter of protest to Reagan. At Downing Street and Whitehall, Nitze found himself facing charges that his government was about to violate international law. He grew angry, saying that this was "tendentious nonsense." It offended him and would offend the President, he said, since SALT II was an expired and unratified treaty. "Legally speaking," he said, "there is nothing to violate! If anyone was violating anything, it's the Soviets!"

He was annoyed to find British officials unwilling to accept what he insisted was the "obvious and incontrovertible fact" of Soviet cheating, especially in what he considered the open-and-shut case of the Krasnoyarsk radar.

In Paris, Jean-Bernard Raimond, the former French ambassador to Moscow who had just become foreign minister, remonstrated with Nitze for "surrendering the high moral ground," an accusation that particularly infuriated Nitze, given France's refusal in April to let American bombers overfly its territory on their bombing raid to punish Muammar Khaddafy for his sponsorship of international terrorism. "Is it the French position that unilateral appeasement is the high moral ground?" Nitze replied.

Nitze returned home satisfied that he had won the debate on points but still deeply worried about the politics of the American decision to break with SALT. At a minimum, he felt, the decision should be kept very quiet, and, he hoped, reconsidered later in the year. He was upset at Perle, Adelman, and Rowny for wanting "to make a big noise and create a lot of trouble with Congress and the allies."[4]

The big noise came in a formal presidential statement on May 27 announcing that the United States was formally discarding the "no undercut" interim-restraint policy that had been in effect since 1981. The next day, Weinberger announced triumphantly, "We are no longer bound by that flawed agreement."

In a press conference on June 11, Reagan seemed to backtrack slightly, suggesting that the decision might yet be reversed. There were sighs of relief at the State Department and mutterings of protest at the Pentagon. The White House spokesman, Larry Speakes, came forward to clarify: "The SALT treaty no longer exists." Reagan then backed him up: "Yes, I think you can trust what Larry Speakes said."

Shultz, like Nitze, defended the decision in public, to visiting foreigners and on television. Privately, the secretary of state was close to despair. "I have no influence at the White House," he told one visitor.

Some members of the Administration believed that the entire issue of whether to remain bound by SALT had arisen because of an artificial deadline. They pointed out that, left to its own devices and given its shortage of crews, the Navy would have preferred to take additional Poseidons out of service as ballistic missile submarines, retiring them or converting them to other missions, so that the United States could have an all-Trident ballistic missile fleet. Similarly, the Air Force's plans called eventually for only ninety B-52s as "standoff cruise missile platforms" that would fire from outside Soviet air space, while the new supersonic American bomber, the B-1, would serve as a "penetrating bomber" that would run the gauntlet of Soviet air defenses to reach targets deep inside the U.S.S.R. The pressure to deploy the 131st ALCM-carrying B-52 was, in the words of one official, "utterly arbitrary: it's a SALT-buster and nothing else."

Quick and Dirty

The SALT-busters continued their campaign on other fronts as well. Caspar Weinberger and Richard Perle seemed to want to break out of the SALT II treaty's limits on offensive weapons in 1986 in part to clear the way for an American breakout from the SALT I antiballistic missile treaty's restrictions on strategic defense in 1987.

Continued American compliance with the ABM treaty was even more controversial within the Reagan Administration than continued compliance with the offensive agreements of SALT. As Paul Nitze repeatedly pointed out, the SALT II treaty had little effect on the Administration's strategic modernization program for America's arsenal of offensive weapons. New submarines like the Trident, new ICBMs like the MX, and new bombers like the B-1 could all go forward even under a policy of interim restraint.

The Strategic Defense Initiative was different. Its essential and presidentially proclaimed purpose was not just a scientific-technological breakthrough but a strategic breakout of the most spectacular kind—a breakout from the confines of traditional deterrence. Therefore, SDI was, by intent and by definition, on a collision course with the ABM treaty. The question was, Would the collision come sooner or later? Weinberger and Perle argued, in effect, the sooner the better.

Like most members of the government familiar with the complexity of the military and political relationship between the superpowers, Perle had, at first, been dismayed by SDI. He was contemptuous of the very idea of an impregnable shield, calling it "the product of millions of American teenagers putting quarters into video machines." When the program was first announced in 1983, he initially feared that SDI would distract attention and resources from the strategic modernization program, giving the public and Congress an excuse to oppose the weapons that SDI was supposed to render impotent and obsolete. Telling the American people that there might be a deus ex machina that would save them not just from the threat of nuclear war but from the toil and trouble and expense of competing with the Soviet Union in the acquisition of raw power would, he later recalled fearing, "only confuse the issue."

Perle had worried about what the President might do ever since he learned about the critical meeting in February 1983 with the Joint Chiefs. "The pivotal event in Reagan's mind was the presentation by the Chiefs," Perle later said. "That was where the President said, 'Isn't it better to save lives than to avenge them?' When I heard that, I knew it was locked in. I was one of those who was not eager."

The incident was, to him, further evidence of the limited strategic wisdom and unlimited sycophancy of the uniformed military leadership: the Chiefs must have been humoring their commander-in-chief, telling him what they knew he wanted to hear. Perle assumed that William Clark, then the national security advisor, was the main direct influence on the President. He did not know fully about McFarlane's role or his secret agenda for arms control. Had he known, he would probably have been even more opposed to the Star Wars speech.

Perle was in Portugal with Weinberger at a NATO meeting in March 1983 when he discovered what the President was about to do. He spent much of the night on the phone with Washington trying to change, or at least delay, the speech. He was so busy trying to talk the White House out of going ahead with the speech that he never told his boss, Weinberger, what was about to happen. As a result, Weinberger went through the meeting and left for home without warning the allies that, in a brief burst of presidential rhetoric, the United States was about to call into question the foundations of deterrence. "I paid a heavy price for that night on the phone," Perle said later.[5]

Throughout 1983 and most of 1984, Perle kept his distance from SDI. When the subject came up in meetings, he smiled indulgently and waited for it to pass. By the end of 1984, however, a number of developments brought about a change in his attitude. His boss, Weinberger, came under pressure from conservative Republicans in the Senate to declare himself a true believer in the program. Weinberger had said he was in favor of continuing SDI research. That was not good enough for Senators Malcolm Wallop of Wyoming and Pete Wilson of California and the other self-styled "Friends of SDI," some of whom were members of the Laser Lobby, which had been instrumental in promoting the program before the President's Star Wars speech in 1983. They told Weinberger that they would not fund a mere research program; they wanted to see evidence of Pentagon commitment to making the research pay off, to fulfilling the President's dream in all its glory. Weinberger began to see gung-ho support for the most ambitious form of SDI as a kind of truth test, a way of demonstrating his fealty to the President and of shoring up his natural constituency on Capitol Hill.

Meanwhile, Perle had begun to take SDI seriously—not as a means of achieving the dream of a nuclear-weapons-free world, in which he did not believe, but as a means of advancing a variety of objectives in which he did believe. He realized that there was no need to take the President too literally. Like others in the government, Perle saw an opportunity in SDI to promote what he wanted the Administration to achieve. It became clear to him that McFarlane and Nitze were trying to use SDI to make progress in arms control; Perle set about to use the program to spike the wheels of the arms-control process so that the cause he cared about—unfettered military and political competition—could go forward.

"You don't influence Presidents by running smack into them," Perle once observed. Following his own advice, he made it appear that in adapting SDI to his own purposes, he was moving with the President. He stopped disparaging the people working on SDI as a bunch of kids in a video arcade. Instead, he began making uncharacteristically euphoric statements like "Spring is breaking out all over. It's the young people who are working on this program. You almost get the sense that they're relieved to be working on defense rather than lethal weapons. These are weapons of life." He turned interagency meetings into pep rallies for the program, delivering upbeat reports on the progress to date and the promise of spectacular accomplishments to come.

President Reagan intended for SDI to be a revolution, an overturning of the status quo. The status quo included SALT, which in turn included the ABM treaty. Perle had never hidden his distaste for the treaty or his determination to see it undone. "I'm sorry to say that [the ABM treaty] does not expire. That is one of its many defects," he said in congressional testimony on February 23, 1982, over a year before Reagan's Star Wars speech. "I would hope that were we to conclude that the only way we could defend our own strategic forces was by deploying defense, we would not hesitate to renegotiate the treaty and, failing Soviet acquiescence in that renegotiation, I would hope that we would abrogate the treaty." A month later, also in testimony, he argued that the "preclusion of strategic defense" in SALT I "is, in my judgment, destabilizing. It was a mistake in 1972, and the sooner we face up to the implications of recognizing that mistake the better." Four years later, on June 3, 1986, he said publicly, "I'd be prepared to replace the treaty with a weapon system."[6]

Yet in these and other statements, Perle revealed the fundamental difference between his idea of SDI and the President's. "Defending our own strategic forces" was emphatically not what Ronald Reagan had in mind for SDI. George Keyworth, the President's science advisor at the time of the Star Wars speech, quoted Reagan as saying to a group of aides in the Oval Office just before he gave the speech, "If there is one thing I do *not* mean by this, gentlemen, it is some kind of a string of terminal defenses around this country."[7] Nor, in Reagan's view, should SDI be seen as a "weapon system" at all. He frequently corrected others when they referred to it as such. He wanted to defend the entire United States and to do so with a system that transcended the very idea of weaponry and that made weapons themselves superfluous.

Perle had never shared that hope. "If I had had my way," he said, "I'd have had [the White House] delay [the original Star Wars] speech by six months. That way we could have spelled out privately to the Soviets what we had in mind. We could also have developed congressional support. One result might have been that we could have said straight out that an early SDI would be too weak and porous to render nuclear weapons impotent and obsolete."[8] But such a system would, in his view, still be desirable because it would, in the jargon, "enhance the survivability" of the American deterrent and "complicate" an enemy attack.

Perle eventually came to see SDI as an ideal instrument for rendering not ICBMs but the ABM treaty itself impotent and obsolete. All that Perle and like-minded officials had to do was play up the inherent contradiction between SDI and the ABM treaty. It was their way of striking back against Paul Nitze's strategic concept and three criteria.

Under the strategic concept, SDI should not be deployed for at least ten years, and even then only if the system met the onerous standards of effectiveness, survivability, and cost-effectiveness at the margins. Under Perle's scheme for early deployment SDI could proceed much sooner, without having to meet what Perle called "the killer criteria" (meaning that they would have the effect of killing SDI).

Perle and others began explaining that whatever millennial vision the President might have for an Astrodome that would protect the entire free world sometime in the twenty-first century—and whatever dazzling experiments the Pentagon might want to carry out to prove that it could bounce lasers off mirrors in space to destroy enemy missiles during their boost or midcourse phase—what SDI really meant, in the near term, was defense of ballistic missile silos, sometimes referred to as ballistic missile defense (BMD). BMD was a latter-day version of ABM, augmented perhaps with some space-based sensors and a first line of defense utilizing newer technologies, but still heavily reliant on ground-based interceptors and having as its goal the protection of critical American military targets, not cities.

In narrowing the scope of the program, Perle had to be careful not to commit too blatant a heresy against the President's dream. Perle's office was often assigned to draft letters for Weinberger to answer pro-SDI congressmen who demanded to know whether the program was still designed to meet the President's objective of saving American lives or "merely" defending missile silos. The approved reply was that SDI would, in its early phases, "protect American lives by enhancing deterrence."

On this issue as on others, the Pentagon civilians' principal allies in Foggy Bottom were Edward Rowny and Kenneth Adelman. In July 1985, Adelman created a minor transatlantic uproar by telling an international gathering of experts at the Ditchley Park Foundation in England that SDI was basically intended to protect ICBM silos and that the rationale of defending the entire population was part of the public relations of the program.

At the same meeting, Perle was represented by his deputy, Frank Gaffney, a young political appointee who had shouldered aside Frank Miller and taken over responsibility for the "SDI account" in Perle's office once Perle himself began to engage on the issue. At Ditchley Park, Gaffney was asked about the now-famous three criteria, particularly "cost-effectiveness at the margin." He responded airily that Paul Nitze did not speak for the Administration on all subjects. When Nitze heard about this comment, he was furious and told Gaffney so in no uncertain terms. Gaffney smiled and replied, "Paul, you're the one who taught us all to keep fighting on these things."[9]

On September 29, 1985, Perle was on NBC's "Meet the Press." Another panelist was Albert Gore, Jr., now a senator and still a leading congressional expert on arms control. Gore pressed Perle hard on whether he was using SDI as a stalking horse for silo defense. Perle dodged the issue on the air, but in discussion afterward he confirmed that that was exactly what he was doing. The goal, he said, should be to "bring SDI down to earth: in the real world, you've got to look at what you can really do."

A month later, when Weinberger appeared in closed session before the Senate Foreign Relations Committee, Gore and another Democrat, John Kerry of Massachusetts, interrogated the secretary of defense on whether SDI would meet the cost-effectiveness criterion. Weinberger replied that calculating and applying such a criterion would be unworkable, but that he could not imagine defense being more expensive than the offense necessary to counter it. Others' imaginations led them to conclude just the opposite: There was far more reason to expect that the advantage would remain with strategic offense—and with countermeasures against strategic defense.

So Perle conceded. In his own appearance before a closed-door session of a subcommittee of the Senate Armed Services Committee on November 6, 1985, he delivered an even bolder repudiation of the cost-effectiveness criterion. Even if it cost $100 billion to put up SDI and only $80 billion for the Soviets to counter it, he said, the United States should proceed with the program because it would complicate the calculation of attack. Besides, Perle continued, the Soviets would never spend the $80 billion in anti-SDI offensive countermeasures anyway. Why was that? asked Senator Gore. Because, Perle replied, the Soviets will always know that the United States would never launch a first strike.

Implicit in this assertion was a corollary of the malevolence factor: Not only were the Americans the good guys and the Soviets the bad guys, but the Soviets themselves accepted the distinction—they *knew* they were the bad guys. The basic problem with the ABM treaty was that it prevented the white hats from protecting themselves from the black hats. During the extraordinarily acrimonious NSC meeting on April 16, 1986—at which Weinberger rudely rebuffed George Shultz's attempt to learn the uniformed military's views on continued compliance with SALT II—the secretary of defense was adamant that whatever was said about other SALT agreements, there should be no mention whatsoever of the ABM treaty. He did not want the NSC even implicitly to endorse the idea that the United States was constrained by its treaty obligations from proceeding vigorously with SDI.

While it was of indefinite duration, the ABM treaty was subject to a review every five years. The third such review was due to begin in 1987. That would be an opportunity for the Pentagon civilians to press for scrapping the treaty. They could make that case on two grounds: Soviet noncompliance with the treaty (exemplified primarily by the Krasnoyarsk radar) and the breakdown in offensive arms control, to which the ABM treaty had always been linked.

In 1986 General Richard Ellis, the chief American representative at the Standing Consultative Commission, came under mounting pressure to hammer away at the issue of Krasnoyarsk. Perle and others had been complaining about Ellis for some time. He was, they said, too inclined to negotiate rather than prosecute. As their dispute with the State Department over interim restraint came to a head back in Washington, they stepped up their attacks on Ellis in Geneva, accusing him of being ''wishy-washy'' and of failing to follow instructions, which were, in Perle's phrase, ''to really stick it to the Russians.'' That sentiment, rather than any real attachment to SDI in its own right, seemed to explain Perle's attitude toward the issue of strategic defense and his deft manipulation of the issue in the second Reagan term.

In mid-1986, Perle went public with the early-deployment silo-defense rationale for SDI, saying at a *Time* magazine conference in Washington on June 3:

I heard the President's speech, as you did, and Presidents give expression to long-term hopes and dreams that can't always be realized in the short term. In my view—and I expect we would all agree on this— the rendering of nuclear weapons impotent and obsolete is not a short-term proposition and it may not be possible in the long term, but there is something to be said for a vision that goes beyond what is immediately feasible.

There are lesser goals, more immediate goals, more tractable problems to be solved. Among those is the defense not of the nation as a whole, not of every city and every person in it, but the defense of America's capacity to retaliate, of our critical defense installations, ballistic missiles, command-and-control facilities, facilities that support elements of our deterrent other than the land-based element. And a partially effective defense, let's say a 50-percent-effective defense, could make a significant and I think vital stabilizing contribution to the security of this country, adjusting the strategic balance so that it represents a proper relationship between offensive and defensive forces.

That summer a document circulating in Perle's office recommended a redefinition of SDI: Instead of billing the program as a way to "transcend deterrence with defense," said the paper, the Administration should explain the purpose and promise of SDI as "using defense to reinforce deterrence for the foreseeable future."

Statements like these—whether public or classified—were a far cry not only from Reagan's explicit disavowal of terminal defense in March 1983 but also from what Weinberger said at a press conference on July 1, 1986: "Terminal defense—that is, defense solely of our military assets, sites, or missile silos—is not and never has been the goal of SDI." Perle and officials in his office were reminded that any early-deployment scheme must be clearly "on the path" to fulfilling the President's objective of comprehensive defense.

Perle seemed unfazed by public contradictions and private remonstrations by his superiors. He knew what he was doing: He was establishing the rationale for rigorous prosecution of the competition with the Soviet Union, free from what he saw as the miasmal distractions of arms control. If SDI served to enhance the survivability of America's deterrent forces, it would not advance the cause of eliminating the need for those forces. If both sides had silo defense, the effect, in the view of proponents, might be to decrease the ability of an attacker's warheads to carry out—while increasing the ability of the other side's forces to survive—a first strike. Theoreticians might debate whether such would indeed be a desirable and "stabilizing" outcome, but it would certainly be very different from the nuclear-free world that Ronald Reagan wanted SDI to make possible. It would certainly be very different from the arms-control "sting" that Robert McFarlane had in mind.

"The Pentagon," McFarlane remarked in frustration, "had to be dragged kicking and screaming into SDI. Now they're treating it like the Holy Grail."

Nitze, meanwhile, had been nurturing the same frustration. "If these guys have their way," he said of the Pentagon enthusiasts for the program, "SDI will lose all connection with rational analysis and planning. It will take on a life of its own; everything else will go by the board."

Fine Print

Arms control is a branch of international law. The superpowers haggle over treaties that are submitted to their legislatures for ratification. The disposition of billions of dollars and rubles in military spending, as well as thousands of megatons of destructive capability, depends on the skill and thoroughness with which diplomats compose the dense legalese of these agreements. During the seventies, attorneys were prominent on the American side of the negotiating table in Geneva. Gerard Smith, Cyrus Vance, Paul Warnke, Ralph Earle, John Rhinelander—these were just a few of the lawyers who played key roles in SALT. Critics of the enterprise often complained that the lawyers had "taken over," and that they were so concerned with practicing their trade and closing deals that they overlooked the unscrupulous nature of their adversary; as a result, their client, the United States of America, was too often gulled and cheated. The Soviets, it was often said, brought to the negotiations the mentality not of lawyers but of soldiers and propagandists; they were looking for advantage, not equity— for loopholes, not precision.

It was neither coincidental nor surprising that when the Reagan Administration came into office, it appointed far fewer lawyers in the upper reaches of its arms-control policymaking apparatus. For example, Edward Rowny, who succeeded Warnke and Earle as chief strategic arms negotiator, was a retired Army general who frequently expressed his contempt for "the legal types."

It was part of Richard Perle's brilliance and success as an infighter that he was able, in 1985, to use the legalistic nature of arms control against the process itself. He took what should have been an arcane footnote to the negotiating history of SALT in the early seventies and turned it into a suspenseful, tumultuous, and potentially critical chapter in the story of START and SDI in the mid- and late 1980s.

George Shultz and Paul Nitze came home from their meeting with Andrei Gromyko in Geneva in January 1985 having impressed on the Soviet foreign minister the principle that however the issues of strategic offense and defense might be resolved "in their interrelationship" as part of an eventual agreement with the U.S.S.R., SDI research must go forward. That was not good enough for Perle. He set about, in the months after the Shultz-Gromyko meeting, to establish the proposition that in addition to conducting research, the United States should consider itself free to develop and test prototypes of a space-based defensive system. It could, in other words, do anything short of deployment of a fully operational system. He based his case on what was called the "new," the "broad," or the "permissive" interpretation of the ABM treaty of 1972.

Article V, paragraph 1 of the treaty consisted of one sentence: "Each Party undertakes not to develop, test, or deploy ABM systems or components which are sea-based, air-based, space-based, or mobile land-based." According to the broad interpretation, that sentence quite simply did not mean what it said. As they pulled out the stops in the program, SDI enthusiasts were already saying, "These are not components we'll be testing, they are subcomponents; nor are they tests—they are experiments." Thanks to the broad interpretation, they could now also say, "And besides, testing isn't prohibited anyway."

The most obvious, yet most heatedly denied, purpose of the broad interpretation was to make SDI even more of an obstacle to arms control. Another, related purpose was to drive an extra nail into the coffin of SALT. In their reading of the ABM treaty, Perle and his colleagues had "discovered" yet another case of perfidy on the part of the Soviet Union and gullibility on the part of the perpetrators of détente: The Americans who brought SALT I to the Senate in 1972 had been played for fools; so, therefore, had the senators who ratified it. The list of suckers included not only Richard Nixon and Henry Kissinger, but also Paul Nitze and even Henry Jackson.

Just as the Nitze criteria had been around for some time, in the thinking and statements of officials like Frank Miller, so the broad interpretation of the ABM treaty had its antecedents in the tangled and largely hidden history of interagency deliberations going back to previous Administrations. Research and development of exotic ABMs, such as chemical lasers, predated Star Wars; so, therefore, did the concern of government officials over whether these projects were legal. During the Carter Administration, lawyers and technical experts drafting "arms control impact statements"—i.e., reports on whether various military programs might contravene or jeopardize various agreements—wrestled with the issue of what exactly the ABM treaty meant with regard to exotic ABMs.

Paul Nitze had once been drawn into that debate himself. He was an authoritative witness, since he and his Soviet counterpart, Alexander Shchukin, had devoted much of their time in SALT I to negotiating the provisions on systems "based on other physical principles." Early in the Carter Administration, when Nitze was working out of his office at the System Planning Corporation in Arlington, he participated in a correspondence among three former SALT I negotiators—the chairman of the delegation, Gerard Smith, the executive secretary, Raymond Garthoff, and the delegation's chief lawyer, John Rhinelander—as well as Donald Brennan, an expert at the Hudson Institute, a conservative think tank, and Abraham Becker, a strategist at the RAND Corporation. At that time, Becker was conducting an analysis of the possibilities of a Soviet breakout from the ABM treaty. He was concerned that ambiguities in the treaty language might be exploited by Moscow.

In a letter to Brennan on July 8, 1977, Nitze refuted Becker: "It was our clear intention that [the SALT I treaty] bar" development and testing of any mobile system that was supposed to "intercept" or "counter" strategic warheads "in flight trajectory." That meant exotic, future systems as well as traditional ABMs. Development and testing of such systems were banned. Nitze conceded that the treaty still needed "cleaning up and mutual agreement" in a number of spots, particularly in its failure to define "development." He recalled that the American understanding of that word was "the engineering development phase, the only phase where there was much chance of monitoring compliance."

There was, however, no doubt in his mind what he and his colleagues had wanted to do—and what he believed they had succeeded in doing: They had intended to ban the development and testing of mobile exotic ABM systems, especially space-based ones. Some of the ambiguity and imprecision in the negotiating record and the final draft of the treaty was the result of *American* reluctance to provide the Soviets with hints about the nature of the Pentagon's secret experiments with lasers from fixed, land-based sites.

In his letter to Brennan and for years afterward, Nitze referred to the job of accurately and usefully interpreting the ABM treaty as "a work of supererogation." He drew the word from his knowledge of theology; it means the performance of good deeds beyond what the Church requires for salvation. He was saying that given the circumstances under which the American negotiators were operating, including the constraints imposed by Washington as well as the obstacles posed by Moscow, SALT I, if not of saintly quality, was at least a piece of negotiation, draftsmanship, and subsequent interpretation of which he could remain proud.*

One point was clear in the otherwise murky thicket: To interpret the ABM treaty as applying only to technologies that existed in the early seventies was to diminish and eventually nullify its value as those technologies gave way to new ones. Yet the treaty was supposed to be of unlimited duration; therefore, it must, by definition, cover new technologies.

A week after receiving Nitze's letter, Brennan wrote Rhinelander capitulating in the face of what he called a "detailed, persuasive, and definitive" defense of the traditional interpretation, "not to mention the essential concurrence of Smith, Nitze, and Garthoff."

"Any further insistence that the Treaty does not necessarily ban the de-

---

*In the dispute over interpretation, the key provisions of the ABM treaty were Articles II and V. Article II defined an ABM system as anything to shoot down enemy missiles. It cited for illustration those systems "currently consisting of" ABM interceptor missiles, launchers, and radars— i.e., technologies that existed at the time. Article V banned the development and testing, as well as deployment, of "sea-based, air-based, space-based, or mobile land-based" ABM systems. But it did not make clear whether that ban applied only to systems based on old, 1970s technology ("currently consisting of," etc.) or to future systems as well. However, Agreed Statement D, which did anticipate the development of ABM systems "based on other physical principles" that might be "created in the future," referred to the treaty's ban on *deployment* of various ABM systems. While the U.S. negotiators understood Agreed Statement D to prohibit what was implicitly prohibited by Article III—i.e., deployment of fixed, land-based exotics—they also believed it stated a general principle that was equally applicable to Article V, the ban on development and testing of mobile and space-based exotics.

This correspondence, conducted in the late spring and summer of 1977 and involving Brennan, Nitze, Becker, Smith, Garthoff, Rhinelander, and Herbert Scoville of the Arms Control Association, is in the Association's files in Washington. For a review of the 1971 negotiations and Nitze's role in them, see, in chapter 6, the section titled "Exotics," pp. 125–30.

velopment of (among others) space-based exotic ABM systems," wrote Brennan, "would have to be reckoned willful, indeed obstinate, stupidity." Or it would have to be reckoned a willful, obstinate, but ingenious attempt to find an escape clause in a contract.

Early in the first Reagan term, when the perennial question arose within the bureaucracy of what sort of R&D the ABM treaty permitted, it was initially decided to leave well enough alone. Administration policymakers and spokesmen accepted the traditional interpretation, which effectively prohibited advanced development and testing of exotic space-based ABMs. Even after the President's Star Wars speech provided a powerful impulse for accelerated R&D on exotic systems, the Administration still hewed to the old line for another two years. The traditional interpretation was implicit in the President's assurance to Margaret Thatcher in December 1984 that SDI was a research program to be conducted in compliance with the ABM treaty.

Paul Nitze had a hand in preparing an interagency report on how SDI would be restricted by the Administration's commitment to remain in compliance with the ABM treaty. He personally assured Congress on March 15, 1985, that these restrictions would dictate Administration policy. Meanwhile, the director of the program, Lieutenant General James Abrahamson, said he could "live with" the ABM treaty for the time being, but that "there clearly will come a time when we enter the development phase, and the development phase will require much more direct testing . . . we will have to have a modified treaty in some way in order to proceed."

As late as April 1985, a Defense Department report described SDI as "a broad research program . . . conducted in a manner fully consistent with all U.S. treaty obligations." An appendix said that a "decision to proceed" from research to development "would almost certainly require modifications to the ABM treaty." The conventional way to modify a treaty was to renegotiate it with the other signatory and then, with the advice and consent of the Senate, to attach the appropriate amendments.

The Reagan Administration, however, was not eager to conduct yet another negotiation with the Soviets or, for that matter, to enter a testy and perhaps losing round of "consultations" with the allies and Congress. One possible way of short-circuiting the usual process would be to reinterpret the treaty unilaterally—to announce to the world that the document meant something quite different from what had long been understood by all parties.

The consensus in favor of the traditional interpretation had already begun to fall apart within the Administration once George Shultz and Andrei Gromyko met in Geneva in January 1985. With that meeting it became apparent that arms-control negotiations were about to resume and that SDI would be a central and contentious issue.

T. K. Jones, who had worked for Nitze in SALT and fanned his concerns about the Soviet civil defense program in 1976, was now an official of the Pentagon's office of research and engineering. Jones was one of those who had grown restless with the narrow interpretation. He complained in a number of meetings that the ABM treaty applied a double standard, tying the hands of the United States more than those of the Soviet Union. He was looking, he said, for "greater flexibility of interpretation." After listening to a member of the Defense Department's legal staff explain why the narrow interpretation was justified, Jones snapped, "I thought you were *our* lawyer!"

It was a telling comment. Just as technical experts in the government were loath to question the scientific feasibility or strategic wisdom of eventual SDI deployment, it was risky for government lawyers to argue the case that a full-scale development and testing program would violate the ABM treaty. They were often reminded, especially at the Pentagon, that the President of the United States was their ultimate client and that their job was to serve him, in effect, by telling him what he wanted to hear.

An example of this occurred when Donald Hicks, a nuclear physicist and senior executive at the Northrop Corporation, was nominated to be under secretary of defense for research and engineering. He would be directly involved with SDI experiments of various kinds. There was already concern on Capitol Hill that the program might soon come into conflict with the ABM treaty. Therefore, during Hicks's confirmation hearings on July 25, 1985, Senator Carl Levin, a Michigan Democrat who was skeptical about SDI, questioned Hicks closely on whether SDI would be conducted within the terms of the ABM treaty. Hicks's reply was reassuring. "SDI is not a development program," he said, "but a fully compliant research program. Research on ABM systems and components is permitted. The objective of the research is to provide a basis for an informed decision in the future on whether to proceed with development and to hedge against a very aggressive research and development program being conducted within the Soviet Union. I believe that it is possible to meet this objective within the framework of the ABM treaty."

At a Pentagon meeting occasioned by Hicks's testimony, Fred Iklé asked, "Why not give them [the senators] an answer that fits *our* interests?"

The senior Defense Department international lawyer, John McNeill, a veteran of SALT and the Arms Control and Disarmament Agency, replied, "Because it also suits our interests to obey the law and honor our treaty obligations."

However, Iklé and Perle had recently hired a lawyer of their own, one who was more likely to reach a finding that supported their case. This was Philip Kunsberg, a former New York assistant district attorney. He had been involved in legal battles against pornography and organized crime and then also worked in the general counsel's office at the CIA, but he had little background in arms control.

As Perle later recalled, "I asked Phil Kunsberg to take a fresh look at the treaty and tell us what it actually said." Kunsberg concluded that the Soviets had neither unambiguously nor consistently agreed to the narrow or restrictive interpretation. Therefore, that interpretation was a unilateral American understanding, not a binding, bilateral one. Hence the United States was free to proceed with testing, development, and perhaps even deployment of SDI if it so desired. Perle said he "almost fell off the chair" when presented with Kunsberg's report. The matter then came before Abraham Sofaer, a former federal judge on the U.S. district court in New York whom Shultz had just brought to the State Department as legal advisor. In that capacity, "Judge" Sofaer, as he was still often called, quickly established a record of interpreting international law to support forceful, unilateral action by the United States. "Abe Sofaer is a great New York lawyer," the state's governor, Mario Cuomo, once remarked. "If they tell him 'Make it legal, Abe,' he'll make it legal."*

Presented with the broad interpretation of the ABM treaty, Sofaer made SDI legal.

Perle was now all the more gleeful. It was one thing to have support from an obscure lawyer within the Pentagon; it was quite another suddenly to have on the Pentagon's side the senior legal expert in Foggy Bottom. "The State Department," said Perle, "ran to Sofaer and said, '[The Department of Defense] has come up with this crazy interpretation. Tell us it ain't so.' They were stunned when he came up with a contrary opinion. You had two smart lawyers [Sofaer and Kunsberg] sit down with this thing, and they found it didn't say what everyone said it said. Immediately it was spread around that I'd known Sofaer intimately and that he was my plant at the State Department. I'd met him exactly once, at a dinner party in New York."[10]

Sofaer consulted on the issue of interpretation with Nitze, who was the only member of the Administration who had been directly involved at a senior level in the negotiation of the ABM treaty. Sofaer did not merely seek Nitze's opinion; instead, he set about—successfully—to influence it.

Sofaer did not dispute what the U.S. government—or, for that matter, what Nitze personally—had intended in SALT I. Instead, he hammered away at what Nitze himself acknowledged to be the "fuzzy spots" in the text of the treaty and in the accompanying, though classified, negotiating record. For example, while Victor Karpov may have indicated on September 15, 1971, that the Soviet side agreed to ban the development and testing of space-based exotics, Kunsberg and Sofaer claimed that the previous and

---

*It was Sofaer, for example, who provided the legal justification for "the Shultz doctrine" of using military force against nations harboring terrorists. He also supported the Administration's decision to deny the jurisdiction of the International Court of Justice after the court ruled against U.S. backing for the Nicaraguan Contras.

subsequent negotiating record was rife with Soviet contradictions and re-
tractions of that agreement. Therefore, according to their reading of the
record, Karpov's September 1971 statement—a key piece of evidence in
favor of the narrow interpretation—had little standing.

Perle and Kunsberg went so far as to argue that the ABM treaty did not
ban even deployment of exotic ABMs. On that point (sometimes called the
"broader than broad" interpretation), Nitze was certain they were wrong,
and he persuaded Fred Iklé to overrule Perle. But on the question of development and testing, Nitze initially wavered and eventually ended up agreeing
with Sofaer, lending his prestige to the broad interpretation. Nitze became
convinced that despite what he and the other American negotiators believed
they had accomplished in SALT I, Sofaer was right: The Soviets had never
unambiguously agreed to a provision banning the development and testing
of space-based exotic ABMs; therefore, no such ban was established by the
treaty.

It was puzzling to many of Nitze's associates then and for years afterward
why he would let his opinion be changed by a newcomer to subjects that
Nitze himself had lived and breathed for decades. The answer, in part, was
that Sofaer was—as Mario Cuomo said—a skillful jurist and advocate. He
may not have been an expert in the arcane field of arms control, but he knew
contract law; he could find and exploit the soft spots in the small print of a
document.

Paul Nitze, while impressively knowledgeable in a number of fields, was
susceptible to the persuasive powers of real experts. Edward Teller had
convinced Nitze in 1949 that he knew how to detonate a thermonuclear explosion before he really did know how. The worst-case scenarists from the Pentagon and CIA had convinced him that the Soviet arsenal was bigger than it
really was in 1950. T. K. Jones had persuaded him in 1976 that the Soviet
civil defense program meant that the Kremlin was preparing to wage nuclear
war against the United States. Similarly, Abraham Sofaer now persuaded
Nitze that the ABM treaty had been the object of a thirteen-year-old misunderstanding on Nitze's own part as well as everyone else's. From the Soviet
standpoint, said Sofaer, it was not a misunderstanding at all—but a dodge.

Sofaer presented his memorandum on the issue to Shultz and Nitze on
Thursday, October 3, 1985. It happened to be the thirteenth anniversary of
the day when the ABM treaty had formally come into force. To mark the
occasion, six former Democratic and Republican secretaries of defense released a statement urging both sides to stop "further erosion of the treaty."
The issue of how much SDI activity was permissible was becoming more
urgent and controversial in public as well as in the dark recesses of the
bureaucracy.

The next day there was a meeting at the White House of a high-level body known as the Senior Arms Control Policy Group.* The principal item on the agenda was the ABM treaty and its implications for SDI. The office of the secretary of defense, emboldened by a legal opinion from the State Department, made the case for the broad interpretation.

Robert McFarlane, the new national security advisor, was in the chair. He later recalled that as he listened to the Pentagon brief on behalf of the broad interpretation, three considerations occurred to him. All were tactical. One concerned his plan for manipulating and outflanking the Pentagon; the other two dealt with his plan for a sting operation against the Kremlin:

(1) The Defense Department and the SDI Organization were pressing hard for a development-and-testing program that might eventually have strained the traditional interpretation of the ABM treaty. McFarlane was hoping that by ''buying onto the broader interpretation,'' he could co-opt and at the same time maneuver around the Pentagon civilians, making it look as though he were on their side. That way, he might be in a better position to argue that the Pentagon and SDI Organization should ''cool it'' in their campaign for what was sometimes called a ''hurry-up'' program of ''demonstrations,'' or treaty-busting tests, lest such a program provoke a damaging public and congressional debate.

(2) The President's popularity was high. His first summit meeting with Gorbachev was scheduled the following month in Geneva. McFarlane hoped that the Administration's promulgation of the permissive interpretation would ''lay down a marker,'' warning the Soviets that the opportunity to negotiate reductions in offense in exchange for restrictions on defense ''was a train leaving the station and they'd better get on board before it was too late.'' The permissive interpretation, said McFarlane, was ''something on which the U.S. could make concessions down the road in exchange for Soviet concessions.'' In other words, like SDI itself, the broad interpretation was bait for the sting. In effect, it was to be another bargaining chip.

(3) The permissive interpretation might also help induce Reagan to go along with the deal that McFarlane hoped the Administration would eventually reach with Gorbachev. The more development and testing that were allowed under such a deal, the easier it would be to persuade the President that his cherished program was still alive.

Taken together, these three points led McFarlane to ''let the Pentagon have its head'' in arguing that the broad interpretation should be the new basis for U.S. policy.[11] He was all the more inclined to do so, since no one spoke up forcefully against the Pentagon during the meeting on October 4.

---

*This body had been known as the SACPG (pronounced ''Sack Pig''), but that was changed to the less colorful acronym SACG, or ''Sack Gee,'' when the word ''Policy'' was dropped from its name.

Kenneth Adelman proclaimed himself to be "on the fifty-yard line," even though the Arms Control and Disarmament Agency's chief lawyer, Thomas Graham, had argued strenuously in favor of the narrow interpretation. Like the Pentagon's McNeill, who had tangled with T. K. Jones over the issue, Graham was a veteran of SALT, so his views were suspect among the Reaganauts.

Nitze had come to the meeting with a memo to pass around the room. It said that the legal issue of how the treaty should be interpreted was open to debate but that it would be politically unwise to reopen the issue after all these years without extensive consultations with the Congress and the allies. However, when he saw how aggressive the Pentagon was in pressing its case, and how little challenge there was from McFarlane or anyone else, he decided not to distribute his memo.

That night after the meeting Nitze lay in bed, unable to sleep, worrying that the new interpretation would put the Administration—and Nitze himself—in an exceedingly awkward position with those members of Congress and European allies whom he had reassured earlier in the year on the basis of the old interpretation. Perhaps, he thought to himself, he had been remiss in not flagging his concerns at the meeting. He decided that the following Monday he would circulate a cautionary memo after all. There was still, he felt, plenty of time for cooler heads to prevail.

He was wrong. Two days after the meeting at the White House, on Sunday, October 6, McFarlane was on "Meet the Press." In response to probing questions about the compatability of SDI with the ABM treaty from Robert Kaiser, an editor of the *Washington Post* and a specialist in Soviet-American relations, McFarlane went public with the new interpretation. "Only deployment [of SDI] is foreclosed," he said. The ABM treaty "does indeed sanction research, testing, and development of these new systems." The language of the pact "provides that research on new physical principles or other physical principles is authorized, as is testing and development."

If what McFarlane said remained Administration policy, the ABM treaty would leave SDI virtually unconstrained and an agreement with the Soviets all the harder to negotiate. As with his part in instigating the President's Star Wars speech unveiling SDI itself, McFarlane's public endorsement of the broad interpretation, which seemed puzzling at the time, in retrospect looked too clever by half. He had played directly into Perle's hands.

So, by his acquiescence, had Paul Nitze. He was furious, at himself as well as at McFarlane. He fired a memo over to the White House warning that there might be hell to pay with Congress and with the allies now that the Administration was unilaterally reinterpreting the treaty in public. It was too late. Through McFarlane, the White House itself had now spoken. The issue seemed resolved in favor of Perle, Kunsberg, and Sofaer. Dissenting memos from McNeill of the Defense Department and Graham of the Arms Control and Disarmament Agency were squelched.

Nitze advised Shultz how to limit the damage. At another contentious meeting of the National Security Council on October 11, Shultz persuaded Reagan to adopt a compromise: The broad interpretation would be accepted by the Administration as a matter of law, but the old, narrow interpretation would remain as a matter of policy. Shortly afterward, in a speech in San Francisco and at a NATO meeting in Brussels, Shultz explained that while the broad interpretation was "fully justified," SDI R&D would "be conducted in accordance with a narrow interpretation." Therefore, said Shultz, the whole troublesome issue was now "moot."

On October 16, Perle said in a meeting with reporters, "With respect to the future elements of the [SDI] program, it remains to be seen which interpretation would apply." He and his supporters would be back to fight another day, pressing for the adaptation of the broad interpretation not just as a point of legal right but as policy. On June 3, 1986, Perle made a confident prediction: "The sooner we remove the [ABM treaty] restrictions that continue, based on the old interpretation, the better. . . . I think it's going to happen in the lifetime of this Administration."

Whatever the ambiguities in the text of the ABM treaty or in the classified negotiating record of SALT I, none was as flagrant as the ambiguity that now beset the Reagan Administration's own position on the subject. Indeed, the Administration had managed to expose itself to two controversies at once. By proclaiming the Perle-Sofaer interpretation of the ABM treaty, the executive branch of the U.S. government had fundamentally altered the meaning and obligations of an international agreement, in defiance not only of the other country that had signed the pact but of the legislative branch, which had ratified it. Then, by adopting the Nitze-Shultz compromise, the Administration was saying, in effect, that the Soviet Union could develop and test its own SDI, since that is what the ABM treaty permitted as a matter of legal right—but that the United States would refrain from doing so as a matter of policy.

The Soviet Union chose to protest the first twist rather than gloat over the second. Marshal Sergei Akhromeyev, the chief of the General Staff, was quoted in *Pravda* as saying that the new interpretation was a "deliberate deceit" that "distorted the essence of the treaty" by "trying to substantiate the lawfulness of experiments" that would lead to SDI. That was essentially the view of Nitze's former colleagues from SALT I, Gerard Smith and John Rhinelander, who joined with others to form what they called the Campaign to Save the ABM Treaty. It was also the view of important members of Congress, who raised their voices against the Administration.

In March 1987, Abraham Sofaer himself was summoned before the Senate

Foreign Relations Committee. Senator Kerry charged him with having created a constitutional crisis by attempting to break with the interpretation that the Senate had in mind when it ratified the ABM treaty in 1972. Another Democrat, Joseph Biden of Delaware, accused Sofaer of an "unconscionable politicization of the office." Under withering criticism, Sofaer defended the broad interpretation but conceded that his "methodology" had been flawed—an error he attributed to "young lawyers" on his staff. In fact, Sofaer had imposed his—and Perle's—reading of the treaty on his staff, causing at least one of the lawyers there to leave. He was William Sims, who came forward at a joint hearing of the Senate Judiciary and Foreign Relations committees. "I had strong reservations about what we were doing," said Sims, "about the procedure and about the conclusions [we] reached. . . . We provided [the President] with a flawed decision memorandum." The Pentagon "seemed to be in the driver's seat" throughout the "rushed" deliberations on the subject. The broad interpretation was by now widely known as "the Sofaer doctrine."

Also in March 1987, Sam Nunn, Democrat of Georgia, now the chairman of the Senate Armed Services Committee and the single most influential and authoritative member of Congress on defense issues, released a series of detailed, blistering reports. After he and his staff had spent many hours studying the relevant classified documents—to which thay had official access—Nunn charged that much of Sofaer's work was based on a "complete and total misrepresentation" of critical parts of the historical record and warned that if the Administration persisted in pressing its view, it would risk a "constitutional confrontation" with the Senate and a congressional backlash against funding for SDI. Nunn's assault had added weight because of his conservative voting record on defense issues. Reinforcing his warning, the Armed Services Committee voted on May 5 to prohibit funding for any SDI tests that would violate the traditional interpretation. The measure was sponsored by Nunn and Carl Levin.

Nitze's more supportive colleagues inside the government, as well as many of his admirers outside, were puzzled and disturbed by the whole episode. "Nobody knows more about the ABM treaty than Paul Nitze," said Rhinelander. "Nobody has more respect for rigorous logic. How could a couple of lawyers who don't know the first thing about arms control come along and turn him around on a dime? It's absurd to think that Sofaer could teach Paul anything he didn't know."

In trying to explain Nitze's role in the affair, some of his friends and partisans made excuses for him. At the time that the battle lines were first forming over the reinterpretation, in the fall of 1985, Nitze himself was in the glare of unwanted publicity. Newspaper articles were depicting him as the Administration's embattled arms controller, impatient for a deal and therefore in danger of losing his influence. Perhaps, it was speculated, Nitze did not want to confirm that impression by opposing the latest ploy by the hard-liners.

Nitze dismissed this theory as "patent nonsense." He did not want to be given the benefit of the doubt, he said, because he had no doubt himself— and no regrets. He remained unrepentant, even defiant. Recalling his sessions with Sofaer, he said, "I came away 100 percent convinced that the permissive, or broad, interpretation was correct."[12]

More than a year later, on April 1, 1987, Nitze gave a speech in the auditorium of the Johns Hopkins School of Advanced International Studies.* The announced subject was the ABM treaty and SDI. A group of senators, including both enthusiasts and skeptics in the SDI debate, had urged him to speak out forcefully and definitively as the Administration's most credible spokesman on the matter. The audience was jammed with experts and former colleagues, many of whom were still counting on Nitze to defeat Perle and win the battle for Ronald Reagan's soul on arms control. They came hoping that perhaps, finally, Nitze would distance himself from the broad interpretation. Sofaer had just been called onto the carpet by the Senate and Sam Nunn had delivered his harsh judgment of the new interpretation. But Nitze was unyielding. He still clung stubbornly to a view that had become not only an embarrassment to the Administration but a major obstacle to progress in arms control.

One irony of the episode was that Nitze and his old rival Henry Kissinger both ended up, in different ways and to different degrees, giving credence to the broad interpretation. Perhaps each was concerned about the vulnerability of his right flank. Whatever the explanation, neither seemed fully to realize that he was thereby endorsing an attack on his own competence as negotiator earlier in his career.†

But the greater irony was that by supporting the broad interpretation, Nitze had strengthened the hands of his opponents at the Pentagon; increased the danger that Congress would cut funds for SDI before it could be used for its bargaining leverage; deepened doubts in Moscow that anyone in the Reagan Administration—including Nitze himself—was interested in a deal; clouded his own reputation, both inside and outside the government; and lessened the chances of the agreement that he was so determined to help achieve.

---

*Not only was he giving the speech at the institution that he had co-founded with Christian Herter in the 1940s and that had provided him with a base during the fifties, but the auditorium was in the school's Paul H. and Phyllis P. Nitze Building—dedicated a year earlier in recognition of the Nitzes' financial and other contributions.

†On February 8, 1987, appearing on "Meet the Press," Kissinger said, "I believe that if you look at the literal text of the treaty, probably the broad interpretation is correct."

CHAPTER 11

The Big Deal

Richard Perle and others worked so assiduously and ingeniously to undermine the ABM treaty partly because they wanted to prevent it from becoming the basis for the defensive half of a two-part strategic arms-control deal: less American defense and less Soviet offense. The idea of a "grand compromise," in which constraints on SDI would be traded for major reductions in Soviet offensive forces, had been around as long as SDI itself. It was inherent in Robert McFarlane's concept of the sting. However, because of Reagan's devotion to SDI and the Pentagon's determination to use the program to block arms control, any sort of compromise, grand or otherwise, could be discussed within the Administration only in muted tones and elliptical terms.

Many government officials were counting on prominent outsiders to make the case for the grand compromise. One of the first to do so was James Schlesinger. On October 25, 1984, he gave a speech in Bedford, Massachusetts, advocating a return to the logic and basic structure of SALT I:

> The Soviets were keenly aware of the inadequacies of the ABM system (whose capabilities we had much exaggerated). When the United States began actually to deploy [its own ABM] system, the Soviets were deeply alarmed about the immense advantages of American technology. They therefore proceeded in the negotiations to insist on a limitation on ABM systems.
>
> That ultimately resulted in the 1972 treaty. Throughout the entire period President Nixon took the position—I believe correctly, and certainly courageously—that there would be no ABM treaty unless the Soviets agreed to limitations on offensive forces. Although the Soviets wanted no agreement at all on offensive forces, their eagerness for the ABM treaty forced them, in effect, to accept the 1972 agreement on offensive forces.
>
> That grand design—of limits on Soviet offensive forces in exchange for constraint on American defense technologies—lies before us again, beckoning.

Arnold Horelick, a Soviet affairs expert at the RAND Corporation who had served as the CIA's senior Kremlinologist in the Carter Administration and who had close ties with the State Department and the National Security Council staff of the Reagan Administration, wrote in late 1984 that thanks in large measure to SDI, the United States had a unique opportunity:

> The still vague but menacing prospect of superior U.S. technology in such areas as sensors, computers, computer programming, signal processing and exotic kill mechanisms being harnessed in connection with President Reagan's Strategic Defense Initiative is bound to increase Soviet anxiety about the possible shape of the strategic balance in the years ahead.
>
> The Soviets could reach a pessimistic assessment of the trends in the strategic nuclear balance and of the high costs and risks that a more competitive U.S. adversary would be likely to impose in an unregulated environment. Such a conclusion could conceivably make Moscow more amenable than in the past to arms control agreements that required the U.S.S.R. to accept substantial reductions in high-value forces in order to constrain the most threatening U.S. programs. . . .
>
> Soviet leaders in the future may be more willing to trade off some existing Soviet strategic nuclear advantages, likely in any case to be eroded in the years ahead, in exchange for constraints on new U.S. programs that would insure against the rejuvenation and significant expansion of U.S. strategic offensive and defensive capabilities.[1]

Paul Nitze remarked in February 1985 that he saw "nothing but good sense" in Horelick's article: "There is nothing one-sided in asking the Soviets to trade reductions in existing systems [i.e., large, MIRVed ICBMs] for a curtailment of future American programs [including, presumably, SDI]. There's nothing unfair about that. Nor is it unacceptable to the Soviets. What they're interested in is precisely curtailment of American modernization. So our negotiation strategy squares with their priorities."[2] The idea of the grand compromise was in accord with many of the positions and principles that Nitze had held for forty years. Here was a chance finally to accomplish what he had advocated as an insider during SALT I and as an outsider during the debate over SALT II: stabilizing reductions in Soviet offense, particularly in throw-weight and MIRVed ICBMs.

On April 13, 1985, at a conference in Atlanta co-sponsored by Gerald Ford and Jimmy Carter, McGeorge Bundy spoke about SDI eventually enabling the United States to strike what he called "the grand bargain." Richard Nixon, who was already beginning to enjoy a degree of rehabilitation as an elder statesman, said he could easily imagine SDI playing the role in the mid- to late eighties that ABMs had played for him in the early seventies at the outset of SALT. The more ambitious dreams for strategic defense were, he believed, "fairyland stuff," but at the right moment, President Reagan might be able to sign what Nixon called a "comprehensive compromise" linking strategic offense and defense.[3]

Great sting operation, grand bargain, grand design, grand compromise, comprehensive compromise—the dramatic billing varied, but the concept was the same. The more neutral term was "offense-defense tradeoff." Whatever the label, it was anathema to Perle and those who shared his distaste for SALT and his determination to block a return to what he called "the folly of the SALT mentality." His supporters waged a campaign of their own against the offense-defense tradeoff, often in public. Henry Rowen—a one-time colleague of Nitze's in the Pentagon, later president of RAND and a CIA official early in the Reagan Administration—wrote in 1985:

> Arms control treaties and agreements have failed to contain the relative growth of Soviet military power. The method that was highly successful in SALT surely commends itself to Gorbachev for the future. Through SALT I, Moscow in 1972 succeeded in killing the nascent U.S. ABM program while preserving the core of its own program (the Moscow ABM system plus an ambitious research and development program), and reinforced the existing American disposition not to invest heavily in offensive forces even as the Soviet Union greatly expanded its own offensive investments. This arrangement ran into serious trouble after the late 1970s and is in need of refurbishment. [The Soviet proposal] for drastic cuts in offensive forces and an end to the U.S. Strategic Defense Initiative is a bold attempt to bring back the old SALT-détente regime.[4]

In July 1986, Kenneth Adelman disparaged the idea of the tradeoff: "We already bought that cow once. In 1972 we gave up defense, in which we had an advantage, in exchange for the Soviets' limiting offense. But they never paid for what they got. The compromise of 1972 has never been fulfilled."[5] On February 2, 1987, Adelman delivered a speech in Bonn titled, straightforwardly, "The Fallacy of the 'Grand Compromise' ":

> SDI may be necessary not only for our future safety but to keep the Soviets honest about any agreement we conclude with them. SDI may be necessary to keep the Soviets constructively involved in the arms control process. To kill SDI, in effect, would be to kill the goose that lays the golden eggs.
>
> At the very least, there is no logical contradiction between progress in arms control and movement to greater reliance on strategic defenses. . . . Logically and strategically, therefore, there is no better way to achieve greater security for both sides than a movement toward strategic defenses in combination with deep reductions in offensive arms.

Defenses are not part of the problem in arms control—they are part of the solution.

I'll leave you with a question: Would you rather base our security on Western ingenuity or on Soviet integrity? If we abandon defenses we may find ourselves trusting heavily to the latter. On the other hand, if we actively pursue the defensive option, there is the possibility of moving simultaneously toward defensive deployment and offensive reductions.

Paul Nitze and Robert McFarlane concurred in the view that the offense-defense compromise of 1972 had never been fulfilled and that the Soviets had not lived up to their end of that earlier version of the bargain. However, they also believed that, thanks to SDI and the offensive strategic modernization program (MX, the Trident II, the B-1 bomber, cruise missiles, etc.), the Reagan Administration had an opportunity to do well what its predecessors had done inadequately in SALT; the Soviets might now make amends for their earlier greediness and bad faith.

Where Nitze and McFarlane parted company with Perle, Rowen, Adelman, and others was over the feasibility and desirability of seeking cuts in offense without accompanying constraints on defense. Nitze said, "We mustn't kid ourselves or try to kid anyone else" into thinking that the Soviets would reduce their offenses if SDI were allowed to "run free." A vigorous, large-scale American defensive system would devalue whatever offensive forces the Soviets would have left after reductions took effect. Therefore, in the absence of constraints on SDI, the Soviet Union would not reduce its offenses at all—it would increase them. And so if there was going to be a deal, some way had to be found to hint at linkage between offense and defense. Somehow, someday, to some extent, SDI would have to end up on the bargaining table. But this hint had to be conveyed to the Soviets without provoking repudiation by the President or galvanizing opposition from the Pentagon.

Round and Round

The communiqué signed by George Shultz and Andrei Gromyko after their meeting in Geneva in January 1985 stated that the issues under discussion in the three forums of the Nuclear and Space Talks (NST)—INF, START, and defense and space—must be resolved "in their interrelationship." Paul Nitze and Robert McFarlane came home from that meeting believing that these three words contained the necessary hint of eventual linkage between START and SDI. What was needed now was to open a negotiation in which the two sides would move from discussion of the concept of interrelationship to the details of a possible agreement. "The devil," Nitze was fond of saying, "resides in the details."

The devil also resided in the semantics. In the two months between the Shultz-Gromyko meeting and the opening of the talks, there was constant bickering within the American bureaucracy over how to define the carefully chosen, hotly disputed word "interrelationship." Even though "interrelationship" had in fact figured prominently in Shultz's own talking points going into the meeting with Gromyko, Richard Perle and other hard-liners began treating it afterward as though it were a strictly Soviet buzzword, a mischievous synonym for the great taboo of "killing SDI."

From the broadest conceptual issues down to the pettiest details where the devil resided, positions within the U.S. government were far apart, and many differences were still unresolved when the talks with the Soviets began. Six options for an opening American proposal went to the President just before the American delegation left for Geneva. They were all recycled versions of the agencies' preferences for START, and they skirted the question of possible tradeoffs between offensive reductions and restrictions on SDI.

McFarlane tried to make a virtue out of the contention and indecision. "Everything is on the table," he said on a number of occasions. "Maximum flexibility is the order of the day." The President, he said, had set forth certain basic, general objectives, and the negotiators could explore various ways of meeting those objectives. It was hoped that the Soviets would join in a kind of creative free-for-all in Geneva from which a compromise would eventually emerge.

In fact, everything was not on the table. There was no agreement among the Americans themselves about when and how, if ever and if at all, SDI was going to figure in the negotiations. Therefore, it could hardly be clear to the Soviets whether an important card in the American hand was available for play.

The absence of clear, unified instructions from Washington made the American delegation in Geneva all the more susceptible to backbiting over questions of procedure and prerogative in the early days of the Nuclear and Space Talks. Time and energy that might have been spent on a proposal were spent instead on such matters as who would be included in the bloated—or what was sometimes called the "MIRVed"—three-in-one delegation (INF, START, and defense and space); who would get what offices in the cramped quarters of the American mission across the street from the botanical gardens where Nitze had once walked and talked with Yuli Kvitsinsky; and whether the mission contained adequate shielding against possible eavesdropping from nearby Eastern Bloc installations. Partly because of the increased size of the American representation and partly because of concern over security, the U.S. arms-control delegation some months later moved into modern, fortresslike headquarters in a more remote setting near the outskirts of the city.

The captain of this cumbersome and fractious team was Max Kampelman, Nitze's longtime friend from the Committee on the Present Danger. Like Nitze, Kampelman had been brought into the Administration largely as a gesture toward bipartisanship and continuity with the past. Also like Nitze, Kampelman was not part of the President's inner circle, and he lacked political backing at the White House. He was like Nitze in yet another respect as well: He proved to be persistent and imaginative in quest of an agreement that would serve the twin goals of blunting the Soviet threat and bolstering strategic stability.*

In the early days of the Nuclear and Space Talks, Kampelman seemed to spend almost as much time mediating among his colleagues as negotiating with the Soviets. Meetings in the "bubble"—the bug-proof chamber inside the American mission—often turned into squabbles over what "interrelationship" might mean. In exasperation, Kampelman waved his hand and said, "Let's not argue about theoretical issues that are not yet before us." When a State Department representative complained to him about the "obstructionists" from the Pentagon, Kampelman replied, "Look, learn to live with them. If you leave guys like that off the delegation, they'll knife you when you come up with something. Let them participate. Let them join in the process of interpreting our instructions to negotiate."

At the first plenary session on March 14, 1985, the chief Soviet representative, Victor Karpov, a veteran of SALT I, SALT II and START, delivered a tough opening statement, insisting on agreement at the outset that there must be a tradeoff between offense and defense. The requirement on defense, he said, was a "ban on space-strike arms"—the phrase Gromyko had used in January. Karpov underscored that his statement had been approved "at the highest level"—i.e., by Mikhail Gorbachev, who had just become general secretary.

A number of the Americans left the meeting discouraged. There were rueful jokes about packing for home and canceling hotel rooms. They had come to Geneva with instructions to convince the Soviets that SDI would alleviate rather than exacerbate the arms race. The superpowers should not be trying to limit, restrict, or trade away strategic defenses at all; rather, they should be negotiating the terms of the "transition" to a world in which there was more defense and perhaps eventually to one in which there was nothing but defense.

---

*Kampelman had been Jimmy Carter's ambassador to the East-West talks, then based in Madrid, on European security and cooperation; the Reagan Administration had kept him on in that post until the end of the talks.

"Transition" was a key word in Nitze's strategic concept, then very much in the news because of his speeches and congressional testimony on the subject. Karpov complained that the strategic concept was a "smokescreen behind which you're seeking military superiority and a first-strike capability." Similar complaints were expressed by another familiar figure on the Soviet side of the table: Yuli Kvitsinsky, who was now the head of the Soviet defense-and-space group. As such, he, too, was Kampelman's counterpart, since in addition to being the head of the American NST delegation as a whole, Kampelman was chairman of the American defense-and-space group. Kampelman tried to get Karpov and Kvitsinsky to be more specific in their objections to SDI and in their proposal for a "ban on space-strike arms." He asked them to "dignify" their proposal with concrete suggestions.

The Soviets replied that the ABM treaty prohibited any research with the purpose of developing systems that would themselves be a violation of the treaty. Kampelman told Karpov and Kvitsinsky, "I want you to understand and to tell Moscow one thing: There's no way we'll give up the right to do research." It was a carefully formulated negative, inviting the Soviets to infer that those more advanced and threatening stages of SDI beyond research—i.e., development and testing—might be negotiable. But Kampelman could not say that outright, lest the Pentagon representatives in Geneva and back in Washington accuse him of signaling a "giveaway" of SDI.

Meanwhile, there were contradictions and perhaps disagreements among the Soviets as well. The Soviet negotiators were repeatedly in the awkward position of taking a harder line on SDI than their political leaders in Moscow. At a minimum, the bureaucracy in Moscow, which was charged with translating Politburo decisions into negotiating instructions for Karpov and Kvitsinsky in Geneva, was having trouble keeping up with Gorbachev.

In a letter to the U.S. Union of Concerned Scientists in July 1985, the general secretary pointedly omitted research from the list of SDI-related activities that must be banned. One of Gorbachev's principal advisors, the physicist Evgeny Velikhov, a vice-president of the Soviet Academy of Sciences, told a visiting American physicist, Sidney Drell of Stanford University, that the United States should "take seriously" this feature of the letter. Drell was a prominent arms-control expert and advocate. He regarded Paul Nitze as "an exceptional case of sanity in the Reagan Administration." Echoing what Paul Warnke had said in 1981, Drell predicted that Nitze "may yet drag the rest of the Administration kicking and screaming into a good agreement." Drell passed along what Velikhov had said, and Nitze relayed the message to Kampelman, who took it up with Kvitsinsky.

"Academician Velikhov has indicated you're not trying to ban research," said Kampelman. "Is that your position?"

"Not at all," replied Kvitsinsky. Gorbachev had said that the U.S.S.R. was against the "creation" of SDI: "That means and subsumes research."

Yet there continued to be hints out of Moscow that research might be permissible, so Kampelman took the matter to Karpov. "One of the confusing things about dealing with you people, Victor," he said over lunch, "is that we don't know where the hell you are." He cited as an example the issue of the research ban.

"Our position hasn't changed," Karpov replied sharply.

However, even during the early days of the talks, there were indications that it was the exotic, space-based aspect of SDI—not necessarily strategic defense in general—that the Kremlin was determined to block in an eventual agreement. Vladimir Medvedev, one of the military representatives, delivered a lecture about how there were "good" defenses and "bad" defenses. SDI was bad defense, particularly the space-based components that would intercept Soviet missiles in their boost phase. He conjured up the Soviet nightmare of American battle stations directly overhead, much as Gromyko had spoken of a sword of Damocles threatening the Strategic Rocket Forces with decapitation.

"We object to your going to nationwide defense," he said, "but if it's point defense you want [i.e., traditional ABMs that would defend missile silos], we'll talk about that." The Americans, however, were not authorized to talk about any limitation on SDI.

In some of his public statements, Gorbachev had spoken about the need to "reaffirm" the ABM treaty. During a luncheon meeting, Kampelman pressed Kvitsinsky on this phrasing: "What does the general secretary mean here? You want us to resubmit a treaty to the Senate for ratification? What provision in international law is there for 'reaffirmation'? Will we have some reaffirmed treaties and some non-reaffirmed treaties?"

Kvitsinsky explained that the Kremlin would be concerned as long as both sides had the right to withdraw from the ABM treaty on short notice: "We need to know you're not going to withdraw for at least ten years." Whatever accommodation was eventually reached on strategic defense, it would have to preclude what Kvitsinsky called "unpleasant surprises": a breakthrough in the SDI R&D that would permit a breakout in the form of deployment. To that end, the Soviets had decided to push for a "nonwithdrawal" clause, effective for a specified period of time, the longer the better from the Soviets' standpoint.

Another, simpler way to protect against SDI breakout would be to inhibit the advanced development and testing of a system. But that would require a reaffirmation of the narrow interpretation of the ABM treaty, and by late 1985, the Reagan Administration had immobilized itself with its internal dispute over the narrow versus the broad interpretation and was on its way toward an impasse with Congress as well.

• • •

During the first round of the Nuclear and Space Talks (March 14–April 23, 1985), the Soviets tried to whet the appetite of the Americans for the offensive reductions that might be possible if and when SDI ever became negotiable. If the United States would just agree to "ban space-strike arms," there could be reductions in offensive forces that would, in the words of one delegate, Grigori Zaitsev, "make your head spin."

The chairman of the American START group was John Tower, the now-retired Republican senator from Texas who had opposed Nitze's nomination as secretary of the navy twenty-two years before and helped block his appointment to a senior Pentagon post at the beginning of the Reagan Administration. Nonetheless, Nitze felt that for political reasons, a well-connected conservative like Tower was "a good man to have on our side," and he had recommended to Shultz that Tower be appointed chief negotiator.

Tower's deputy in START was Ronald Lehman, a former aide to Perle and, before that, to Tower himself. Lehman had more recently worked for McFarlane on the NSC staff. Just before the end of round one, Karpov told Lehman that he hoped in the next round, beginning at the end of May, the two sides would begin to "talk turkey."

Later, at a cocktail party, Karpov said to Tower, "Let's hope for more flexibility in the future on the part of both of our governments."

"Well, Victor," Tower replied, "I'll be ready to hear whatever you've got to say when you come back. I'm a good listener. My Methodist clergyman father taught me the value of patience." The implication was clear: It was up to the Soviets to make the first real moves; there was not much chance of flexibility on the American side in the next round.

Kampelman all but invited Karpov to strengthen the hand of the would-be arms controllers on the American side against the anti-arms-control faction. "You make it too easy" for the hard-liners and stonewallers on the American side, Kampelman told Karpov. "You don't come up with what you want to do in START. You talk about radical reductions. But it's just talk. Give us some numbers. Tempt us."

At the end of the first round, Kampelman said to Kvitsinsky, "I've given you and your proposition the dignity that every partner in a negotiation has a right to expect. You have not been giving us and our proposals that dignity. I hope that when you get back [in May], you'll do the same that we've done." Echoing Tower, he added, "I've got time. I've got patience."

Shortly before the beginning of round two, Gorbachev in effect took Kampelman's advice; he made the Soviet offer on offenses more ambitious and more attractive. In a speech in Warsaw on April 26, he said that his government would go beyond the offensive reductions it had been willing to make in START as long as they were tied to restrictions on SDI. The Soviet Union, he said, had "already suggested that both sides reduce strategic offensive arms by one quarter as an opening move"; it had "no objections to making deeper reductions. . . . All this is possible if an arms race does not begin in space.''

In Geneva, Karpov followed his leader in reaffirming the generality, but dragged his feet when the Americans pressed him for specifics. Not until more than halfway through the round did the Soviets make a formal statement with their position on offensive reductions. ''It was so convoluted and cryptic,'' one of Kampelman's deputies noted wryly, ''that we knew it must be significant.'' The Soviet side said it took cognizance of repeated American expressions of concern about the possibility that one side or the other would be able to concentrate an inordinate amount of its firepower on a certain type of weapon; in order to meet that concern, the Soviet side might be willing to agree to percentage limits, whereby no more than a particular portion of weapons would be allowed on a particular type of strategic nuclear delivery vehicle.

The United States had contended for years that some kinds of weapons were more destabilizing than others: Bomber weapons, cruise missiles, and SLBMs were considered retaliatory, while ICBM warheads were deemed instruments of a first strike. Therefore, an agreement should include subceilings not just on ICBM launchers but on ICBM warheads, particularly those atop large ICBMs. Now, after years of resistance, the Kremlin seemed inching in that direction. The latest Soviet statement sounded like an offer to cap not just ballistic-missile warheads in general (i.e., including those on SLBMs) but ICBM warheads in particular. By extension, that might mean reductions in heavy ICBM warheads (those on SS-18s).

This presaging of a major concession, if that was what it turned out to be, had been designed and approved back in Moscow. Once again, the Soviet negotiators in Geneva seemed uncertain what their new instructions meant. Under questioning from the Americans, they offered hesitant and widely differing answers about what the percentage limitations might be, whether there would be a single percentage applicable to all types of weapons (say, 50 percent for SLBMs, ICBMs, and bombers) or whether there would be different percentages for different types (say, 60 percent for ICBMs, 40 percent for SLBMs, and 20 percent for bombers). Tower and Lehman found Karpov to be uncharacteristically nervous and vague. He brought along the chief military man on the delegation, General Victor Starodubov, to handle the more probing questions of the Americans. On at least one occasion, Starodubov had to correct Karpov when he got an answer wrong. As on the issue of strategic defense, Gorbachev and his advisors back in Moscow were sweetening the pot in Geneva without telling their assistant chefs what the recipe was.

The Kremlin had accepted the principle of sublimits on warheads. But it had not yet accepted the principle, equally important to the Americans, that such sublimits be ''preferential''—that is, that they actively discourage some kinds of weapons (MIRVed ICBMs) over others (bombers, cruise missiles, and SLBMs).

"You have repeatedly told us that you're concerned about the concentration of certain weapons," said Karpov. "Well now, our proposal would preclude such concentration."

"It's not just concentration per se that bothers us," replied Lehman. "We would be delighted if you concentrated all your weapons on bombers. It's particular concentrations that bother us—namely, the concentration of your allotment of nuclear weapons on land-based ballistic missiles."

The Soviets understood that perfectly well. They knew that their large, MIRVed ICBMs gave them their principal leverage in the talks. For just that reason, they were not about to expend that capital—or indicate a willingness to do so—until they had a clearer idea of what they could get in return by way of concessions on SDI. And so far, the official American position was that SDI was, for all intents and purposes, non-negotiable.

The Monday Package

Paul Nitze was a past master of what he considered justifiable insubordination. "Sometimes," he once remarked, "when the system has broken down, you've got to devise a system of your own." The most dramatic example had been his walk in the woods with Yuli Kvitsinsky during INF. For the sake of an agreement he felt both necessary and possible, he was willing to defy his superiors' insistence on the Zero Option, leave the Soviets with some INF missiles in both Europe and Asia, and cancel the prospective deployment of the American Pershing IIs. In 1985, with the walk-in-the-woods precedent very much in his mind, Nitze once again departed from the beaten track of Administration policy.

Nitze had been thinking about a bold initiative for some time, discussing it with an inner circle of his most trusted personal advisors. These included James Timbie, one of the most knowledgeable and experienced technical experts of the Arms Control and Disarmament Agency. He had helped Nitze in the star-crossed effort to salvage the walk-in-the-woods plan when it came under attack, primarily from Perle, in the fall of 1982.

Under the directorship of Perle's ally Kenneth Adelman, ACDA had become enemy territory for would-be explorers of the grand compromise. Timbie was transferred to a less visible and less vulnerable corner of the bureaucracy, on the staff of the deputy secretary of state, John Whitehead. Timbie was not only a veteran of Nitze's earlier campaigns in the bureaucratic wars of the Reagan Administration; he was a survivor of the Carter

Administration as well. Before helping Nitze with the walk in the woods and the grand compromise, he had worked with Cyrus Vance and Paul Warnke on SALT II. His unadvertised but steady presence at Nitze's side in the eighties was a reminder, for those who noticed, of continuity with the past.

Nitze also derived encouragement and concrete ideas for the grand compromise from conversations with outsiders who were promoting their own versions of the plan. One of these was Jeremy Stone, director of the Federation of American Scientists. For years, Stone had been pushing the idea of an agreement whereby the superpowers would reduce their offensive arsenals each year by a set percentage. At a conference in Moscow in early April 1985, he tried to persuade an audience of forty Soviet scientists that dramatic offensive reductions might be a way of inducing the United States to accept restrictions on SDI:

> You people are saying that if we go ahead with Star Wars, there can be no disarmament. I agree, but you should turn it around. You should see that if both sides go ahead with disarmament, there can be no Star Wars. Disarmament in and of itself might be the answer to Star Wars. With offensive reductions underway, there would be no political support for Star Wars [in the United States]. On the other hand, if there are no offensive reductions in prospect, there will be all the more support for Star Wars. You need political restraints, not further legal assurances concerning the ABM treaty. And only one number needs to be negotiated—the percentage for annual reduction of SALT II limits.

Stone discussed this proposal with Velikhov and Roald Sagdeyev, director of the Space Research Institute outside Moscow. They accepted his basic point, although they argued with him about which side should go first—the Soviet Union in proposing dramatic reductions in offense or the United States in signaling a willingness to put SDI on the table. Stone kept saying, "Why don't you make us an offer we can't refuse?"

This was the same exhortation with which Kampelman was trying to wheedle concessions in START out of Karpov in Geneva.

On May 3, after his return to Washington, Stone called on Nitze and urged percentage reductions in offense, linked to "perpetuation" of the ABM treaty. Nitze was at first resistant, then listened attentively and receptively, although with a touch of discouragement and apprehension. "Jeremy," he said, "people in this Administration already treat me like a radical dove without any interest in national security."

In spite of those anxieties, Nitze made his move later that month. In mid-May, Andrei Gromyko and George Shultz met in Vienna for the thirtieth anniversary of the Austrian State Treaty, which had ended the partial Soviet occupation of Austria and guaranteed the neutrality of that country.* Nitze and Robert McFarlane accompanied Shultz to Vienna. The three men had many hours together, and they shared frustrations over the dilemma of SDI and arms control. Nitze said the answer might be to "streamline the process," bypass the haggles in Geneva and the backbiting in Washington, and go straight to the Soviets with a package deal. McFarlane asked Nitze to come up with a detailed proposal.

As soon as he returned to Washington, Nitze went to work. The plan he eventually assembled provided for a "schedule" of percentage reductions in strategic offenses every year for ten years, so that by the end of 1995, each side would have come down by approximately 50 percent from a 1986 "baseline" derived from the various SALT II ceilings and subceilings.

The ideal of 50-percent reductions had been around since Reagan's first term. It had acquired a talismanic standing with the left as well as the right, ever since George Kennan had promoted the idea in 1981. Shultz felt that if Reagan was ever going to accept any limits on SDI, it would have to be in exchange for something as dramatic and simple-sounding as a 50-percent cut in offense. The magic number of 50 percent was necessary, Shultz felt, for him to go to the President and say, "Here is a good START agreement." Without 50 percent, Shultz remarked on a number of occasions, "all the fun goes out of it"—that is, the grand compromise would lose its appeal to the President; the offensive reductions would not seem to justify the necessary constraints on SDI.

Nitze had always been worried about "reductions for their own sake." In a moment of near-despair over Administration policy and the impasse with the Soviets, he once remarked, "The horrid truth is that deterrence works better with *higher* levels of offenses and no defense. Defense only deters if there is no offense."[6] These two sentences crystallized the case against SDI in its presidentially sanctioned form.

When Nitze set about to incorporate the goal of 50-percent reductions into his scheme for the grand compromise, he chose the numbers carefully so that the reductions would cut deeper into each side's inventory of warheads than into its inventory of launchers, thus reducing not just overall numbers but the ratio of warheads to targets and thus the plausibility of a first strike. His overall proposal was meant to encourage de-MIRVing, the evolution of both side's arsenals toward what Nitze called "one-warhead-per-launcher weapons" like Midgetman.

The defensive side of the tradeoff he envisioned would require both sides

---

*Richard Perle was fond of saying that this treaty was the only agreement in the otherwise dismal annals of Soviet-American diplomacy that had truly served the interests of the West. He would then add pointedly that it had taken ten years to negotiate the Austrian State Treaty: "That's the precedent we should have in mind [for arms control in the eighties], not SALT."

to commit themselves to conducting research and development of SDI within the terms of the ABM treaty.

Speaking at the time, in mid-1985, Nitze put the case for the grand compromise negatively: "Absent a change in Soviet offensive capability—that is, unless they're prepared to reduce the destructive power of their offense and end a situation in which they've got the ability to take out our hard targets on a far greater scale than our ability to take out theirs—we've got to look at defenses." He went on, however, to imply the converse: If the Soviets were willing to reduce offenses in a way that contributed to stability, the United States might consider "not just a perfected ABM treaty but perfected implementation of the ABM treaty, since the Soviets' view of what's permissible under the treaty and ours differ so radically."[7] He was referring primarily to the Krasnoyarsk radar—an example of the need for "removal of the ambiguities" in the pact. But there would also have to be, he believed, a negotiation on what R&D activity would be permissible under a "perfected" treaty.

This was before the debate broke out within the Administration over the narrow versus the broad interpretation of the treaty—and before Nitze allowed himself to be maneuvered by Perle and Sofaer into the uncomfortable position of seeming to advocate American exploitation of ambiguities in the treaty and the negotiating record. In the spring and summer of 1985, Nitze was still thinking in terms of the narrow interpretation, which would ban testing of space-based exotic systems.

McFarlane had his doubts about some features of Nitze's plan, particularly its bias toward Midgetman, but he was glad to find what he called "real brainstorming on the specifics of how to capitalize on the leverage that SDI gave us in arms control." He had been counting all along on Nitze to lead the way. Somehow, that way had to bypass the Pentagon while leading through the Oval Office. Nitze had learned from the experience of the walk in the woods that McFarlane cared about form and procedure as well as about substance. This time, he was determined to have not just McFarlane's support but at least the tacit authorization of the Joint Chiefs of Staff and of the President as well.

McFarlane and Shultz had been holding a series of talks with Reagan on SDI and arms control, sometimes in a regularly scheduled Wednesday-afternoon meeting, sometimes when one or the other would get time with the President alone on Air Force One. They went through the logic of the grand compromise with deliberate, exaggerated simplicity, starting with a reductio ad absurdum and working backward to what McFarlane called a "doable deal."

As McFarlane later reconstructed the argument he and Shultz used with Reagan: "If the Soviets did not have any ballistic missiles at all, we would not need SDI; if the Soviets had fewer ballistic missiles, we would not need as much SDI; if we got the Soviets down to the point where their ballistic missiles didn't threaten us with a first strike, we could live with constraints on SDI.''

The President would nod and say yes, that made sense. But then Caspar Weinberger would get equal time. He had virtually instant and automatic access to Reagan whenever he wanted it, and he frequently used his visits to the Oval Office to stiffen the President's back against what Shultz and McFarlane had been telling him. At a minimum, SDI must proceed unconstrained in order to find out what was possible. It would be irresponsible and dangerous to deny the American people the protection of their own technology. The grand compromisers did not dare to let the people find out for themselves. The United States should look to its own resources. If SDI fulfilled the President's own highest hopes and fondest dream, Weinberger said, it would allow the United States to stand tall in the face of the Soviet nuclear threat. Let the Soviets fire their missiles; the American people would protect themselves with their high-tech, high-frontier shield.

The President found that idea more appealing than the rather more complicated one that Shultz and McFarlane were quietly trying to sell him. It was a well-established fact of life in the Administration that the decisive argument with Reagan was often the most recent one he heard, particularly if it came from an old friend from Sacramento days. Knowing this and exploiting it, Weinberger pulled out all the stops to be sure that his was the last word before any presidential decisions on SDI or arms control.

Shultz and McFarlane became increasingly disillusioned with Reagan's notion of ''cabinet government.'' Out of this frustration came the idea of getting Reagan to approve, in its vaguest terms, a secret negotiation: The Administration would open a back channel to the Soviets in a way that at least initially excluded the Pentagon civilians; McFarlane would quietly enlist the support of the uniformed military. With luck and skill, the negotiation might produce an agreement that could be presented to the President as virtually a done deal. Nitze would be both the chief designer and the chief negotiator of the American position.

Nitze knew that as soon as Weinberger learned what had happened, he would ''fight like hell,'' but by then, he and McFarlane hoped, it would be too late. The alliance between the State Department and the Joint Chiefs of Staff on behalf of a deal that the Soviets had already accepted would be unbeatable. With the grand compromise a fait accompli, and with his own soldiers and diplomats as well as the Soviets lined up to support it, Reagan would impose it on Weinberger.

Shultz, McFarlane, and Nitze were scheduled to hold a meeting with Ambassador Anatoly Dobrynin at the State Department on Monday, June 17, 1985. Shultz's talking points for the meeting were to be a broad hint to

Dobrynin that someone of authority on the Soviet side enter back-channel talks with Nitze.

There had to be a name for the venture. Nitze recalled that during the sixties, there had been a super-secret document called "the Sunday Paper." He dubbed the talking points for the Shultz-Dobrynin meeting on June 17 the "Monday Paper," or "Monday Package." The key passages in a revised version of the document, which ended up in the White House, read:

> This paper outlines a package approach covering the three areas of the NST negotiations and [takes] account of the interrelationship [among] them. Its essence is an agreement of indefinite duration providing for deep and continuing cuts in offensive nuclear arms, both strategic and [INF], and agreement by the sides not to develop, test or deploy ABM systems or components in contravention of an agreed, strict interpretation of the provisions of the ABM Treaty as it currently stands . . . *as long as* both sides complied with the reduction schedules spelled out below for strategic and [INF] arms* . . . In order to facilitate the above, the sides would reach a mutual understanding of the demarcation between research which is permitted, and development and testing which is prohibited under the ABM treaty.

According to this plan, the United States would be relinking START and INF with a resolution of the problem of SDI and reaffirming the ABM treaty in its narrow interpretation.

McFarlane saw to it that the paper was "run past" Reagan. As the documentary legacy of the Iran-Contra scandal later demonstrated, Reagan often did not read the options papers that came to him for decision. His initials next to the approve/disapprove boxes were frequently accompanied by handwritten notes from his national security advisor saying that the President had been "orally briefed" on the contents of the paper. In the case of the Monday Package, McFarlane took advantage of what was later called Reagan's casual, often inattentive, sometimes oblivious "management style." He passed the paper before Reagan's eyes, summarized it in the most low-key, cursory fashion, and elicited a presidential shrug and a nod. Reagan could now be said to have approved the plan.

---

*For START, there would be yearly reductions that would commence in 1986 from starting points of 9,000 ballistic missile warheads and 12,000 ballistic missile warheads plus air-launched cruise missiles. The paper spelled out various formulas for annual reductions that would have the effect of reducing the two warhead categories by 50 percent over the first ten years, then another 50 percent of the remainder—down to 25 percent of the starting point—after twenty years. Thus, by the end of 1995, the two sides would be down to 4,500 ballistic missile warheads and 6,000 for the aggregate of warheads and ALCMs; by the end of the year 2005, they would be at 2,250 and 3,000 for the two categories. The paper also proposed roughly parallel reductions in INF.

Enlisting the support of the uniformed military was just as tricky. Nitze at first counted on McFarlane to approach the Joint Chiefs but in the end took on that task himself. He discussed the concept of the Monday Package first with the chairman at the time, General Vessey, then with the Chiefs as a group in their meeting room, "the Tank." Nitze was careful to present the offense-defense compromise as his own idea, and the Chiefs, while they raised no objections, were equally careful not to endorse the plan.

It was a bizarre sort of shadow play. Nitze was still relying on McFarlane to give the Chiefs a more complete and candid briefing later—and to signal that the idea was more than just Nitze's own. The Chiefs were not about to lend even their tacit support to the plan unless they were sure that it had coordinated, high-level backing from the State Department and the White House.

The encounter with Dobrynin in Shultz's office on Monday, June 17, was no less ambiguous, and no more conclusive, than the earlier steps in this peculiar process. Working from talking points prepared by Nitze, then revised by McFarlane, Shultz hinted at the contents of the Monday Paper and indicated that the American side would be amenable to exploration of a deal in a confidential, discreet channel. It was all indirect, if not downright cryptic. The hope was that Dobrynin would put two and two together. As an astute observer of a blatantly divided Administration, he would see—and seize—an opening to enter into a kind of conspiracy with the State Department, in the persons of Shultz and Nitze, as well as the White House, in the person of McFarlane, against the Pentagon. As Henry Kissinger's one-time partner in many tête-à-têtes that had bypassed Geneva negotiators and Washington bureaucrats alike, Dobrynin would understand the value of a back channel. He would agree with Shultz to have the Kremlin designate someone as Nitze's counterpart for an extended, highly confidential super-negotiation that might lead to the grand compromise.

Dobrynin seemed to miss the hints of willingness to trade SDI for START—either that or he chose to ignore them. Instead, he concentrated on the procedural issue of the back channel itself, and there he seemed not to want to play the game that was being proposed in such a Delphic fashion. He may have been protecting his own prerogatives. In a subsequent meeting, Dobrynin pointedly told Shultz that he was the Soviet representative in Washington, and Gromyko's successor as foreign minister, Eduard Shevardnadze, was the representative in Moscow. He seemed to be saying that if there was business to be done, Shultz could deal with Shevardnadze or with Dobrynin himself. There was no need to enlist the special services of Paul Nitze.

Nitze had been hoping to build on the precedent of the walk in the woods and his reputation as the American who was most determined and most able to deliver a deal. But the experience of the walk in the woods may have cut the other way, leaving in Moscow lingering doubts about whether he could deliver his President. He had failed, after all, to do so in 1982 on the critical issue of whether the United States was willing to live without the Pershing II in Europe.

The issue of the Pershing II came up again in a telltale way during the skittish maneuvering over the Monday Package and the grand compromise in 1985. The Soviets still professed to be deeply worried about the military potential of the weapon, now deployed in West Germany. Two Soviet negotiators in Geneva, Boris Ivanov and General Starodubov, asked of their American counterparts: "If you were a Soviet defense planner, which would you really rather have facing you, a Minuteman II or a Pershing II?" The answer to this rhetorical question was clear: The Pershing II was more threatening than the single-warhead version of Minuteman, because of its mobility, its greater accuracy, its short flight time, and its deployment in West Germany, near the Soviet Union.

At the end of August, Shultz flew to Helsinki for yet another ceremonial meeting of foreign ministers to celebrate an East-West pact. This was the tenth anniversary of the Conference on European Security and Cooperation, which had produced the 1975 "Helsinki Accords." Nitze accompanied Shultz. Shevardnadze brought along Kvitsinsky. Shevardnadze relied heavily on Kvitsinsky, once referring to him as "my teacher" on arms-control matters.

At that time some Soviets were dropping hints that perhaps the way to break the logjam at the Nuclear and Space Talks in Geneva was, in the words of Vladimir Pavlichenko, a veteran of INF now assigned to NST, "to reactivate the Nitze-Kvitsinsky walk-in-the-woods channel."

Nitze and Kvitsinsky met for dinner at a restaurant in the suburbs of Helsinki. Nitze outlined at some length the concept of the offense-defense tradeoff, stressing that SDI could be held within the terms of the ABM treaty (the narrow interpretation) in exchange for significant but negotiable reductions in START.

Kvitsinsky was aggressively skeptical. "You've made proposals on two subjects," he said, referring to SDI and START. "What about INF?"

Nitze said that the walk-in-the-woods formula still made sense.

"What do you think now about giving up the Pershing II?" asked Kvitsinsky.

"I personally can't think of a better substantive outcome," Nitze replied.

"So!" snapped Kvitsinsky, as if slamming shut the door of a trap. "Now you've made proposals in all three areas."

"They're not proposals," Nitze retorted. "They're personal thoughts, not solutions."

The next morning, at breakfast in the hotel restaurant, Kvitsinsky asked

Nitze's closest aide, Norman Clyne, "Was your boss serious about what he said last night? Was he serious about the walk-in-the-woods formula? Would you really give up your Pershings?"

"Ambassador Nitze is always serious," Clyne replied, but he stressed once again that Nitze had been speaking personally, not on behalf of the Administration.

Kvitsinsky had heard that distinction before, and he seemed uninterested in negotiating on that basis. In October, when Nitze accompanied Shultz to Moscow for a meeting to lay the groundwork for the first Reagan-Gorbachev summit, to be held in Geneva the following month, he encountered Kvitsinsky again and tried to raise the Monday Package "on a personal, exploratory basis." There were no takers on the Soviet side.

"The woods," remarked one of Kvitsinsky's Soviet colleagues later, "had turned out to be a jungle for Yuli. Much treacherous footing. Many nasty creatures. Not a place he wanted to return to. Not all alone, at least. And not with Ambassador Nitze. Some Americans may have regarded it as a precedent for what to do next. Our people, or some of them at least, regarded it as a warning of what *not* to do."

This postscript to the walk-in-the-woods episode of 1982 augured badly for the Monday Package of 1985–86.

Squeeze or Deal

As the episode of the Monday Package demonstrated, the grand compromise was so controversial within the Administration that it was virtually impossible to have the necessary technical work done by the bureaucracy. Any interagency group with the task of studying and developing the concept would unavoidably include Caspar Weinberger and Richard Perle or their representatives, who would make sure that the idea went nowhere and that its advocates were denounced for entertaining impure thoughts about SDI.

In parallel with Paul Nitze's effort to circumvent the Pentagon, there was another, equally extraordinary, roughly similar attempt undertaken by a small circle of experts at the RAND Corporation. They in effect became a kind of shadow NSC staff for Robert McFarlane, helping him with the great sting. Later, after McFarlane's departure from the government, they served as an occasional brain trust for George Shultz, supplementing and complementing the advice he was getting from Nitze.

Ironically, RAND's involvement grew out of its close ties to the Pentagon. In 1983, the year SDI was unveiled, the Air Force sponsored a number of RAND studies on various aspects of strategic defense. This work was supervised by Donald Rice, the president of RAND, and one of his vice-presidents, James Thomson. Others involved were Arnold Horelick, the Soviet affairs specialist who had laid out one of the most persuasive rationales for the grand compromise in *Foreign Affairs,* Arnold Kanter, and Ted Warner.

On August 21, 1985, McFarlane, who had accompanied Reagan to his ranch in Santa Barbara, traveled down the Pacific coast to RAND's headquarters in Santa Monica for a series of briefings on its analysis of SDI. In that discussion, the RAND analysts stressed the opportunities that SDI represented if it was used for leverage in arms control—and the dangers it posed if it was pursued unilaterally, and if Soviet offenses were allowed to proliferate in reaction to American defenses.

The Geneva summit was coming that fall. McFarlane was frustrated at the inability of the government to address the issue of how arms control might affect SDI. "I can't get this kind of work done in the government," he said. He asked the members of the RAND group to provide "informal" assistance, and to keep it quiet that they were doing the work at his request.

For nearly two months—carefully using funds from nongovernmental sources rather than from Pentagon contracts—the RAND team prepared a report raising the possibility of trading constraints on SDI for deep cuts in Soviet offenses. It was a classic options paper—a menu from which a policymaker could make a choice. It listed five possible ways of limiting SDI as part of a deal on strategic reductions: a reaffirmation of the ABM treaty for seven years, until 1992; a reaffirmation for fifteen years, until the year 2000; a ban on testing weapons based in space or against targets in orbit; and two versions of an even more extensive ban that would prohibit the development of defenses against short-range, or tactical, ballistic missiles as well as intercontinental ones.

The report concluded with a "vu-graph," a visual aid that the briefers could refer to as they talked:

NEXT STEPS WITH THE SOVIETS

- WE FACE A STRATEGIC CHOICE
    I. DEAL: BUILD ON POSITIVE ELEMENTS OF SOVIET PROPOSAL
      TO TRY TO REACH AGREEMENT
          or
    2. SQUEEZE: USE SDI AND STRATEGIC FORCE MODERNIZATION
      TO COMPEL CHANGES IN SOVIET FORCE STRUCTURE

- IF WE DECIDED TO SQUEEZE, THEN DEFENSIVE OPTIONS I OR 2
  LOOK BEST [reaffirmation of the ABM treaty for seven or fifteen years]
      —LITTLE OR NO EFFECT ON SDI: CONTINUED
      MAXIMUM LEVERAGE ON SOVIETS

      —MITIGATES POLITICAL COSTS IF [THERE IS] NO
         ARMS CONTROL AGREEMENT

* IF WE DECIDE TO DEAL, THEN DEFENSIVE OPTIONS 3, 4 OR 5
  LOOK BEST [reaffirmation of the ABM treaty coupled with a ban
  on space testing]
     —PROTECTS AGGRESSIVE SDI RESEARCH PROGRAM
     —PROVIDES REAL INCENTIVES FOR SOVIETS TO
        DELIVER ON PROMISE OF DEEP CUTS
     —MAKES SOVIETS SOLELY RESPONSIBLE IF NO
        AGREEMENT EMERGES

While the report was supposed to appear neutral on the either/or choice between "squeeze" and "deal," there was no question that its authors favored a deal. They felt that some combination of options 3, 4, and 5 would trigger major Soviet concessions on offense yet keep SDI alive as a research-and-development program. Such an outcome would not preclude eventual deployment if the R&D ever produced a system that met the Nitze criteria of military effectiveness, survivability, and cost-effectiveness at the margin.

Yet the continued observance of the ABM treaty (which the report stipulated must be narrowly or restrictively interpreted), combined with the ban on some forms of testing in space, would provide the Soviets with what the RAND experts called "SDI breakout insurance." That meant the Soviets would have time to respond if American R&D produced a breakthrough in the laboratory and an ambitious testing program, since such a breakthrough might lead to deployment of an operational, comprehensive, and highly effective system that would upset the strategic balance. With the guarantee of a long lead time between permissible R&D and possible deployment, the Soviets could afford to cut their offenses as their part of the bargain.

The idea of using the ABM treaty as a way of providing breakout insurance was already in the air, just as it was at the heart of Nitze's Monday Package. In his July 1985 reply to the letter from the American Union of Concerned Scientists, Mikhail Gorbachev had written that the ABM treaty was "the key link in the entire process of nuclear arms limitation"; SDI, he warned, "would invariably lead to the breakup of the document"; "strategic stability and trust would, no doubt, be strengthened if the United States agreed together with the U.S.S.R. in a binding form to reaffirm its commitment to the regime of the treaty on the limitation of antiballistic missile systems."

Shortly afterward, at the Nuclear and Space Talks in Geneva, Max Kampelman had asked Yuli Kvitsinsky to elaborate on Gorbachev's statement. Kvitsinsky replied that the Soviets were looking for "some element of predictability" and would need at least ten years' warning time on SDI.

On October 15, Thomson and Kanter took their charts and vu-graphs to Washington and met with McFarlane for an hour and a half. McFarlane had many questions about the plan and much anxiety about keeping the meeting secret. His appointment with Thomson and Kanter was deliberately not listed on his calendar.

Meanwhile, Horelick was consulting more openly with the State Department on Soviet affairs in general. On October 18, he and Kanter gave one of Shultz's deputies, Michael Armacost, under secretary of state for political affairs, a set of talking points they had prepared for possible use inside the government in preparation for the summit. This paper was less detailed than the briefing Thomson and Kanter had given McFarlane three days earlier, but it also stressed the opportunities for an offense-defense tradeoff. Since it was in the form of a script that Shultz might possibly use in a conversation with Reagan, the arguments were couched in terms meant to reassure the President that he could reconcile his two dreams—comprehensive defense in the distant future and dramatic reductions in offense in the fairly near term.

To negotiate constraints on strategic defense would not, the paper stressed, mean " 'bargaining away' SDI. We should continue to pursue a vigorous program." The paper outlined the choice between squeeze and deal. It warned that choosing to squeeze "will mean rough—perhaps dangerous—times ahead. . . . Alliance relations will become increasingly strained."

Then came a key passage. Shultz might tell the President that SDI "depends on sustained congressional and public support which may not be forthcoming"; the long-term survival of the program and the eventual achievement of Reagan's dream of SDI "requires that your [the President's] successor be committed to the same strategy and be able to stand the heat and stay the course." In other words, the greatest danger to SDI might be not from the Soviets or from domestic critics of the program but from the next President, who would not share Reagan's commitment to it, or from the next Congress, which would not have the benefit of Reagan's persuasive powers as it faced hard choices about levels of funding for the program.

Therefore, the RAND talking points concluded, the way to assure the survival of SDI in the post-Reagan era might be to make a comprehensive arms control agreement the crowning achievement of the Reagan presidency in foreign policy—and to make the guarantee of a continuing R&D program for SDI the jewel in that crown.

The peroration of these talking points for Shultz abandoned all pretense of neutrality over the choice between squeeze and deal:

> Our negotiating position may never be stronger. If we exploit our advantages and bargain hard, we may be able to achieve the kind of agreement which produces deep reductions in strategic forces; sharply reduces Soviet throw-weight and first-strike potential, objectives which have

eluded all previous efforts . . . ; protects our strategic modernization; creates conditions which, if SDI pans out, would pave the way from assured destruction to assured survival.

The paper stressed that "to get an agreement, we will have to take some account of Soviet concerns; we, too, will have to be serious and not simply seek a propaganda advantage."

To that end, Shultz might tell Reagan: "I think you should put Gorbachev to the test when you see him [at the summit] next month in Geneva. You could indicate that we are prepared to abide by a strict interpretation of the ABM treaty and negotiate an interim ban on tests of weapons in space or against targets in space until the year 2000, in exchange for Soviet agreement on offensive, defensive, and compliance issues of concern to us."

In Shultz's sessions with Reagan, White House officials noticed that the secretary of state steered clear of the treacherous issue of the narrow versus the broad interpretation, not least because his own legal advisor, Abraham Sofaer, was now the principal advocate of the broad interpretation and Shultz's senior arms-control advisor, Paul Nitze, had shifted to that side of the debate. But even though he did not follow the script exactly, Shultz did use the basic rationale of the RAND analysts for the grand compromise. He told the President repeatedly that SDI must be "put into an arms-control context"—emphasizing that this would result not in trading the program away but, quite the contrary, in making sure that it survived.

Hanged in a Fortnight

Geneva was a busy and crowded city in the fall of 1985. In addition to the third round of the Nuclear and Space Talks (September 19–November 7), the city also hosted Ronald Reagan and Mikhail Gorbachev themselves for their first meeting, from November 19 to 21.

Both sides amended their positions in order to increase the chances for progress at the summit. "The very possibility of a summit," remarked Max Kampelman, "is, in a positive sense, like the prospect of being hanged in a fortnight: It concentrates the mind wonderfully." Confirming that the same dynamic was at work on the Soviet side, Boris Ivanov said, "Let's agree on something. We must be able to come up with an agreement on something in time for our leaders."

Throughout the year, the Soviets had been hurling at the United States a dizzying barrage of proposals in various channels. Sorting out the tricks, traps, and teasers from the genuine offers was a complicated task, but the contours of what Moscow might be willing to offer for the sake of a grand compromise began to emerge as the summit drew closer.

At the beginning of October, the Soviets proposed a ceiling of six thousand "nuclear charges," a term meant to subsume ballistic-missile warheads, cruise missiles, and bomber weapons (gravity bombs and short-range attack missiles). The Americans considered this another step in the right direction, although they objected that bomber weapons should not be lumped together with ballistic missiles, since the bombers themselves were slow and vulnerable to enemy air defenses. During the round, the Soviets hinted at a willingness to exempt gravity bombs and short-range attack missiles (SRAMs) from the limit on "nuclear charges."

More important, they offered a new formula for subceilings under the six thousand ceiling. Refining their so-called force concentration rule, put forward earlier in the year, they now indicated that no more than 60 percent, or 3,600, of the nuclear charges could be on any one "delivery means," such as ICBMs.* Some U.S. negotiators were encouraged. If the Soviets were willing to accept subcategories below the overall ceiling, they might eventually accommodate the American insistence on "preferential" limits on first-strike weapons, notably ICBM warheads. There were also Soviet hints of additional subceilings on MIRVed, land-based, and heavy ballistic missiles. Karpov said in a plenary statement that his side's proposal would result in a reduction of up to 50 percent in ballistic missile throw-weight. What Nitze had long considered the cutting edge of the Soviet threat might finally be dulled.

On INF, too, there was some give. INF was the sleeper of the three groups. For the first two rounds, the Soviets had hung tough. On a number of issues, they had even backtracked from where they had been in 1983, at the time that the American missiles were deployed and the talks collapsed. Early in 1985, the chief American negotiator, Maynard Glitman, who had been Nitze's deputy in 1981–83, chided his Soviet counterpart, Aleksei Obukhov: "You may take six hours or six days or six weeks or six months to get back to the positions you took in 1983. We don't care. But know this: When you get back to your old positions, you get no credit for it with us."†

During the first round, in March and April, the Soviets seemed to grant that, while a settlement had to provide for the eventual removal of all the

---

*The Americans preferred the term "differentiation rule," since it underscored their point that arms control should differentiate between those weapons that were destabilizing (MIRVed ICBMs) and those that were retaliatory (cruise missiles and bombers).

†In the early sixties, Obukhov was an exchange student in the United States, working under the historian Hans Morgenthau at the University of Chicago. He was a member of the Soviet START delegation during the first Reagan term, and he impressed the Americans with his intellect and debating skills. Apparently he was equally impressive to his own comrades. Their nickname for him was "our heavy"—a reference to the most formidable of Soviet ICBMs, the SS-18.

American missiles as well as an allowance for some Soviet missiles as "compensation" for the British and French forces, some of the U.S. missiles already deployed might remain for a decent, perhaps even an open-ended, interval. In the second round, May 30–July 11, they backed away from even that modest concession: All American missiles had to come out immediately. Obukhov subjected Glitman to constant harangues that echoed the hardest line of the Brezhnev period in '81. Once, Glitman asked a simple question and, in response, got a sixty-five-minute filibuster on the perfidy of American policy and the illegitimacy of the American nuclear presence in Europe.

A number of Americans sensed that the Soviets were hanging tough on INF because, paradoxically, it was the negotiating forum in which progress would be the easiest to achieve, if and when the Kremlin decided to move.

"Let's assume we agree fully with the position you've taken in INF," said Glitman. "We could see reaching an INF agreement without linkage" to START and space and defense.

Obukhov agreed. A few days later, having checked with his home office, he said, "I can tell you that my answer was correct." Karpov subsequently reconfirmed to Kampelman the Kremlin's willingness, in principle, to sign a separate deal in INF. Gromyko had insisted at the beginning of the year that all three of the issues on the table in Geneva—INF, START, and space and defense—must be resolved "in their interrelationship." Now it looked as though INF might stand on its own.

By the third round, from September to November, with the summit in prospect, the Soviets returned to their earlier willingness to leave some American missiles on the continent when an INF deal was signed. They began pushing hard for an "interim agreement" on INF whereby the United States would keep some of its cruise missiles in Europe (the Pershing IIs would have to go) in exchange for a drawdown in Soviet SS-20s within range of Europe and a freeze on those in Asia. An INF agreement to this effect could be signed before there was a resolution of the other, strategic issues. However, the Soviets were still holding out for eventual withdrawal of all American INF missiles, and they were holding START hostage to that outcome: Their offer to accept a START ceiling of six thousand nuclear charges was conditioned on the elimination of all American missiles from Europe. Karpov told Kampelman there would be no agreement on strategic weapons as long as there was a single American missile in Europe.

Nevertheless, the stage was set for a separate deal on Euromissiles.

The Reagan Administration, too, moved slightly during the fall 1985 round of the Nuclear and Space Talks. Near the end of the round, with Shultz about to fly to Moscow to prepare for the summit and the Reagan-Gorbachev meeting less than three weeks away, Kampelman and his colleagues arrived at the Soviet mission on November 1 for a "joint plenary." All three negotiating groups were assembled, facing each other across the phalanx of bottled mineral water and clusters of colored pencils. "I want you to listen carefully," said Max Kampelman with a wide smile and a twinkle in his eye. "And I want you to listen with your constructive ear." Victor Karpov smiled back, though somewhat more guardedly.

Kampelman introduced a new American proposal for START. It was based on a combination of numbers from the Soviet position already on the table and a schedule for offensive reductions similar to the one at the center of the still highly secret Monday Package: an overall ceiling of 6,000 on "nuclear charges" (the combined total of ballistic missile warheads and air-launched cruise missiles); 4,500 ballistic missile warheads; 3,000 ICBM warheads; 1,500 heavy ICBM warheads (i.e., a 50-percent reduction in heavy SS-18s). While the Americans presented their proposal, one of the Soviets, Gennadi Khromov, took out a pocket calculator and busily figured what the new American numbers would do to the Strategic Rocket Forces—and to the United States Air Force.

One number that was meant both to surprise and to please the Soviets was a provision that would, in effect, squeeze the American air-launched cruise missile force to a smaller size than expected.*

There was also, however, a feature in the new American proposal that came as an unpleasant surprise, not only to the Soviets but to many Americans as well, notably including Nitze. It was a proposed ban on mobile ICBMs. Nitze would have welcomed a ban on MIRVed mobiles, since that would serve the cause of stability by reducing the ratio of warheads to targets, but a ban on all mobiles outlawed what he felt was one of the most welcome and stabilizing prospective weapon systems, the single-warhead Midgetman. More immediately and pertinently, however, the ban would outlaw the Soviets' two new ICBMs, the SS-24, roughly the equivalent of the MX, and the SS-25, the three-stage, intercontinental, although only single-warhead, version of the SS-20.

The ban on mobiles was shoehorned into the American position at the behest of Perle and the Pentagon, with the enthusiastic support of McFarlane. Defense Department planners wanted to stop the SS-25 because it was considerably harder for the commanders of American missile forces to target a Soviet mobile system than stationary silos. There were already over

---

*Under the American formula, each side would be allotted "free" only 1,500 air-launched cruise missiles (6,000–4,500 = 1,500). ALCMs were fungible—that is, if either side wanted more than 1,500 ALCMs, it could have them, but it would have to pay a price in ballistic missile warheads. Some American plans had called for as many as 4,000 cruise missiles on bombers, and the Soviets, in their own worst-case projections, feared that their air defense system might eventually have to contend with as many as 8,000 American ALCMs.

forty SS-25s deployed in a mobile basing mode, and they were causing problems for the "targeteers" of the Pentagon.

McFarlane's reason for backing the ban was more general and already well established. One of his disagreements with Nitze stemmed from his doubt that the United States would ever overcome political resistance to mobile land-based missiles and be able to deploy Midgetman.

Partly in order to preserve the appearance that it was consulting with Congress on arms control, the Administration did not include the proposed ban on mobile ICBMs in Kampelman's November 1 presentation. The delay gave the Administration just enough time to warn key congressmen that one of their favorite programs—a program on which they had insisted in exchange for their support of Administration defense and arms-control policy— was about to be declared illegal under the new American proposal.

The principal bearer of this bad news was, as usual, Nitze himself. In the eyes of many senators and representatives, he had the highest standing of anyone in the Administration on arms control. That he opposed the policy in question was nothing new. He had been in a similarly awkward and ironic position with the Europeans, for similar reasons, many times before, and would be so again.

As Nitze expected, Democratic advocates of Midgetman on Capitol Hill were upset. These included Senators Sam Nunn and Albert Gore, Jr., who had been collaborating closely and quietly with Nitze in making the case for Midgetman, as well as Congressman Les Aspin. They tried to get the Administration to reverse the decision. But before these protests could have any effect in Washington, the ban on mobiles was put to the Soviets in Geneva. John Tower, the head of the American START group, summoned Victor Karpov on a Saturday afternoon and told him the bad news. Ostensibly, Tower was extending Karpov a courtesy: Better Karpov should learn of the ban on mobiles from Tower than find out about it through press leaks out of Washington or feedback from Moscow once Shultz arrived there. But the real reason for giving Karpov a sneak preview of the proposal was to make sure that it was, in the words of one American diplomat in Geneva, "locked in stone—immune to the appeals of the Midgetmanners who were raising such a stink back in Washington."

Perle waved the furor aside. He saw the no-mobiles proposal as being a perfectly reasonable negotiating ploy. It lent itself to an obvious fallback later in the talks: a "set-aside" for one unMIRVed—that is, single-warhead—mobile ICBM per side, so that the Soviets could keep the SS-25 if the United States proceeded with Midgetman.[8] This was not a characteristic tactic for Perle. In the past, he had often denounced others, like Paul Nitze, for even considering fallbacks.

"The Highest Plane of Reason"

The Soviets, meanwhile, continued their effort to tantalize the Americans in Geneva with breathtaking concessions in START if only SDI were to become negotiable. Some of the discussions in which they dropped these hints took place in a rathskeller, called the Albatross, on the grounds of the Soviet mission on the outskirts of town. In keeping with Gorbachev's new antialcohol campaign, the featured beverage was now orange juice when the Soviets entertained the Americans.

The Soviet negotiators seemed to have a harder time following their general secretary's lead when he publicly signaled flexibility in the Soviet Union's own position on SDI. In August, Gorbachev had given an interview to the editors of *Time* magazine. "If there is no ban on the militarization of space, if an arms race in space is not prevented, nothing else will work," he said. "In Geneva the Soviet Union has proposed a ban on the creation—including research, testing and deployment—of space-strike weapons. Therefore, as we see it, our proposed ban would embrace all stages in the birth of this new kind of arms. Research is something we regard as part of the overall program for the development of space weapons."

That seemed to be a reiteration of the blanket ban that his negotiators had indeed been seeking in Geneva. But Gorbachev continued:

> Now, when the question comes up about research, and the question of banning research, what we have in mind is not research in fundamental science. Such research concerning space is going on and it will continue. What we mean is the design stage, when certain orders are given, contracts are signed, for specific elements of the system. And when they start building models or mockups or test samples, when they hold field tests, now that is something—when it goes over to the design state— that is something that can be verified . . . by national technical means of verification. There will have to be field tests of various components. After all, if we can now, from our artificial earth satellites, read the numbers of automobiles down on earth, surely we can recognize these things when they come to that stage.

With those words, Gorbachev considerably amended the Soviet position, bringing it somewhat closer to what some American experts believed to be a reasonable—and verifiable—interpretation of the ABM treaty and its prohibition on development and testing of exotic ABMs other than land-based ones.

All of a sudden, a passage from the record of the Nixon Administration's testimony at the time of the ratification of SALT I became highly germane. On July 18, 1972, during Senate hearings on the ABM treaty, Senator Henry Jackson had asked the chief negotiator, Gerard Smith, at what point development of exotic systems would become impermissible. Smith's answer was drafted by the Pentagon and approved by an interagency committee:

> The obligation not to develop such systems, devices or warheads would be applicable only to that stage of development which follows laboratory development and testing. The prohibitions on development contained in the ABM treaty would start at that part of the development process where field testing is initiated on either a prototype or breadboard model. It was understood by both sides that the prohibition on "development" applies to activities involved after a component moves from the laboratory development and testing stage to the field testing stage, wherever performed. The fact that early stages of the development process, such as laboratory testing, would pose problems for verification by national technical means is an important consideration in reaching this definition. Exchanges with the Soviet delegation made clear that this definition is also the Soviet interpretation of the term "development."

Like Smith in 1972, Gorbachev in 1985 was not just improvising; he was working from talking points prepared by his advisors. According to one of them, they had reread the Smith testimony from 1972 and were using the *Time* interview to send a signal to Washington that the Soviet position on SDI might be compatible with the traditional American interpretation of the ABM treaty.

They did not, however, transmit that signal through—or even, apparently, to—their own negotiating team in Geneva. When Kampelman asked Kvitsinsky what the general secretary had meant in his *Time* interview by "research in fundamental science," the Soviet diplomat replied, "Such things as splitting the atom." Would anything visualized for SDI be permissible?

"No," replied Kvitsinsky; any purposeful research, wherever conducted, was forbidden.

Only some time later did the Soviets amend their position slightly to conform with what Gorbachev had said in *Time,* explaining that the ban on "development, including scientific research," would apply to any activity that was "observable by national technical means of verification"—i.e., testing outside the laboratory that could be observed by the other side's spy satellites.

The Reagan Administration's response to the steadily evolving Soviet position was a stubborn display of sales resistance. Whatever the Soviets did the United States pointedly referred to as a "counterproposal." That word was meant to convey the impression that the Soviets were playing black on the chess board, countering bold moves by the United States, which was playing white. The reality for some time had been the opposite. The Reagan Administration had not really made a new proposal at all in the Nuclear and Space Talks. It had dusted off its old START and INF positions from the first term, before the Soviet walkout in 1983, and coupled them with an argument—implausible not only to the Soviets but to many Americans as well—that SDI should be allowed to proceed independent of whatever happened on the offensive side of the equation.

When the Soviets made their own moves, either in new proposals put on the table in Geneva or in statements issued by Gorbachev in Moscow, the Administration complained about whatever was patently unacceptable in the Soviet position (e.g., counting U.S. forward-based systems as strategic) and pocketed whatever concessions were to the liking of the U.S. (e.g., the ICBM warhead ceiling).

Publicly, Paul Nitze was the most outspoken and authoritative American naysayer. His skepticism partly served as his own protective coloration in an Administration that prided itself on toughness. In speeches, congressional testimony, and interviews, he made the case throughout 1985 that it was the Soviets who were dragging their feet and imposing artificial obstacles to progress. They had, he said repeatedly, yet to demonstrate "seriousness." But his complaints, if read carefully (as they were at the Soviet embassy in Washington), were almost always couched in terms that subtly indicated where progress could be made through mutual flexibility. His grievances and exhortations were a disguised appeal on behalf of the grand compromise.

For example, in a speech at the National Press Club on May 1, Nitze said, "It is the Soviets who, by focusing their energies on an attempt to derail SDI research, are contradicting the January [Shultz-Gromyko] agreement to deal with all the issues in their interrelationship." Decoded in Moscow, this message might read: Stop trying to ban research, and maybe we can get serious about an offense-defense tradeoff.

Speaking to the American Defense Preparedness Association on October 24, Nitze argued that "in its impact, the Soviet counterproposal [tabled in round three, for a ceiling of six thousand nuclear charges] would . . . actually decrease rather than enhance stability." He meant that the ratio of Soviet ICBM warheads to American hardened military targets would go up rather than down unless the Soviets also agreed to subceilings on their ICBMs. But this tough-sounding message, which earned him applause with his immediate audience of American hard-liners, could also be read in Moscow to mean that if the Soviet Union accepted subceilings on ICBMs and ICBM warheads, the offensive side of the grand compromise would be in place, perhaps triggering some American concessions on the defensive side.

The Soviets were playing much the same game as Nitze: In the way they berated the Americans, they were probing possible points of compromise. The Soviets were still conducting their end of diplomacy as part of a broader anti-SDI campaign. They did not want to talk about what the ABM treaty permitted; rather, they wanted to concentrate in the negotiations on what the treaty did not permit. Nevertheless, the glimmer of a compromise was beginning to appear. By denouncing the United States for taking an extreme position, they were suggesting that a less extreme position might be acceptable to them.

On June 4, 1985, Marshal Akhromeyev, the chief of the General Staff, gave an interview to *Pravda* commenting on various statements coming out of Washington, including some by Nitze himself, about the ABM treaty. Akhromeyev attacked the United States for "trying to exploit the treaty's provisions for possible amendments" and defended the Soviet strategic defensive program, including the controversial radar at Krasnoyarsk. But he did so in a way that seemed to leave some room for negotiation over what might be negotiable and permissible.

Nitze read the text closely and concluded that Akhromeyev was "threading his way beyond pure polemics" and addressing the issue of strategic defense on the "highest plane of reason." This was stunning praise for the chief of the Soviet General Staff. The Akhromeyev piece confirmed Nitze's long-standing preference for dealing with Soviet military men rather than diplomats. He hoped that this military man in particular might at some point enter the negotiations.

After Gorbachev's interview in *Time* appeared at the beginning of September, Nitze noted cautiously that the Soviets now seemed willing to distinguish between what he called "basic conceptual research" and "engineering research." The former, as Nitze read it, "would be excluded from limitation" under an agreement; restrictions on the latter, he suggested, might be included. He told a House Foreign Affairs subcommittee in October that while "the research program is not on the table . . . other aspects of the program" were negotiable—as far as he was concerned, at least.

That same month, while in Moscow with Shultz to lay the ground for the summit, Nitze told the Soviets, "We ought to put our heads together and work out what the ABM treaty permits."

With these statements, clearly implying give on SDI, the President's senior advisor on arms control was coming dangerously close to heresy.

Meanwhile, Nitze grew annoyed at criticism offered in anticipation of a possible deal from a number of prominent Americans, and one in particular. With the summit coming and talk of an offense-defense tradeoff in the air, Henry Kissinger was beginning to lob objections and exhortations in the direction of advocates of such a deal. In a syndicated column that appeared on September 8, Kissinger attacked Gorbachev's interview in *Time* as an attempt to equate "success at Geneva with abandonment of the Strategic Defense Initiative." He urged the Administration to hang tough. He hailed SDI as a promising alternative to mutual deterrence, which he said was "clearly losing relevance." Unless the West found a way to base deterrence on defense rather than offense, "democratic publics will sooner or later retreat to pacifism and unilateral disarmament."

This was a theme to which Kissinger would return many times. It reflected a deep pessimism on his part about the psychological balance of power. He made it seem that the West was inherently, incorrigibly soft in contrast to the steely-eyed, utterly ruthless Soviets. The traditional doctrine of offense-dominant deterrence was not mutually applicable or mutually beneficial, for it favored the tougher of the two superpowers.

That was a Spenglerian view. It was also a Nitzean view. Nitze had worried for years that the Soviet Union, with its supposed capability and presumed willingness to fight a nuclear war, would be able to checkmate the West, to "deter our deterrent." However, in the 1970s pessimism about the ruthlessness gap had not stopped Kissinger, then inside government, from making arms-control deals that were intended to bolster traditional deterrence—deals that Nitze criticized from the outside. In 1985, their positions were reversed.

Kissinger's column was a preemptive attack on precisely the position that Nitze was trying to advance for the summit. Kissinger disparaged as militarily "marginal" and "strategically meaningless" the offensive reductions that the United States might be able to get in exchange for yielding to the Soviets' "vicious campaign" against SDI. Instead of accepting constraints on the development and testing of SDI, he urged the Administration to press for an agreement to regulate deployment. Strategic defenses, he said, should be phased in over a ten-year period with two objectives: "protection of the retaliatory force (i.e., ICBM and bomber bases)"; and "a defense of population against limited attacks and accidental launches by a superpower, as well as attacks by third nuclear countries."

Kissinger was going back to square one in the ABM debate of the sixties and seventies. Whatever promising new technologies might be available—whatever a space-based chemical laser or a "pop-up" bomb-pumped X-ray laser might be able to do in the 1990s that a ground-based interceptor had not been able to do twenty years before—there was still nothing in the laboratory, or in the mind of man (no "conceptual breakthrough," as Kissinger might once have termed it), to answer the original nagging question: How could one side convince the other that its antimissile system was purely defensive and not potentially part of a capability to carry out a one-two punch? It was the inability to answer that question that had led Kissinger, Nitze, and others, thirteen years before, to accept strict limits on strategic defenses as part of SALT I, and that led Nitze now to look for ways to "perfect" the ABM treaty and its implementation as part of a grand compromise that included stabilizing reductions in offense.

Nitze was exasperated with what he regarded as Kissinger's mischievous carping. After reading Kissinger's column, Nitze said he was deeply skeptical whether it would be possible to "define 'retaliatory' and to confine defense in that definition." Moreover, he continued, Kissinger "doesn't even give house room to negotiability. Negotiability shouldn't be the *summum bonum* of arms control, but it shouldn't be ignored either."[9]

In the Ford Administration a dozen years before, it had been Kissinger who complained that Nitze was making unreasonable demands on diplomacy as the art of the possible.

The Fireside Document

Ronald Reagan and Mikhail Gorbachev were to meet in Geneva in mid-November. On the eve of his departure for the summit, Reagan gave a series of interviews, primarily to elaborate on his hopes for SDI. In a session with Soviet journalists on October 31, Reagan said, "We won't put this system in place, this defensive system, until we do away with our nuclear missiles, our offensive missiles."

All over the government, on both sides of the Potomac and on both sides of the ideological divide over arms control, officials winced. It was a vivid example of the way Reagan's thinking often short-circuited on the subject of nuclear-weapons policy. He had been listening for months to George Shultz and Robert McFarlane explain how less offense would require less defense. They had been trying to implant in the President's mind the most rudimentary rationale for the grand compromise. He had oversimplified their point even further, and now regurgitated it as the astonishing suggestion that the elimination of all offensive weapons would be a precondition for, rather than a consequence of, deployment of SDI.

Taken at face value, the President's statement should have been cause for rejoicing in Moscow. It would have made the Soviets' task easy: All they would have had to do to block SDI would be to refuse to eliminate their offenses—not a difficult choice under any circumstances. Larry Speakes dismissed what he called a "presidential imprecision."

A week later, on November 6, in another interview, this time with the wire services, Reagan clarified:

If . . . we had a defensive system, and we could not get agreement on [the Soviets'] part to eliminate the nuclear weapons, we would have done our best and, now, we would go ahead and deploy it. But even though, as I say, that would then open us up to the charge of achieving a capacity for a first stike—we don't want that. We want to eliminate things of that kind, and that's why, frankly, I think that any nation offered this under those circumstances that I've described would see the value of going forward. Remember, the Soviet Union has already stated its wish that nuclear weapons could be done away with.

Now, with a bit more preparation, Reagan was saying that the American priority was a negotiated transition to a world with less offense and more defense than was currently the case; whatever the outcome of the negotiations, the United States would seek to structure its own mixture of offenses and defenses in a way that minimized the appearance of seeking a first-strike capability.

Reagan was so grossly oversimplifying the problem that he inadvertently underscored how daunting it was. Before the United States could "have" a shield that it would then "go ahead and deploy," it must first build a massive, complex system involving thousands of elements extending over thousands of miles; such a "supersystem," as the experts sometimes called it, would require extensive testing before the United States could be said to "have" an effective defense. Building the technology without putting it in place would offer little benefit.

On November 12, in a third interview, this one with foreign broadcasters, Reagan portrayed SDI as an inducement for both sides drastically to reduce, even eliminate, their nuclear weapons:

Let me give you my dream of what would happen. We have the weapon. We don't start deploying it. We get everybody together and we say here, here it is, and here's how it works, and what it'll do to incoming missiles. Now we think that all of us who have nuclear weapons should agree that we're going to eliminate the nuclear weapons. But we will make available to everyone this weapon. I don't mean we'll give it to them. They're going to have to pay for it [*laughter*]—but at cost. But we would make this defensive weapon available.

Now, some can say, if you're going to do away with the nuclear offensive weapons, then why does anyone need this? Well, because we all know how to make it, and someday there may be a madman in the world, as there have been before, who would start in secret to produce these weapons. But it's like when in Geneva in 1925 all the nations of the world after World War I got rid of poison gas. Everybody kept their gas masks. Well, the same thing—this is [like] the gas mask. We could say look. We'll never, any of us, have to fear that maybe someone of us is cheating or maybe there is going to be that madman someday, if we all have the ability to defend ourselves against nuclear missiles. And

I think this would make far more sense than for us to say, oh, we found it, we'll go ahead and deploy it now while we still keep our other missiles.

In his use of the gas mask analogy, the President was in close accord with what he had been hearing from George Shultz. The secretary of state had, in his conversations with the President, recently adopted the notion of SDI as an "insurance policy." This view of the program appealed greatly to Reagan, but it was also reminiscent of the anti-Chinese rationale for the "thin" ABM late in the Johnson Administration. What might be called a "thin SDI" could take account of the political appeal of strategic defense (in this case, its appeal to a popular and determined President), while at the same time signaling to the Soviets a willingness to negotiate limits on deployment as part of a deal that covered offenses.

During his November 12 interview, Reagan was asked outright about the negotiability of SDI. In his answer he spoke from the heart while following the advice that Shultz had been giving him. He would not, he said,

> compromise in the sense of giving up on the research. . . . Since this research is all going on within the bounds of the ABM treaty, we're going to continue, because I think it would be the greatest thing in this century if we could come up with the idea that, at last, there is a defensive measure—a system against nuclear missiles. . . . And so, this isn't a bargaining chip in that sense of being willing to trade off the research and stop what we're doing in order to get X number of missiles eliminated. We'll continue with that. Then, as I've said many times, . . . before deployment, I think we sit down together and decide how we use this to bring about the elimination of nuclear weapons—offensive weapons—and to make the world safe.

Every presidential mention of the ABM treaty was a point for Shultz, McFarlane, and Nitze in their struggle against Weinberger and Perle. Now they were about to carry that struggle to the summit. With the help of the White House chief of staff, Donald Regan, Shultz and McFarlane arranged for Weinberger to be left out of the entourage that would accompany the President to Geneva.

On the very eve of the meeting, the Pentagon struck back. *The New York Times* and the *Washington Post* carried front-page articles about a letter drafted by Perle and sent to Reagan over Weinberger's signature, recommending that the President not commit the United States to continued compliance with the ABM treaty. The letter rehearsed the case that the Pentagon had been making for the broad interpretation of the ABM treaty: "In Geneva, you will almost certainly come under great pressure . . . to agree formally to limit SDI research development and testing to only that research allowed under the most restrictive interpretation of the ABM treaty, even though you have determined that a less restrictive interpretation is justified legally.''

Acceding to such pressure—which the letter implied would come not just from the Soviets but from the State Department—would be to play into the hands of SDI opponents on Capitol Hill: "The Soviets doubtless will seek assurances that you will continue to be bound to such tight limits on SDI development and testing that would discourage Congress from making any but token appropriations.''

As the President set off for his first meeting with the leader of the Soviet Union, the letter was a dramatic display of dissension within the ranks of his Administration. McFarlane, in the guise of an unnamed official aboard Air Force One who was quoted in the newspapers the next day, fumed that ''someone'' was trying to ''sabotage'' the summit. He left no doubt that Perle was the leading suspect. In Geneva, Perle denied the charge and suggested that the State Department had leaked the letter to make the Pentagon look bad.

Whoever slipped the letter to the *Post* and *Times*, Weinberger and Perle's motivation in sending it to the President was clear: The letter was meant to head off what Nitze and McFarlane wanted to do—use the ABM treaty as the basis for the grand compromise. That had been a key feature of the Monday Package, and it was carried over into a plan that McFarlane and Nitze had for the summit.

At his first meeting with Gorbachev, in a villa on the shore of Lake Geneva, Reagan tried to persuade him that they had a historic opportunity to free the world from the ''uncivilized doctrine'' of assured destruction. ''I simply cannot condone the notion,'' said Reagan, ''of keeping the peace by threatening to blow each other away. We must be able to find a better way.'' SDI, he said, was a better way. Anticipating Gorbachev's objection that SDI was simply a cover for achieving an American first-strike capability, Reagan repeated his vow not to deploy the system unilaterally, to negotiate a transition to a new defense-dominant world, to share defensive technology, and to open American laboratories so that the Soviets could see that the work there was indeed ''purely defensive.''

As the President wound up his presentation, Gorbachev was sitting back, his eyes locked onto Reagan's. He was silent for a moment before beginning his response. He started calmly, slowly, in his confident, authoritative baritone. But his vehemence grew as he spoke. He needed no help from notes or from his comrades. He extemporized passionately about the danger of ''space-strike arms.'' He hammered away at the suspicion that ''what you call research'' on SDI had the potential of producing ''offensive nuclear weapons circling the earth.'' Gorbachev said that he could neither accept the "faulty and deceiving justification" for SDI nor bring himself to believe that the President meant what he said on the subject. The United States was "plotting" to use SDI to re-establish a "one-sided advantage" over the U.S.S.R. The very concept of SDI, he said, was "founded on emotions rather than on facts.''

In reply, Reagan reminded Gorbachev that the United States had enjoyed a monopoly in nuclear weapons after World War II but had not employed those weapons for aggressive purposes. "Why don't you trust me?" Reagan asked.

Gorbachev turned the question around: Why didn't Reagan trust *him?*

The President replied that any American leader must plan according to the other side's capabilities.

That was just the point, said Gorbachev: SDI had the capability of disastrously upsetting parity and the strategic balance.

There was a long, tension-charged pause, and finally Gorbachev said, "It looks as though we've reached an impasse.''

Reagan invited him to go for a walk. They bundled up against the cold, left their aides behind, and went to an adjoining pool house, where a fire had been prepared. Accompanied only by their interpreters, the two men removed their overcoats and sat in stuffed armchairs on either side of the fireplace. Reagan had brought with him a manila envelope. He removed the papers inside and handed Gorbachev a Russian translation of the key document. The Soviet leader put on his reading glasses. The two men spent a few moments studying the papers before discussing their contents.

The paper was an American proposal for a set of "guidelines" that the two leaders might issue to their negotiators at the Nuclear and Space Talks. Paul Nitze had been closely involved in the preparation and drafting of the document. The key sentences were on offensive nuclear weapons and strategic defense: In addition to accepting a 50-percent cut in strategic offensive forces, "the sides should provide assurances that their strategic defense programs shall be conducted as permitted by, and in full compliance with, the ABM Treaty.''

Unlike the Monday Package, the summit guidelines had been, in the slang of bureaucrats, "massaged" in the interagency process—including by the strong fingers of the office of the secretary of defense. Therefore, the paper also contained a transparent endorsement of SDI: "The sides should agree to begin exploring immediately means by which a cooperative transition to greater reliance on defensive systems, should such systems prove feasible, could be accomplished.''

The nub of the Monday Package was still there, but it was now couched in terms that would appeal more to Reagan and less to Gorbachev. In presenting the paper, the President stressed to the general secretary that the guidelines were a package deal: The Soviet side could not pick it apart, accepting only the provisions they liked and discarding the others.

"But this allows SDI to continue," said Gorbachev.

"Yes," said the President, now speaking for himself, not needing to refer to carefully prepared talking points. "It must continue." He did not dwell on the subtle point in the guidelines about how it would continue as an R&D program within the terms of the ABM treaty.

"Then we just disagree," said the Soviet leader.

Much of the rest of the summit was devoted to the negotiation of a joint communiqué. There was considerable haggling within the American delegation as well as intense, sometimes acrimonious negotiation with the Soviets. Perle was particularly proud of the communiqué. Afterward, he said in a number of background interviews with reporters that it was one of the first documents of its kind that was devoid of ritualistic Soviet generalities about the "inadmissibility" of nuclear war. Instead, the communiqué contained the more categorical and straightforward assertion that "a nuclear war cannot be won and must never be fought."

Since the mid-1970s, it was widely believed in the West that Soviet military doctrine and deployments were based on the proposition that a nuclear war could indeed be fought and won. That was certainly the strong conviction of many members of the Committee on the Present Danger, including Paul Nitze. One of the principal pieces of evidence adduced to support this suspicion was the size and capability of the Soviet MIRVed ICBM force, particularly the heavy SS-18s. Nor had the Soviets themselves done much to discourage these ominous inferences. In their public statements, including earlier joint communiqués that they signed with foreign leaders, even when asserting their peaceful intentions, Soviet statesmen had been careful not to contradict what Soviet generals were telling their subordinates: If it comes to a war with the forces of imperialism and capitalism, we can and will prevail.

Then, starting in the late seventies, there were indications that perhaps both the political and military leaderships were rethinking the wisdom of this position; perhaps Soviet doctrine, especially against the backdrop of Soviet deployments, was provoking the West into more hostile attitudes and more threatening weapons programs of its own. Gorbachev's willingness in Geneva to associate himself with American phraseology that repudiated the doctrine of fightable, winnable nuclear war was one of the most striking and authoritative indications of such rethinking. It augured well for the more practical and meaningful step of actually reducing Soviet MIRVed ICBMs in a START agreement.

In the struggle within the American delegation over the communiqué, Perle fought successfully against any reference to the ABM treaty that would have hinted at limitations on, or the negotiability of, SDI. Even a reference to the desirability of preventing an arms race in space proved contentious. That phrase had appeared in the Shultz-Gromyko communiqué of the previous January, but Perle opposed it at the summit anyway. McFarlane insisted that it go in and got his way, though only after strenuous argument.*

"You've got to work pretty hard around here just not to move backward," McFarlane later commented in some disgust.

From Reagan's standpoint, his first encounter with Gorbachev had gone extremely well. He got credit both among the allies and in the United States, from the left and the center of the political spectrum, for meeting with the leader of the Soviet Union and holding what were obviously serious and apparently amicable discussions. At the same time, he got credit from the right for holding firm on SDI—for letting Weinberger's admonition on the eve of the summit be his guide. In the eyes of the Pentagon and the Laser Lobby on Capitol Hill, the summit seemed a success precisely because there seemed to be no progress toward the grand compromise.

Probably for just that reason, Gorbachev's reception back in Moscow was less enthusiastic, especially on the part of the military. In a number of pronouncements, Marshal Akhromeyev, who had accompanied Gorbachev to Geneva, was noticeably cool about both the general secretary and the accomplishments of the summit.†

In a memo assessing the meeting, Nitze judged it to have "turned out to be a media triumph for the President. A failed summit was closely averted, and on substance the score was zero-zero."

Shortly afterward, in early December, after constant sniping from the Pentagon and often losing battles over turf and prerogatives with White House Chief of Staff Regan, McFarlane resigned as national security advisor. Nitze lamented that he had "lost a friend and an ally." The idea of SDI as the greatest sting operation in history would have to proceed without its originator. McFarlane's way to the exit had been paved with good intentions, but he had been outmaneuvered and outsmarted at almost every turn by Perle in the struggle over how to use SDI.

---

*The communiqué committed the two sides to accelerate negotiations to "prevent an arms race in space and to terminate it on Earth, to limit and reduce nuclear arms and enhance strategic stability."

†Kremlinologists commented particularly on Akhromeyev's lukewarm endorsement of Gorbachev's handling of the meeting in the November 28 issue of *Pravda* and a postsummit editorial in *Krasnaya Zvezda* (Red Star), the armed forces journal, warning about the "illusions of people who, despite facts to the contrary, still believe . . . that the U.S. Administration is capable of heeding the voice of reason."

Back to Zero

The communiqué released at the end of the 1985 summit committed both sides "to accelerate the work" of the Nuclear and Space Talks, so that there might be "early progress, in particular in areas where there is common ground, including the principle of 50-percent reductions in the nuclear arms of the U.S. and the U.S.S.R. appropriately applied, as well as the idea of an interim INF agreement." Yet the most immediate and evident acceleration was not in the negotiations in Geneva but in the workings of the Soviet public-relations machinery in Moscow.

In their eagerness to play to the gallery of world public opinion, the Soviets took little notice of the forms of diplomacy. Shortly before noon on January 15, 1986, Dobrynin's deputy, Oleg Sokolov, gave George Shultz a letter from Gorbachev to Reagan. Shultz immediately sent the letter to the White House. It arrived while Administration officials there were telling a gathering of reporters not to expect any changes in the Soviet negotiating position until after Gorbachev had consolidated his political position at a Communist party congress the following month. Only three hours later, the anchorman on the Soviet television evening news spent half an hour reading aloud the entire document while TASS distributed the text around the world.

The proposal was nothing less than a schedule for the elimination of all nuclear weapons "by the end of 1999." The Soviet Union was back in the business of general and complete disarmament. The proposal was in three stages—front-loaded with the reductions most beneficial to the military and political interests of the Soviet Union. The first stage featured a START agreement along the lines already proposed (50-percent cuts to 6,000 "nuclear charges," of which 3,600 could be on any one kind of launcher, such as ICBMs). In the second stage, beginning in 1990, other nations would join in reducing their nuclear weapons toward zero. The third stage called for the elimination of all remaining nuclear arms. All these reductions would be possible "only if both the U.S.S.R. and the U.S.A. renounce the development, testing, and deployment of space-strike weapons."

While this proposal was more ambitious, elaborate, and sudden in appearance than those of the past, its main purpose was obvious and familiar—to block SDI. Gorbachev had laid down his own logic chain, and it looked like this:

Ronald Reagan has said that he will bring about the millennium of total nuclear disarmament. His way of doing so is Star Wars. SDI will, he says, render offensive weapons impotent and obsolete. But his is a dangerous and dishonest scheme. It masks ominous, even aggressive intentions. Moreover, it is a pie-in-the-sky promise. He does not even say when this meretricious dream of his will supposedly come true. I, Gorbachev, have a better idea. It, too, will bring about the millennium—literally by New Year's Day in the year 2000; it, too, will eliminate nuclear weapons from the face of the earth. Moreover, it will do so in many of our lifetimes (very likely during my own tenure as the leader of the Soviet Union). By following my plan, we will have actually achieved the goal that President Reagan pretends to offer you in the dim, doubtful, and dangerous future. My plan will be fulfilled before SDI could possibly be deployed. We will have accomplished all this without unleashing the specter of an arms race in space and a new generation of space-strike arms.

In Geneva the next day, Karpov opened round four of the Nuclear and Space Talks with a verbatim reading from the eleven-page Gorbachev millenarian proposal as a "plenary statement." It was marked *sekretno* (secret) on the top page, yet virtually every word had appeared the day before in TASS.

The Soviets had apparently decided to concentrate on exploiting the proposal for everything it was worth in the public arena. There was little amplification in diplomatic channels, and what follow-up there was tended to be confused and confusing. The Soviet negotiators in Geneva still seemed to be operating on the basis of inadequate, sometimes even contradictory instructions from their home office over how to interpret the bold public statements of their leader.

Perhaps because Gorbachev was so clearly going over their heads, appealing directly to public opinion, the Soviet negotiators were in a testy mood. Early in the round John Tower made a plenary statement saying that there were a number of areas of "convergence" in START: As the Reagan-Gorbachev communiqué had said, both sides were committed to the principle of 50-percent reductions and to the goal of narrowing the gap over how to define and apply those reductions. Tower suggested to Victor Karpov that they establish working groups to explore "common ground" between the two positions—a phrase that had actually appeared in the communiqué.

"There is nothing to discuss," snapped Karpov. "There is no common ground, no convergence. The important areas are those where we differ." His polemical tone continued for much of the round. On a number of occasions he launched into philippics on the sins of the United States. Tower would reply with low-keyed sarcasm, "Thank you, Victor. We subscribe completely to your characterization of the American position. Now let's get down to business."

Business in START was anything but booming. Karpov and his colleagues emphasized that 50-percent reductions in offense were contingent on a complete ban on SDI (as well as inclusion of forward-based systems), and they seemed determined to hold further progress on offensive reductions in abeyance until they extracted some indication of American flexibility on defenses. Grigori Zaitsev noted smugly that under Gorbachev's comprehensive proposal, all nuclear weapons would be abolished in fifteen years, so there would be no need for SDI; only when the Americans recognized that the rationale for SDI had disappeared and were prepared to make the program itself go away would there be opportunities in START.

One of the surprises in Gorbachev's January 15 comprehensive proposal was that the first stage included the elimination of all INF missiles from Europe. Just as the general secretary and his advisors were willing to meet the American demand for deep cuts in strategic offense if doing so would get rid of SDI, they decided to play back to Washington a version of its own old Zero Option for INF as a way of forcing the elimination of American missiles from Europe. Thus, the Soviets were subjecting American INF forward-based systems to double jeopardy: U.S. weapons in Europe were still defined as "strategic," therefore part of the Soviet count in START, and they were marked for elimination in an INF agreement as well.

As an "interim" agreement in INF, the Soviet negotiators explained, they might eliminate all their SS-20s from Europe and perhaps even freeze the number of SS-20s in Asia. At the same time, they dropped their demand for direct compensation for British and French nuclear forces. However, there was a provision in their new proposal that would prevent Britain and France from building up their nuclear forces (for example, MIRVing their SLBMs) and another that would eventually make those weapons subject to reduction and elimination as part of the overall timetable.

It was not at first clear whether INF could truly be unlinked from SDI and START and resolved in a separate agreement in the relatively near future, or whether the implementation of an INF treaty would somehow remain contingent on the bigger, more troublesome, and strategically more significant issues of intercontinental weapons and SDI. Yuli Kvitsinsky kept telling Max Kampelman that INF remained "closely tied" to START and defense and space, but Aleksei Obukhov, the Soviets' chief INF negotiator, waffled and dodged on that question with his counterpart Maynard Glitman.

Once again, it took Gorbachev to clarify and advance the matter. On February 6, he received Senator Edward Kennedy in Moscow and told him that there was no linkage between an INF interim agreement and the other issues. Only then did the Soviet negotiators in Geneva seem to have their signals straight. Over lunch, Kvitsinsky said grudgingly, "Well, you got a gift from us on this one."

On the issue of defense and space, the Soviet document tabled at the beginning of round four dropped the earlier ritualistic reference to a ban on SDI "research" per se. The operative noun was now "creation" *(sozdaniye,* sometimes translated as "development"). Edward Ifft, a State Department representative, asked the old question: How did this word apply to research? General Victor Starodubov referred to Gorbachev's interview in *Time* of the previous autumn: "fundamental research" would be permitted; "purposeful research" would be banned. Back in Washington, Nitze said that this was "an obnoxious and clearly unacceptable word game: Our research is 'purposeful' because of the President's March 1983 speech, while theirs is 'fundamental' because they've never declared what its purpose is."

Kvitsinsky advanced in the defense-and-space group a proposal that looked more constructive: The two sides, he said, should negotiate measures to "strengthen" the ABM treaty. The proposal was ambiguous and vague, but it seemed to have some promise. Largely through Perle's efforts, the ABM treaty had not been mentioned in the summit communiqué, but it had figured in the guidelines, which Nitze had helped draft, that Reagan had given Gorbachev during their fireside chat in the pool house. A senior Soviet official in Moscow later confirmed that his side "had noted the mention of the ABM treaty in guidelines with some interest. It was a straw in the wind, which we grasped. With enough such straws, perhaps we could make a basket."

For his part, Kampelman stepped up his effort to set the stage for the grand compromise, which he confided to other Americans was a "theoretically possible and desirable outcome." Picking up on Gorbachev's proposal to eliminate all nuclear weapons by the year 2000, Kampelman told Karpov and Kvitsinsky: "Mr. Gorbachev is saying, 'You won't need defense because we'll have no offense.' My reply is that if our two countries could agree on eliminating all offensive nuclear weapons between us, we'd still want to be able to take care of the Khaddafys of this world. Also, you can't put the genie back in the bottle. We're not going to trust you any more than you're going to trust us. You have to have some element of safety on top of trust. We can decide on the numbers; we can discuss these things jointly."

Kampelman was using a variant of the insurance-policy rationale for SDI that Reagan had seized upon the previous year and that also figured prominently in Shultz's thinking and talking about how to reconcile the program with diplomacy.

Since the beginning of the Nuclear and Space Talks in 1985, Kampelman had been urging the Soviets to "tempt us" with concessions in START—to "sweeten the pot" with offensive reductions, so that American advocates of the grand compromise would be in a stronger position back in Washington. He intensified this effort during round four. He tried to use the summit communiqué and its reference to 50-percent reductions in offense to pry loose more Soviet concessions on defense. "Your leader makes an agreement,'' Kampelman said to Karpov. ''I assume it's bona fide. Yet he can't carry the day. Why not? Who is your leader?''

Karpov bristled at this taunt, perhaps taking it to suggest that the Soviet delegation in Geneva was somehow in league with an anti-Gorbachev faction back in Moscow. He, too, referred to the summit communiqué, but he used it to bolster his contention that American concessions on defense had to come first.

''I helped write the November 21 communiqué,'' said Karpov, ''and I can tell you that the most important sentence there was the reaffirmation of the [earlier] January 8 statement [at the end of the Shultz-Gromyko meeting] on the objective of preventing an arms race in space''—precisely the sentence that Perle had tried to keep out of the Geneva communiqué.

During a long conversation over lunch, Kampelman became more explicit about the dilemma on the American side: ''Look, Victor, I don't know if you know what 'wiggle room' means.'' He pointed to his shoe. ''It means room for the toe to move around in. At this moment I have no wiggle room. None. That's because you're handling these negotiations badly. You are desperately eager to have us show you wiggle room [on SDI], but I can't do it. I don't even want to ask for it back in Washington. However, if you can come up with significant reductions—not promises, but realities—I might get *some* wiggle room. But I won't even try to get that unless you show us something. I can't even explore with you what is possible unless you show us more on the price you're willing to pay in reductions. We need something so that Ron Lehman will say, 'There! That's good! That's in our interest!' ''

Lehman had been Tower's deputy in START, but he was also a key NSC aide on arms-control issues. He was doing double duty as the Geneva team's principal emissary to Washington. By the end of round four in March 1986, Tower had grown impatient with the slow pace of the enterprise and resigned. Lehman was promoted to replace him. Kampelman was telling Karpov that the bureaucratic balance of forces within the Administration would not shift in favor of limits on SDI and the grand compromise unless and until a prospective START agreement had Lehman's approval.

The end of round four also saw the first major change in the top ranks of the Soviet team. The Americans had long since noticed tension between Kvitsinsky and Karpov. Kvitsinsky was Kampelman's counterpart for the defense-and-space talks, but he did not disguise his desire to broaden his mandate so that he could discuss INF, which he obviously knew well, and START, which entailed the other half of the offense-defense tradeoff. Karpov was jealous of his prerogatives as overall captain of the Soviet team, and he held Kvitsinsky back.

During one of their private talks, Kampelman remarked to Kvitsinsky, ''You know, Yuli, you should get out of this business and become ambassador to Bonn. That's your first love." Near the end of the round, Kvitsinsky was recalled to Moscow for what was supposed to be a brief consultation. He did not return. He sent a message to Kampelman through the executive secretary of the Soviet delegation in Geneva: "Max, I took your advice."

Karpov himself took over Kvitsinsky's portfolio on defense-and-space issues ("That's where the action isn't," he quipped). Aleksei Obukhov, who had been in charge of INF, took over START, and Obukhov's deputy, Lem Masterkov, moved up to be chief INF negotiator. Masterkov had a reputation as an "iron pants" negotiator of the old school. There was debate among the Americans over whether his appointment meant that the Kremlin was indeed ready to move to closure in INF and wanted someone who would get the best deal in the final stages, or whether his assignment would be to stall the talks.

One reason the Kremlin had for sending Kvitsinsky to Bonn was that the issue of INF was, once again, proving divisive within the alliance. The Soviets no doubt wanted an envoy in West Germany who could argue their case in the most up-to-date terms, and in fluent German, against the youthful, high-powered, and well-respected new American ambassador, Richard Burt, who had formerly been an assistant secretary of state and an occasional thorn in the side to Nitze.

The Soviets were now suggesting elimination of all the SS-20s in Europe, but not the so-called shorter-range INF missiles (SS-12s and SS-23s). These could reach West German territory from bases in Eastern Europe. During one of his frequent visits to Bonn, Nitze found the Germans as adamant as ever that an agreement must deal with those shorter-range missiles, too. Meanwhile, on a similar mission to Asia, Edward Rowny reported that the Chinese and Japanese were dissatisfied, since the Soviet proposal for a freeze on SS-20s east of the Urals would leave intact the missiles that were arrayed against them.

The allies seemed difficult if not impossible to please. They had one set of anxieties when arms control was in deadlock (the Western Europeans felt the chill of the relationship between the superpowers), another set when an agreement seemed in prospect (the giants were negotiating over the West Europeans' heads). In 1977, many Europeans complained that there were no U.S. INF missiles on the Continent; in 1983, many protested when the American deployments began; now, in 1986, there was a sudden burst of alarm that perhaps the American missiles would be removed. As for America's strategic partners in Asia, they had not paid the political price of accepting American missiles on their territory, yet they were asking for military relief from the Asian SS-20s as part of an INF deal.

Nitze's and Rowny's missions abroad led to a frenzy of bureaucratic infighting in Washington, resulting in a further adjustment in the American INF position in late February. The Reagan Administration now came full circle, returning to an insistence on the "global" Zero Option of 1981 (i.e., the elimination of Asian as well as European SS-20s).

"The Old Man"

The middle months of 1986 saw considerable movement on the Soviet side of the Nuclear and Space Talks, but virtually none on the American. Some Soviet concessions in Geneva were presaged during the spring, when representatives of the foreign-policy institutes in Moscow inundated their American contacts with "speculation" about the concessions the Kremlin might make to accommodate the Administration's "more legitimate and reasonable" objectives. Gorbachev seemed to be relying increasingly on a flying squad of academicians and *institutchiki* to provide sneak previews of proposals that he would later announce himself or instruct his negotiators to put forward at the bargaining table.

Among the best known and most effective spokesmen were Evgeny Velikhov, vice-president of the Academy of Sciences; Roald Sagdeyev, director of the Space Research Institute; and Georgi Arbatov and a number of specialists from his staff at the Institute for the Study of the U.S.A. and Canada. They fanned out to conferences in the West, where they buttonholed American arms-control experts, former government officials, and others who could be counted on to report to the Reagan Administration and promote the grand compromise.

In exchange for limiting SDI to "laboratory research," said these emissaries, the Soviet Union might be willing to drop its "reach criterion" for including American forward-based systems in START (any weapon that could reach the territory of the other side was "strategic") and accept deep reductions, perhaps even elimination of the SS-18, as well as subceilings on MIRVed ICBMs that would diminish the ratio of Soviet warheads to American silos.*

One of the Soviet institute representatives was asked why his government did not make its offers through the front channel in Geneva. "Because," he replied, "negotiating with Kampelman is like negotiating with the entire Reagan Administration, and that is impossible. There are people who want one thing and people who want another. Whenever we make a proposal— for example, thirty-six hundred [the proposed limit on ICBM warheads] or something really quite significant and for us difficult—your side says, 'That's

---

*Other features of these "unofficial" Soviet suggestions were a limit of five warheads per ICBM, which would also serve to ban the SS-18 (with ten warheads) and the SS-19 (with six), and the proposed elimination of two American "counterforce" weapons, the MX and the Trident II SLBM.

nice, what else are you willing to do?' Our people are fed up with that; they feel as though they are being manipulated and played for suckers."

He then launched into a lengthy discourse on how the Soviet side, too, had its factional and interagency disagreements. There were two schools of thought in Moscow, he said. One held that Gorbachev should make the moves necessary to test American willingness for an offense-defense trade-off. That would mean dropping the reach criterion and accepting subceilings in START, particularly ones that would force reductions in MIRVed ICBMs and heavy missiles. The other school held that Moscow should give up on Soviet-American arms control "until the early 1990s" and concentrate meanwhile on "playing the European card"—using INF to sow discord in the alliance.

The blast of mixed signals and platoons of semiofficial spokesmen from Moscow had already begun to annoy the American government. "If you've got something to say to us," said George Shultz to Eduard Shevardnadze when they met in Helsinki in late 1985, "say it to us in Geneva." Early in round five of NST, in May 1986, Kampelman complained to Karpov about the discrepancy between what the Soviet delegation was saying and the tantalizing talk from the institutes and the Academy of Sciences about less onerous restrictions on SDI and a more "forward-leaning" position in START.

"What are you trying to do here?" asked Kampelman. "Either the right hand doesn't know what the left hand is doing, or what these other people are saying is disinformation that complicates our negotiations."

Karpov replied tartly, "When it's said here by our delegation, that's when it counts. You know how some of our academicians think they are experts. The same is true on your side."

The approximate American equivalent of Velikhov and the Soviet *institutchiki* were the RAND specialists who had been helping McFarlane refine the terms of the great sting and Jeremy Stone of the Federation of American Scientists, who had been consulting with Nitze. After the Geneva summit and McFarlane's resignation from the government at the end of 1985, the RAND experts gave their squeeze-or-deal briefing to a wider audience, including members of Congress. In April 1986, they incorporated their analysis into a comprehensive study of U.S. arms-control options—once again carefully paid for out of nongovernmental funds—and presented it to RAND's own board of trustees. The board included Harold Brown, Brent Scowcroft, and Frank Carlucci, who had served as deputy secretary of defense under Weinberger at the beginning of the Reagan Administration and would return to government at the end of the Administration, first as national security advisor, then, replacing Weinberger, as secretary of defense.

Later, the RAND experts took this analysis to Washington, visiting offices on both sides of the Potomac. On July 10, they called on Fred Iklé, Perle's ostensible boss, who was also a former RAND executive and an important sponsor of RAND projects. He was not, however, about to endorse this one, although later he seemed cautiously interested in the extent of the reductions in Soviet offenses that RAND calculated would be possible. But he remained acutely nervous about the other half of the grand compromise. "The very act of raising options about limiting SDI," he warned, "could be misinterpreted."

Nitze's reaction was naturally much more favorable. On May 14, 1986, Donald Rice and James Thomson called on Nitze at the State Department. "Bud McFarlane asked us to do some work last year on possible tradeoffs between offense and defense," explained Rice.

Nitze arched his eyebrows with interest. "Oh?" he said. "Tell me about it."

Rice and Thomson laid out the details of the squeeze-or-deal plan. As he showed Rice and Thomson out, Nitze said, "Keep it up, boys."

A month earlier, Nitze had begun to let it be known outside the government that he favored the grand compromise even if others in the Administration did not. Meanwhile, he privately tried to reactivate the idea of a back channel that would bypass the bureaucracy and the Pentagon civilians as well as the Geneva talks.

On April 4, Nitze used a seminar with a group of arms-control specialists to hint broadly at both his intentions and the obstacles he faced. As so often in the past, he couched his real, hortatory message to his own government in a skeptical, pessimistic analysis of the Soviets' position then on the table: "If they were really offering something attractive, we could offer something on defense." He paused, looked around the room, and added with emphasis, "That isn't the executive branch's point of view; that's my point of view." He continued, "However, the issue of a tradeoff doesn't arise until there's something on offense. If they did offer anything on offense and they talked to me about it, I'd be interested in talking to them, although not everybody in the U.S. government agrees with that approach."

Asked what the Soviets would have to do to demonstrate willingness for what he had called "a doable deal on the offense-defense trade," he said, "If they drop the requirement of counting noncentral strategic systems [i.e., American forward-based systems], then all kinds of things are possible."

The following week, Dobrynin had appointments with Shultz and Nitze. Shultz suggested that in preparation for the next summit, each leader should delegate the back-channel negotiation to special representatives. He said that the American side was prepared to designate Nitze and Jack Matlock, then the principal Soviet affairs expert on the NSC staff.* (Matlock had been

---

*Matlock was later appointed U.S. ambassador to Moscow.

included in the small circle of officials who knew about the Monday Package. McFarlane had been replaced by his deputy, Admiral John Poindexter. Poindexter did not share McFarlane's intense interest in arms control and secret high-level diplomacy. Nor was he entirely trusting of Nitze, so he expected Matlock not only to help Nitze but also to keep an eye on him.)

Dobrynin frowned thoughtfully. He still seemed concerned about procedure, protocol, and logistics. "How would we do this?" he kept asking. Nitze said he traveled a great deal; there would have to be a "cover," such as a "summit preparatory trip"—either he could go to Moscow or his Soviet counterpart could come to Washington.

Dobrynin might now be a candidate for that job himself. For the first time in nearly a quarter-century, he was no longer calling on the secretary of state and the President as Soviet ambassador. His visits to the State Department and the White House in early April 1986 were farewell calls. The previous month, Gorbachev had recalled him to Moscow, putting him in charge of the Central Committee's foreign affairs department. Dobrynin was now roughly the equivalent of the American national security advisor, at least with regard to Soviet-American relations. He was therefore a plausible counterpart to Nitze if the Kremlin decided to accept something like the Monday Package.

Shortly afterward, one of Dobrynin's associates said that there was serious consideration in Moscow of taking Shultz up on his suggestion of a Dobrynin-Nitze channel. The view had prevailed that the Soviet Union had better get the best deal it could out of Ronald Reagan rather than betting on his successor. That left the question of how to negotiate with a divided American government. Many in Moscow were increasingly pessimistic about whether anybody in the Administration was in a position to deal seriously with the full authorization of the President. "The State Department can't do it," this Soviet mused, citing Weinberger's recent, much-publicized defeat of Shultz on the issue of whether to continue abiding by SALT II. As for the White House, "Are we going to negotiate with Donald Regan? Or Admiral Poindexter?

"But," the Soviet continued, "there is of course another possibility: *Starik* [the old man], whom the Reagan Administration has proposed might be designated as an underground czar to meet with Dobrynin somewhere in Europe." Dobrynin and his colleagues were "very impressed with *starik*"— although they were struck by the irony that Nitze could now be considered by anyone as a dove.

The Soviet side had yet to respond to this suggestion for two reasons. One was that Soviet-American relations were disrupted in the wake of two events in April—the American bombing raid against Libya on April 14 and the accident at the Chernobyl nuclear plant on April 25, which touched off an outburst of American criticism tinged with gloating. The other reason had to do with the reshuffling in Moscow over foreign policy. Dobrynin, while an old hand with plenty of experience in back-channel diplomacy, "is still learning his way around the Central Committee apparatus, and relationships are still being established."

Dobrynin's associate even mused about where a secret meeting might take place. The traditional venues of neutral ground—Vienna, Helsinki, Geneva—"won't work," he said. "Too many people would know. Why doesn't *starik* fly to Moscow?"—adding with a slight smile, "There are now four flights a week from the United States." He concluded that there was a distinct possibility that Dobrynin's successor as ambassador to the United States, Yuri Dubinin, might bring with him in early June an acceptance of the American proposal for the back channel and an invitation for *starik* to come to Moscow.

Dobrynin's invitation to Nitze never came, via Dubinin or by any other route.

As with the walk in the woods, the ambiguity and secretiveness of the Monday Package made it difficult to determine, then and subsequently, what the Soviets made of the whole exercise and why they did not respond more favorably. Jack Matlock commented in August 1986, "The Soviets have had a couple of chances to pick us up on our hints. They have two names [Nitze's and Matlock's own]. They know who to call. The Soviets haven't got their act together. They don't know what they want. There's no evidence that Gorbachev has pulled together a negotiable position on strategic offense. We're waiting for Moscow to come up with a negotiable response."

The Soviet explanation was quite different: The back channel entailed risks. The Soviets would not just have to tip their hand; they would have to lay all their cards on the table. They would have to go straight to their bottom line on offense and defense alike, with the largest reductions in START and the least stringent constraints on SDI that they could tolerate. They would also have to take the chance that, as with the walk in the woods, the deal might still fall apart on the American side.

Perhaps using those arguments, the Foreign Ministry apparently asserted itself and prevailed. After the Shultz-Dobrynin meetings in April, the next major Soviet move occurred very much in the front channel, in June 1986, at the end of round five of the Nuclear and Space Talks in Geneva.

Temptation

The dialogue between Max Kampelman and Victor Karpov in Geneva was becoming almost surrealistic in its monotony, with each using the same old arguments to needle or cajole the other into making new concessions. Kampelman complained about the lack of Soviet follow-through on Gorbachev's commitment at the summit to the pursuit of 50-percent cuts in offense. "Has the military overruled Gorbachev?" he asked on one occasion. "Has the Politburo overruled him? Has Gorbachev changed his mind?"

Bridling, Karpov again reminded Kampelman that the communiqué of the previous January had been just as explicit in committing the United States to a ban on an arms race in space. That meant "talking seriously" about SDI. Before there could be further Soviet flexibility in START, said Karpov, there would have to be American flexibility on SDI.

"Tell Moscow they've got it backwards," said Kampelman. "They're asking us to pay a price but not letting us see what they're selling us. It's like this: You've got a closet full of chocolates, but you won't let us see what's in the closet. Are they still good? Have they gone rancid? Are they with almonds or without almonds? . . . You want to make the ABM treaty whole. Well, the ABM treaty provides for offensive reductions"—he meant that the ABM treaty had been linked to the prospect of offensive reductions in SALT II. "We're due for those reductions fourteen years later."

"That's not our fault," replied Karpov.

"The issue isn't who's at fault, Victor. The issue is what can we accomplish."

Sensing that perhaps Gorbachev's agreement to the 50-percent goal had been a publicity stunt and had become an obstacle to the Soviets as they tried to develop a concrete proposal, Kampelman asked, "Do you want to get off of 50 percent? If so, what do you want to do instead?"

Karpov said that the problem was not deep cuts in offense; it was the constant American attempt to discuss such cuts "in a vacuum," separated from the issue of SDI.

"Well, Victor," said Kampelman, "you've got to understand—and Moscow has to understand—that we're not going to accept anything that cuts back on our research activity." It was yet another negatively worded inducement for the Soviets to make a proposal for an arrangement that would allow SDI to continue as an R&D program. Kampelman was resorting to his old tactic of daring the Soviets to "tempt" the Administration by making a proposal that would be hard to refuse.

At the end of May, Karpov and his colleagues received new instructions authorizing them to accept Kampelman's dare, on both offense and defense. As though to underscore their priorities, the Soviets moved first on defense. They had for some time been putting out feelers on whether the United States would agree to "partial limitations as an interim measure toward the goal of a ban on space-strike arms." The measure would consist of a ban on antisatellite (ASAT) weapons, a ban on "space-to-earth weapons" (such as lasers mounted on orbiting battle stations), and a "strengthening of the ABM treaty." "Taken together," said Karpov, these "strengthening modifications" in the ABM treaty would constitute "a ban on space-strike arms."

Both in the defense-and-space group and in the one-on-one Kampelman-Karpov exchanges, the Soviets suggested adding a new protocol to the ABM treaty that would prohibit either side from withdrawing for fifteen to twenty years. They also asked the United States to agree to "certain definitions" of the "development" of ABM components, prototypes, and mock-ups that would guarantee "unswerving compliance" with the treaty.

It was not clear exactly what the Soviets meant by some of their language. Nor, for that matter, was it clear that they knew themselves. But it looked as though they were trying to extend the definition of impermissible activity beyond what the American drafters of the treaty had intended in 1972. The Soviets, in short, had now come up with their own reading of the ABM treaty, and theirs was more restrictive even than the traditional one then under such fierce attack from Perle and Sofaer back in Washington.

So Perle himself was quick to point out. On June 3, shortly after the Soviets made their proposal for "partial measures" in Geneva, he dismissed it as "a tactic to define 'component' in a way that is so far-reaching it would shut off all space-based experiments. A piece of anything that can be used for interception of a ballistic missile would be banned. If you put a computer chip up there that would be part of the final system, it would be illegal. They've moved Smith indoors." He was referring to Gerard Smith's 1972 definition of illegal development activity as starting with the construction of a "breadboard model," presumably outside the laboratory, that could be seen by the other side's spy satellites.

Kampelman saw the Kremlin's proposal in a more positive light. The Soviets appeared finally to be moving away from insistence on a blanket ban toward more practical, reasonable, and negotiable measures. He pointed out to Karpov that some key words in the Soviet proposal, like "prototype" and "mock-up," did not appear in the text of the ABM treaty. "Do you want to amend the treaty to include the word 'mock-up'? If so, give us some proposed amendments." Nor was the word "development" clearly defined in the treaty.

That, said Karpov, was just the point: There should be a straightforward negotiation "to clarify what is permissible." The Soviets said repeatedly that progress in such a negotiation—which they defined as agreement on nonwithdrawal from, and "unswerving compliance with," the ABM treaty— would "clear the path," "open the way," and "improve the conditions" for 50-percent reductions in offense.

What those reductions might look like in practice became clearer on June

11, when the Soviets made a new proposal for START. As so often, they took two steps forward and one step backward. For the first time, they officially abandoned their "reach criterion" for defining strategic weapons; American forward-based INF missiles and bombers would no longer count under the START ceilings. They were at last yielding on what Nitze had identified in early April as the principal sticking point in START. They also loosened their terms on cruise missiles, agreeing to permit those weapons on heavy bombers and submarines.*

That was the good news. The bad news was that the Soviets' new START proposal would allow them to retain more ICBM warheads than their old position. The overall ceiling on strategic launchers would now have to cover bombers and submarines armed with cruise missiles, and the one on "nuclear charges" would have to cover the now-permitted cruise missiles as well as ballistic warheads. Therefore the Soviets proposed new numbers for both ceilings: 1,600 launchers, a figure close to one that had been discussed since the early days of START, and 8,000 nuclear charges—2,000 higher than they had proposed earlier. By raising the nuclear-charges ceiling from 6,000 to 8,000, they were indirectly also raising the subceiling on ICBM warheads. Under the 60-percent "force concentration" rule that they had already proposed, the new nuclear-charges aggregate would allow them 4,800 ICBM warheads instead of the 3,600 implicit in their earlier position.

The lower number would have forced the Soviets to dismantle many, perhaps most, of their SS-18s, while the new, higher number left them with much more flexibility to retain large MIRVed ICBMs. Ominously, Soviet negotiators now also turned evasive on what sort of reductions in throw-weight would result from their proposal. Earlier they had indicated that they might agree to a stipulated 50-percent cut in throw-weight; they now said only that there would be "significant reductions."

The Americans could only hope that the earlier, lower figure for warheads would turn out to be a concession that the United States could eventually "pocket" even though it had for the time being been formally revised upwards.

"You've been at 6,000 before," said Kampelman to Karpov. "Perhaps you'll be there again."

"We'll see," replied Karpov.

While there were still obvious problems with the Soviet START position,

---

*Throughout most of the 1982–83 round of START, the Soviets had sought to ban long-range cruise missiles entirely, including air-launched and sea-launched (ALCMs and SLCMs). Toward the end of those negotiations, they had yielded on ALCMs. In their September 30, 1985 proposal in NST they were back to banning ACLMs and SLCMs. Their June 11, 1986 proposal, while permitting SLCMs on submarines, would have created mischief with the American SLCM program, since it would have halted the U.S. Navy's plan to put Tomahawk SLCMs on surface ships.

there was also much that was meant to be accommodating—and, in terms of Kampelman's frequent exhortation of Karpov, "tempting." The biggest obstacle to real negotiations with the Soviets on SDI was still the Reagan Administration's inability to overcome its internal divisions and the resistance of the President himself.

CHAPTER 12

Sages and Owls

Perhaps because he saw that the American Administration was so hopelessly paralyzed over the negotiability of SDI, in late 1986 Mikhail Gorbachev made the extraordinary move of going over the heads of the U.S. government directly to Ronald Reagan himself. Gorbachev did so by luring Reagan to a hastily arranged meeting in Reykjavik, Iceland, on the pretext of putting the finishing touches on a separate INF deal and then, at the last minute, offering the President the grand compromise on strategic offense and defense instead. It was a classic bait-and-switch operation—Gorbachev's own attempt at the great sting.

After their first meeting at the Geneva summit in 1985, Reagan and Gorbachev had entered into an exchange of letters. With little progress at the negotiations in Geneva and none at all in Shultz and Nitze's effort to interest the Kremlin in a back channel, the Reagan-Gorbachev correspondence became a conduit for new proposals as the leaders tried to maneuver each other toward a second summit and a breakthrough in arms control.

For his part, Reagan was eager to encourage a continuation of the dialogue that he had begun at the Geneva summit. He seemed convinced that by a combination of his own personality, his persuasive powers, and the merits of his position he could, as he put it, "bring Gorbachev around"—convince the Soviet leader that SDI was good for both sides.

In his public statements directed at Gorbachev as well as in a number of confidential letters, Reagan adopted a soothing, come-hither tone. "Accentuating the positive," he called it. In February, Reagan wrote Gorbachev welcoming his January 15 comprehensive proposal for eliminating nuclear weapons by the year 2000, even though that proposal had as its central goal the elimination of SDI as well.

By the summer of 1986, Reagan's more conciliatory instincts had been reinforced by domestic American political developments. Administration national security policies in general and SDI in particular were once again in trouble on the home front, and the Soviets were pressing harder than ever for a deal. There was a near-mutiny on Capitol Hill and among the Western European allies over the presidential decision, announced May 27, to break with SALT II at the end of the year.

Considerable sentiment was brewing in Congress to hold SDI funding hostage to the restoration of a promising arms-control process. It was increasingly apparent that Reagan would pay a political price, perhaps including a disastrous congressional backlash against SDI, unless, at a minimum, there was a return engagement with Gorbachev—another round of smiles and handshakes to dramatize that the President still had the most important and dangerous of the country's foreign relationships under control.

In a series of statements, Reagan markedly adjusted his characterization of the Soviet-American strategic balance. Instead of talking about Soviet superiority or the need for an American "catch-up" effort to re-establish a "margin of safety," he began to try out the concept (although he avoided the term) of offsetting asymmetries between the arsenals of the superpowers. In an interview with the *Los Angeles Times* on June 23, Reagan said, "I think because of the mix that each of us sees, we have chosen a different way to go—with what we call the triad—than they have. They've placed more reliance on the intercontinental [ballistic missile]. And so there are things that have to be negotiated and worked out." An advocate of SALT II and the grand compromise could hardly have said it better.

Reagan temporarily backed away from a commitment to breach SALT II at the end of the year, saying that the decision to exceed the treaty ceilings had been tentative and that he might reconsider in the light of Soviet behavior in the Nuclear and Space Talks. If, however, SALT II did pass into history, Reagan stressed, he had every intention of replacing it with a new pact.

In a speech to a high-school graduating class on June 19, he said that in their latest proposals "the Soviets have begun to make a serious effort"; he expressed the hope that, at a meeting later in the year, Gorbachev would "join me in taking action—action in the name of peace." Reagan gave that speech in Glassboro, New Jersey, where nineteen years before, Lyndon Johnson and Robert McNamara began the process of SALT by trying to persuade Aleksei Kosygin that strategic arms control depended on limiting defense and offense alike.

If the choice of Glassboro as the site of Reagan's speech was intended as a symbol of reconciliation with his predecessors and continuity with the past, the gesture was one of spirit, not of substance. The President was still a long way from echoing Johnson and McNamara's basic message to Kosygin—that strategic defense was, ipso facto, destabilizing. Quite the contrary, on his own visit to Glassboro, Reagan sounded just the opposite message: SDI, he proclaimed, held out the hope of a "shield that could protect us from nuclear missiles just as a roof protects a family from rain." The purpose of the speech, said a number of Reagan's aides at the time, was to signal not a willingness to trade SDI but an eagerness to have another crack at persuading Gorbachev that it ought not to be traded.

Four days after the Glassboro speech, the new Soviet ambassador, Yuri Dubinin, arrived at the White House and delivered a letter from Gorbachev. It repeated what the Soviet negotiators in Geneva had been saying about the possibility of finding an area of compromise on SDI-type research and promised that the recent Soviet concessions in START would be followed by a new INF proposal in round six of the Nuclear and Space Talks, which was due to begin in September. Abandoning its usual display of sales resistance, the White House was quick to say that the Gorbachev letter was "positive" and "practical."

However, a more detailed American response was slow in coming. The principal cause of delay was disagreement over what now to say about SDI. Officials at the State Department suggested proposing not to deploy anything in violation of the ABM treaty for five to eight years, since it would be at least that long before the technological feasibility of SDI deployment could be determined. The Pentagon civilians bitterly opposed any such ban, arguing that it would put the United States on a "slippery slope" leading to the effective cancellation of the program; if the United States agreed to constrain SDI in accordance with any diplomatic agreement, particularly the ABM treaty, Congress would use those constraints to rationalize cuts in funding. The Laser Lobby and friends of SDI on the Hill had long since made clear to Weinberger that they would not fund a mere research program; they wanted a program virtually guaranteed to lead to deployment, and the sooner the better.

This latest State-versus-Defense dispute was summed up in a single exchange between Paul Nitze and Richard Perle in a meeting over how to reply to Gorbachev:

"We're not saying we won't eventually deploy," said Nitze. "We're saying we won't deploy until we've got something that's ready to deploy and that makes sense to deploy."

Perle replied, "Once you agree to the principle of limiting deployment, you've prejudiced the chances of there ever being deployment. You might as well kiss the whole program goodbye."

As so often in the past, the interagency process reached an acrimonious impasse. There were competing drafts of a presidential letter, and the competition itself became a state secret of acute sensitivity. Under the new national security advisor, Admiral John Poindexter, the coining of code words and the compartmentalization of the bureaucracy were raised to a higher art form. There was, in the corridors of the State and Defense departments, hushed talk about new entities, the Owl Compartment and the Sage Compartment: "Are you cleared for Sage?" "Is your boss an Owl?" (The answer in both cases for Nitze was yes.)

Membership in these ad hoc, high-level offshoots of the Senior Arms Control Group was overlapping and on a strictly "need to know" basis.

Only the members themselves were supposed to know what went on at the meetings. Agendas and minutes were even kept out of the highly classified memos that flickered through the NSC's interoffice word-processing and distribution system in the Old Executive Office Building. These were small, elite, but not very collegial debating societies. They made little progress, and there were still leaks about the discord and backbiting.

Around the Fourth of July weekend, when Reagan and some of his top advisors were in New York City to celebrate the one-hundredth anniversary of the Statue of Liberty, Poindexter ordered up a new draft of the letter to Gorbachev. It was yet another attempt at a compromise between State and Defense, but it ended up lopsidedly in favor of Defense. The United States and the Soviet Union would continue to abide by the ABM treaty for five years (a concession to State); if after that period either side decided to proceed toward deployment of strategic defenses, it must put forward a plan for sharing the benefits of research on strategic defenses—and eliminating all ballistic missiles.

This last feature of the proposal was to be the biggest bombshell since Reagan unveiled SDI itself just over three years earlier. In due course, it became sanctified with its own euphonious set of initials: ZBM for zero ballistic missiles.

Ballistic missiles were by far the most formidable and cost-effective weapons of the nuclear age. Under this new American proposal they would not have to be intercepted and destroyed by SDI. Instead, they would, by mutual agreement, be destroyed before SDI was even deployed.

The antecedents of this idea were scattered through the confused history of the past two years. The President's original Star Wars speech had envisioned a world in which ballistic missiles would be removed from the scene— i.e., rendered "impotent and obsolete." Shultz and McFarlane, in their quiet, subtle, but persistent attempt to persuade Reagan that lower levels of defense might be possible if there were lower levels of offense, had explained how the elimination of all offenses might, theoretically, permit the elimination of all defenses—or the retention of only a scaled-down defensive system as an insurance policy. Reagan had told Soviet journalists before the Geneva summit in 1985 that the United States wanted to eliminate all offensive weapons before SDI was deployed, only to have Larry Speakes explain that this was a "presidential imprecision."

By the summer of 1986, Weinberger had seized on the idea of no ballistic missiles and made it the centerpiece of his office's recommendation during the secretive, conflict-ridden letter-drafting exercise of June and July. Fred Iklé had been toying with the idea of no ballistic missiles for some time, and Richard Perle had been looking for a "boffo" arms-control proposal with which to counter Gorbachev's headline-grabbers of the previous months.

When, at Weinberger's behest, the no-ballistic-missiles feature was inserted into the text of the President's letter to Gorbachev, the secretary of defense encountered little resistance. Only three other presidential advisors even saw the final draft: Shultz, Poindexter, and Regan. Poindexter was concerned with brokering a compromise between the various agency positions, and he had less sophistication and interest in arms control than his predecessor McFarlane. Regan had even less than Poindexter, yet he was asserting himself increasingly in foreign policymaking.

Shultz was never an enthusiast for the proposal. When later chided about the unrealistic idea of doing away with ballistic missiles, Shultz snapped defensively, "Don't look at us. That idea didn't come from the woolly-headed types over here. It came straight from DoD"—the Department of Defense. But at the time that the President made his decision to include the Pentagon suggestion in the letter to Gorbachev, Shultz conceded that it had "merit." The principal merit was that it appealed to Ronald Reagan. It was a simple, bold comeback to Gorbachev's plan for the elimination of nuclear weapons by the year 2000. Like Gorbachev in January, Reagan would now be proposing a concrete schedule for progress toward an ideal outcome. Unlike Gorbachev's plan, however, Reagan's would not only preserve SDI— it would make SDI the bulwark of peace, to replace what Reagan called "these God-awful missiles."

Even though he had all the Owl- and Sage-level clearances, Nitze was left in the dark until the White House had approved a final draft of the letter. He was appalled. The goal of eliminating ballistic missiles by agreement with the Soviet Union seemed to him no more realistic than the goal of rendering them useless by unilateral means. It was, as he said, "pie-in-the-sky stuff." Moreover, making such a proposal would have an unwelcome impact in the short term on the U.S. strategic modernization program. Nitze asked what the chances were that the U.S. Congress—in an era of huge federal deficits and legislatively mandated budget cuts—would continue to fund a new generation of ballistic missiles such as the MX and the Trident II SLBM, not to mention Nitze's own favorite, Midgetman, if the President suddenly committed himself to the goal of banning all such weapons.

Nitze's other concern, as so often in the past, had to do with the allies. The White House draft of the letter said that not only would the United States and Soviet Union have to give up their ballistic missiles—so would third countries, such as Britain, France, and China. The United States was about to make a proposal, directly and secretly to the Kremlin, for an agreement in which two American allies in Europe and one of its principal strategic partners in Asia would have to give up their own independent nuclear deterrents because Washington and Moscow told them to. Knowing the sensitivity of the Europeans about the superpowers' negotiating over their heads, Nitze was afraid that this feature of the proposal might "destroy the alliance."

This was the kind of dire warning that had, during the INF debate of 1982–83, earned Nitze the reputation in Washington of being a Chicken Little—someone who was inclined to exaggerate the extent and the consequences of the allies' nervousness. Yet precisely because he was known to be so concerned with perceptions and sensitivities on the far side of the Atlantic, Nitze was, just as he had been during INF, the ideal messenger to brief the Europeans on what was afoot in Washington; they would be more likely to go along with the latest American proposal if they learned of it from him.

The reaction Nitze encountered, particularly in London, was much as he expected, although less apocalyptic in tone than he had suggested it might be. A British official dismissed as "heresy" the idea that British and French nuclear forces should somehow be "put up for grabs" as a result of an American proposal. After his consultations, Nitze could, in good conscience and with some satisfaction, report that the allies wanted no reference to the ballistic missiles of third parties in whatever letter Reagan finally sent to Gorbachev.

With that deletion, the letter was dispatched to Gorbachev on July 25. Some of it—the proposed continuation of the ABM treaty—was promptly leaked. However, not until nearly a month later (in *The Wall Street Journal* on August 21) did the world learn of the proposed ban on ballistic missiles.

Initially, the letter was described as an offer to "delay" the deployment of SDI. This was widely interpreted as a hint of American willingness eventually to accept significant constraints on strategic defenses in exchange for deep reductions in offensive nuclear weapons—a victory for the State Department. James Schlesinger, who had long disparaged what he called Reagan's "voodoo strategic defense," welcomed press reports of the letter as an indication that "in principle the President is prepared to constrain defense in exchange for reductions in offense."[1]

Actually, the letter represented a bigger victory for the Pentagon supporters of SDI. According to the new American plan, SDI would not really be delayed at all, since there was no way the program would be ready for deployment sooner than seven years in any case. While Reagan had signaled a willingness to put SDI on the negotiating table, he did so in the context of reaffirming his determination to proceed toward eventual deployment; moreover, in effect he asked the Soviet Union to agree to the inevitability of deployment. The United States would abide by the ABM treaty for five years, but at the end of that time the treaty would be dead—not of old age but because a death sentence would have been carried out on schedule—and the United States would be free, without renegotiation or constraint, to deploy an exotic ABM system anywhere, including in space.

There was also a new wrinkle in the old debate within the Administration over what would be permissible even during the final five years that the ABM treaty remained in force. The esoteric but potentially critical issue of the broad-versus-narrow interpretation had come up again during the preparation of Reagan's letter. The State Department wanted the letter to affirm the Nitze-Shultz compromise that effectively fudged the question, while the Pentagon was pushing for its permissive interpretation. In the final version, Reagan proposed to Gorbachev that during the seven and a half years before deployment would be allowed, the United States would reserve the right to proceed with a program of SDI development and testing, "which is permitted" by the ABM treaty. That subordinate clause and the comma preceding it were the object of fierce semantic and bureaucratic guerrilla warfare. The Pentagon won. Parsed carefully, the letter affirmed the broad interpretation.

Three days after Reagan sent his letter to Gorbachev, Deputy Foreign Minister Alexander Bessmertnykh arrived in Washington for discussions with Shultz and Nitze on a possible summit. Bessmertnykh was a relatively young star of the Soviet diplomatic corps, yet an old hand in dealing with the Americans. He had been Dobrynin's deputy in Washington for twelve years. He was well versed in the nuances of the seemingly endless wrangle over SDI.

When Bessmertnykh was shown a copy of the letter from Reagan to Gorbachev, one of the first things he noticed was the wording that suggested development and testing of SDI were permitted by the ABM treaty. He accused the Administration of trying to pull a fast one—of reasserting the permissive interpretation and hoping that no one would notice. Nitze insisted that that was not the case and that the issue of what was permissible under the ABM treaty was still open to negotiation.

Like Gorbachev—and, for that matter, like Shultz and Nitze themselves—Bessmertnykh was obviously impatient with the slow pace of the Nuclear and Space Talks, although his government was not ready to open a true back channel. Instead, he spoke of the need for "extraordinary" talks. These would not be an extension of the Geneva negotiations but instead, in his words, "a free-for-all discussion" with only three or four "authoritative" people on each side who might force a breakthrough. The Kremlin proposed that this "experts' meeting" take place in Moscow in August. Soviet officials were known to take their August vacations seriously, so Bessmertnykh seemed to be indicating a high degree of urgency and seriousness. He also said that the Soviets wanted the two delegations to be "home-office, non-Geneva types," and implied that a higher-ranking official than Victor Karpov would be the chairman.

The United States accepted the Soviet proposal and planned to assemble a comparable high-level team that would outrank the Geneva regulars. The delegation would be led by Nitze and include Kampelman and Robert Linhard, an Air Force colonel who was the principal specialist on arms control for the NSC staff.

Weinberger insisted that Perle be included, too. Shultz agreed that in the absence of an airtight back channel through which Nitze might explore the Monday Package in complete secrecy, Perle should be directly involved in the negotiations. Shultz was encouraged in this view by Kampelman, who believed that Perle might eventually be co-opted into supporting a strategic agreement. Kampelman and Perle were both Democrats. For some time Kampelman had been trying to persuade Perle that "an agreement during the Reagan Administration considerably undercuts pacifist movements and will strengthen the Sam Nunns and the [Henry] Jackson wing of our party." Simultaneously, Kampelman had been urging Shultz to "get Richard into the tent and onto our side. He can be destructive and irresponsible when he's outside the process. He wants to live up to the stereotype. But he can be constructive if he's on the team."

When the Soviets presented the roster of their own delegation for the August experts' meeting, the Americans were unpleasantly surprised to see that Karpov was to be chairman after all; the other members were Aleksei Obukhov, Nikolai Detinov, and General Nikolai Chervov. Chervov was head of the arms-control directorate of the Soviet General Staff, but the other three were all part of the Geneva delegation. That gave the Americans no choice but to include Ronald Lehman and Maynard Glitman, the heads of the START and INF teams respectively. Otherwise, said Shultz, "we'd be undercutting the prestige and credibility of our own negotiators." Then Edward Rowny demanded to be included as well, and he threatened to resign if he was left home. While Rowny was hardly regarded as indispensable, his quitting in a huff would have stirred up a furor among right-wing, pro-SDI, anti–arms-control members of Congress.

So it was that, with Perle and Rowny as members, the group that set off for the August meeting in Moscow was as diversified, and as divided, as the bureaucratic interests and philosophical positions in the Administration as a whole. In such company, it would be difficult for Nitze to pursue the Monday Package.

Meanwhile, Nitze's right-wing critics were on their guard back in Washington. Shortly before the mission to Moscow, the conservative Center for Peace and Freedom called a news conference to denounce the "SDI sellout danger," and another group, the Coalition for SDI, issued a similar warning. On August 6, the week before Nitze left, President Reagan felt compelled to quiet conservative fears:

There's been some speculation that in my recent letter to General Secretary Gorbachev, I decided to seek some sort of "grand compromise" to trade away SDI in exchange for getting the Soviets to join with us in the offensive reductions. . . . Let me reassure you right here and now that our response to demands that we cut off or delay research and testing and close shop is: No way. SDI is no bargaining chip, it is the path to a safer and more secure future. And the research is not, and never has been, negotiable.

In an appeal for further funding, Reagan went on to say, "This is the worst time to undermine vital defense programs and take away America's needed negotiating leverage."

One of the leading pro-SDI congressmen, Representative Jack Kemp, a Republican of New York, who was already planning to seek the 1988 Republican presidential nomination, pronounced himself pleased by what the President had said but added: "I wish people in the State Department would stop trying" to get the President to trade SDI.

Such references seemed aimed straight at Nitze, and he certainly took them that way. "It gets me down," he remarked to a colleague, "to be identified as a giveaway artist."

Not surprisingly, little was accomplished in Moscow. In thirteen hours of discussion, the Soviets concentrated on the importance of adhering to the ABM treaty, more narrowly interpreted even than under the traditional American view, and the importance of limits on defense as a condition for reductions in offense.

It was Richard Perle's first visit to the Evil Empire. In public, he appeared blasé, giving a newspaper interview in which he professed disappointment with the quality of the ice cream sold on the streets of Moscow. At the negotiating table, he made the strongest case he could for the proposition that an agreement should eliminate all ballistic missiles—and that such an outcome would be in the interests of the Soviet Union. The Soviets listened attentively, almost deferentially. Perle was something of a celebrity in their eyes. Like Shultz, they set about to co-opt him—smothering him if not with kindness then with respect.

"Richard Perle has, in his way, been very helpful," Karpov told Kampelman.

General Chervov, a gruff, jowly caricature of a Soviet military officer, who conducted his side of a conversation as though he were barking orders, particularly enjoyed the chance to tackle head-on this most notorious of American hawks.

"I have a high regard for Mr. Perle," Chervov said later. "I like arguing with him. We know where he stands. It is a challenge to deal with him."[2]

The following month, Perle and Nitze both sat in on discussions in Washington between Shultz and Shevardnadze on a Saturday at the State Department. The Soviet foreign minister called Perle "your side's heavy artillery," saying that some of the ideas that Perle had been expressing about the mutual benefits of eliminating ballistic missiles were more interesting than "Professor Nitze's." This was a curious compliment to Perle, given the Soviets' obvious and continuing attachment to ballistic missiles as the mainstay of their strategic forces—and a gratuitous insult to Nitze. He was taken aback, then looked intensely uncomfortable.

Perle took it all in stride. Soviet blandishments seemed to confirm his long-held belief that toughness was the only thing the other side understood. He excused himself early from the Shultz-Shevardnadze meeting, politely explaining that he had to attend his seven-year-old son's birthday party.

The superpowers seemed finally to be moving toward closure in START as well as in INF. At a second experts' meeting in Washington, the Reagan Administration presented what it called ''new ideas.'' These included a joint ceiling of 1,600 strategic nuclear delivery vehicles or launchers (ICBM silos, SLBM tubes, and intercontinental bombers) and revised the proposed sub-ceilings on various types of weapons.

The Soviets came to Washington with some new ideas of their own. They were still not willing to accept subceilings that discriminated against ICBM warheads per se, but they floated a suggestion for a new version of their earlier force concentration rule that would limit the number of warheads on ballistic missiles.*

In INF, too, a compromise seemed to be emerging, and it looked like a good deal for the United States. It represented a number of significant concessions by the U.S.S.R. and the preservation of a number of important principles for the West. The centerpiece, it appeared, would be equal ceilings of one hundred intermediate-range missile warheads on each side in Europe. That would mean a large reduction in SS-20s; the United States would have prevailed in asserting its right of offsetting deployments on the Continent; and NATO would have dodged, once again, Soviet efforts to shoehorn the British and French deterrents into a superpower arms-control agreement.

At round six of NST in Geneva (September 18–November 12), each side formally proposed the concessions that had been discussed at the experts' meeting in Washington. There was some maneuvering over which side got credit for making the last move, leading Ronald Lehman to express exasperation at the Soviets for playing ''silly, coy games.'' But he complimented

---

*The United States proposed a ceiling of 7,500 for the combined total of ballistic missile warheads and air-launched cruise missiles (the Soviets were proposing 8,000 ''nuclear charges''), with a set of SALT II-type subceilings: 5,500 for all ballistic missile warheads (on ICBMs and SLBMs)—3,300 on ICBMs alone, and only half of those could be on the Soviets' most heavily MIRVed weapons, the SS-18s and the new, stationary version of the SS-24, which was the Soviet equivalent of the MX. Mobile ICBMs were still to be banned.

Under the Soviet force concentration rule, no more than 80–85 percent of the 8,000 ''nuclear charges'' could be on ballistic missiles. That would mean 6,400–6,800 ballistic missile warheads.

them for taking "steps in the right direction." Once again, Max Kampelman began to talk hopefully about "convergence" between the two positions. This time Karpov did not contradict him.

That convergence, however, was taking place almost entirely in the realm of offensive arms control, in INF and START. Discussion of how to limit SDI remained an American taboo in the negotiations. Nonetheless, the offense-defense tradeoff was still the subject of intensive if furtive brainstorming at the State Department.

In anticipation of a summit at the end of the year, George Shultz invited outside experts to come to the department on Saturday mornings for a series of seminars on Soviet-American relations. After one of these meetings, on September 13, Arnold Horelick mentioned to the secretary the latest refinement of the RAND analysis. Earlier in the week, RAND experts had briefed White House Chief of Staff Donald Regan, Senator Sam Nunn, and some key military officers. Shultz asked for a paper outlining the idea. Four days later he received a six-page paper warning that "time may be running out for the Administration" and recommending a "phased agreement which links progressive implementation of 'deep cuts' in START" to a five-to-seven-year extension of the ABM treaty and delays in tests of space-based missile-killing devices until the mid-to-late 1990s. Together, these measures would "ease Soviet anxieties that the U.S. could combine START cuts and SDI deployments to achieve first-strike advantages" and would therefore constitute "SDI breakout insurance."

As a nod to the White House, the RAND paper maintained that this so-called "phased approach" would "build on the structure proposed in the President's July letter to Gorbachev." In fact, Reagan's letter had asked Gorbachev to join in mutual commitment to the eventual deployment of SDI and the elimination of ballistic missiles. Together, those goals, if translated into concrete policies, would serve not to insure against breakout from traditional, offense-dominant deterrence but to increase the chances that such a breakout would occur.

Shultz, meanwhile, asked Nitze for "some bold ideas" on how to "square the circle" by reconciling with the President's letter the main ingredients of the Monday Package and other ideas like the RAND plan. That, Nitze noted wryly, was "a first-rate intellectual challenge."

The Lost Weekend

It was once again Mikhail Gorbachev who had the boldest ideas, not only about what to propose but about how to make the proposal.

On September 19, Eduard Shevardnadze, who was in the United States for a visit in the UN, called on President Reagan at the White House and delivered yet another letter from Gorbachev. The general secretary wrote of the need for the two leaders to provide an "impulse" to the stalled diplomatic process. He proposed that they meet roughly halfway between their capitals, in Reykjavik. If the encounter went well, it could lay the foundation for a full-dress summit in Washington at the end of the year.

President Reagan was immediately inclined to accept. He was encouraged by Donald Regan, who felt that the President had proved in Geneva the year before that he could deftly handle his Soviet counterpart. Besides, a mid-October meeting in Reykjavik would come a few weeks before the congressional elections of November 4, in which the Republican party would be fighting—in vain, as it turned out—to keep control of the Senate. The meeting would remind the electorate that the Republican flag was still firmly planted on the diplomatic high ground.

Gorbachev's letter and accompanying comments by Soviet officials led the Americans to expect that INF would be the focal point both of the Reykjavik meeting and of the year-end summit. For nearly a year, Soviet spokesmen had been indicating that their leader was prepared to sign an INF interim agreement that would leave the United States with some missiles in Europe and that would be unlinked from START and SDI. As Anatoly Dobrynin's deputy in the foreign affairs department of the Central Committee, Georgi Kornienko, put it in Moscow the day after Shevardnadze delivered Gorbachev's letter in Washington, "We feel it is important to make progress somewhere, and INF appears to be the only area of opportunity."[3]

Thus, Reagan went to Reykjavik with high hopes that he could get an arms-control agreement with the Soviet Union without having to sacrifice anything in SDI—and with the expectation that an "INF only" agreement, as it was sometimes called, would be signed in Washington at the end of the year. The Reykjavik meeting was to be purely preparatory, not a full-fledged summit. To underscore that feature of the event, a cozy, modest site was selected—Hofdi House, a two-story, turn-of-the-century residence owned by the local city government, with a view of snow-covered bluffs across a frosty bay.

However, at the beginning of the first session, on Saturday, October 11, it became apparent that INF was, in the Soviets' mind, still a secondary issue, a means to an end—and the end was restriction of SDI. The two leaders initially met one-on-one across a table, with only their interpreters present. Gorbachev expressed satisfaction with the "businesslike setting," saying he was glad that it would not be another inconclusive fireside chat of the sort they had had in Geneva the year before. Reagan expressed mild surprise at the thickness of the folder that Gorbachev had brought with him. Gorbachev explained that he had a proposal; he hoped the two of them could "wrench arms control out of the hands of the bureaucrats."

With Shultz and Shevardnadze joining them, Gorbachev laid out a set of "principles" for a broad agreement—on strategic as well as intermediate-range weapons, on defense as well as on offense—that he and Reagan might sign in Washington at their summit. These were, in effect, his reply to the American "guidelines" that Reagan had given to him at the fireside in Geneva eleven months before.

Opening his surprise package, Gorbachev gave prominence to the once stunning, now almost commonplace idea of a 50-percent reduction in strategic offenses. He knew that this would be the most enticing feature to Reagan. To make it all the more so, Gorbachev promised that in addition to across-the-board cuts in all categories of strategic weaponry, there would be "substantial—I don't mean trivial but substantial—cuts" in heavy missiles. He later said that these cuts would be 50 percent.

Gorbachev repeated and underscored concessions that had trickled out during the months before, ever since his comprehensive January 16 proposal. The Soviet Union, Gorbachev told Reagan, would accept "your definition" of "strategic"—i.e., only ICBMs, SLBMs, and intercontinental bombers would count in START; no more "reach criterion"; no more double-counting forward-based systems in both INF and START. And no more counting the British and French independent deterrents. Intermediate-range missiles in Europe would be "eliminated," he said, reminding Reagan that this was "your own Zero Option."

Not quite. The Zero Option had been "global in scope," requiring the elimination of SS-20s in Asia as well as Europe. But Gorbachev was taking a big step toward accepting the first arms-control proposal Ronald Reagan had made in 1981, and he indicated that a solution might be found to the problem of Asian missiles, too. At the same time, he was moving closer to achieving the long-standing Soviet objective of keeping all American missiles off the European continent.

Gorbachev treated the issue of SDI almost as an afterthought, a low-key reiteration of a point that had already been well established, couched in terms of yet another Soviet concession. He understood, he said, how strongly Reagan felt about SDI. Therefore, the program could go forward. But both sides must remain in compliance with the ABM treaty for at least ten years. Previously, the Soviets had been insisting on a fifteen-year "nonwithdrawal" agreement.

The leaders recessed, and Reagan met with his advisors in the cramped, bug-proof "bubble" in the American embassy to consider the American reply. Reagan summarized the first session by saying, "He's brought a whole lot of proposals, but I'm afraid he's going after SDI." Paul Nitze called Gorbachev's package of offensive reductions the best Soviet proposal he had ever seen: "I'm excited by it." Others, particularly Richard Perle, Kenneth Adelman, and Edward Rowny, were more skeptical, warning that the START proposal was almost sure to be rigged in a way that would preserve Soviet advantages in MIRVed ICBMs and throw-weight. Shultz suggested that Reagan propose to Gorbachev the appointment of "working groups" to hash out various issues.

In their second session, Reagan and Gorbachev locked horns on SDI. Reagan repeated what was becoming his favorite analogy—comparing SDI to gas masks during World War I—and Shevardnadze remarked that gas masks "did not have offensive capabilities." The President said that he favored a new treaty that would supersede the old ABM pact and commit the United States to sharing SDI technology with the Soviet Union. Gorbachev said he did not believe that America would ever keep that promise, and besides, "The ABM treaty must be strengthened, not scrapped."

The leaders agreed on little except the establishment of working groups. Paul Nitze chaired the American team, and the Soviet side was led by Marshal Akhromeyev. His selection was significant. After the Geneva summit of the year before, there had been speculation, encouraged by comments from Soviet officials and institute representatives, that Gorbachev's failure to secure any concessions on SDI had disturbed powerful members of the military establishment, who had made it a condition for their support of his arms-control policies that the Americans not be allowed to evade the issue again. Gorbachev had apparently decided to overcome any problem he was having with the military in part by designating the chief of the General Staff as his alter ego at the "working level" in Reykjavik.

For Nitze, the ensuing all-night session was one of the high points of a long and eventful career. His counterpart was the senior military officer of the Soviet Union, who was operating on direct instructions from the general secretary of the Communist party, who in turn was monitoring the talks from his headquarters aboard a Soviet ship tied up at the dock in Reykjavik harbor. Nitze and Akhromeyev were grappling with the great issues of the strategic debate: What constituted stability in the nuclear balance? What exactly should be the "interrelationship" between offense and defense? How should that interrelationship be defined, structured, and enforced through arms control?

In many respects, Nitze and his American colleagues were ill prepared for this meeting. They had come expecting a much more focused, less ambitious agenda. Had they known what to expect, they would have been sharply divided within their own ranks over what their position should be. That division was personified by the disagreement between Paul Nitze and the man at his side, Richard Perle. Nonetheless, the encounter with the Soviet marshal across the table was one for which Nitze had spent forty years preparing.

Having come with a sweeping proposal that caught the Americans by surprise, Akhromeyev initially had the advantage, and he pressed it hard.

He elaborated on the paper that Gorbachev had given to Reagan earlier. The marshal first reviewed its contents, then asked, "How should we set about discussing this? Item by item? Paragraph by paragraph? Sentence by sentence? We can discuss the philosophy behind it if you want."

For nearly six hours, starting at 8:00 p.m., the Americans probed what Gorbachev's idea of 50-percent cuts would look like in practice. Akhromeyev explained that the proposal would entail cutting in half the arsenals of the two sides "category by category" (ICBM launchers, SLBM launchers, ballistic missile launchers, heavy bombers, ballistic missile launchers plus heavy bombers, and total "charges," or warheads, on strategic nuclear delivery vehicles).

As Nitze pointed out, in those categories where the Soviets were ahead, such as ICBM warheads, their proposal would let them keep their advantages. The result, he said, would be "unequal reductions that would lead to unequal end levels." Therefore, he said, an agreement must stipulate equal ceilings—1,600 launchers and 6,000 warheads—and equal subceilings of the kind that the United States had already presented in Geneva.

Reinforcing Nitze's objection, Perle complained that the Soviet proposal for a 50-percent cut would "freeze your superiority" because the Soviets had more launchers. The resulting inequality, he noted, would be "against American law." As Victor Karpov acidly pointed out, the "law" to which Perle was referring was the 1972 Jackson amendment to the Senate's approval of SALT I—which Perle himself had been instrumental in drafting.

Akhromeyev took a more patient tone. "By setting the number of weapons in each category," he said, "you are in effect telling us how to restructure our forces. That is unacceptable to us." He appealed to the old Kissingerian concept of offsetting asymmetries: "You have more warheads, so it balances out." He meant that the American lead in submarine missile warheads and bomber weapons would compensate for the Soviet lead in ICBM warheads.

Perle responded that it was ICBM warheads that mattered most, since they were hard-target killers and first-strike weapons; while the Soviet Union was ahead in that category, the Soviet proposal made no specific provision for 50-percent cuts there.

The Soviets were, for purposes of their argument, counting weapons carried by airplanes as equivalent to missile warheads. This led Nitze to remark to Akhromeyev, "As a marshal of the Soviet Union, you must understand that there is a big difference between a gravity bomb on a B-52 and a reentry vehicle on a SS-18." Therefore, the United States must insist not only on equal ceilings overall but on subceilings that would restrict the most threatening weapons.

"We're already prepared to cut ICBMs," replied Akhromeyev. "All that your subceilings and arithmetic do is just cut us further."

At Akhromeyev's side, Karpov was increasingly sullen, casting dark glances across the table, rolling his eyes and engaging in heavy, theatrical sighs. Some of his impatience seemed directed at Akhromeyev for indulging the Americans in a rehash of old debates. Another member of the Soviet delegation, Georgi Arbatov, also grew vocally annoyed and caustic, and Akhromeyev had to calm him down. The chief of the General Staff seemed to be playing good cop to his civilian comrades' bad cop.

Eventually, though, Akhromeyev, too, complained that the talks were leading nowhere, and this complaint turned into a threat: "We have instructions to discuss this document and come to an agreement, then report to our principals by morning. We seem to be getting nowhere. It looks as though we can't come to agreement on any points, so I guess we should report to our principals that we've failed."

To avert a breakdown and provide some sort of American counterproposal, Nitze started to adjust upward the subceiling that the United States was seeking for ICBM warheads, from 3,000 to 3,600.* But Edward Rowny grew agitated and passed Nitze a note demanding a break. When the Americans conferred in another room, Rowny strenuously objected that the United States must not let the Soviets have an additional six hundred ICBM warheads.

Nitze said not only that he found Akhromeyev impressive but "I believe he wants to be helpful. I want to offer him something." Even if raised, the ICBM warhead subceiling would still be equal.

"But ICBMs are the Soviet specialty," protested Rowny.

"I *know* that, Ed," said Nitze with growing exasperation.

Rowny was adamant that any American retreat would be "dangerous and unwise," and Perle and Adelman sided with him.

"You're forcing me to be as rigid as the Russians are at their worst," said Nitze. "I'm absolutely furious."

After the break, the American team put forward what was essentially the U.S. position already on the table at the Nuclear and Space Talks in Geneva. So Akhromeyev noted. His voice laden with sarcastic solicitude, he asked, "Please, Mr. Nitze, tell us on what points does this proposal differ from the one you introduced in September?"

There was an awkward pause, then Nitze said, "Yes, it doesn't differ, but that is because it is a good proposal."

Akhromeyev turned the screw: "We have explained already why these

---

*The 3,600 figure had the potential appeal of picking up on an earlier Soviet proposal: At one point in START, the Soviets had been willing to accept an overall ceiling of 6,000 nuclear charges and a "force-concentration rule" of 60 percent—i.e., no more than 60 percent, or 3,600, on any one leg of the strategic triad, ICBMs, SLBMs, or heavy bombers—which would have meant 3,600 ICBM warheads. See p. 273.

proposals of yours are not acceptable. Now it is clear that you are not ready to negotiate on the basis of our proposal. In that case we have to report to our superiors. I see no other way out.''

Shortly before 2:00 A.M., Akhromeyev requested an adjournment. Nitze woke Shultz, and Akhromeyev went to the Soviet ship and consulted with his superiors. Shultz assured Nitze that he had the authority to adjust the numbers for the subceilings, and Akhromeyev received instructions that allowed the Soviet side to make a similar move. "In the name of good will," said Akhromeyev on returning to the meeting at 3:00 A.M., "we agree to equal ceilings" on launchers and warheads.

The session, which continued until six in the morning, resulted in agreement on what those overall ceilings should be: 1,600 launchers (ICBMs, SLBMs, and intercontinental bombers) and 6,000 nuclear charges. That was 1,500 lower than the previous American proposal and back to the figure the Soviets had been proposing before June, when they raised the ceiling to 8,000 as part of their maneuvering over INF; 6,000 was also genuinely closer to the magic 50 percent, since there were roughly twelve thousand strategic warheads on both sides.

Differences remained on how to define nuclear charges. The U.S. definition would have included strategic ballistic missile warheads and air-launched cruise missiles. Under a Soviet compromise formula, gravity bombs and weapons other than cruise missiles (i.e., short-range attack missiles) would be included also, but at a greatly discounted rate, in the aggregate of nuclear charges. This was a surprise bonus for the United States, since it implicitly acknowledged the retaliatory nature and stabilizing virtues of "slow-flyers" or "air-breathing" weapons, as opposed to ballistic missiles, and eased the burden of an agreement on the U.S. bomber force.*

The issue of sea-launched cruise missiles was set to one side, but only after much haggling over what to say in a joint statement. The Soviets were willing to permit SLCMs on submarines but wanted to ban them on surface ships; the United States wanted to let them run free. Perle tried to persuade Akhromeyev that there was no need for special verification measures on SLCM. How could SLCMs be verified anyway? he asked. Akhromeyev replied, "We have constraints on ALCMs [they were allowed on specially designated and externally distinguishable bombers]—we can do the same sort of thing with SLCMs." This was a telling, ironic exchange, since Perle had been, and would continue to be, a stickler for the toughest verification measures when the weapon system in question was one in which the Soviets

---

*Under Akhromeyev's proposal, a bomber armed with gravity bombs and short-range attack missiles would count both as one launcher and as one nuclear charge (no matter how many bombs and SRAMs it actually had on board). By contrast, a bomber armed with ALCMs would count as one launcher, and each of its ALCMs would count as a nuclear charge.

enjoyed an advantage. It took more than an hour to agree that the joint statement would say that the two sides would work toward a mutually agreeable solution.

On the question of subceilings the two sides remained at an impasse. For Nitze—never enthusiastic about reductions for their own sake—a world in which each superpower had 6,000 warheads could be more dangerous than one in which each had 12,000. If the Soviets kept a disproportionate number of their 6,000 nuclear charges on large, MIRVed ICBMs, the resulting ratio of Soviet warheads to American targets—the index of vulnerability—might actually increase. Indeed, one of the disadvantages, in Nitze's view, of the 1,600 launcher ceiling was that it provided an inducement to keeping MIRVs (since if the number of launchers was to be limited, there would be a temptation to put multiple warheads on those that were permitted). Therefore, Nitze bore down on the need for specified subceilings on ICBMs, MIRVed ICBMs, and heavies.

Akhromeyev countered that subceilings were superfluous and unjustified, especially now that the Soviet side was willing to reduce the overall ceiling on nuclear charges from 8,000 back to 6,000. With only 6,000 warheads allowed, his country would be foolish to keep a large number of them on heavy missiles. The logic of the situation alone would require deep cuts in heavies.

Fine, said Nitze. He was a great believer in logic. But he was also a great believer in embodying logic in agreements. Let a START treaty simply ratify the logic of what Akhromeyev was saying by including subceilings. At a minimum, he said, any joint statement coming out of the meeting should say that either side had the right to raise the issue of subceilings in subsequent negotiations.

Akhromeyev replied that of course either side could raise any issue it wanted, but the United States did not have a right to dictate to the Soviet Union how its Strategic Rocket Forces should be structured under a START agreement. Therefore, nothing about subceilings could be spelled out on any piece of paper that his government signed. He was reflecting an attitude characteristic of military planners on both sides, who want as much flexibility as possible about how to implement whatever limitations and reductions are imposed upon them by their diplomats and political leaders.

Finally, as Nitze summarized it later, ''we agreed that we would not work out the sublimits there, but that it was an issue of major importance. Akhromeyev acknowledged this.''

Nitze asked for, and was sure he received, Akhromeyev's personal assurances that the issue remained open for future negotiation. The question of subceilings had already been a critical sticking point at the Nuclear and Space Talks in Geneva, and it would become the most contentious and important issue in START for more than a year after Reykjavik.

All in all, Nitze later recalled concluding, "we were on the road to something we could agree to in the important issues of START. If we're going to get a deal, this was the direction we would have to go. That's how it is— you chew away and chew away."[4]

On the even more difficult question of what to do about SDI, the all-night session produced no reason to expect a breakthrough. Akhromeyev's line of argument was familiar and unyielding: The ABM treaty prohibited the deployment of a territorial defense; SDI was intended to provide territorial defense; therefore, nothing associated with SDI could go beyond fundamental research. The confines of permissible R&D seemed to be the four walls and ceiling of a laboratory; the Soviets were still, in Perle's phrase of the previous summer, trying to "move Smith indoors."

Like Gorbachev at his opening session with Reagan, Akhromeyev acted as though his government were making a generous concession when he said that the Soviet Union was willing to let the United States "test components designed to be deployed in space—as long as they are tested in the laboratory." That led Perle to ask, "What if we put the laboratory in space?"

The Soviets treated the question as a wisecrack, although in the months to come it became much more than that: Eventually the superpowers would almost certainly have to determine what sort of R&D activities in space were permissible either under the old ABM treaty or under a new accord of some kind.

As they finally concluded their talks, Akhromeyev congratulated Nitze on his stamina, and Nitze remarked, "As regards strategic arms cuts, we've made more progress than in years." But on SDI, he said, "We've left much for the President and the general secretary to do."

On Sunday, Reagan and Gorbachev met again, with Shultz and Shevardnadze present, for what was supposed to be the last time. They gave their sanction to the work done by their subordinates during the night on offensive weapons, but the disagreement on defense once again loomed large. Reagan tried at one point to remand the issue to the Nuclear and Space Talks, but Gorbachev, who had come to Reykjavik largely to leapfrog over the slogging negotiations, objected: "If it goes back to Geneva, we'll be eating this porridge for years." They agreed to hold an unscheduled meeting in the afternoon and told their foreign ministers to get together after lunch for one last attempt to reach a compromise.

Shultz summoned Nitze, Poindexter, Perle, Kampelman, and Robert Linhard of the NSC staff. "We're at a very serious impasse" on SDI, said the secretary of state. The meeting failed to produce a new strategy. That was partly because it was brief, partly because the Americans had come to Reykjavik unprepared to deal with the offense-defense tradeoff, but also because in Nitze and Perle, the group advising Shultz included both the Administration's leading advocate and its leading opponent of such a tradeoff.

When Shevardnadze and his aides arrived, Shultz began by stressing what had already been accomplished on offense and other issues. Shevardnadze interrupted: "I'm not going to talk about those things. There's one issue before us. Is the President prepared to agree on a period of time, ten years, when there will be no withdrawal from the ABM treaty and strict adherence to its terms? That's got to be settled. If it's not, nothing else is agreed. We're prepared to come down to ten years, but no lower. If not, let's go home."

Turning first to Kampelman, the Soviet foreign minister said, "You are a creative person—can't you think of something?" Then he looked at Nitze: "You are so experienced—can't you come up with something?"

The Americans did improvise a way of reconciling Reagan's and Gorbachev's positions, but its authors were Perle and Linhard, who were sitting on the other side of Shultz from Nitze and Kampelman. While Shevardnadze was talking, they put their heads together and scribbled on a pad of paper, hastily stitching together bits and pieces of ideas that they had discussed during earlier brainstorming sessions. They passed a note to Poindexter, who gave it to Shultz. He read it and said to Shevardnadze: "You've seen some writing at that end of the table. This is an effort by some of us here to see if we can't break the impasse." Shultz added that the idea had acquired the status of an American proposal there on the spot, and that when Reagan heard it, "the sound you hear may be the President banging my head against the wall."

Shultz then read the Perle-Linhard formulation: The two sides would agree to abide by the ABM treaty for five years; during that time strategic offenses would be cut by 50 percent along the lines of what the negotiators had agreed during the all-night session (presumably with the addition of the subceilings that the Americans were seeking); then there would be a second five years of adherence to the ABM treaty if all remaining ballistic missiles were eliminated during that time. After a total of ten years of compliance with the ABM treaty and the elimination of all ballistic missiles, either side would be free to deploy strategic defenses.

The supposed concession was that the United States would be "coming up" from the seven and a half years of compliance that Reagan had offered in his July 25 letter to Gorbachev, meeting the Soviet insistence on ten years. The more germane and problematic feature of the proposal was that Reagan's goal of zero ballistic missiles, which in the letter had been open-ended, was now also shoehorned into the ten-year time frame. The United States would be imposing a specific deadline for the elimination of the most powerful weapons and the mainstays of deterrence.

Approximately a year before, on the eve of the Geneva summit, Larry Speakes had dismissed as a "presidential imprecision" Reagan's statement to a group of Soviet journalists that strategic offense should be reduced to zero before SDI would be deployed. Now Perle and Linhard were, through Shultz, unmistakably proposing the same thing. This proposal, if accepted, would commit the Soviet Union to the inevitable deployment of SDI. For just that reason, Shevardnadze warned that while Reagan was bouncing Shultz's head on the wall, Gorbachev might be rejecting the proposal for his own reasons. However, the foreign minister continued, it was still worth exploring.

The Americans could only guess at the strategy the Soviets were pursuing. Perhaps Shevardnadze and his advisors sensed an opportunity to turn the American proposal to their own advantage. Phase one, the first five years, amounted to the deal the Soviets themselves had been seeking: continued adherence to the ABM treaty and 50-percent reductions in offense. Phase two, the second five years, which would occur in the post-Reagan era, might turn out to be never-never land. Moreover, since under Reagan's proposal SDI deployment was ultimately contingent on the prior elimination of ballistic missiles, the scheme had its own built-in slippery slope: Phase one might be stretched out indefinitely if, as was likely, the two sides found it neither desirable nor feasible to reduce their missiles to zero.

The meeting adjourned so that the ministers could report to their principals and prepare them for the final session. Shultz and Poindexter presented the new version of the American proposal to the President, stressing its consistency with his July letter to Gorbachev. Reagan said that the idea was imaginative: "He gets his precious ABM treaty, and we get all his ballistic missiles. And after that we can deploy SDI in space. Then it's a whole new ball game."

Reagan asked Perle whether the United States could afford to eliminate its own ballistic missiles within ten years.

"I think we can," said Perle, explaining that there were programs under way that would assure American security in a world without ballistic missiles. He was referring in particular to "stealth" technology that could make bombers and cruise missiles—i.e., strategic delivery vehicles other than ballistic missiles—all but invisible to radar and, therefore, more effective instruments of deterrence and retaliation. Indeed, it was largely because of American superiority in the technology of nonballistic, air-breathing weapons that the elimination of ICBMs and SLBMs on both sides would redound to the net advantage of the United States.

When Gorbachev arrived for the final session with Reagan, he countered with a Soviet proposal for the elimination after ten years not just of ballistic missiles (in which the Soviet Union had an overall advantage) but of all offensive strategic arms, encompassing bombers and cruise missiles (in which the United States was ahead) and short-range weapons as well. He was making sure that even in its stipulation of a utopian goal, the Reykjavik agreement, if there was to be one, would represent Soviet-American equality in nuclear weaponry—the equality of zero—while leaving the Soviet Union with its numerical superiority in conventional arms, particularly in Europe. He was also all but guaranteeing that phase two of the American plan would remain forever in the future, while phase one would dictate what actually happened as a result of the agreement.

"Suits me fine," said the President. He and his aides subsequently maintained that he had not intended to endorse Gorbachev's call for total nuclear disarmament within ten years—only to reiterate his long-standing hope that a nuclear-free world would be achieved one day.

What did not suit Reagan was Gorbachev's adamancy about confining SDI to the laboratory. The President kept saying it was just that one word, "laboratory," that stood between them and success. It was a synonym, said Reagan, for the Soviet effort to "kill" SDI. He suggested again setting the issue aside to be resolved in Geneva or at the summit he was hoping shortly to host in Washington.

Gorbachev still refused, saying that an agreement on reductions in offensive weapons was impossible as long as SDI could proceed outside the laboratory, building momentum toward deployment.

In his "laboratory" formulation, Gorbachev was demanding the sort of "SDI breakout insurance" that the RAND group and Nitze had been advocating for a long time. He told Reagan that he would be regarded in Moscow as "the village idiot" if he agreed, even in principle, to deep cuts in offense without a clear and restrictive understanding about what the defensive half of the agreement would entail. Later he said publicly, "It would have taken a madman" to leave the issue of SDI unresolved. These comments seemed to confirm Gorbachev's concern that he not repeat the mistake for which Akhromeyev and other comrades may have chastised him after the Geneva summit in 1985.

By now, both men were beginning to gather their papers. Finally, Reagan closed his briefcase and stood up. The meeting ended in a failure all the more spectacular because of the suspense and high expectations that had been growing throughout the weekend. Hopes and plans for a follow-up summit in Washington exploded in a burst of public disappointment and mutual recrimination. Shultz and Gorbachev gave press conferences before going home. Standing at the entrance of the crowded foreign press center at a downtown hotel while Shultz talked, Kampelman fought back tears. In a nearby room, Nitze prepared to meet with journalists.

"We tried," he said, his voice heavy with exhaustion. "We tried, we tried. By God, we tried. And we almost did it."

One of the strangest episodes in the annals of nuclear diplomacy had ended. The two leaders seemed to have been caught up in a make-or-break atmosphere, engaging in a bout of feverish one-upmanship, with each trying to outdo the other in demonstrating his devotion to the dream of a nuclear-free world while at the same time protecting his preference for the real world. In Reagan's case, it would be a world with large-scale strategic defenses; in Gorbachev's, a world where safety continued to be the sturdy child of terror.

Despite the collapse of the talks, however, and despite the ensuing dispute over who had agreed to what during the final manic-depressive encounter of what some of the Americans involved called "the lost weekend," there had been a genuine breakthrough. During the small hours of that Sunday morning, Nitze and Akhromeyev had laid the foundation for a triad of agreements: the elimination of all American and Soviet land-based intermediate-range missiles; a major—and stabilizing—reduction of strategic offenses; and a joint pledge not to withdraw from the ABM treaty or to deploy SDI for a defined period of time. A large number of relatively small issues remained. But there were only two major ones: concurrence on sub-ceilings in START and agreement on how the ABM treaty applied to SDI, especially in its definition of permissible research, development, and testing.

CHAPTER 13

Battle Lines

In early November 1986, George Shultz and a group of aides undertook a salvage mission. They met in Vienna with a Soviet delegation led by Eduard Shevardnadze. The object of the meeting, said Paul Nitze to Victor Karpov on arrival, was to "capture the good things on which our leaders were able to agree at Reykjavik."

At the same time, the U.S. government unceremoniously jettisoned the more unrealistic vestiges of the lost weekend. One of the first pieces of the Reykjavik package to disappear was ZBM—the goal of achieving zero ballistic missiles in the course of the next ten years. The Joint Chiefs of Staff were appalled that their Commander in Chief had agreed, however conditionally, to a deadline for the elimination of the most potent weapons in the American arsenal. Even if that goal proved to be a mirage, as almost everyone believed it would, the Chiefs feared that the President's embrace of a plan for phasing out all ICBMs and SLBMs was likely further to erode congressional support for new ballistic missile programs, the MX and the Trident II.

Paul Nitze was similarly concerned about the fate of his own preference for a new ballistic missile, the Midgetman. Unwisely, in his view, the Administration had already proposed in START to ban mobile ICBMs. Now the President had further undercut Midgetman by proposing to ban all other ballistic missiles as well, both existing and prospective ones.

Shortly after Reykjavik, at a meeting in the White House on October 27, Admiral William Crowe, chairman of the Joint Chiefs, read a hard-hitting prepared statement objecting to the plan. He warned that it jeopardized both the necessary modernization of the American deterrent and the stability of the superpower relationship. "As your chief military advisor," Crowe told the President, "I don't advise you to submit this proposal."

ZBM was equally unsettling to the allies. "Zeroing out" intermediate-range American missiles in Europe was problematic enough. Doing the same thing to U.S. ICBMs and SLBMs was almost unthinkable. American strategic missiles were a guarantee of European security; they were the great equalizers, assuring that their protector, an ocean away, could retaliate against aggression by the Warsaw Pact. Once again, it was British Prime

Minister Margaret Thatcher who intervened directly—though discreetly and confidentially—with the President to coax him away from his own proposal.

The Soviets, who were even more attached to ballistic missiles, were also glad to let ZBM die an unmourned death. So when Shultz and Shevardnadze met in Vienna, they concentrated instead on the more practical goal of filling in the gaps of a START agreement that would allow each side 1,600 strategic launchers, including ballistic missiles, and 6,000 warheads.

For the United States, the most important piece of unfinished business from Reykjavik was to get the Soviets to agree to subceilings that would further restrict the number of warheads allowed on ballistic missiles, particularly ICBMs. The U.S. proposal now called for one subceiling of 4,800 warheads on the aggregate of SLBMs and ICBMs, and another of 3,300 warheads on ICBMs alone.

In Vienna, Shultz and Nitze maintained that Marshal Akhromeyev had agreed at Reykjavik that the United States was free to raise the subject of "stabilizing subceilings" in the future. Shevardnadze's deputy, Alexander Bessmertnykh, demurred: Gorbachev, he said, had implied nothing of the kind; moreover, for the United States still to be harping on the matter of subceilings was a "retreat from what our leaders did agree in Reykjavik."

Victor Karpov went further. "It was clear," he said, "that we agreed in Reykjavik there would be no subceilings."

Now it was Nitze who took umbrage: "Pardon me, Victor, but I have to say that is an outright lie. There are eight of us here who were witnesses to the exchange between Akhromeyev and me."

Karpov shrugged. He had met with Gorbachev shortly before coming to Vienna, he said, and the general secretary had dismissed as "nonsense" the idea that the United States could continue to raise the matter of subceilings. The battle lines were drawn even more starkly than at Reykjavik on what would be the most contentious and important issue in START for over a year to come.

In early December, when the Nuclear and Space Talks resumed, Max Kampelman tried his hand at getting Karpov to budge. They met, along with their principal deputies, for four days in Geneva. The session quickly fell into an old pattern—a chicken-and-egg argument. Kampelman tried to convince Karpov that new Soviet concessions in START, particularly on subceilings, might induce the United States finally to give up something on SDI.

"Look, Victor," said Kampelman over lunch, arranging a knife, a fork, and a folded napkin before him. The napkin represented the compromise that the two sides might eventually reach; the knife, at the far edge of the table, was the Soviet position; the fork, a few inches from the napkin, was the U.S. position in START. "Let's assume you want to end up here in the middle. Nothing says you can't start off way over here. Let's assume we want to end up an inch away from you. But we can't start way off over here—at the other extreme from you—because we have to convince our public and our allies that we're starting from a reasonable position. You're going to have to make more concessions than we are in the endgame, so why not start making them now?''

Karpov accepted neither the premise that the Soviet position was unreasonable nor the conclusion that his side should make the next move. ''We're already making all the concessions,'' he said, ''and that's not the way a negotiation should take place.''

Cap's End Run

While in Geneva Max Kampelman was trying discreetly to nurture what he called ''the arms-control potential'' of SDI, back in Washington Caspar Weinberger and Richard Perle were doing the opposite—generating momentum for early deployment of a system that would force the United States out of the ABM treaty and preclude concessions on strategic defense in the Nuclear and Space Talks.

On December 17, 1986, Weinberger, Perle, Frank Gaffney, and General James Abrahamson, the director of the SDI organization, gave President Reagan an exuberant briefing on progress in the program, particularly for an early-deployment plan then taking shape. Space-based kinetic kill vehicles (KKVs), which were subsequently called space-based interceptors, were becoming the technology of choice, since they were more likely than lasers, particle beams, or rail guns to be available before the year 2,000. The Pentagon had claimed a stunning success in September with an experiment in which one device launched on a rocket booster tracked and collided with another device moving at approximately the velocity of a warhead. The experiment was in a sense rigged: A reflector on the target rocket magnified its image one thousand times—an aid to interception that the Soviets were not likely to provide if they fired missiles at the United States.

Weinberger contended that it might be possible in the mid-1990s to orbit a space-based ''overlay'' of 300 huge satellites, called ''garages,'' each capable of launching ten or so smart rocks that could intercept Soviet missiles. The system would also include an ''underlay'' of ground-based smart rocks capable of striking warheads as they re-entered the atmosphere. Such a system, unless it was radically miniaturized, would require putting more than six million pounds into orbit, the equivalent of more than 125 space-shuttle loads. The whole complex was a prime candidate for what was now called ''phased deployment.'' The term ''early deployment'' had been retired, in part because it smacked too much of traditional ABM silo defenses and of deliberate treaty-busting. ''Phased deployment'' was meant to suggest the first phase ''on the path'' to realization of the President's original and enduring dream for SDI.

Weinberger used the December 17 meeting with the President to recommend higher levels of funding for SDI, particularly for the development of a ''heavy lift launch vehicle''—a huge rocket that could put all the ''overlay'' hardware into orbit—as well as for unambiguous adoption of the broad interpretation of the ABM treaty. Implicit in what he said was a strong rebuttal to the idea that any aspect of SDI should, in any way or under any circumstances, be traded away.

President Reagan listened approvingly to all this good news about his favorite program. ''Cap,'' he said, ''that's great! Good for all of you over there. It looks like we're going full speed ahead.'' He had only one question: How did all this square with what he had told Mikhail Gorbachev two months before in Hofdi House? Reagan had agreed in Reykjavik to delay deployment of any SDI system for ten years if ballistic missiles were eliminated at the same time. Weinberger, caught momentarily off guard, replied that his office would study the question and get back to the President. Thus, Reagan's endorsement at Reykjavik of continued compliance with the ABM treaty presented an obstacle to the Pentagon in its attempted end run around the would-be deal-makers elsewhere in the Administration.

Weinberger had chosen his moment carefully. The holidays had begun. Shultz was attending a Christmas party at the State Department. The National Security Council staff—which was supposed to referee disputes between the State and Defense departments and prevent one agency from sneaking its preferences past another—was in greater disarray than usual because of the Iran-Contra affair.

John Poindexter had resigned as presidential national security advisor on November 25, and Frank Carlucci was designated to succeed him. Carlucci was a former subordinate of Weinberger's. He had been deputy secretary of defense at the outset of the Administration. Earlier, in the Nixon Administration, he had been Weinberger's deputy at the Office of Management and Budget and at the Department of Health, Education and Welfare. Therefore, according to conventional wisdom, the bureaucratic correlation of forces had, if anything, shifted in Weinberger and Perle's favor against the State Department.

In fact, however, Carlucci's appointment was a turning point in the opposite direction. As a trustee of RAND, he had been following the quiet attempt by a group within the think tank to explore an offense-defense trade-off. Therefore, unknown to most of the government, the RAND analysis of the grand compromise now had a sympathetic ear in the second most important office of the White House. In 1987, Carlucci received from Abrahamson a briefing entitled ''How Defenses Work.'' It was nicknamed in the bureaucracy "The Yellow Brick Road" because it was supposed to show the way to the Emerald City and the Wizard of Oz. Afterward, Carlucci remarked curtly to a colleague, "There's nothing there."

Still, Carlucci was determined to move slowly and cautiously. He was not going to take sides as long as he could help it. There seemed little profit in opposing Weinberger outright. Not only was the secretary of defense personally close to the President, but his enthusiasm for SDI and his opposition to compromise on the program made him philosophically close as well.

Not until later did Paul Nitze get wind of what Weinberger and Perle had been up to from his own conversations with Abrahamson and pro-SDI congressmen. He was, he said, "outraged" at the "treachery" of the Pentagon for "maneuvering the President on policy while excluding the secretary of state."

George Shultz's own language was, as usual, much cooler, but his annoyance, too, was intense. "Cap just won't let stand the good arrangement we reached a year ago" on the interpretation of the ABM treaty, remarked the secretary of state to a colleague. "The trouble with the way this government works sometimes is that there's no ninth inning. People keep replaying the last inning until it comes out the way they want."

In the midst of all this interagency warfare, Attorney General Edwin Meese fired a shot of his own across the State Department's bow. He had neither technical expertise about SDI nor bureaucratic responsibility for it, but he was one of the President's oldest personal friends and closest advisors in the government. His views both reflected and influenced Reagan's. Deployment of SDI, said Meese publicly on January 16, should be accelerated "so that it will be in place and not tampered with by future Administrations."

Weinberger was worried about his colleagues Shultz and Nitze tampering with SDI in the present Administration. On January 22, he was in "Star Wars City"—Colorado Springs, Colorado—regaling an audience of SDI officials and military contractors with a speech that promoted phased deployment of a kinetic kill vehicle system, which would have been in violation of both the narrow and the broad interpretation of the ABM treaty.*

---

*The Administration was uncertain whether kinetic kill vehicles (or space-based interceptors) should be considered an exotic system, "based on other physical principles" (OPPs), as envisioned by the ABM treaty, or whether they were traditional antiballistic missile interceptors. There was in this question—sometimes expressed in jargon, "Are KKVs OPPs or ABMs?"—a dilemma. While the technology used to fire and guide them was highly sophisticated, KKVs themselves were projectiles or interceptors, bullets to hit bullets. They were not Buck Rogers–like laser or particle beams. If KKVs qualified as traditional antiballistic missile interceptors, the development and testing, as well as the deployment, of a space-based KKV system would be prohibited even under the broad interpretation. If, on the other hand, they were designated an exotic, or OPP, system, development and testing might be permitted, but deployment would of course still be forbidden, even under the broad interpretation. Either way, the Pentagon would be thwarted in its desire to make KKVs the centerpiece of an early-deployment system—unless, of course, the United States was to pull out of the ABM treaty altogether.

Perle himself tried to explain to Shultz that phased deployment was not the same as early deployment and that the Pentagon was now explicitly recommending *against* early-deployment systems while pushing hard for a phased-deployment one. The difference between the two was about four years in target dates. Shultz chose not to be drawn into the semantics of the issue. Nor did he frontally challenge the Pentagon's advocacy of any particular scheme, but he objected that the State Department had been "excluded from the process." It was, he said, "too early to make a deployment decision and unnecessary to do so." That was almost identical to Carlucci's position. A new alliance was forming against Weinberger and Perle.

Permitted/Prohibited

On January 22—the same day Weinberger was speaking in Colorado Springs—Academician Evgeny Velikhov called on Nitze at the State Department. The two men fell into an intense conversation about the possibility of establishing "quantitative limits" or "parameters"—for example, the power or brightness of a laser beam—that might be used to define a device as an ABM component. They also discussed the kinetic kill vehicle program and how it related to the ABM treaty.

For some months there had been hints coming out of Moscow that the Kremlin might be willing to adopt a definition of permissible research less stringent than the "laboratory" formulation that Gorbachev had used to such unsatisfactory effect with Reagan at Reykjavik. Shevardnadze had told a number of foreign visitors to Moscow that the U.S.S.R. was prepared to offer a more lenient definition, and Georgi Arbatov was saying much the same thing, although carefully adding that "unlimited testing would constitute a carte blanche to break out of the ABM treaty."

At the Shultz-Shevardnadze session in Vienna in November 1986, the Soviets had proposed setting up a separate "experts group" that would conduct a new negotiation on what SDI activity was permissible, and what was impermissible, under the ABM treaty. Nitze favored such talks, for he accepted the Soviets' contention that their need for breakout insurance should cover SDI testing. As he put it, the two sides must "put their heads together and figure out a way to fill in the holes in the treaty . . . to fix it where it needs fixing . . . to make it whole . . . to perfect it." That meant precise stipulation of permissible and impermissible testing as well as research and development, an idea he had included in the Monday Package of 1985.

His purpose was not merely to "fix" the old treaty on strategic defenses but to get a new treaty on strategic offenses. It was, he said, a matter of "absolutely indisputable logic that if you want a START agreement resulting in stabilizing reductions, you've got to repair the gap in the way the existing treaty deals with new technologies." The ABM treaty was a diplomatic instrument; it could be repaired only through diplomacy.

Nitze found his conversation with Velikhov on January 22 a stimulating and encouraging model of the kind of constructive, productive interchange that might take place in the new negotiations that the Soviets were now proposing. His advocacy of what became known in shorthand as "permitted/prohibited talks" was the antithesis of Weinberger and Perle's phased-deployment scheme. If Nitze had his way, SDI would be on the table once and for all. If Weinberger and Perle had theirs, there would be no table.

In what passed for Solomonic wisdom in the Reagan Administration, the White House quickly stymied both of these recommendations, leaving the State Department and the Pentagon—and therefore the Administration as a whole—in deadlock. On February 3, there was a meeting at the White House of the National Security Policy Group, the expanded NSC. Weinberger wanted a decision in favor of early deployment on the spot. Admiral Crowe, the chairman of the Joint Chiefs of Staff, balked. "The Chiefs support SDI and support phased deployment," he said, "but we don't have enough in hand to decide now." He cautioned particularly against scrapping the ABM treaty. Like SALT II, the ABM treaty provided a degree of predictability that the Chiefs valued highly. Their experience the year before with the zero-ballistic-missiles proposal had been sobering for the Chiefs. Weinberger had concocted that proposal despite their misgivings, and Perle had made it more onerous at Reykjavik by setting a ten-year deadline for the elimination of ICBMs and SLBMs. Crowe was beginning to show independence from Weinberger—and to edge over to the side of the Shultz-Carlucci alliance that was now forming, enabling Nitze to add a new line to the set piece he was delivering within the government: "I'm with Crowe on the ABM treaty: We're better off with it than without."

Shultz used the February 3 meeting to argue against an early-deployment decision and in favor of "feeling out" the Soviets on their views.

Weinberger objected. "We shouldn't debate with the Soviets what can and can't be prohibited," he said.

The President clearly agreed. "Why don't we just go ahead on the assumption that this is what we're doing and it's right?" he asked. "Don't ask the Soviets—tell them."

Within forty-eight hours, Gregory Fossedal, a pro-SDI journalist, wrote an article with excerpts from the top-secret minutes of the meeting. It appeared in the capital's conservative newspaper, the *Washington Times*, which was owned by business interests affiliated with the Unification Church of a Korean evangelist, the Reverend Sun Myung Moon.[1] The leak prompted an

FBI investigation into the source. Advocates of SDI hoped that the story would commit the government publicly to the position that the President and the secretary of defense had taken in the meeting—against any "giveaway" of SDI under the guise of permissible/impermissible talks with the Soviets.

But the political effect of the leak was quite different from the probable intent. The revelation that Weinberger was accelerating his campaign for early deployment of strategic defenses and adoption of the broad interpretation of the ABM treaty prompted Senator Sam Nunn to reiterate in stern tones his warning that the Administration was on the brink of a "constitutional confrontation of profound dimensions." Messages of more muted concern poured in from Europe, including from Prime Minister Thatcher, Chancellor Helmut Kohl of West Germany, and Lord Peter Carrington, the secretary general of NATO.

A second high-level White House meeting produced another, by-now-familiar something-for-everyone compromise: The Administration would study the possibility of "restructuring" SDI to take full advantage of additional latitude for testing available under the broad interpretation. Shultz told the House Appropriations Committee on February 11, "We don't think any further negotiations are necessary" on how to interpret the ABM treaty; the Administration, he said, planned to proceed on the basis of "what we think it says."

Paul Nitze was dispatched to Europe to consult with the allies. Once again, he was given the mission precisely because he was so highly regarded in Europe. Yet he was less trusted than ever in his own government. Such was his reputation for "wandering off the reservation"—and such was the Pentagon's concern that he might use the trip to stir up support for "further negotiations" with the Soviets on the ABM treaty—that he was accompanied by Perle. In a particularly farfetched effort to make a virtue out of necessity, there had even been some thought in the Administration of designating Nitze and Perle to conduct back-channel negotiations with the Soviets. The two Americans, it was hoped, would "keep each other honest." But the Soviets gave this idea the back of their hand, citing Perle's proposed role as proof that it was not "serious."

On their trip to Europe, Nitze and Perle passed through Geneva, where the Nuclear and Space Talks were in session. The two men were there on Saturday, February 28, which turned out to be a big day. Also in Geneva was another in a steady stream of "codels," or congressional delegations. This one was particularly influential. It was led by the Democratic chairman of the Senate Foreign Relations Committee, Claiborne Pell, and it included two prominent Republicans, Richard Lugar and Ted Stevens, as well as Albert Gore, Jr. All four were members of the Senate Arms Control Observers Group, which, to the occasional annoyance of the Administration and its negotiators in Geneva, was empowered to look in on the talks from time to time.* The senators reflected the widespread unease among moderates on Capitol Hill about a number of aspects of Administration policy, notably the broad interpretation of the ABM treaty. Like Nitze, some senators believed that SDI gave the United States leverage to get a good START agreement—and that Congress's own power of the purse gave it the leverage to force the Administration to use SDI for that purpose.

The delegation from Washington met at noon that Saturday with Kampelman, Nitze, and Perle in the bubble of the U.S. mission. A consensus emerged and was committed to paper. For a fixed period, such as the fiscal year 1988, the Administration would not carry out SDI development or testing in violation of the restrictive interpretation of the ABM treaty. In exchange, the Senate would support a "respectable," but also negotiable, level of funding for SDI "research and other actions within the narrow interpretation." The Senate would also "forego legislative action to lock in the strict interpretation of the ABM treaty for a specified period of time or express formal Senate endorsement of the strict interpretation." Gore wanted the bargain to include an understanding that Kampelman would have greater "flexibility" on SDI in his negotiating instructions. "Flexibility" was understood to be code for the "permitted/prohibited" talks that Nitze wanted.

This arrangement did not last long. Attempts at follow-up negotiations back in Washington came to nought. Over time, the Pentagon's continuing adamance provoked congressional opponents of Star Wars in general and the broad interpretation in particular to toughen the conditions of a deal for which they would settle. Some felt that the senators in Geneva had given the Administration too much leeway. Sam Nunn eventually became more determined than ever to achieve what Gore and the others had been willing to forgo: legislation that would lock the Administration into the narrow interpretation.

Nonetheless, the compromise hammered out in the bubble in Geneva—short-lived as it was, and inadequate as it was deemed by some back in Washington—was still a turning point. For a few hours at least, the American mission to the Nuclear and Space Talks became the scene of negotiation and compromise not only between the United States and the Soviet Union but between the executive and legislative branches of the U.S. government as well—and, implicitly, between opposing factions of the executive branch represented by Nitze and Perle.

· · ·

---

*During the first Administration, as part of the price to maintain support for the President's strategic modernization program and his arms-control policies, the White House reluctantly agreed to let the Senate establish the Observers Group with a mandate to monitor the Nuclear and Space Talks and a license to kibitz on what was happening there.

Later that same day, February 28, Kampelman met with his new Soviet counterpart. The month before, Victor Karpov had been recalled to Moscow, where he was put in charge of the arms-control office of the foreign ministry. He was replaced by Yuli Vorontsov. As a member of the Central Committee and a first deputy foreign minister, he outranked Karpov; having previously served as Anatoly Dobrynin's number two in Washington, he also had close ties to the Central Committee Secretariat, where Dobrynin was now in charge of foreign policy.

Kampelman, too, now wore a second, "home-office" hat: In addition to being chief NST negotiator, he was made counselor of the State Department. It was hoped in Washington that the Kampelman-Vorontsov connection might become a new special channel.

In his meeting with Kampelman on February 28, Vorontsov brought up a long-standing Soviet complaint: The continuing talk out of Washington about the broad interpretation of the ABM treaty posed an obstacle to progress in the strategic talks. Caspar Weinberger's widely reported statements in Colorado Springs, along with news stories like the *Washington Times* account of the February 3 White House meeting, suggested that the broad interpretation was now Administration policy and that the President had already decided to proceed with deployment of SDI.

"What are we negotiating about?" asked Vorontsov in some pique. "What are we doing here if the President has already decided?"

Having just sat through an intense negotiation with Albert Gore and his senatorial colleagues, Kampelman knew just how troublesome the broad interpretation already was and how much more troublesome it might become. He felt more than ever that the American domestic debate over the 1972 treaty was a no-win proposition, threatening to cripple him as a negotiator. Aggressive promotion of the broad interpretation would needlessly provoke the Soviets and mainstream senators like Gore and Nunn, while outright advocacy of the narrow interpretation would cause trouble for the advocate himself with the Pentagon hard-liners and Star Wars enthusiasts in Congress.

Kampelman had been telling members of his own staff that the narrow-versus-broad issue was "irrelevant but politically complicating." To those who were true believers in the broad interpretation, he said, "Put away your sabers and your scalpels. Give us time to get an agreement without making a mountain out of a molehill. If we fail, then we'll have a big fight and sell tickets." In the meantime, he said, the best course was to set aside the whole issue for as long as possible and hope that in the course of the negotiations attention would shift from pedantic disputes over the old treaty to serious negotiation of a new agreement.

Kampelman now set about to downplay the issue with Vorontsov as well. "You're making too much of all that," he said. "Even if the President goes for the broad definition while we're here negotiating—and I'm not saying that he will—then if we get a treaty and it's ratified, that treaty will become the supreme law of the land and supersede any tentative decision by the President.''

Kampelman himself was, as he reminded Vorontsov, a lawyer. He knew when haggling over the fine points of a contract mattered and when it did not. What mattered to the Soviet Union was insurance against deployment of SDI. Whatever differences there might be between the two sides—for that matter, whatever disagreements there might be within the U.S. government—about the permissibility of development and testing, the Reagan Administration was prepared to accommodate Soviet concerns about deployment; Reagan had said as much to Gorbachev at Reykjavik.

Later in the evening on that busy Saturday of February 28, Nitze also met with Vorontsov. He, too, treated the narrow-versus-broad controversy as an annoying but avoidable "distraction," "beside the point," "something we should put behind us"—in effect, the same line Shultz had taken a year earlier.

Yet when Perle returned to Washington, he pressed harder than ever for adoption of what some in the Pentagon called "the legally correct interpretation," or LCI. Like zero ballistic missiles (ZBM) the year before, the broad interpretation now had the ultimate bureaucratic endorsement—its own set of initials.

"The Last Twenty Minutes"

While strategic arms control remained at an impasse, the talks on intermediate-range nuclear forces (INF) moved steadily forward. At Reykjavik, Mikhail Gorbachev had incorporated the Zero Option for Europe into his comprehensive proposal; but at the end of the dizzying weekend, the deal had fallen apart over the old issue of linkage. Gorbachev made an INF deal, like a START agreement, conditional on a comprehensive strategic agreement, which in turn was contingent on limiting Star Wars. Therefore, the Zero Option for INF, like the zero-ballistic-missile feature of START, seemed to have evaporated.

There was an almost audible sigh of relief from NATO capitals and in many offices in Washington as well. Military officers associated with the Joint Chiefs of Staff, strategic experts in Western Europe, and various congressional moderates who had been skeptical about the seriousness of the Zero Option when Reagan proposed it in 1981 were equally skeptical about the strategic wisdom of the proposal when it looked as though the Soviets might accept it after all in 1986–87. They were concerned about the effect of removing all long-range, land-based American missiles from Europe, fearing that the move would "decouple" the United States from its allies.

However, if the ZBM proposal in START was doomed to fail, the Zero Option in INF was doomed to succeed. It had a powerful appeal in the Kremlin precisely because it meant the complete withdrawal of the American missiles from Europe, and Reagan remained as attracted as ever to the "elimination of the entire class of land-based missiles." That bold and simple idea was far more compelling to him than recondite concerns over alliance coupling, escalation dominance, and extended deterrence.

"I'm not going to pull away from Reykjavik," Reagan told Max Kampelman when they discussed various interim measures for INF. Neither, apparently, was Gorbachev. A few days after Reykjavik, he had complained publicly that the United States was "distorting" the Soviet position in the talks. He scorned the idea that the U.S.S.R. would "recognize" the "right" to deploy American missiles in Western Europe.

The Americans had now seen Gorbachev alternately delink and relink INF to SDI so often that they calculated it was only a matter of time before he delinked again—in part to provide momentum to the otherwise stalled arms-control process, but also to achieve the Soviet objective of forcing the withdrawal from Europe of the Pershing IIs and Tomahawk cruise missiles.

"We need to look back at the matters discussed at Reykjavik," said Yuli Vorontsov to Kampelman in Geneva. "Then we must decide which ones can be singled out for progress soon." To that end he made a procedural suggestion. Joint plenaries of the umbrella Nuclear and Space Talks lent themselves to propagandistic posturing if only because they brought together the negotiators from all three forums and therefore emphasized the linkage that was proving such an obstacle. Vorontsov suggested scaling back the number of joint plenaries to leave more time for separate negotiations, particularly on INF.

Kampelman asked, "I hear comments coming out of Moscow: 'Reagan is no good; we can't do business with him.' What's your position?"

Vorontsov's predecessor, Victor Karpov, had usually dodged such questions, using them as a pretext for rehearsing his litany of complaints against the United States. Vorontsov, by contrast, seemed eager to reassure. "We want to deal with Ronald Reagan," he said. "He's your President. We know he wants an agreement."

As before, it remained for Gorbachev himself to spell out exactly what kind of business he was prepared to do. On February 28—the same busy Saturday when Kampelman, Nitze, and Perle met with Pell, Gore, and the other congressional observers in Geneva—the Soviet news agency, TASS, released a statement in the general secretary's name. The most important sentence was: "The Soviet Union suggests that the problem of medium-range missiles in Europe be singled out from the package of issues, and that a separate agreement on it be concluded, and without delay."

Max Kampelman recalled a famous Soviet remark that the last twenty minutes of a negotiation are the most important. Round eight of the INF forum of the Nuclear and Space Talks, predicted Kampelman, would be "the last twenty minutes."

The Soviets began working with gusto on what was formally known as the joint draft text of a treaty, a document in which agreed passages were spelled out and disputed ones were in brackets. Negotiation became largely a process of removing brackets. Aleksei Obukhov, who, as Vorontsov's deputy, had resumed overall responsibility for the INF talks, surprised Maynard Glitman by serving champagne and caviar. One of Glitman's deputies observed that the normally dour Obukhov "smiled for the third time in the history of NST."

Kampelman and Glitman's toughest job was convincing the Soviets to accept a "double global zero"—essentially Richard Perle's preference for the Zero Option back in 1981, no SS-20s or shorter-range SS-12 and SS-23 INF missiles anywhere in the U.S.S.R. Kampelman stressed to Vorontsov that such a sweeping treaty would help eventually with the politics of ratification in the U.S. Senate. "A big concern of the senators," he said, "will be verification. It will be far easier to verify a treaty that achieves a global zero outcome than one that leaves some shorter-range missiles in Europe and SS-20s in Asia."

To underscore the political obstacles that Reagan might face at home, Kampelman showed Vorontsov an article that Richard Nixon and Henry Kissinger had written for the *Los Angeles Times* on Sunday, April 26. It was highly critical of the prospective INF treaty, complaining in particular about the possibility that the Soviet Union would be able to keep SS-20s deployed in Asia.

The article was galling to Paul Nitze. It was another in a series of attacks not from the right but from the center of the political spectrum, from moderate members of Congress like Sam Nunn and Les Aspin and former government officials closely associated with détente and SALT. Kissinger had been using his syndicated column for some time to snipe at both the Zero Option and the grand compromise for START and SDI. James Woolsey, one of Nitze's former aides, had co-authored with Brent Scowcroft an article in the *Washington Post* on March 31 warning against "the danger of the Zero Option" and urging that the United States go back to the interim formula of a hundred INF warheads on each side.*

---

*A third co-author of this article was John Deutch, a scientist who had served with Woolsey and Scowcroft on the presidential commission on strategic forces.

Nitze wrote a number of articles of his own replying on behalf of the Administration to these criticisms. On Saturday April 25 he saw an advance copy of the Nixon-Kissinger collaboration, and it made him fume. "My God!" he said. "There are many things that are desirable, but we've got to think about what's negotiable. We've got to think about what we can get. Then we've got to get the best we can, and move on from there. We can't let ourselves be stopped from getting anything by these outsiders who unreasonably want us to get everything." He called Kissinger "that traitor."

Except for this characteristic epithet, Nitze's furious lament might have come from Kissinger himself—and been directed at Nitze—at any of a number of points between the spring of 1974 and the summer of 1976, when Kissinger was trying to negotiate something in SALT II while Nitze, the outsider, attacked him for not accomplishing more.

These were hard months for Paul Nitze. His wife of fifty-five years was in the terminal stages of emphysema. She assembled the family, including most of her eleven grandchildren and her one great-grandchild, for Easter weekend at the farm in Maryland. Back at their home in Washington, she required round-the-clock nurses. She was in bed or a wheelchair most of the time, constantly requiring oxygen and rapidly losing weight. A few friends came to sit and talk with her or to play bridge.

In spite of her frailty, she tried to maintain the normality of the household, and she encouraged her husband to keep up his demanding schedule. In the evenings, shortly before he came home from the State Department, she would put on makeup, pearls, earrings, and a long dressing gown. He would sit and talk with her as long as she was able. But she could stay downstairs for only a short time. She often insisted that he then go out to other people's homes for dinner. He would put on a tuxedo, climb into his Mercedes, and drive to Georgetown for an elegant party at which he would frequently be called upon to defend either the Administration's INF policies against one set of critics or his own views on SDI against another.

At one such black-tie dinner in April, Nitze encountered Bruce Jackson, a young Army captain on Weinberger's staff at the Defense Department. Nitze had known his father, William Jackson, who had been a prominent investment banker and an advisor to Dwight Eisenhower. Nitze enjoyed debating SDI with Bruce Jackson, who stoutly defended the Pentagon position and jabbed away at Nitze's. Their disagreements remained civil, but Nitze grew heated when he spoke of the larger forces that he saw out to get him within the Administration. He was fed up, he said, at being depicted by Richard Perle, Edward Rowny, Kenneth Adelman, and others as in any sense "against" SDI. "Who has defended SDI more vigorously than I?" Nitze demanded. "No one has!"

Yet in the next breath he confirmed his opponents' principal charge against him—that he was "defending" SDI largely for the diplomatic leverage it gave the United States in START: "SDI is a relative benefit, not an absolute benefit. The trick is to get something for it. START is the main thing."

He expressed his admiration for the career legal experts at the Pentagon, men like John McNeill, who had been patiently telling Weinberger for years "the facts of life" about SDI and the ABM treaty. McNeill was "someone of integrity." Weinberger, by contrast, was another sort of lawyer—"a contemptible type like Dulles who would bend the truth, show no respect for the law, in pursuit of what his client wants." Weinberger and Perle were "dishonest pricks who are arguing against the truth."

He paused, then became aware of the ladies around the table, now staring at him wide-eyed. "I'm sorry," he said, "but I feel rather strongly about these things."

The one-on-one sparring continued through dessert and into coffee and brandy, when the guests were supposed to adjourn to the living room. Nitze and Jackson stayed at their table, locked in combat, both clearly enjoying themselves. Their hosts had invited a number of senators, who now found themselves excluded from this extremely relevant debate. Finally Claiborne Pell wandered over and sat in a free chair, looking for a chance to contribute to the discussion. At the first lull in the duel, he ventured a general observation on the strategic military competition: "Frankly, I think we'd all be better off if we went back to bows and arrows." Nitze looked at him sharply and said, "Oh, come on, Claiborne." He then resumed his struggle with Jackson. Pell lingered for a moment, then excused himself.

These lapses of etiquette on Nitze's part may have reflected a degree of conflict not just with his colleagues but within himself. Once again, as with his role in SALT II, he was rewriting an awkward chapter in history. McNeill had been, and continued to be, a lonely champion of the narrow interpretation of the ABM treaty at the Pentagon. Weinberger and Perle had rammed the broad interpretation—so convenient to the wishes of "their client" Ronald Reagan—through the government, over the objections of career public servants like McNeill and Thomas Graham, the chief lawyer of the Arms Control and Disarmament Agency. Weinberger and Perle succeeded in part because, with Abraham Sofaer's help, they had enlisted the support of Nitze himself in 1985.

A Moon of Mars

The remaining obstacles to an INF treaty began to crumble in mid-April 1987. George Shultz visited Moscow, and Mikhail Gorbachev told him almost casually that the Soviet Union was now willing to eliminate the shorter-range SS-12s and SS-23s as well as the SS-20s. Eduard Shevardnadze said that this feature of an agreement would be "global"—that is, it would apply throughout the U.S.S.R.

As usual, the Soviet delegation in Geneva was slow to catch up with its home office. Yuli Vorontsov at first said that his government was prepared to "zero out" shorter-range missiles only in Europe, not in Asia. It took some weeks before his position fell into line with what Gorbachev had already told Shultz in Moscow. By July, the Soviets had accepted global double zero—elimination of longer- and shorter-range INF missiles throughout the U.S.S.R.

Even as the Soviets accelerated progress toward a separate INF treaty, Vorontsov stressed that the Kremlin was by no means giving up on strategic arms control. The INF pact, he said, should "lead the way" to a START treaty, and a START treaty, in turn, would depend on resolution of what to do about SDI. To that end, Vorontsov proposed what he called a "framework" agreement, establishing in the near future broadly defined objectives for a START treaty that might be concluded later. A number of Soviet officials, including Georgi Arbatov and Deputy Foreign Minister Vladimir Petrovsky, said they were hoping for what they called an "INF plus" summit when Gorbachev came to Washington later in 1987: the Zero Option treaty plus a framework agreement for a START treaty that might be signed in 1988.

"If we have only an agreement on INF and nothing else," said Arbatov, "people will not be sure what will happen next in arms control. Therefore, perhaps something should be added, perhaps at the summit itself."[2]

Under the Soviets' new proposal, one of the "key elements" of a framework agreement would be a commitment by both sides to continue to abide by the ABM treaty for ten years, "with strict implementation of all its provisions, including the obligation not to create or experiment with components of a system." Nor could there be experiments in space with "devices" that might constitute components. Defining such devices would be a matter for the proposed new talks that Nitze—almost alone among senior officials of the U.S. government—wanted to hold.

In the spring of 1987, a controversy arose concerning a Soviet device that was already being built in a giant laboratory on the outskirts of Moscow. Under the aegis of the Institute for Space Research, headed by Nitze's occasional interlocutor Roald Sagdeyev, the Soviet government was preparing an unmanned mission to Phobos, a moon of Mars. The instrument-laden spacecraft would pass within fifty meters of the surface of the moon and perform experiments on its composition by disturbing its surface with tiny laser and particle beams, then analyzing the cloud of dust kicked up by the disturbance. The plan was hardly a secret. The Soviets had been vigorously soliciting international participation in the project, including from the United States.

The Reagan Administration refused to cooperate. A number of officials inside the government, as well as Star Wars advocates outside, claimed that they saw the Phobos program as nothing less than an attempt by the Soviet Union to advance its own version of SDI under the guise of peaceful space exploration. And to compound the perfidy, the Soviets were trying to trick other governments into providing some of the high technology that might someday be used for space-based weaponry. If that was the case, Soviet star warriors were starting small and had a long way to go. The beams aboard the Phobos probe were one quadrillion times weaker than the ones envisioned for SDI and at least ten million times too weak to have any antimissile capability.

In Nitze's speech on April 1 at the Johns Hopkins School of Advanced International Studies, in which he stubbornly reaffirmed his acceptance of the broad interpretation of the ABM treaty, he said, "It would be difficult to prove that the power, brightness, and tracking and aiming characteristics of these devices [on board the Phobos probe]" were not sufficient to constitute components of a weapon system and therefore a violation of the ABM treaty as narrowly interpreted.

But Nitze was not saying that the Phobos probe *was* a violation. Rather, he was underscoring his contention that there had to be a new negotiation to determine what exactly constituted a violation. The laser and particle beam devices on board the Phobos probe were clearly technologies based on "other physical principles," as envisioned in 1972. But were they large enough and strong enough to constitute components of an antimissile system? There was no agreed answer to that question in the ABM treaty or anywhere else. Neither the broad nor the narrow interpretation would settle the matter. Hence his assertion, in his April 1 speech and on other occasions, that the narrow-versus-broad debate was "irrelevant." Americans should set aside their squabble over what was agreed about hypothetical devices in 1972 and negotiate a new agreement in 1987–88 that would cover real devices like those in Sagdeyev's laboratory.

Amplifying in a letter three weeks later, Nitze wrote, "My intent is not to preclude legitimate space exploration (and this experiment [the Phobos probe] would seem to qualify as such), but rather to point out that the treaty language gives little help in setting standards of capability reliably to differentiate between such exploration and of testing useful to the creation of potential ABM components."[3]

He had in mind a precedent from his experience during SALT I. In order to define permissible and impermissible radars for purposes of the ABM treaty, he and Alexander Shchukin had agreed first that a specified "power-aperture product" could serve as an appropriate threshold, below which a radar would be judged too weak to serve as part of an ABM system, then to a number for that threshold (3 million watt-meters-squared).

The lesson in that experience for the present situation was, to him, obvious: The two sides should establish parameters for defining when a laser— or a laser-bouncing mirror, or a particle beam, or a kinetic kill vehicle— was powerful enough to qualify as an antimissile weapon, then negotiate numbers to go with the parameters. Testing of devices below those levels would be permitted; testing above those levels would be prohibited.

That was exactly what the Soviets were proposing, too. In April, Gorbachev suggested to Shultz that the question of permitted/prohibited SDI activities be turned over to the Standing Consultative Commission, which reviewed and, if possible, resolved matters of compliance with SALT. The Soviet leader urged that a special session of the SCC meet under the chairmanship of the two defense ministers or their deputies. Shultz believed that the Soviets were trying to co-opt Caspar Weinberger, giving him a central position in the next stage of the process, so that he would not have to worry about anyone else being soft in the talks.

If that was the Soviet tactic, it did not work. As far as Weinberger was concerned, all American activities were permissible, and it was outrageous for anyone—whether Mikhail Gorbachev or Paul Nitze—to be suggesting otherwise; the SCC, furthermore, was a disreputable vestige of SALT.

No one at the White House wanted to overrule the secretary of defense. Neither, for that matter, did George Shultz himself. The very mention of "permitted/prohibited activities" had acquired the same stigma that already marked "negotiability," "bargaining chip," "offense-defense tradeoff," and any talk of the grand compromise itself; these were taboo words. They were synonyms for the ultimate heresy—making constraints on SDI part of an arms-control deal.

That taboo was honored almost everywhere in the Administration except in "the Nitze shop," his suite of offices on the seventh floor of the State Department around the corner from Shultz's. There, and in his many forays out around the city and across the Atlantic, Nitze continued to argue for "active study" of the Soviet proposal for thresholds. He considered enlisting the help of some prominent outsiders who would form an advisory group on the subject of SDI and the ABM treaty. Nitze thought of inviting James Schlesinger, one of the original proponents of the grand compromise, and Ashton Carter, a physicist and expert on space weaponry who was associate director of Harvard University's Center for Science and International Affairs.

Nothing came of the idea of the advisory group, but Carter became a consultant to the State Department and worked closely with Nitze. At an arms-control seminar in Aspen, Colorado, the previous August, Carter had presented a paper on how limited SDI development and testing could be pursued within the confines of the ABM treaty. Nitze was impressed by the paper and hired Carter to spend a few days a week in Washington providing technical advice as Nitze refined his own plan.

Exit the Prince

At Reykjavik, Gorbachev had said that the ten-year period in which neither side could withdraw from the ABM treaty must be followed by three or four years of negotiation about what would happen next, and that even then there could still be no deployment unless the two sides agreed on the form it would take. So the nonwithdrawal commitment really had a span closer to the fifteen years that the Kremlin had sought earlier. Nor were the Soviets conceding that deployment could ever occur.

When Shultz visited Moscow in April 1987, Gorbachev and Shevardnadze modified their stance. They explained that two or three years before the expiration of the ten-year nonwithdrawal period, there would begin yet another negotiation on what to do after the ten years were up. If there was no agreement, and if one side decided to proceed with "the practical establishment of an ABM system," the other side would be released from its obligations to reduce or limit its offensive weaponry.

This was a qualified but still significant concession. The Soviets now seemed willing to accept language that the Reagan Administration might interpret as allowing eventual deployment of SDI. To be sure, the concession was accompanied by a warning if not a threat: An American decision after ten years to exercise the right to deploy SDI would trigger Soviet offensive countermeasures; defensive breakout would provoke offensive breakout—just as Robert McNamara had predicted in 1967. The Soviets were still insisting on linkage between restrictions on strategic defense and reductions in strategic offense. But they seemed now, in effect, to be postponing the moment of truth well beyond the lifespan of the Reagan Administration; they were saying that offense-defense linkage in the longer term need not stand in the way of an offense-reductions agreement in the near term.

Shultz commented approvingly to Shevardnadze, "You're beginning, it seems, to talk about a real ten years."

Yet Shultz's own government was no longer talking about ten years. At the insistence of the Pentagon, the Administration had shortened the length of time that the United States would remain bound by the ABM treaty. At Reykjavik, Reagan had committed the United States to abide by the treaty for ten years. Now, six months later, the American side was willing to stay within the treaty only through 1994—seven years as of late 1987.

The Pentagon civilians justified this hardening of the American position by saying that the earlier commitment to remain within the ABM treaty for ten years had been conditioned on the elimination of all ballistic missiles during that period. Under the Reykjavik timetable, SDI would have been necessary only as insurance against cheating on the zero-ballistic-missiles rule. But now that the goal of ZBM had been abandoned and START would achieve "only" a 50-percent reduction in ballistic missiles, American security would require more SDI—and require it sooner.

It had been Richard Perle, along with Robert Linhard of the NSC staff, who at Reykjavik had linked the ten-year nonwithdrawal from the ABM treaty to the ten-year deadline for the elimination of all SLBMs and ICBMs. That idea had been the most quickly discarded and least mourned component of the Reykjavik package. Yet now Perle was able to use it to impede progress on the surviving components.

This was a characteristic ploy. As it became apparent that the superpowers were moving to closure in INF, Perle and the Administration hard-liners noticeably toughened their stance on START and SDI. On earlier trips with Shultz, since his first one in January 1985, Perle had been on his best behavior, encouraging Kampelman and even Shultz himself to hope that he could be coopted to support an eventual strategic-arms agreement. Now, however, on the April 1987 trip to Moscow, Perle was once again living up to his old nickname the Prince of Darkness, exuding harsh and gratuitous anti-Sovietism and raising objections to any suggestions of American movement.

Perle was preparing to resume his role as critic of arms control who could speak freely from outside the government. On March 12, he had submitted his letter of resignation, "effective this spring after an orderly transition in my office." He told an assoicate that it was "getting to be springtime for arms control around here," and he did not want to be part of it. He arranged for his deputy, Frank Gaffney, to succeed him. When Perle finally left office in June, Gaffney became acting assistant secretary of defense for international security policy, although, having offended many on Capitol Hill, he was never confirmed by the Senate.

Perle had been talking about resigning for years. Sometimes the threat seemed to be a bluff or pressure tactic in whatever showdown he was having with the State Department; sometimes it seemed to reflect a desire to spend more time with his wife and young son and to lead a more leisurely life. Perle had never been a workaholic. If he was afflicted with Potomac fever, it was a different strain from the one that led others to cling to their presidential commissions and the perquisites of office. Perle, quite simply, had had enough. He wanted to make money lecturing, consulting, and writing a novel based on his experience in government. Besides, he had accomplished much of his agenda, perhaps as much as he could accomplish from the inside. His brainchild, the Zero Option—indeed, his original preference from 1981, the global double zero—was about to become a reality. Even in the springtime of arms control, the sweet smell of vindication was in the air.

Perle's conduct during and after the Shultz mission to Moscow in April confirmed the long-standing suspicion of many that he was interested in an INF agreement primarily as a sop to the Congress, to the allies, to public opinion, and to those in the Administration, like Paul Nitze, whom Perle called "weak sisters." INF was, in a phrase sometimes heard around the civilian corridors of the Pentagon, a "firebreak"—a way of satisfying some constituencies' misguided enthusiasm for arms control in the militarily marginal area of Euromissiles rather than in the centrally important sphere of strategic weaponry.

Major General William Burns, who had been on Nitze's INF delegation and who was now in the State Department's Bureau of Politico-Military Affairs, came out of a meeting with Perle during the spring and told a colleague he was convinced that "Cap and Richard see INF as something we can afford to give away because it'll give the arms controllers something to chew on while the tough guys circle the wagons on SDI and START."

The List Approach

When, in Geneva, Yuli Vorontsov proposed an "agreement of principles" to be signed at a Reagan-Gorbachev summit in late 1987, Max Kampelman was dismissive. Such a document would be "meaningless," he said; it would not have the force of law; it would not be binding on the next President— "and I can't say that he won't be Jack Kemp," the Republican congressman from New York who was the presidential candidate most committed to Star Wars.

Back in Washington, Paul Nitze was more receptive to the idea of a framework agreement. "By and large we've been stung by agreements in principle," he said, but such an agreement in 1987 might be acceptable "if it will be helpful to a negotiation that will translate it into a treaty next spring," in 1988. "If that's what the Soviets want, okay."

By the late spring of 1987, the Soviet delegation in Geneva was officially proposing a version of the idea that Nitze had been discussing with Evgeny Velikhov, Roald Sagdeyev, and others for many months. It was a list of devices associated with SDI-type technologies—lasers, mirrors, particle beams, kinetic kill vehicles—that would be prohibited in space if their size or power was greater than certain specified levels. A so-called "threshold limits approach" had also been developed and urged on the Soviets by John Pike, associate director for space policy of the Federation of American Scientists and a close colleague of Jeremy Stone. Pike came up with a detailed proposal on how to apply the ABM treaty to the new technologies that might be developed under SDI. He had presented the plan to Soviet scientists as early as May 1984. He and colleagues refined the details and continued to press the proposal with the Soviets through 1985 and 1986.

After the Reykjavik meeting between Reagan and Gorbachev in October 1986, Roald Sagdeyev indicated that the idea was catching on in official circles in Moscow. The levels were clearly negotiable, and Nitze was more than ever in favor of having that negotiation. He became not only the most vigorous advocate of the so-called list approach to dealing with SDI but virtually the only such advocate at a high level of the U.S. government. "The ABM treaty has a hole in it as to what are components of ABM systems based on other physical principles," he said. "The list approach would give us a way to fill that hole with the right definitions. Whenever we've left holes in treaties in the past, we're the ones who have ended up falling into them."

Kampelman had a serious heart attack on March 19. He was hospitalized and lost twenty pounds before he returned to work in mid-April. At first he came into his office only part-time, but soon he threw himself back into work with a vengeance. His secretaries affectionately referred to him as "the same old tornado." Kampelman was upset to find that Nitze had been trying to get the U.S. delegation's negotiating instructions changed to authorize exploratory talks on the list approach. Kampelman wanted no such change. He said, "It's not necessary for us to advocate moves that the President is incapable of making in order to bring the Soviets into a deal." His opposition to the list approach had little to do with the technical challenge of filling in holes in the ABM treaty; it had everything to do with the political challenge of trying to get Ronald Reagan and the Republican right wing to accept an eventual agreement.

Kampelman said that Nitze's logic was "impeccable—it's the politics of Paul's position that are faulty. He can make an iron-clad case for quantitative limits on testing, but it's still not going to happen in this Administration. Why? Because Ronald Reagan believes it would open the way to SDI restrictions not justified by the broad interpretation."

It was a telling and perhaps accurate comment: However disputed or even discredited the broad interpretation might be in the eyes of most experts, including influential senators like Sam Nunn and Albert Gore, it still reflected the President's preferences and established the boundary of what he would be likely to accept in an agreement.

Kampelman believed that even if the President could somehow be made to accept limits on testing—and however much Nunn, Gore, and other moderates might approve of such an outcome—there would be an uprising by the Laser Lobby. He was thinking about the kind of agreement that would be ratified by two-thirds of the U.S. Senate. "I'm looking for what the President and sixty-seven Senators will buy," he said, "or what will keep thirty-four Senators from coming together against it." As a result, Kampelman believed, "we've got so little to give [the Soviets] that I'd like to save it for the last ten or fifteen minutes of the negotiation."

He hoped that a pledge on nondeployment of SDI, combined with a pledge on nonwithdrawal from the ABM treaty, would give the Soviets the breakout insurance they were looking for, and that more specific limitations on testing would be unnecessary, at least in the near term. He instructed his deputy in the defense-and-space talks, Henry Cooper, to look for a way to replace the list approach with a nondeployment pledge.

Kampelman was trying to make a virtue out of ambiguity: Let the vagueness of the ABM treaty with regard to exotic space-based defenses work to the advantage of both sides, permitting a compromise between them; let the Soviets think that the treaty permitted as little SDI testing as possible while the Americans claimed that it permitted as much as possible. Reagan would be out of office before the program reached the point where the two sides' claims would collide.

Nitze found Kampelman's position intellectually unsatisfying and politically risky. He hated ambiguity; he always had. Abraham Sofaer had convinced him in 1985 that the language and negotiating record of the ABM treaty were ambiguous; that was the basis for the vastly troublesome broad interpretation. The task now, in 1987, was not to perpetuate the ambiguity, or to wave it aside, or to exploit it. Rather, the task was to resolve the ambiguity, to get rid of it once and for all.

While Kampelman was glancing nervously over his shoulder at the Laser Lobby, Nitze was looking to congressional moderates who were increasingly impatient with the financial cost of SDI, with the incompatibility between an unfettered program and the chance of achieving new agreements in arms control, and with the combined stubbornness and fractiousness of the Administration on the subject. As a military-technological program requiring public support and congressional funding, SDI was in real trouble; therefore, warned Nitze, as a source of bargaining power in START, it was a "diminishing asset." And so he said, "Let's use it before we lose it" for the leverage it gave the United States in START.

"Paul," Kampelman advised, "stop asking for trouble. If you press for a presidential decision on this, the answer will be negative."

Frank Carlucci, then national security advisor, and Howard Baker, who had replaced Donald Regan as White House chief of staff, were natural allies of the State Department. Carlucci had stayed quietly in touch with the RAND experts who continued to refine and promote their own version of the grand compromise. Baker, a moderate Republican and the former leader of the party in the Senate, could see political support for SDI steadily eroding and pressure for an arms-control deal rising. Both men were concerned that Weinberger's fight-to-the-death attitude toward SDI—what Baker called his "aggressive and dogmatic style"—was becoming a liability not just for the SDI program itself but for the Administration as a whole in its dealings with Congress. In private, Carlucci was extremely critical of Weinberger and of Perle for having exploited SDI as a battering ram against the edifice of arms control and for having overpromised, to the President and to the nation, the prospective benefits of deployment. He also felt Weinberger and Perle had needlessly riled key senators, notably Nunn, and picked unseemly fights within the Administration, contributing to the appearance—and the reality— of constant division and frequent paralysis.

However, their day-to-day visits to the Oval Office constantly reminded Carlucci and Baker how devoted Ronald Reagan was to SDI—and how resistant he was to any suggestion that smacked of trading it away. They did not want to seem any less devoted themselves. Carlucci commented on a number of occasions—to Nitze and Kampelman as well as to the RAND specialists who came to brief him on their own project—that "asking this President to sign on to restrictions on SDI testing would be the same as asking him to raise taxes tomorrow." Like Kampelman, he believed that the trick was in finding some way to satisfy the Soviet need for breakout insurance while satisfying the President's insistence on preserving a "robust" SDI research and development program, that would almost certainly have to include some testing.

The list approach did not seem to fit that bill, and Nitze's persistence on its behalf made him something of a foil for Carlucci and Baker as well as for Kampelman; they were able to position themselves between Weinberger's intransigence and Nitze's perceived overeagerness for a deal. In one meeting, Baker warned that the list approach, with its restrictions on SDI testing, could turn out to be a "dangerous gambit that would innocently but severely constrain the most promising areas of technology." On another occasion, he said: "None of us should urge anything that would interrupt the continuum of research to development to deployment—when available and appropriate." Never mind if deployment were never available or appropriate: Baker could say that he was "on board" the program in a way that Nitze was not.

After yet another unsuccessful visit to the White House, Nitze commented to a colleague, "Everyone else says my position is too complex, that it leads us into a wilderness. But we're already in a wilderness!"

In mid-June, Nitze's isolation became public. He and Carlucci were together at a weekend seminar on arms control at a retreat in Maryland. Carlucci bluntly told the assembled experts from outside the government that the President was dead set against negotiating on permitted/prohibited activities. Nitze was then asked his view, and he was equally forthright in laying out his differences with Carlucci. The *New York Times* specialist in arms control, Michael Gordon, was present for this exchange and alluded to it in print. That article prompted newsmen at a breakfast meeting with Nitze back in Washington to ask him about the possibility of trading constraints on SDI testing for stabilizing reductions in offense. "I see a hope of it," he replied, "but I'm not sure anyone else in this Administration agrees with me."

This comment, too, was widely reported. Proponents of SDI were indignant. "The list is a technical way to kill off" the program, charged Daniel Graham. Nitze's bureaucratic opponents, Edward Rowny, Kenneth Adelman, and Frank Gaffney, reacted with much finger-wagging and eye-rolling. They treated the incident as a replay of the walk in the woods: Nitze had "wandered off the reservation," then been caught, publicly exposed, and severely rebuked.

Vigorous Doubles

Yet Nitze persisted. He next tried to sell the grand compromise, including concessions on SDI, to the two men with the greatest sales resistance of all—Ronald Reagan and Caspar Weinberger.

August was vacation month. President Reagan was chopping wood and riding horseback at his ranch near Santa Barbara. Frank Carlucci was in California with the traveling White House. On August 28, much as his predecessor Robert McFarlane had done two years before, Carlucci traveled down the coast from Santa Barbara to Santa Monica for a visit to the RAND Corporation. He was given an update on the brainstorming there about why and how to join an INF deal with a START/SDI tradeoff.

"An INF agreement would be a significant accomplishment," said the latest set of talking points prepared by the RAND team. "But, absent a START agreement or other limitations on strategic nuclear forces, it also would raise tough—perhaps unanticipated—issues for the U.S." None of the Soviet INF missiles slated for elimination under the Zero Option could reach the territory of the United States. With the Reagan Administration's decision not to observe the SALT limits, and in the absence of a START agreement, there would be nothing to prevent the Soviet Union from replacing the intermediate-range SS-20s with intercontinental-range SS-25s, the "Midgetmanskies" about which Robert McFarlane had been so concerned. Without a START agreement, the United States could end up facing more Soviet missile warheads than before. Furthermore, those SS-25 ICBMs could cover targets in Europe as well, nullifying the benefits for NATO of the Zero Option.

The RAND paper offered a number of options, each with clearly acknowledged drawbacks. The one that a number of RAND analysts obviously favored, however, was the last: "START reductions in exchange for negotiated constraints on testing and development of strategic defenses." Following their own logic chain, they had reached a destination close to Nitze's.*

Carlucci was interested in the plan, but he had his own reservations about establishing definite limits on testing and was in any event doubtful that the President would buy it. The name of the game, he said once again, was to find some way of giving the Soviets their breakout insurance without imposing explicit limits on SDI testing.

In the view of the RAND analysts, that was a tall order, but perhaps not impossible. One said that he and his colleagues would "go back to the drawing board" and see if they could identify other options that might take into account "the apparent constant in the equation," which was the President's "neuralgia" about testing limits.

Meanwhile, Nitze was still convinced that the need for negotiated testing limits was the constant and the President's attitude was the variable.

When George Shultz was getting ready to make his own call on the President in Santa Barbara, Nitze tried, yet again, to persuade him to make the case for a negotiation on permissible/impermissible activities. Nitze drafted a paper for Shultz laying out the argument: By proposing the list approach, the Soviets had finally accepted the President's contention that the ABM treaty did not constitute a prohibition against SDI; Moscow had caved, and the United States needed now only to nail down the terms of surrender.

However, Nitze continued, the Soviets had always made clear that reductions in offense would depend on restrictions on SDI; Congress was imposing similar linkage by holding SDI funding hostage to progress in START and by forcing the Administration to adhere to the restrictive interpretation of the ABM treaty. The Soviets were asking for a "strengthening of the ABM treaty"; so far, that meant a narrower-than-narrow interpretation. In order to forestall congressional cuts in the SDI budget, the United States must have a credible counterproposal; what was needed was a "clarification" of the ABM treaty that would protect various aspects of the R&D program which might otherwise be declared illegal by the Soviets and forbidden by the Congress.

Now it was Nitze who was presenting his position as a middle ground between the all-or-nothing extremes—the "all" that the Laser Lobby (and

---

*The RAND options also reviewed—and found fault with—Kampelman's choice. "START reductions in exchange for non-deployment until 1994," said the paper, would impose "no constraints on [the] SDI program, including plans for early, interim deployments, *but* [the] Soviets [are] very unlikely to agree: instead of achieving their objectives it would virtually give their sanction to SDI deployment after 1994."

the President himself) wanted and the "nothing" that the de facto unholy alliance between Congress and the Kremlin was likely to accept.

Shultz balked. As he told a member of his staff, "Paul doesn't give up, does he? It's something I greatly admire about him. But this time he's asking for too much. He's asking me to break my pick at the White House, and I'm not going to do that."

Nitze had even less success with the secretary of defense. Both men vacationed near Northeast Harbor on the coast of Maine; so did Bruce Jackson, with whom Nitze met frequently back in Washington to spar over strategic defense and arms control. The August holiday of 1987 was Nitze's first alone. His wife had died on June 27 at the age of seventy-five. Jackson came over almost every morning to play vigorous doubles at a nearby tennis club with Nitze and two other men, both, like Jackson, in their thirties. They would switch teams between sets, and the pair that included Nitze usually won. After tennis, Nitze and Jackson frequently went back to his cottage overlooking the harbor to continue their spirited argument about the negotiability of SDI. Nitze told Jackson that he had been thinking for weeks about "tackling Cap on this subject, wrestling him to the ground, and pinning his ears back by sheer force of logic and argumentation."

Jackson laughed and said he thought it would be "the battle of the century." He volunteered to serve as promoter—"as long as I can have a ringside seat."

Jackson arranged for Nitze and Weinberger to be invited to an elegant dinner at the summer home of Susan Mary Alsop, a prominent Washington hostess and the former wife of Nitze's old friend Joseph Alsop.* Just as Jackson had intended, Weinberger and Nitze fell into an intense tête-à-tête over lobster and white wine.

Nitze made the same case that Shultz and McFarlane had used with Reagan since 1985: Far from killing SDI, putting it "in an arms-control context" would save it; making it negotiable and incorporating limited constraints on the program in an agreement would assure the survival of research, development, and testing. On the other hand, to keep SDI off the negotiating table was to invite "disaster"; it would produce the worst of all possible worlds: no funding from the Congress and no deal with the Soviets. It was Congress, Nitze kept saying, not the State Department or himself, that was bent on killing SDI: "Congress is taking away our bargaining leverage even as it ruins the chances of success for the program."

He then launched into a long, hortatory reminiscence about the halcyon

---

*Alsop himself had once mediated a partial and temporary truce in the Nitze-Kissinger feud in 1977; see p. 151.

days of the Marshall Plan, when a Democratic Administration was able to work its will on a Republican-controlled Congress. He expatiated on the brilliance of George Marshall and Robert Lovett, who had cleverly let Senator Arthur Vandenberg take credit as the hero of bipartisanship. The Reagan Administration, said Nitze, should do the same thing now with Sam Nunn.

Weinberger replied that Nunn's reputation for wisdom in military matters was considerably exaggerated; Nunn was more inclined to adopt the consensus than to shape it; he did not understand either the defense budget or grand strategy; the Administration's proper objective was not to accommodate Sam Nunn or the Soviets but to protect from their opposition the President's dream of strategic defense.

That, Nitze kept saying, was exactly what he was trying to do, too. But Weinberger was having none of it.

Shortly afterward, Nitze was close to despair. He had the secretary of defense fighting him, the secretary of state resisting his advice, and his old friend Max Kampelman sniping at him. This was not a pleasant experience for Kampelman, either. "It hurts me," he said. "I don't like the President to keep saying no to the Department of State and to Paul Nitze."

Nitze's unrelenting advocacy of the list approach probably cost him a promotion. Following in the footsteps of his ally Richard Perle, Kenneth Adelman had announced in late July his intention to resign as director of the Arms Control and Disarmament Agency after the year-end Reagan-Gorbachev summit. Shultz recommended to Reagan that Nitze be appointed to the job. It would have been a satisfying capstone to his career. Once again, however, the right wing rose up and smote him. On September 3, the *Washington Times* ran an article saying that Reagan had chosen Nitze for the ACDA job and that there was already a firestorm of protest from hardliners in the agency and on Capitol Hill. It was a classic example of the press leak as preemptive attack—a phony scoop intended, by its source if not its author, to prevent from happening what the article said had already happened. The incident was eerily similar to other setbacks Nitze had suffered over the years, particularly when the *Washington Herald*—an ideological forerunner of the *Washington Times*—sabotaged Nitze's appointment to the Pentagon in 1953.

Weinberger had his own candidate for the ACDA job—Ronald Lehman. Frank Carlucci and Howard Baker were not inclined to urge the President to overrule Weinberger and pick Nitze, especially since he had been publicly identified during the summer as a maverick if not a heretic on SDI. Baker also warned Shultz and Reagan that, if nominated, Nitze would face resistance from the right in the Senate. The last thing the Administration needed was a confirmation fight.

The President needed no convincing. His aides had noticed that he had for some time been reacting negatively to the very mention of Nitze's name, which he had now come to associate with the "giveaway" of SDI.

The Chief Sword-Carrier

While Paul Nitze kept pushing a change in the U.S. position on SDI right away, Max Kampelman in Geneva continued to treat it as an eventual reward that the Soviets might earn by changing their own position in START, especially on subceilings. "I will not ask the President for anything that modifies our position [on SDI]," Kampelman told Yuli Vorontsov, "unless and until we've got sublimits that satisfy the Joint Chiefs."

The Soviets' proposed framework still offered no satisfaction on this score. It allowed each side to reserve the right to determine the structure of its strategic forces; the United States could not dictate to the Soviet Union the proportion of its six thousand nuclear charges that would be allowed on ballistic missiles in general or on ICBMs in particular.

On August 7, Kampelman had a chance to press the matter with Eduard Shevardnadze himself during a visit by the foreign minister to Geneva. Shevardnadze complained that "sublimits are designed to interfere with the structuring of our forces." In reply, Kampelman repeated that the principle of subceilings had been embedded in earlier Soviet proposals—the "force concentration" rules of 1986 and Gorbachev's bold talk at Reykjavik about huge cuts not just across the board but in those weapons that worried the Americans most. The United States, said Kampelman, was merely agreeing to something that the U.S.S.R. had already proposed. "We can't have an agreement without subceilings," said Kampelman. "And you know that. You've already acknowledged it in the past. Why can't you give us your old yes for an answer now?"

It was a deliberate echo of the taunt that the Soviets often made when the Americans squirmed over the Zero Option in INF ("The Zero Option was your idea—why can't you take yes for an answer?").

Of the subceilings that the United States was seeking, continued Kampelman, the most important was a limit of 4,800 ballistic missile warheads (an aggregate of ICBM and SLBM warheads). He implied that if the Soviet side would accept that subceiling, it might not be necessary to have a separate limit of 3,300 on ICBMs alone—the U.S.-proposed feature that the Soviets considered most onerous and unacceptable.*

---

*The American goal was still to wean the Soviets away from their reliance on large, MIRVed

The Soviets apparently took the point. When Shevardnadze came to Washington in mid-September, he resurrected an old idea that his side had first floated in 1985: There could be a limit of 3,600 nuclear charges for each leg of the triad—ICBMs, SLBMs, and bombers.

The good news was that the Soviet-proposed ICBM subceiling was now only 300 higher than the American one of 3,300. The bad news, particularly for the Joint Chiefs of Staff and the U.S. Navy, was that the same ceiling would apply to SLBMs. Concern about the vulnerability of American Minutemen to Soviet attack and political difficulties in replacing Minuteman with a mobile MX or Midgetman made the Chiefs want to preserve as much latitude as possible to "move out to sea" with the Trident II SLBM program.

All this the Soviets knew perfectly well. They were sending a clear message: You Americans want to force us to restructure our arsenal, giving up the ICBMs on which we have traditionally relied. Fine. But as part of the deal, you will have to restructure your arsenal, giving up the SLBMs in which you are heavily investing.

Reading that signal, Nitze could see a compromise. It was the same one that Kampelman had been exploring with Vorontsov in Geneva: The United States would drop its pursuit of a separate ICBM warhead subceiling; the Soviet Union would reciprocate by dropping an SLBM warhead subceiling; and the two would sign an agreement that retained only the limit of 4,800 on the aggregate of all strategic ballistic missile warheads, land-based and sea-based alike.

Nitze was even more hopeful about the latest refinement in the Soviet position on SDI. The Kremlin was now proposing that the two sides agree strictly to abide for ten years to the ABM treaty "as signed and ratified" in 1972—in other words, the narrow interpretation. ABM research would be confined to ground-based laboratories—in other words, Gorbachev's formulation at Reykjavik.

Then came the sweetener that interested Nitze. The Soviets brought with them a new version of their list of "potential components" of a system (i.e., ones based on "other physical principles" such as lasers, mirrors, particle

---

ICBMs. In computerized studies of the effects of various proposals on the arsenals of the two sides, Pentagon analysts had concluded that the United States could go far toward achieving its goal if the overall ceiling of 6,000 nuclear charges was accompanied by the subceiling of 4,800 ICBM/SLBM warheads. These two numbers— 6,000 and 4,800, combined with 50 percent cuts in SS-18s—would have the desired effect because, together, they would constitute an incentive to the Soviets to build up their bomber force in order to take full advantage of the allowance of 1,200 bomber weapons, and to redistribute their ballistic missile warheads away from fixed ICBMs toward mobile ICBMs and/or SLBMs.

The 4,800 figure was less onerous to the Soviets than the 3,300 ICBM warhead ceiling, since the 4,800 left the U.S.S.R. with some discretion on how many of its warheads to keep on land and how many to put at sea. It was felt that the United States could afford to leave the Soviets with this "freedom to mix," since they were already beginning to rely more on mobile, survivable submarine-based missiles and less on fixed, highly vulnerable and heavily MIRVed ICBMs.

beams, kinetic kill vehicles) and a list of "associated critical parameters" (power of lasers, size of mirrors, velocity of kinetic kill vehicles) with specified "capacity thresholds."

It was the most forthcoming and authoritative version yet of the list approach to permitted/prohibited talks. Even though Nitze had already failed repeatedly, and at considerable personal cost to his standing and influence, to sell the idea within his own government, he now set about to try again, this time by enlisting the Soviets' help directly. During a long, hard working group meeting in Washington, with Victor Karpov in the chair opposite him, Nitze got the Soviet delegation to rewrite its proposal on the spot so as to acknowledge that the testing of devices with parameters below the thresholds would be permitted anywhere, including in space.

Afterward Nitze told Shultz, "We've now got a clearer statement of the Soviet position than we've had before. It's basically a good position if we can get the right numbers plugged into the capability thresholds."

Having held Nitze at bay for months on any such plan, Shultz was now willing to support him, but only passively. There was still "a lot of missionary work" to be done, he said, and Nitze himself should be the principal missionary—"the chief sword-carrier," as the secretary put it—with Carlucci, the SDI Organization, and the Joint Chiefs of Staff, but ultimately and most essentially with Weinberger. "Then," said Shultz, "Cap will sell it to the President."

"A most challenging assignment," replied Nitze, recalling his futile encounter with Weinberger in Maine. "Am I merely to carry this sword or fall on it as well?" He understood, however, why Shultz did not want to lead the way. "I know it would be poison for you to differ with the President on this issue," he told the secretary of state.

In the days that followed, Nitze's consultant from Harvard, Ashton Carter, wrote an analysis of the latest Soviet list proposal, criticizing the specifics but endorsing the general concept and suggesting ways in which the United States could, with a counterproposal, protect a vigorous R&D program likely to satisfy all but the most zealous Star Warriors. This paper became the basis of Nitze's missionary work with the Joint Chiefs of Staff.

Shultz and Shevardnadze had begun a global shuttle to arrange for the summit. A National Security Policy Group meeting was called on October 13 primarily to discuss Shultz's negotiating instructions for his next visit to Moscow. Shultz himself was not at the NSPG meeting because he had to be on Capitol Hill testifying on the budget. Nitze, who spoke at the meeting, did not ask explicitly for Shultz's instructions to be broadened or for the United States to make a formal counterproposal on the list approach. There was, he said afterward, "no point in breaking spears against windmills." Instead, he urged that there be an interdepartmental "study of the question of what is involved" in a list and the threshold approach: "Are there thresholds that the United States could live with while pursuing vigorous SDI research, development, and testing?'' He concluded his recommendation by warning, ''We won't be able to justify to the Congress closing our eyes to the issue.''

Admiral Crowe agreed, saying that the Chiefs were already ''studying the question'' (he did not say that they were doing so partly on the basis of Nitze's briefings and Carter's paper) and that the Soviet proposal ''should not be dismissed out of hand.''

Weinberger fulminated against the list approach. It would, said the secretary of defense, be ''absurd'' and ''outrageous'' to retreat an inch from the American position then on the table: a willingness to defer deployment (but not testing) for seven years, through 1994, and to abide by the broad interpretation of the ABM treaty (which permitted unlimited testing) in the meantime.

Carlucci seemed to side with Weinberger when he said that there was ''no need to show leg to the Russians at this time.''

With this implicit repudiation of his own recommendation ringing in his ears, Nitze set off for Moscow with Shultz. En route, Shultz gave him the news that he was no longer even a candidate for the directorship of ACDA.

The Sakharov Finesse

During a meeting in the Kremlin on October 23 with Shultz, Carlucci, and Nitze, Gorbachev presented a new proposal for subceilings: 3,000–3,300 ICBM warheads, 1,800–2,000 SLBM warheads. The SLBM subceiling was still much too low to be acceptable to the Joint Chiefs of Staff. But the sum of the lower of the two sets of numbers for ballistic missile warheads— 3,000 and 1,800—was 4,800, exactly the number that the United States was seeking for the aggregate. Gorbachev seemed to be saying: Let's drop the separate subceilings for ICBM and SLBM warheads, go with the aggregate subceiling for both, and we've got a deal . . . if, that is, we can reach compromise on SDI.

Toward the end of the meeting, the general secretary asked what could be accomplished at a summit beyond an INF treaty, whether there was a chance of getting a framework, or key-provisions, agreement on START and SDI. Shultz and Carlucci replied that President Reagan would not agree to anything that would have the effect of ''crippling'' SDI.

In that case, said Gorbachev, he did not feel comfortable setting a date for the summit. It was a shocking but, as it turned out, only momentary instance of relinkage. Gorbachev had attempted the same bait-and-switch scam he had used at Reykjavik. This time, however, when it became apparent the ploy had backfired, he reversed himself almost immediately. Within a week, he dispatched Shevardnadze to Washington to put arrangements for an INF-only summit back on track.*

During those few days when it looked as though relinkage had reared its head again, Nitze did not share the consternation of much of the rest of the government. "Gorbachev," he said, "has been more or less consistent in his demand all along that he get something on the space issue. He wants it—and if we want a favorable START deal, we should consider it."

Meanwhile, Sam Nunn and a number of other influential Democrats were making clear that unless the Administration abandoned the broad interpretation of the ABM treaty, they would hold hostage not only funding for SDI but possibly ratification of the forthcoming INF treaty as well. As part of his campaign against the broad interpretation of the ABM treaty, Nunn was suggesting that he might ask to see the entire classified negotiating record of INF in order to make sure there were no "ambiguities" of the sort that the Reagan Administration had discovered to such mischievous effect in SALT I.

Building on the basis of the agreement that Nitze, Perle, and Kampelman had reached with Pell, Gore, and the other senators in Geneva in February, Howard Baker was trying to work out a compromise with key senators on a tradeoff between Congress's willingness to fund the program and the Administration's willingness to negotiate limits on it within the terms of the narrow interpretation.

Each turn of the screw—whether applied by the Kremlin or by Congress— was welcome to Nitze. Perhaps Gorbachev and Nunn in tandem would succeed where Nitze himself had so far failed. Perhaps, faced with Soviet inducements in START and congressional threats against SDI, the Reagan Administration would go for the grand compromise after all.

He had all the more reason to hope so, since the Soviets were adjusting their own position on SDI in a way that seemed calculated to make compromise palatable to President Reagan.

From October 26 to 28, the week after George Shultz was in the Soviet Union for his talks with Gorbachev, a delegation from the U.S. National Academy of Sciences attended a conference in Vilnius, the capital of Soviet Lithuania. The Soviet side consisted of a number of academicians, led by Roald Sagdeyev, the space scientist active on arms-control issues. Another participant was Andrei Sakharov, the renowned physicist and winner of the

---

*Gorbachev was under intense internal political pressure from two camps—"conservatives" who opposed his reforms and "adventurists," like Moscow party chief Boris Yeltsin, who wanted to push the reforms faster and harder. Also, the American stock market had crashed the previous Monday, October 19, and Soviet informants said later that Gorbachev's advisors told him he might be able to exploit Reagan's increased political vulnerability by upping the ante on the summit.

Nobel Prize for Peace whom Mikhail Gorbachev had released from internal exile a little over a year before.

During 1987, Sakharov's rehabilitation had taken a curious turn. He had emerged as an important and influential voice in the debate over SDI, sharply criticizing the U.S. government for undertaking the program but urging his own government not to make stringent limits on SDI a precondition for a START agreement.

In February, as one of the speakers at an international symposium on disarmament in Moscow, Sakharov had argued for at least partial de-linkage of limits on SDI from progress in START, or what he called "untying the package." He said that SDI was simply too rudimentary and unpromising to constitute a threat to strategic stability in the foreseeable future; therefore, it need not pose an obstacle to reductions in offensive forces. The technical difficulties of developing a system of impregnable defense, combined with the strategic unwisdom of deploying it, constituted all the insurance that the Soviet Union needed to begin cutting back on its ICBMs in START.

"I believe," said Sakharov, "that the package approach [linkage between START and SDI] can and should be revised. A significant cut in ICBMs and medium-range and battlefield missiles, and other agreements on disarmament, should be negotiated as soon as possible, independently of SDI, in accordance with the understanding laid out in Reykjavik. I believe that a compromise on SDI can be reached later. In this way the dangerous deadlock in the negotiations could be overcome."

A number of Soviet scientists who were as much insiders as Sakharov had been an outcast acknowledged that his argument carried a certain force. "We came to realize," said Sagdeyev, "that we had not helped ourselves by screaming so much about SDI. We had encouraged some Americans to think that anything the Russians hate so much can't be all bad. And we had overestimated how much damage SDI could do to strategic stability in the short and even the medium term."[4] During the year, Sagdeyev, Evgeny Velikhov, and other Soviet scientists seemed almost to be following Sakharov's lead, implying that stringent, explicit restrictions on SDI, while eventually necessary to preserve strategic stability, need not necessarily be a precondition for preliminary reductions in START.

In September, when President Reagan praised Sakharov in a speech at the United Nations as a brave and eloquent spokesman for the cause of liberalization in the Soviet Union, Eduard Shevardnadze retorted by citing Sakharov's criticisms of SDI: "If we are to believe an academician in one area, why shouldn't we believe him in another area—where he is really a qualified expert?"

The Kremlin was still a long way from taking Sakharov's advice entirely, but it had nonetheless come a long way from its original attempt to ban all "purposeful" SDI research. The Soviets were now saying that not only could research go forward—so could testing, as long as it fell within the realm of what was permitted by the ABM treaty. That was close to the view of a number of the American scientists who went to Vilnius in late October. They were critics of SDI and supporters of the ABM treaty, and they came prepared to discuss ways to reconcile the two governments' positions.

Before the group left for Vilnius, one member had a discussion with James Timbie, and on the delegation's return, it offered the State Department a brief report on their impression of Soviet policy. For thirty years, exchanges like this were standard procedure when private groups of experts had contacts with their Soviet counterparts, but in the politically supercharged and suspicion-filled atmosphere of the Reagan Administration in the fall of 1987, the incident gave rise to a new controversy centered on Paul Nitze.

On November 3 Gregory Fossedal published another of his scoops in the *Washington Times,* this time asserting that Nitze ''has been assisting a group of American scientists in private discussions with top Soviet experts aimed at developing what could become a U.S.-Soviet agreement to limit weapons in space.'' The source and the motive behind the story were apparent from one sentence in particular: ''A Defense Department official who has begun monitoring its activities said the [U.S. National] academy panel, though unofficial, has become 'a de facto negotiating team' and that its proposal on 'Star Wars' would probably be submitted by Soviet negotiators to their U.S. counterparts, possibly this week.''

There was no truth to the allegation that the scientists had been covertly negotiating on behalf of Nitze or anyone else in the Administration, but the article nonetheless did considerable damage. Five conservative Republican congressmen requested an FBI investigation into the alleged unauthorized negotiation, and it became riskier than ever for anyone in the government to raise the possibility of bargaining on SDI.

Cap's Last Shot

It took one more high-level meeting to nail down a date for the summit. From November 22 to 24, George Shultz once again met Eduard Shevardnadze, this time in Geneva, and once again Caspar Weinberger moved to discourage compromise. The secretary of defense set up a screening for Ronald Reagan of a pro–Star Wars film, *SDI: A Prospect for Peace,* which had been produced by the American Defense Preparedness Association and funded in part by SDI contractors. It drew an analogy between the SDI program and medical research on incurable diseases. The President sent the association a videotaped message hailing the film as ''worth four stars.''

Weinberger also arranged for Reagan to schedule a visit a few days later to a plant in Denver where the Martin Marietta Corporation was building an orbiting chemical laser system named Zenith Star. Having the President agree to sanction the program publicly was a victory for Weinberger in his ongoing battle with the State Department.

It was also, however, one of his last acts in office. His wife, Jane, had been in poor health for some time and had been urging him to quit. He did not want to leave. Among other things, he did not want to abandon the field of battle over SDI to Shultz, Nitze, and other advocates of flexible arms-control policies. When, reluctantly, he concluded he must resign, he set about to ensure that his deputy, William Howard Taft IV, would succeed him. "Will can be counted on to stand firm on SDI," Weinberger told an associate. He indicated to Taft that the job was his, then went to the Oval Office to make the case for him.

Howard Baker sat in when Weinberger called on Reagan. Baker listened to Weinberger's appeal for Taft, then urged that Frank Carlucci be made secretary of defense instead. Taft, said Baker, was a fine public servant who came from a distinguished line of great Republicans, but Carlucci would "better be able to cement the improvement of relations" among the State Department, the Defense Department, and the National Security Council staff.

"But I've already promised Will!" protested Weinberger.

Baker persuaded the President to defer a decision, giving George Shultz a chance to intervene in favor of Carlucci at his regular weekly luncheon meeting with Reagan and Baker.

The President chose Carlucci, and the White House promptly let out the word. Weinberger seemed surprised and annoyed when the news of his impending departure broke on November 3. At his formal retirement two weeks later, with President Reagan at his side, he denounced the idea of trading on SDI as "one of the most dangerous ideas ever to infect our political discourse." The President seemed to agree. On November 23, he said in a speech on arms control, "SDI is not a bargaining chip. It's a cornerstone for our security strategy for the 1990s and beyond. We will research it. We will develop it. And when it's ready, we'll deploy it. Just remember this: If both sides have defenses, it can be a safer world."

Carlucci, however, wasted no time in signaling that there was a major change in the offing. A few days before being formally named to his new post, he remarked—in private, but to a large group of influential citizens— that a compromise on SDI "should be manageable." He laughed at the idea of "sharing" SDI technology with the Soviets, saying it "sounds really nice. I'm sure the President is sincere." Even Nitze's list approach, which Carlucci had so disparaged earlier, now seemed not entirely unthinkable. "These things can be negotiated," he said.

One of his first moves on taking office was to replace Perle's protégé Frank

Gaffney with Ronald Lehman as assistant secretary for international security policy. He also called in Lieutenant General Abrahamson, the director of SDI, and told him sternly, "From now on, I want you to be strictly a program manager, not a salesman." Crossing to the other side of the barricades, he tried to make peace with Sam Nunn, urging the senator, "Let's call off the fight over the ABM treaty and look at SDI as a program in its own right."

On the eve of Gorbachev's arrival in Washington, the correlation of forces within the Administration had shifted dramatically. Perle, Weinberger, Gaffney were all gone; Adelman was on his way out the door, about to be replaced by Major General William Burns, an arms-control moderate, experienced in negotiation, with close ties both to the Joint Chiefs of Staff and to Nitze himself. Edward Rowny, whose influence on the inside had never matched his support among conservative outsiders, was now further undercutting his position by criticizing the impending INF treaty. Carlucci, Shultz, and Crowe were working together in a degree of harmony unprecedented in the Reagan presidency. And Nitze himself, while bruised by the battles of the year, was still in place, still determined to work the problem as much in his way as American colleagues and Soviet counterparts would permit.

"As Required"

Mikhail Gorbachev came to Washington on December 7, 1987, to sign the INF treaty and also to lay the ground for a START agreement in 1988. At Reykjavik, the two leaders had begun and ended their frenetic encounter with a disagreement over how the ABM treaty related to Star Wars. In Washington fourteen months later, they found a formula for avoiding a clash on SDI while letting their negotiators, once again led by Paul Nitze and Sergei Akhromeyev, move ahead in START.

The subject of Star Wars was not even discussed by the principals until Reagan outlined his position on the third of Gorbachev's four days in Washington. "We are going forward with the research and development necessary to see if this is a workable concept," the President said to the general secretary, "and if it is, we are going to deploy it." He made it clear that he knew the Soviets still hoped to hamstring his program and that he would not allow that to happen.

Gorbachev listened intently, looking Reagan hard in the eye. When the President finished, the Soviet leader replied forcefully but without rancor or sarcasm: "Mr. President, you do what you think you have to do. . . . And if in the end you think you have a system you want to deploy, go ahead and deploy it. Who am I to tell you what to do? I think you're wasting money.

I don't think it will work. But if that's what you want to do, go ahead.'' But he added: "We are moving in another direction, and we preserve our option to do what we think is necessary and in our own national interest at that time. And we think we can do it less expensively and with greater effectiveness." Then the general secretary suggested, "Let's talk about something else."

As at Reykjavik the year before, the leaders left the detailed negotiations to a working group co-chaired by Nitze and Akhromeyev. At American insistence, the two delegations focused their efforts on the joint draft text of a START treaty that was already on the table at the Nuclear and Space Talks in Geneva, rather than on a statement of principles or a framework agreement of the sort that the Soviets had been proposing. Many important provisions of that document were in brackets, indicating that they were in dispute.

Meeting at the State Department, the working group whittled away at the brackets. The two most important and difficult issues were the Americans' quest for what they called "stabilizing subceilings" in START and the Soviets' desire for insurance against breakout in SDI. The United States had been holding out for a subceiling of 4,800 strategic ballistic missile warheads; the most recent Soviet proposal had been 5,100 for the subceiling.

Nitze and Akhromeyev tried to trade off concessions on offense by one side for concessions on defense by the other. Nitze offered to agree to a figure closer to the 5,100 level the Soviets preferred if Akhromeyev would accept American language on SDI. Akhromeyev balked, for the Reagan Administration was not just asserting the right of either side to deploy space-based defenses at the end of a specified period of nonwithdrawal from the ABM treaty; it was also asking the Soviet Union to affirm that right in a communiqué that would be released at the end of the summit. In the meantime, while the nonwithdrawal agreement was in effect, the two sides would, according to the U.S. position, have the right to conduct "their research, development, and testing [of SDI-type systems], which are permitted by the ABM treaty." This formulation was borrowed from Reagan's letter to Gorbachev in July 1986. The comma and the word "which" had been the object of intense struggle within the Administration, since they implied the broad interpretation. Now, for good measure, another phrase had been added: Permissible activity should include "testing in space, as required."

This opening bid had been proposed by the Defense Department at a National Security Planning Group meeting on the eve of the summit. To many in the State Department, the position looked not just tough but retrograde. There were grim jokes about Weinberger's ghost stalking the corridors of the Pentagon. It was true that, even with the departure of Weinberger, Perle, and Gaffney, there were still plenty of holdovers from their regime in the Pentagon bureaucracy, such as Nitze's tennis and debating opponent Bruce Jackson. But the real explanation lay with Weinberger's successor, Carlucci, who was genuinely skeptical about how far the United States had to go in accommodating Soviet concerns about SDI and who, in any event, did not want to fuel suspicions among SDI enthusiasts that he was going to "give away the store" at the first opportunity.

One of Carlucci's aides remarked with a wink after the NSPG meeting that it was a chance for the new secretary of defense "to demonstrate to the President that his heart is in the right place. Frank has now gone on record seeking the best possible deal, with the accent on 'best.' Then, over time, we can shift the accent to 'possible.' "

Some State Department officials were afraid that the Soviets would take one look at the American proposal and throw up their hands. Shultz said he would have preferred "a somewhat more realistic approach." But the President, in a directive promulgated December 9, the day Gorbachev arrived, had decided to ask for the maximum and see what his negotiators could extract.

Therefore Soviet complaints and intransigence were predictable. Once again playing the heavy, as he had at Reykjavik and Geneva a year earlier, Victor Karpov demanded that the Americans "stop wasting our time" with old and patently unacceptable positions. Marshal Akhromeyev was more temperate but no less adamant. There was no way, he said, that the Soviet Union would endorse the permissibility of testing in space or the inevitability of deployment.

Then, attempting the tactic that Nitze had tried, only in reverse, Akhromeyev offered to lower the Soviet number for a subceiling on ballistic missile warheads, bringing it closer to the American figure of 4,800—if the Americans would soften the wording on SDI.

The haggling over START and SDI began shortly after Reagan and Gorbachev signed the INF treaty on Tuesday, December 10, and it continued throughout the next day. While many other government officials were at the Soviet embassy for a formal dinner Wednesday evening, the working group toiled over sandwiches at the State Department until 12:30 A.M.

At one point, a disagreement developed among the Americans somewhat like the one that had interrupted the all-night bargaining session at Reykjavik the year before. Nitze was looking for areas of possible compromise on SDI when he ran into opposition within his own delegation. He did not want to accept language that would restrict America's ability to test or eventually deploy SDI—he knew better than that—but he did want to find wording that would embody a Soviet-American agreement to disagree on the question. Max Kampelman called this objective "kicking the can down the road." Nitze called it "papering over our differences."

That was not good enough, however, for Henry Cooper, Kampelman's deputy in the defense-and-space group in Geneva, or for the President's science advisor, William Graham. They still wanted to get the Soviets not just to acknowledge the American position on SDI but to accept it. They were holding out for the hard-line Pentagon position on SDI that had been sanctioned by the President on the eve of the meeting, while Nitze and Kampelman were for abandoning it. During a recess, Nitze told Cooper and Graham that their position was "neither saleable with the Russians nor necessary to protect the President's program." If, however, they insisted on pressing the matter further, they were welcome to try doing so themselves. Cooper took Aleksei Obukhov aside for a mini-negotiation that was acrimonious and unsuccessful.

From that moment on, the Pentagon's opening bid was part of the history of the negotiations; Nitze's and Kampelman's advocacy of artful dodging carried the day.

On Thursday—the last day of the summit—Shultz and Nitze called on Eduard Shevardnadze at the Soviet embassy to attempt a breakthrough. The essence of a compromise would be that each side would be able to interpret a joint statement in its own way; the postsummit communiqué would become the means of both consecrating the progress that had been made in START and agreeing to disagree on SDI. Shevardnadze was receptive but said he would have to check with Gorbachev.

Later, while Reagan and Gorbachev were preparing for the departure ceremony, the two teams assembled again in the Cabinet Room. They were joined by Frank Carlucci and his successor as national security advisor, Lieutenant General Colin Powell. With the band warming up on the South Lawn of the White House, the negotiators put the finishing touches on a settlement that split the semantic and numerical differences between them. On the ballistic missile subceiling, they agreed to a figure of 4,900—100 more than the U.S. had long been seeking, 200 less than the last Soviet proposal. The contentious matter of whether there should be additional subceilings for ICBM and SLBM warheads, as well as a variety of other tangles involving cruise missiles and mobile ICBMs, were put back on the agenda of the Nuclear and Space Talks in Geneva.

On SDI, the Americans dropped the reference to testing in space and the explicit claim of a right to deploy, and they combined two passages from their earlier position: The United States would still have the right to conduct "research, testing, and deployment as required, which are permitted by the ABM treaty."

These were clearly American code words for the broad interpretation. Therefore, the Soviets insisted on some offsetting code words of their own: The ABM treaty must be observed as it was "signed and ratified" in 1972. As Sam Nunn and other powerful members of Congress had reminded the Administration continually, the treaty that the Senate had ratified in 1972 was one that could only be interpreted narrowly, forbidding advanced development and testing in space of exotic defenses. In fact, under pressure from Nunn and other influential senators, including a number of moderate Republicans, Reagan had already signed legislation that would have the effect of keeping the narrow interpretation in force almost until the end of his term. While the President's dream and rhetoric remained unchanged, the Congress, with Nunn in the lead, had imposed its will on the Administration, at least for the time being.

Shultz persuaded Shevardnadze to leave well enough alone. It would be inappropriate, said the secretary of state, for a Soviet-American communiqué to refer, even obliquely, to the American domestic political process of ratification or to a dispute between the executive and legislative branches over treaty interpretation. In the end, the Soviet words "and ratified" ended up alongside the American words "in space" on the cutting-room floor of the summit. But the remaining reference to the ABM treaty "as signed in 1972" still served the Soviets' purpose, since they could always maintain that their government had signed the pact with the narrow interpretation in mind.

With help from Carlucci, who joined the negotiations at the last minute, Shultz and Nitze got Shevardnadze to agree to a provision whereby each side would be "free to decide its own course of action" at the end of the nonwithdrawal, nondeployment period. This could be taken to mean that the United States would indeed deploy SDI. But it was also consistent with what Gorbachev had already said to Reagan: If the United States exercised its right to deploy, the Soviet Union would be entitled to take whatever offensive and defensive countermeasures it deemed appropriate.

With minutes to go before he said goodbye to Gorbachev, Reagan saw the final version of the communiqué. Shultz leaned over and explained that the superpowers could pursue their strategic defense programs "as required."

Reagan looked inquiringly at Colin Powell. "Mr. President," said Powell, "I think we're fully protected."

Gorbachev, meanwhile, was receiving similar assurances from his advisors, who included Velikhov. If the Soviets agreed to set aside SDI—to "kick the can down the road"—they would be doing so in a way that preserved the maximal option of each side while accelerating progress in START. The closer the reality of a START treaty, the more the Americans might be willing to tinker with the dream of SDI, especially in 1988, when they would be up against the deadline of an election in which the Republicans would be eager to point to a diplomatic triumph.

Gorbachev recognized that the compromise meant that Reagan would be able to claim, just as he had after the Geneva summit in 1985 and again after the Reykjavik meeting in 1986, that he had, for a third time, protected his favorite program against Soviet efforts to kill or cripple it. But that was now a claim that Gorbachev seemed willing to let Reagan make, for it had an increasingly hollow ring against the backdrop of mounting skepticism and the political calendar. When Reagan proclaimed his satisfaction that SDI was alive and well and proceeding toward full deployment, there would be Sam Nunn, much of the U.S. Congress, and most of the American foreign-policy establishment all rolling their eyes and looking at their watches. From Gorbachev's standpoint, Reagan's attachment to SDI had become less a threat perpetrated by the Soviet Union's principal adversary and more an object of indulgence, the fanciful obsession of an eccentric lame-duck President whom Gorbachev could afford to humor.

Besides, Gorbachev, too, could claim to be giving up nothing. The communiqué preserved the Soviet Union's ability to press its contention that advanced development and testing of SDI were illegal under the ABM treaty. The U.S.S.R. could at any time relink a START treaty with resolution of the SDI issue. The communiqué merely allowed the Soviet Union to procrastinate in deciding what form that resolution should take.

"All right," said Gorbachev to a cluster of his own advisors. "We'll go with it."

The Sakharov finesse seemed to have become the Gorbachev finesse.

CHAPTER 14

So Close . . .

Ronald Reagan had intended the Washington summit to set the stage for the happy ending of his presidency. He and Mikhail Gorbachev announced that they would meet again, in Moscow in mid-1988. Reagan wanted a START treaty so that he could claim to have achieved his long-sought goal of "radical," 50-percent cuts in the most dangerous and powerful weapons in the superpowers' arsenals. The President could then say—and it could be said on his behalf—that his buildup in offensive weaponry and SDI had served not only to bring the Soviets to the START negotiating table but ultimately to draw them to the treaty-signing table as well.

A START pact in 1988 would have other benefits for Reagan. It would help offset the political damage that the Administration was suffering elsewhere in its foreign policy during its last year in office. Congress had effectively vetoed the President's use of the Nicaraguan Contras to bring the Sandinista regime to heel in Managua. Anti-American rioting broke out in Honduras in April, and the State Department bungled an attempt to oust General Manuel Noriega, the military dictator of Panama, whom an American court had indicted for drug trafficking. The Middle East, so often a source of frustration and disappointment for American statesmen, was particularly so in early 1988, when the Palestinian population of the occupied territories in Israel rose up against the government. George Shultz tried in vain to use the crisis to jump-start the stalled machinery of the Arab-Israeli peace talks.

Against this background, the prospect of springtime in Moscow looked all the better to the President and the secretary of state.

For Gorbachev, too, a clear-cut diplomatic triumph would be welcome in a year of troubles. He had to cope with an outbreak of ethnic unrest in the Caucasus and a recurrence of labor strife in Poland. In Afghanistan, the Soviet Union was cutting its losses and withdrawing the forces that for nine years had waged a quagmire war against the local anti-Communist resistance. Gorbachev's internal reforms were a major preoccupation for him and the rest of the leadership, arousing resistance if not outright opposition at virtually all levels of Soviet society. *Perestroika* (restructuring) at home required *peredyshka* (breathing space) abroad. Superpower summitry would help to that end, and reductions in strategic arms of the kind envisioned for START would be consistent with Gorbachev's political, military, and economic priorities.

So at the beginning of 1988, one of the prerequisites for a breakthrough—political will at the highest levels on both sides, in the White House and in the Kremlin—was clearly present. So, too, were the main ingredients of the START treaty itself. The overall ceilings on launchers and warheads had been agreed at Reykjavik in October 1986, and the long-sought subceilings on ballistic-missile warheads, heavy missile warheads, and ballistic-missile throw-weight had finally been added to the package at the Washington summit. Agreement on those numbers represented a landmark in the twenty-year quest for stabilizing reductions in the most destabilizing strategic weapons.

Moreover, there were at hand the makings of a de facto if not de jure tradeoff between offense and defense. By the spring of 1988, five years after Reagan's Star Wars speech, the prospects for the program bore little resemblance to the presidential dream. A majority of Congress had resisted the Administration's requests for large funding increases and ruled out SDI tests that would violate the ABM treaty. Caspar Weinberger's drive for early demonstrations of SDI technology, and early deployment of an actual system, had failed. So had the presidential campaign of Jack Kemp, the one candidate who had made all-out advocacy of Star Wars a centerpiece of his bid to succeed Reagan. The new secretary of defense, Frank Carlucci, had—as soon as he took office—forcefully applied the brakes to the SDI juggernaut within the Pentagon. In testimony on Capitol Hill, Carlucci offered assurances that tests scheduled over the next few years would "probably not raise the treaty compliance issue."

Earlier, it had been fashionable to pay lip service to the desirability, if not feasibility, of a comprehensive antimissile shield; by 1988, while almost no one wanted to be an apologist for the idea of leaving the United States forever entirely naked to nuclear attack, the new fashion in strategic defense was minimalism. Suddenly virtually everyone was in on the act of scaling back the goals and the cost of SDI. The uniformed military had closed ranks behind one proposed system that might stop about half of the Soviets' SS-18 warheads and only 30 percent of the entire missile force in a massive first strike. Such a defense would perhaps complicate the Kremlin's calculations and thereby bolster deterrence, but it was a far cry from what the Commander in Chief had originally wanted and still seemed to want. Senator Sam Nunn proposed something much more modest—what he called an accidental-launch protection system (ALPS), a land-based defense against stray missiles.

SDI had reached the point that the ABM program had reached twenty years earlier: "Thin" defense was the order of the day, whether against a fraction of the Soviet missile force or against a lone ICBM fired by mistake, by a rogue colonel, or by some third-world madman. Just as the adoption of the thin ABM in the late sixties had laid the ground for the offense-defense tradeoff in SALT I, so the emergence of a thin SDI in 1987–88 seemed to make possible a similar breakthrough in the Nuclear and Space Talks.

Even the obstacle of Ronald Reagan's continuing attachment to an unfettered testing program in space seemed surmountable after he and Gorbachev put their names, at the Washington summit, to a joint formulation of their willingness to set aside the hard issues of SDI. The most important, and most contorted, passage in the communiqué was the statement that the two sides would "observe the ABM treaty, as signed in 1972, while conducting their research, development and testing as required, which are permitted by the ABM treaty, and not to withdraw from the ABM treaty, for a specified period of time." The commas and subordinate clauses in what Paul Nitze called "the peculiar sentence" left deliberately vague what level of testing would be permissible during the nonwithdrawal period. That Soviet-American agreement to disagree on SDI, combined with increasingly apparent circumstantial constraints on the program, laid the basis for the defensive half of the offense-defense tradeoff.

Among those who had never liked SDI for its own sake but had nurtured it in its early days for what Robert McFarlane had called its "arms-control potential," there was a distinct note of relief, satisfaction, even vindication. McFarlane himself had by now returned to the public spotlight as a central figure in the Iran-Contra scandal. The humiliation and trauma of his new notoriety led him to attempt suicide in 1987 and, in March 1988, to a plea bargain with the special prosecutor. Yet McFarlane could take some consolation from the evolution of SDI and the course of events in arms control since his personal fall from grace. To a surprising degree, his original hope for SDI had worked: The American declaration of intent back in 1983 had indeed helped induce the Soviets to agree in 1986–88 to deep reductions in their most threatening offensive forces—deeper and more one-sided in favor of the United States than they had been willing even to consider in the first round of START during the first Reagan term. The greatest sting operation in history had very nearly worked; the superpowers had all but settled on the terms of the grand compromise.

. . . Yet So Far

"The main thing," said Nitze, "is that we've broken the back of what we mean by 50-percent reductions. And that means we've solved 90 percent of the problem in START." But it was in the last 10 percent that the two sides came up hard against the details where Nitze had always seen the devil to reside. As a result, Reagan and Gorbachev were not able to meet the goal that they had set themselves the previous December. They kept to their timetable for their fourth summit, meeting in Moscow from May 29 to June 2, but they were unable to reach final agreement in START. Instead, they had to settle for a communiqué that indicated progress only on secondary and tertiary matters while acknowledging that "serious differences remain on important issues."

A number of factors combined to thwart the hopes of the two leaders and of their hardworking aides, of whom none had worked harder than Nitze.

One problem was a result of the disconnection between Reagan's notion of SDI and everyone else's. The President had long been the object of manipulation, if not deception, by his deputies. Since he did not fully understand the part he was assigned to play in the script they had in mind—nor would he have accepted the part if he had understood it—he was all the less likely to speak the right lines as the drama approached its denouement.

No sooner was Mikhail Gorbachev out of town in December than Ronald Reagan claimed that the summit had "resolved" the dispute over SDI and the ABM treaty. Three days later Colin Powell, the national security advisor, tried to clarify what the President had meant—and thereby inadvertently demonstrated how unhelpful clarification was in the case of a muddle on the American side and a standoff with the Soviets. Appearing on "Meet the Press," Powell said, "The President has preserved the right to go ahead with the SDI program. The Soviet position is clear. They think SDI is the wrong way for us to be going. . . . They would prefer that all of our testing and research and development were restricted to the so-called narrow interpretation of the ABM treaty. The President did not accept that, and the joint statement does not put a girdle around us in that way."

The next day, Gorbachev struck back. In a televised address in Moscow, he complained that "certain persons . . . are trying to assert that the talks in Washington have removed differences on such a problem as SDI, and under that pretext made calls for speeding up work on the program."

Now it was Reagan who felt provoked. "Gorbachev took his position," he said, "we took ours, and it was put that way in the joint communiqué. We are going forward [with SDI]."

The December communiqué had included agreement that a defense-and-space pact would have the "same legal status" as a new START treaty and the old ABM treaty. In Geneva, the American delegation at NST tabled a draft text for a treaty "On Certain Measures to Facilitate the Cooperative Transition to the Deployment of Future Strategic Ballistic Missile Defenses." Anatoly Dobrynin's deputy in the Central Committee, Georgi Kornienko, visited Washington in late January and early February and called on

Nitze to complain that the mere tabling of such a document, not to mention its title, was contrary to the spirit of the summit, since it presumed not only the inevitability of a deployed American SDI but Soviet acquiescence in that deployment. At a press conference at the Soviet embassy, Kornienko said that instead of leaving the "conceptual dispute" over SDI to be resolved at "some later time" as agreed at the summit, the "U.S. delegation [in Geneva] again tries to convince the Soviet delegation that it would be good to move forward toward deployment of outer-space ABM systems."

So much, it seemed, for the artful dodging that Shultz and Nitze had managed to choreograph for the two leaders at the summit. The finesse was turning back into an impasse.

Meanwhile, the INF treaty ran into unexpected trouble in the Senate. The Administration's resulting defensiveness over a treaty that it had already signed and the long delay in its ratification created a drag on progress in START. Not until Reagan had already departed for Moscow in late May did the Senate finally (though overwhelmingly) approve the INF treaty.

Some of the opposition came from predictable quarters, ultraconservative senators like Jesse Helms, Republican of North Carolina. He and other die-hards on the right used the INF treaty as a kind of voodoo doll in which they could stick pins in order to inflict pain on the body of arms control more generally and START in particular. Seizing on discrepancies among American intelligence experts over how many undeployed, uncounted SS-20s the Soviets had, Helms accused the State Department of "cooking the books" to conform with Soviet lies about their SS-20 inventory.

Richard Perle and Frank Gaffney, now private citizens associated with the American Enterprise Institute, released a 48-page report listing "drafting errors" and "loopholes" in the treaty that would make it easier for the Soviets to cheat. In congressional testimony, Nitze replied that while it might not be possible to know exactly how many missiles the Soviets had hidden away, the INF treaty contained "the most comprehensive and intrusive" safeguards for verification in the history of arms control.

That was not good enough for the critics of arms control, who were now laying down markers that they would be able to pick up and use to powerful effect later, when the battle was joined over START. In attacking INF, Perle and Gaffney made clear that their objections were aimed in part at making sure that "the proper lessons are drawn for the future" and that "far more intrusive" verification measures be written into START.

Moderates, too, took potshots at the INF treaty. David Boren, Democratic chairman of the Senate Select Committee on Intelligence, contended that the government would have to improve its coverage of the Soviet Union with spy satellites to monitor compliance with the treaty.

Sam Nunn had his own concern about INF. It carried special force be-cause it came from him, and special irony because it meant that one of the most brazen ploys of the anti–arms controllers was coming back to haunt the Administration as a whole now that it finally had an agreement in hand. Nunn wanted to know from executive-branch witnesses who came before the Senate Armed Services Committee how the INF provisions enforcing the elimination of the SS-20s, ground-launched cruise missiles, and Pershing II ballistic missiles would apply to future intermediate-range weapons that might be based on exotic technologies. How could he and his fellow senators be sure that their reading of the INF treaty they were ratifying in 1988 would be respected by subsequent administrations?

In pressing these questions, Nunn was using the executive branch's obvious eagerness for ratification as leverage to establish once and for all the Senate's prerogatives with regard not only to the new treaty on INF but to the old one on ABMs as well. He later said that it probably would not have occurred to him to ask about exotic INF weapons had it not been for the dispute over the ABM treaty.[1]

Nitze was dispatched to the Hill to reassure key senators that the Administration considered the Senate's interpretation of the treaty to be binding. In the end, the Senate made its ratification conditional on the stipulation that the President could not change the interpretation without congressional approval.

Max Kampelman, too, was now spending most of his time serving as a witness in the INF hearings rather than as chief negotiator at the Nuclear and Space Talks in Geneva. Not that he could have accomplished much there, anyway. George Shultz had agreed to hold a series of "ministerial talks" with Eduard Shevardnadze approximately once a month in preparation for the late-spring summit. Virtually all the important negotiating went on at the Shultz-Shevardnadze level. The U.S. delegates in Geneva were left with little to do but rehash old arguments with the Soviets (and with each other) and draft treaty language for whatever agreements their superiors were able to reach during the ministerial talks.

The first months of 1988 had been envisioned at the Washington summit as the climactic period of NST. Instead, the negotiating process between the superpowers and the decision-making process in Washington both seemed to be enacting Zeno's paradox: How does an arrow that gets halfway along its path of flight, then half of the remaining distance, then half of what is left, ever actually reach its target?

The Revolt of the Chiefs

Admiral William Crowe and the Joint Chiefs had never been enamored of an all-out, accelerated SDI. Nor had they ever shared Caspar Weinberger's and Richard Perle's antipathy toward arms control. Speaking in mid-1988, Crowe summed up his differences with the former secretary of defense: "I was never sure he was for an agreement, and I knew I was." He remembered how Weinberger had, for years, heaped "sophomoric sarcasm" on Paul Nitze, whom Crowe regarded as "one of the really distinguished defenders of our national interest that this country has ever had. His persistence in the face of adversity and vested interests is a great tribute. He has furnished much of whatever continuity we've been able to maintain around here. I know how he gets disgusted when people keep coming along trying to reinvent the wheel, or laying siege to battlements he captured a long time ago."

Early in 1988, Crowe hosted Nitze for an intensive round of brainstorming with the Chiefs. It was, in effect, a celebration of the new regime at the Pentagon. Crowe expressed pleasure at how the atmosphere of governmental deliberations had improved: "For the first time, people can come in here, bring up ideas, and not fear the consequences." He assured Nitze that the Chiefs wanted to do everything they could to "advance the endgame" in the Nuclear and Space Talks.

Still, Crowe's admiration for Nitze had its limits, and he had growing doubts about the START treaty Nitze was championing: "Having been in the business as long as he has, and having reached an advanced age, Paul is feeling pressure to get an agreement and to do so quickly. That's the most dangerous thing that can happen."[2] As the year went on, it became increasingly apparent that the Joint Chiefs of Staff differed sharply with many officials in the State Department and some in the White House on both the pace of negotiations and the substance of some details of the emerging treaty.

This was not a personal clash between Nitze and Crowe, nor an institutional one between the Chiefs and the State Department. It was broader than that. As the nation's senior military officers, the Chiefs were deeply concerned about the future of American defense programs. They, like others (including Nitze), saw arms control as an auxiliary to national security policy. National security policy in the mid-1980s was, in their view, a mess. As the Reagan Administration, wounded by Iran-Contra and other debacles, limped into its last year in office, the Chiefs had an opportunity to assert themselves, to insist on a pause in arms control while there was a reassessment of the nation's strategy and weapons programs.

Their major grievances went back at least as far as the inception of SDI itself. The President's meeting with the Chiefs on February 11, 1983, had been the point of no return on his path toward the Star Wars speech. He had misconstrued their concerns about the disarray in American offensive programs as an endorsement of an all-out program to develop defenses. Over time, the Army, the Air Force, and the Navy all came increasingly to see SDI as a potentially troublesome competitor for a shrinking pool of defense dollars. Crowe had been uncomfortable with Weinberger's tendency to "cheer-lead" for SDI. Even while Weinberger was still in office, the admiral spoke up in meetings at the White House against "some people's obsession with a program that has been skewing strategic judgments and military budgets alike."

He and the other Chiefs were uneasy over Weinberger's and Perle's impatience to break out from SALT II and dismayed by the Pentagon civilians' zero-ballistic-missile proposal that had worked its way into the American arms-control position in 1986.

By 1988, Weinberger was gone, but questions remained over what kind of military forces the United States wanted to have and could afford to have ten or twenty years into the future. The emerging START treaty featured ceilings and subceilings that *could* be conducive to strategic stability—that is, the treaty might have the effect of not just reducing numbers of weapons but also reducing the danger that any of the remaining weapons on one side might be used in a first strike against those on the other. "We're basically in favor of this treaty as it's shaping up," Crowe told Shultz, Nitze, and Kampelman over breakfast at the Pentagon in February. Whether START in fact turned out to be stabilizing, however, depended on how the United States chose to fill its allotment of 1,600 launchers, 6,000 nuclear charges, 4,900 ballistic missile warheads, etc. More specifically, it depended on what steps the United States took to ensure that its reduced forces of ICBMs and SLBMs were less vulnerable than before.

For ICBMs, that meant some sort of mobility. On this subject the Chiefs felt the United States government, notably including Congress, was too far from a consensus to proceed in START. "Diplomacy," said Crowe, "has gotten out in front of planning." The Administration was still formally proposing to ban mobile ICBMs in the START treaty, yet the Air Force was moving ahead with a plan to deploy the hydra-headed MX on railroad cars, while key members of Congress were pushing Midgetman. The Chiefs continued to believe that Midgetman, because it carried only one warhead per launcher, would turn out to be too expensive and that funds for developing it would have to come out of other corners of the defense budget. The worst outcome, Crowe feared, was that the de-MIRVing enthusiasts would block the MX while the cost-cutters would block the Midgetman, and the United States would end up with no mobile ICBMs while the Soviets proceeded with both of their own mobile systems, the SS-24 and the SS-25.

At a White House meeting, Crowe told the President in some exasperation, "We find it extremely difficult to deal with this problem as long as we have no idea what our mobile program will be. We can't advise you properly on what we should seek with the Soviets until we know what we're going to have on our side."

Crowe had similar misgivings about the way the SDI issue had been handled in the communiqué released at the end of the Reagan-Gorbachev meeting in December. He and his fellow officers had to think in concrete terms about what weapon systems to develop, test, procure, and deploy. It did them little good, they felt, for political leaders to be agreeing to disagree and calling that progress in diplomatic language that could be read any of a number of different ways. Crowe considered the cryptic but critical sentence on SDI and the ABM treaty to be a gimmick, adequate perhaps as an exercise in mutual face-saving at the time of the summit itself but not as the basis for an eventual arms-control pact that would entail constraints on American military programs. In a meeting with his staff, Crowe warned that it would be "crazy" to base a defense and space treaty on the language of the communiqué. He was afraid that the Soviets would use the ambiguity to develop their own strategic defenses to the maximum, while the U.S. Congress would use it to hold the American program to the minimum.

"Why would we set ourselves up with language that is imprecise?" he asked. "That will lead to loopholes of the sort the Soviets have used to cheat in the past."

Crowe made the same point in a letter to the National Security Council. The key recipients of this letter were General Powell and his principal deputy for arms control, Colonel Robert Linhard. As military men themselves, they were sympathetic to the admiral's appeal, and they sent the State Department a draft of new instructions to the American team in Geneva: A defense-and-space treaty must be "clear" in establishing "our" interpretation of what the ABM treaty said.

But what exactly did that mean? What was "our" interpretation? The issue of strategic defense was still profoundly contentious, not only between the United States and the Soviet Union but within the Administration itself. The President was still committed to his original vision of a comprehensive shield that would protect the entire United States and its allies as well. There were those in the government who were privately contemptuous of that goal but were interested in a scaled-down version of SDI to protect U.S. missile silos and other critical military installations. Still others doubted that even limited point defenses could be deployed without provoking Soviet offensive countermeasures that would upset the strategic balance to the detriment of American security. There was not even a unified official American position on whether the broad interpretation permitted the testing of space-based kinetic kill vehicles.

Paul Nitze agreed with Admiral Crowe that imprecision and ambiguity had no place in Soviet-American agreements. He had never given up pushing his own idea on how to achieve the precision that Crowe urged: an agreed list of permitted and prohibited SDI-related activities. Crowe had supported Nitze's uphill and, it seemed, losing battle to win authorization for the so-called list approach. At one White House meeting in 1987—in Weinberger's presence and to his obvious fury—Crowe had said, "Paul, the Joint staff will study your idea with interest, with care, and of course with respect." Nitze assiduously cultivated Crowe's deputy, Robert Herres, an Air Force general who had previously been head of the U.S. Space Command. In early March 1988, Herres told a symposium on space defenses at the Brookings Institution that Nitze's proposal was "not without merit," that it had "some interesting ramifications" and "certainly should not be summarily cast aside."

In Frank Carlucci's view, "the Nitze list," as it was now called, still smacked too much of the kind of testing limits that he knew Reagan would never sanction. Yet Nitze kept reminding anyone who would listen that it was illogical to declare the list approach a taboo. Sooner or later, something of the sort would be unavoidable—otherwise, there would be endless confusion over how the SDI program squared with America's obligations under whatever agreement it ultimately made with the Soviet Union. Crowe's letter to the White House asking for "precision" on SDI was a reminder that the Administration could not have it both ways: Either it could make a virtue out of its own uncertainty and settle for deliberate vagueness, as Shultz and Nitze had gotten the President to do in the December communiqué, or it could press for specificity, as Crowe was now urging. But the latter course would, by definition, mean being specific about what testing SDI entailed—and what testing a defense-and-space agreement permitted.

Shortly after receiving Crowe's letter, Linhard mused about what kind of a deal might be possible. One outcome, he said, might be a framework agreement embodying the list approach, although he acknowledged with a wry smile that these phrases—"framework agreement" and "list approach," along with any reference to "laboratory" and "permitted/prohibited activities"—were "bumper stickers banned in all the parking lots around here." There would have to be a "change in the words, the situation, and the timing." But the framework agreement and the list approach, he concluded, "may be exactly right as concepts."

Arms-control policymaking had become in part an exercise in finding the right euphemism for good ideas that had been rejected for bad reasons.

Drones

The trickiest problem in START had nothing to do with the reduction of strategic ballistic missiles, mobile or otherwise, or with the relationship between strategic offense and defense. The weapon that posed what seemed to be an almost insurmountable obstacle to final agreement was a small, low-flying, slow-flying drone that did not even figure in the so-called Single Integrated Operational Plan, or SIOP, the Pentagon's top-secret, highly detailed master plan for waging nuclear war against the Soviet Union. This was the nuclear-armed sea-launched cruise missile, or SLCM.

The United States enjoyed a significant lead in the miniaturized guidance and propulsion systems for SLCMs. Partly for that reason, the Soviets wanted severely to constrain them in START. SLCMs had been one of the thorniest issues with which Nitze's and Akhromeyev's delegations had grappled during the otherwise productive all-night session at Reykjavik in October 1986. It had taken more than an hour to agree on a joint statement saying no more than that the two sides would work toward a mutually agreeable solution.

Some American military experts argued that nuclear-armed SLCMs were one of the nastier creatures ever to have emerged from the Pandora's box of the arms race, and that the United States would be well advised to accept stringent restrictions on them while the Soviets were still interested. Perhaps there was a lesson to be learned from the history of MIRVs: The U.S. might live to regret its own innovation once the Soviet Union mastered the technology involved.

One skeptic about the wisdom of nuclear-armed SLCMs was Brent Scowcroft, the retired Air Force general, national security advisor in the Ford Administration, and, more recently, chairman of Reagan's advisory panel on strategic forces. Scowcroft believed that the American technological edge in SLCMs would prove temporary while the geographical asymmetries between the superpowers were permanent—and permanently favorable to the Soviet Union. Key American cities and military installations were near the coasts and therefore easy marks for Soviet SLCMs, while many comparable Soviet targets were deep inland and protected by the most extensive air defenses in the world. A number of NATO officials, particularly from Norway and Canada, made the same point, and Sam Nunn said that he found this view "most persuasive."[3]

There was another consideration that militated against nuclear-armed SLCMs. By any standard, the U.S. Navy was superior to the Soviet fleet. America could outfight the Soviet Union on the high seas—as long as the war was confined to conventional forces. However, if the Soviets "went nuclear" in battles at sea, American aircraft carriers and battleships might disappear in mushroom clouds. In that event, the Soviets would have used their naval nuclear weapons as equalizers to compensate for America's maritime superiority, much as the United States counted on its own nuclear weapons to make up for NATO's numerical inferiority in conventional land-based forces in Europe. From the American standpoint, therefore, it was better to raise the so-called nuclear threshold as high as possible in the naval arena; that meant no nuclear-armed SLCMs.

Paul Nitze was the principal proponent within the Administration of the view that possession of nuclear-armed SLCMs by both sides made those weapons "inherent losers" for the United States. As secretary of the navy in the Johnson Administration, he had been responsible for taking nuclear-armed carrier-based aircraft out of the SIOP on the grounds that they were unlikely to survive long enough to be of any use in a nuclear war. Recalling that decision of a quarter-century earlier, he now asked a number of admirals whether the Navy would not be better off with a simple, radical measure: a ban on nuclear-armed SLCMs, as well as on nuclear-armed torpedoes, depth charges, surface-to-air missiles, and other launchers. Each side had roughly two thousand such "nonstrategic" naval nuclear weapons that would be eliminated by a ban. The only nuclear weapons remaining in the super-powers' navies would be submarine-launched ballistic missiles.

Nitze's longtime technical advisor, James Timbie, devised a series of moves for the endgame of START, a step-by-step plan for American con-cessions intended to trigger a series of roughly matching Soviet responses that would bring the two sides to a final agreement. (Among some of the hard-liners still in middle-level posts at the Pentagon, this document was contemptuously nicknamed "the Timbie surrender plan.") Nitze hoped that American willingness to do away with nuclear-armed SLCMs would be a central part of what he called a "more forward-leaning" package of new American START proposals which George Shultz could take to Moscow for a ministerial meeting with Shevardnadze at the end of February.

But Secretary of Defense Carlucci and the Joint Chiefs of Staff vetoed the idea. Carlucci regretted that the Pentagon had ever agreed even in principle to put SLCMs on the agenda for START. He and the Chiefs concluded that the United States must preserve the option of deploying ship-to-shore (or "land-attack") nuclear-armed SLCMs as a means of bolstering nuclear de-terrence on behalf of NATO, particularly West Germany, now that the Per-shing IIs and ground-launched cruise missiles were going to be removed as a result of the INF treaty. They concluded, therefore, that START should permit each side more than 700 nuclear-armed SLCMs as well as more than 3,000 conventionally armed ones. That meant coming up with a verifiable way of differentiating between the two. SLCMs were small and easy to hide, and it was almost impossible to distinguish the nuclear- from the conven-tionally armed version, especially at a distance, and neither side was willing to permit the other to conduct on-board inspection of its ships.

At the conclusion of the Washington summit in December, Gorbachev had touched off a minor stir by claiming at a press conference that it was tech-nically feasible for one side to determine from a distance whether the other side's ships had nuclear-armed SLCMs on board. American experts were extremely doubtful about this claim; they were sure that it would be possible to shield nuclear warheads so that the rays they emitted could not be detected by remote sensors.

Carlucci felt that the Soviets knew perfectly well that the nuclear/conventional distinction was impossible and that their real purpose was to "capture" the entire American SLCM program. The Pentagon-sanctioned solution was for each side simply to declare how many SLCMs it planned to deploy. This made a mockery of the long-standing American insistence that each side must be able independently to monitor the other's compliance with all provisions of an agreement. President Reagan had learned, and repeatedly quoted, a Russian proverb, *"Doverai no proverai"* ("Trust but verify"), as his watchword for arms control. Yet where SLCMs were concerned, the American position was "Trust," period. Carlucci's way of dealing with this awkward fact was eventually to assert, in a television interview during the Moscow summit, that SLCMs were not really strategic weapons anyway.[4]

What for years had been a bothersome detail in strategic arms control had at the eleventh hour become a treaty-blocker, if not a treaty-buster. The more movement there was on other details (such as how to count air-launched cruise missiles), the more serious an obstacle SLCMs became. In conversation with the Soviets, Max Kampelman floated the idea of finessing the problem in somewhat the same way as SDI had been finessed at the Washington summit. "Maybe we can kick this can down the road, too," he said.

That was not good enough for the Soviets. Unlike SDI, SLCMs represented a technology that was already available. Therefore, Moscow wanted them to be subject to verifiable limits as part of a START treaty. "Otherwise," said Marshal Akhromeyev, "you'll be able to circumvent the treaty by surrounding the U.S.S.R. with long-range nuclear weapons." A number of Soviet civilian experts, including Roald Sagdeyev of the Institute for Space Research, favored a version of Kampelman's idea; they wanted to set aside the SLCM problem for a separate negotiation so that Gorbachev could sign a START treaty with Reagan at the May–June summit. But Akhromeyev was as unyielding with his own countrymen as he was with the Americans. "We can't have a START treaty and an unconstrained American SLCM program," he told Sagdeyev.

Uncertainty about its own military strategy exacerbated the Administration's natural instinct, particularly on the part of the Pentagon, to engage in nickel-and-dime negotiating tactics with the Soviets. As the bottom line of a START treaty became clearer, each of the armed services paid closer attention to the various line items it cared about most, sensing that it had better wage a last-ditch effort on behalf of its own favorite programs before the two sides wrapped up a final deal.

In that spirit the Air Force dug in its heels on the treatment in START of air-launched cruise missiles. On the theory that the bomber carrying an

ALCM gave that missile much of its operational range, SALT II had defined as strategic any ALCM that could travel on its own more than six hundred kilometers. At Reykjavik, the Soviets astonished the Americans with a proposed method of counting ALCMs that was extremely accommodating of the U.S. program. Instead of merely pocketing that concession, the Reagan Administration, at the behest of the Defense Department, tried to see if perhaps it could get something even better—a still more permissive counting rule that represented a "discount" for ALCMs, since they were slow-flying and therefore supposedly stabilizing weapons. From the Washington summit through the early spring of 1988, the United States proposed that ACLM-carrying bombers be counted as having only six missiles per plane, even though they were capable of carrying two or three times that number. The Americans also wanted an exclusion of ALCMs with ranges less than 1,500 kilometers (in short, a more favorable definition of "strategic" ACLMs than the one in SALT II).

Nitze was uneasy with what he regarded as petty overreaching. He was prepared, as he put it, to "move in the Soviet direction" by adopting a counting rule that corresponded more closely to the load capability of the bombers. But movement itself had now become suspect. In meeting after meeting, Admiral Crowe warned that "the arms-control dialogue is acquiring a momentum of its own" and argued for "applying the brakes" to the bilateral negotiating process until America's own unilateral defense planning could catch up.

Wearied by wrangles in Washington that were almost as intense as those at the negotiating table in Geneva, Robert Linhard offered a stunning acknowledgment of the core problem in American arms-control policy. "Even if the Soviets didn't exist," he remarked, "we might not get a START treaty because of disagreements on our side." Kampelman put it differently. The whole experience reminded him of last-minute, drawn-out snags in contract law: "After you've got the major issues in your pocket, the minor issues become major issues. The big problem now may be whether we can live with a 'yes' from the other side."

START had all but stopped because of the opposition of the military establishments on the two sides. None of the men responsible for the snag, Soviet or American, was in any sense a Bonapartist, too big for the britches of his uniform. Nor was any of them an opponent of arms control. They all seemed genuinely to believe that treaties like SALT II and START could serve the common cause of nuclear deterrence. Carlucci had ushered in a new and welcome collegiality between the Defense and State departments. On Capitol Hill, he was now probably the single most respected official of the executive branch, largely because, unlike Weinberger, he seemed willing to make prudent compromises with budget-minded senators as well as with the Soviets.

For his part, Crowe continued to impress the State Department with his commitment to the validity of arms control even as he balked at Nitze's proposed formulas for resolving the SLCM issue. Crowe felt that the United States needed a clearer idea of the future of its own military forces before it made any more concessions in START. Yet he asserted this view without arousing suspicions that he had a secret agenda to torpedo the negotiations. Colin Powell, too, was a military man, an Army lieutenant general; and he, too, impressed the civilians at the State Department as an honest broker in the way he discharged his duties as national security advisor. Yet he shared many of the career military's anxieties and biases, and these led him frequently to side with the Pentagon.

Meanwhile, Mikhail Gorbachev seemed to have come up against a similar problem with his own good soldiers. In May 1987, a quixotic West German peacenik had evaded the vaunted Soviet air defense system and landed in Red Square in a single-engine Cessna (in effect, a piloted cruise missile), and the incident had given Gorbachev an excuse to purge the defense ministry. He had hand-picked the new defense minister, Marshal Dimitri Yazov. As for the chief of the General Staff, Marshal Akhromeyev, ever since Reykjavik he had struck Nitze as "a worthy partner, serious about the negotiating process as well as dedicated to his own side's goals."

Yet when push came to shove in the spring of 1988, it was these military men on both sides who came together in a perverse sort of joint venture to thwart their bosses' desire for a more upbeat, conclusive ending to START in the Reagan Administration. They could be accused of defending parochial military interests, and indeed, that is exactly what they were doing. But that is what they were paid to do. In a relationship that was still rooted in the paradox of deterrence, the soldiers would have their say, including a veto over what the diplomats—or, for that matter, the President and the General Secretary—could accomplish at their forthcoming meeting in Moscow.

Going for the Gold

Increasingly, the division within the U.S. government was not so much over how START should deal with a particular issue, such as mobile ICBMs or SLCMs, as over how realistic it was to expect, or how prudent to attempt, to have a treaty at all before the Administration left office. Admiral Crowe believed that the difficulty in "getting our own act together" was too deep-rooted for negotiations with the Soviets to proceed at a pace that would yield a treaty in time for a summit. "We just can't move as quickly as you gentlemen want," he told Shultz, Nitze, and Kampelman during one of their many visits to the Pentagon. Meanwhile, on his own trips to Capitol Hill, Carlucci was hearing much criticism, exhortation, and warning to the effect that START would encounter even more trouble than the beleaguered INF treaty. William Webster, the director of Central Intelligence, shared Senator Boren's concern that the United States did not have sufficient spy satellites to verify the ambitious new treaties. The President's Foreign Intelligence Advisory Board echoed that warning in a meeting with Reagan himself.

Nitze had little patience with these misgivings. "These fellows are getting cold feet," he said. He dismissed as nonsense the danger of being rushed into a bad agreement. "Who in God's name is rushing?" he demanded. "It's not as though we've just started in this business. I personally have been working on these problems since 1969. So we're not dealing with these subjects for the first time."

At a number of points in his own career, Nitze had vehemently denounced the idea of negotiating against the deadline of a summit. He had resigned from the SALT II delegation in 1974 largely on those grounds. But now he saw matters differently. He recalled that just a few months before, in the fall of 1987, there had been considerable pessimism about whether the many sticking points in INF could be resolved in time for there to be a treaty for Reagan and Gorbachev to sign in Washington; yet the demands of the calendar and the expectations of the leaders had served to keep the INF negotiators' noses to the grindstone. That could happen again now in START, he believed, and to good effect. Nitze helped persuade Shultz, who in turn persuaded the President.

At a meeting at the White House just before Shultz left for the Moscow ministerial meeting in February, Carlucci warned, "We won't play well if we go into a two-minute drill." Shultz replied, "If you talk like that, you'll never get anything. We won't know what we can accomplish until we try. Let's not base policy on a self-fulfilling prophecy."

Howard Baker sided with Shultz. "I have but one constituent," he said, referring to the President, who was chairing the meeting. "And I understand that he wants to overcome these obstacles and push ahead. We have a presidential commitment. We have an obligation to make a real effort."

The President agreed. Borrowing a phrase from the Winter Olympics then under way in Calgary, Canada, he said that the United States should "go for the gold."

But Shultz made little progress toward the finish line on START during his talks with Gorbachev and Shevardnadze in Moscow on February 21 and 22. While the Americans had a presidential mandate to strive for a treaty by the summit, they did not have sufficient flexibility in their negotiating instructions to do so. Nor were the Soviets forthcoming at the meeting. As the spring wore on, there was only incremental progress in START.*

From Shultz's visit to Moscow in February through Reagan's trip there for the summit in late May and early June, the Soviets kept repeating that if the two sides could only make a deal in START, there was no reason for their differences on SDI to stand in the way of an agreement. All that was necessary was to reiterate the peculiar sentence in the Washington communiqué. "Nothing should be changed from the Washington summit joint statement," said Shevardnadze in February, "other than possible additions of some legal aspects."

In that last qualifying phrase, Nitze saw a fresh opportunity to work the problem. What was required, it seemed, was a refinement of the Washington finesse that met three quite different sets of interests: Reagan's insistence that an agreement must preserve a robust SDI program, including the testing of devices in space; Gorbachev's refusal to endorse eventual deployment; and the Joint Chiefs' desire, shared by Nitze, for greater precision in defining what the testing program would look like.

On Shultz's plane coming home from Moscow in February, Nitze and Kampelman worked out a series of what they called "predictability measures" that would govern the two nations' programs to do research and development on strategic defenses during the period of nonwithdrawal from the ABM treaty. According to a draft of the scheme, each side would give the other a "statement of its planned program" of testing for the next five years: "After discussions, and mutual adjustments if agreed, each side will state its lack of objection to the other's planned test program." One year after the entry into force of that agreement, there would be negotiations on an "agreed dividing line" between, on the one hand, "sensor" systems and devices and, on the other, kill vehicles, defined with language taken directly from the ABM treaty. The "testing or deployment" of "sensor systems and devices in space" would be permitted. There would be another "agreed dividing line" between what constituted testing and what constituted de-

---

*As of February, the Soviets were still resisting a subceiling on ICBM warheads, which the United States wanted, unless it was accompanied by an equal subceiling on SLBM warheads, which the United States did not want. And, as though for good measure—perhaps because their defense ministry was attempting some nickel-and-diming of its own—the Soviets had suddenly added to their proposal a new subceiling, of 1,100, on bomber weapons. The United States eventually adjusted its proposed counting rule for ALCMs, inching upward from six to ten the number of missiles that would be attributed to each bomber. On subceilings, the United States dropped what had always been regarded as a throwaway in its package: an aggregate limit of 1,650 warheads on mobile ICBMs (like the rail-garrisoned MX, the SS-24, and the SS-25s), heavy ICBMs (the remaining 154 SS-18s that the Soviets would be allowed after a 50-percent cut in their heavy force), and ICBMs with more than six warheads (such as a stationary MX). For their part, the Soviets abandoned their quest for a subceiling on bomber weapons, and Akhromeyev repeated something he had said in Washington in December: "We have no plans to go beyond 3,300" ICBM warheads. "Good," said Max Kampelman. "Let's find a way to express that in the treaty."

ployment of kill vehicles. "Neither side will deploy" kill vehicles. A body comparable to the Standing Consultative Commission for SALT would be set up to adjudicate disputes.

Nowhere did the document mention a "threshold." Instead, it spoke of an "agreed dividing line." There was no explicit reference to what would be "permitted," only to what each side would state its "lack of objection to." Nor was anything to be "prohibited"; rather, "neither side will . . ." Behind these semantic feints, Nitze, now in collaboration with Kampelman, was pursuing his list approach as doggedly as ever. He continued doing so through the spring, sending a series of memos to Shultz, Carlucci, Powell, and others, with exhortations that "we cut the Gordian knot."

The Chiefs, in their own quest for clearer rules of the road as the superpowers embarked into space, were taken with the idea of distinguishing between kill vehicles and sensors and exempting sensors from whatever restrictions applied to kill vehicles. "Let's get at least that much established with the other guys," said Crowe, referring to the Soviets. There was an opportunity to do so through a military-to-military channel in mid-March, when Carlucci held an unprecedented meeting with his Soviet counterpart, Dimitri Yazov, in Bern, Switzerland. With the backing of Robert Linhard, Carlucci used the meeting to propose that space-based sensors should be allowed to "run free"; their testing and deployment would not be affected by any mutually agreed constraints on space-based kill mechanisms.

Yazov and the Soviet delegation plunged into a lengthy wrangle over how to define a sensor. They wanted to know whether this new proposal meant that the Americans would finally "stop the campaign" against the Krasnoyarsk radar. Since Krasnoyarsk was a ground-based "sensor," would not it, too, be allowed to "run free"? Absolutely not, said Carlucci; the U.S.S.R. must take down the installation before there could even be a negotiation on space-based sensors.

Back in Washington, some of Carlucci's own civilian colleagues at the Defense Department, who had been left out of what Linhard called "the Yazov gambit," were upset when they found out about it. Ronald Lehman, the former aide to Perle who had gone off to Geneva to negotiate START, was now back in the Pentagon, sitting in Perle's old chair as assistant secretary for international security policy. Lehman felt that it would be one thing for the United States to announce unilaterally that it intended to proceed for its own good reasons and in its own good time with the testing and deployment of sensors in space; it was quite another to put the matter before the Soviets for discussion. Once the Soviets addressed the issue, the ABM treaty—far from receding into the mists of history, if not oblivion, as some in the Administration wanted—would be front-and-center once again, an object not only of dispute with Congress but of renegotiation with the Soviets. The ABM treaty prohibited the deployment of traditional missile-tracking radars either on mobile platforms or in space, and it stipulated that exotic tracking devices that could be substituted for ABM radars, such as high-tech sensors of the sort envisioned for SDI, would have to be the subject for new talks with the Soviets. Lehman feared that Carlucci had inadvertently invited the Soviets to join in just such an exercise.

For just that reason Nitze was pleased. What Carlucci had proposed might be a step in the direction of the negotiation that Nitze had long been seeking on what aspects of SDI were permissible under the ABM treaty. His office helped draft a proposed text for a defense-and-space treaty that would establish a so-called "test range in space." It would be a designated, agreed set of orbits—for example, above the Equator—that could be used for a specified number of platforms from which experiments could be conducted under the close scrutiny of the other side; and it would be analogous to the test ranges on earth sanctioned by the ABM treaty. Once again, Nitze was attempting to update his own handiwork of the early seventies.

Nitze's obvious impatience and aggressive ingenuity to that end continued to make others nervous. There were grumbles from the other side of the Potomac that Nitze was pushing too hard, that he was getting out in front of the Administration as a whole. The intelligence community, which designed and administered the top-secret American spy-in-the-sky system, was extremely nervous about putting any aspect of the program on the agenda of Soviet-American negotiations. Powell told an NSC staff meeting that he was tired of having to "keep driving a stake through the heart of Paul Nitze's plan" for the list approach. Finally, the national security advisor came close to issuing a public reprimand. On May 5, he told a meeting of SDI supporters and contractors, with a number of reporters present, that the President would "accept no cute way of listing permitted/prohibited activities" for SDI testing in space. There was no question what, or whom, Powell was talking about.

Once again, as with the walk in the woods six years before, Nitze's never-say-die efforts on behalf of his own proposed solution to what seemed an otherwise insoluble problem had earned him a rebuke from the White House.

"A Time for Reaffirmation"

George Shultz had come home from the first Moscow ministerial in February reasonably upbeat about having kept alive the possibility of a START deal by the summit. That was just what worried some of the Administration's critics. In a newspaper column in mid-January Henry Kissinger warned, "The current nuclear arms control negotiations are too one-sided." He urged that a START treaty be linked to major reductions in Soviet conventional forces. In late February Kissinger repeated that recommendation while testifying on INF before Congress.

The March 1988 issue of *Commentary*—which had frequently been a forum in the past for the views of members of the Committee on the Present Danger—carried an article by Patrick Glynn that was sharply critical of the prospective START treaty. It was titled "Reagan's Rush to Disarm." That headline hardly seemed fitting to anyone familiar with the course of the Nuclear and Space Talks. When a group of influential senators, including Sam Nunn and Robert Byrd, the Democratic majority leader, visited Geneva, they found the American and Soviet diplomats there discouraged about the treadmill-like quality of the negotiating process. On their return to Washington, the senators called at the White House and conveyed to Reagan and Howard Baker their pessimism about the chances of a breakthrough in time for the summit. Nunn added that he had deep reservations about whether it was wise to proceed toward a START agreement when there was still so much division, uncertainty, and confusion on the American side over the future of American strategic offensive programs, including both ICBMs and cruise missiles.

Talking with Reagan afterward, Baker recommended that the President begin lowering expectations for the summit and indicate that he was more interested in a good deal than in an early deal. The President did just that in an interview with Lou Cannon of the *Washington Post* on February 25. "I have to tell you that common sense indicates that the time is too limited for us to really think that we could bring a treaty ready for signature to [the summit]," said Reagan. "This one [START] is so much more complicated with regard to verification and everything else than the INF treaty, which we were able to bring together. But even that took a few months to do. So we're not going to be disappointed . . . we're not at this moment anticipating that it would be ready for signature then." Perhaps, Reagan added, a few extra months might make the difference in START, and a fifth summit would be possible later in the year: "I believe with the amount of time that would still be remaining that, if there is sincerity on both sides with regard to getting such an agreement—and I think there is—I think that could be done . . . before my time expires."

Reagan's statement was read with relief at the Pentagon and dismay at the State Department. Nitze was at first furious. He told associates that the President had undercut Shultz, who was committed to the proposition that a deal was possible by the summit. Later, however, Nitze managed to put a good face on what had happened. Reagan's statement, he said in an interview of his own, was "brilliant because it dealt with the main opposition that has been expressed by my old colleagues on the Committee on the Present Danger and others who are warning that we're going too fast, that we shouldn't negotiate against the deadline of the summit, that we should hold our horses."[5]

There were other constituencies with very different concerns that also needed to be allayed. The first week in March, the President attended a meeting in Brussels of the leaders of the sixteen NATO member states. He found the allied leaders, especially his old friend Margaret Thatcher, eager for guarantees that Moscow would not be another Reykjavik; when Reagan sat down with Gorbachev, there must be no flights of fancy into a dream world of zero ballistic missiles or total nuclear disarmament. That assurance was written into the final communiqué of the NATO meeting: "While seeking security and stability at lower levels of armaments, we are determined to sustain the requisite efforts to ensure the continued viability, credibility and effectiveness of our conventional and nuclear forces, including the nuclear forces in Europe, which together provide the guarantee of our common security. . . . We will continue to be steadfast in the pursuit of our security policies, maintaining the effective defenses and credible deterrence that form the necessary basis for constructive dialogue with the East, including on arms control and disarmament matters."

The title of the document was "A Time for Reaffirmation." What was being reaffirmed was deterrence. What was being repudiated, therefore, albeit only implicitly, was not only a relapse into excessively ambitious and ill-considered schemes for offensive arms control but the presidential version of SDI as well.

In a letter to the editor of *Commentary*, which appeared in the May issue, Nitze rebutted Patrick Glynn's denunciation of START: "I believe an agreement will be seen as a good agreement if it reduces the imbalance in the destabilizing forces arrayed against us and makes it more feasible for us to assure and to maintain deterrence; INF is such an agreement. START can be an even more important step." Practiced as he now was in avoiding taboo words, Nitze managed throughout his long letter to keep away from the four-letter word SALT. But there was no mention of SDI either. Moreover, he did note that START was the continuation of a process begun in the Johnson Administration, adding, "I have personally been involved in that effort for much of those twenty years."

Paul Nitze was coming to the defense of the arms-control policies of an Administration under attack from its critics on the right, whose ranks now included Henry Kissinger. Nitze was basing his defense on what amounted to a ringing endorsement of traditional means, both diplomatic and military, of keeping the nuclear peace.

. . .

By the eve of the Moscow summit, George Shultz felt that the best the two leaders could do would be to "take a photograph of where we are" by consecrating the work that had already been done on the joint draft text of a START treaty and leave it to their subordinates to remove the remaining brackets that indicated points of disagreement.

En route to Moscow, Air Force One stopped in Helsinki for three days to give the President a chance to catch up on jet lag. During the layover, on May 28, Colin Powell gave a briefing for the traveling White House press corps. He spelled out his own hope for the summit, acknowledging what had become the number-one sticking point: "If we make some progress on sea-launched cruise missiles—if not a breakthrough, we might make sufficient progress that we can return to work in Geneva, finish it over the summer, and in the fall at a ministerial meeting or higher, should that come about, we could go to closure on it."

There was no breakthrough—in fact, no progress at all—on SLCMs at the summit, and only the most modest, inconclusive progress on other, less troublesome issues. For all the important political symbolism of Ronald Reagan strolling through Red Square arm in arm with Mikhail Gorbachev, the theme of nuclear diplomacy at the meeting was in a distinctly minor key. There was a sense of fatigue on the American side and of impatience on the Soviet side—not only impatience with the same old disagreements but impatience to deal with a new American leadership. Reagan tried yet again to persuade Gorbachev that SDI was benevolent, posing no threat to the Soviet Union. "We just don't believe that," said Gorbachev wearily. "We believe it's an offensive system."

"But it would not kill or hurt anyone," Reagan replied.

"Let's talk about something else," said Gorbachev.

At another point during the meeting, Reagan trotted out his favorite three words of Russian, *"Doverai no proverai."* Akhromeyev later made a sarcastic joke about SLCMs: "Your President seems to think that because that's a Russian proverb, it applies only to Russian weapon systems. Or perhaps he thinks it means we're supposed to trust while the Americans alone are supposed to verify."

Once again, just as they had at Reykjavik and Washington, Akhromeyev and Nitze co-chaired the arms-control working group. But this time there were no all-night sessions.

When the summit ended, Nitze was assigned to brief the hundreds of reporters assembled in a ballroom at the Mezhdunarodnaya Hotel on the bank of the Moscow River.* It was a melancholy event, pervaded by a sense

---

*The traveling American press included Richard Perle, who was in Moscow as a contributor to *U.S. News and World Report* and a commentator for "The MacNeil-Lehrer Newshour."

at once of finality and of inconclusiveness. Questioner after questioner probed Nitze for some sign of meaningful progress on the important outstanding issues and for some hint that there might still be a START agreement before Reagan left office. Nitze could offer little news for them, and little comfort for himself. Finally, Helen Thomas of UPI, dean of the White House press corps, decided to ask a more general question: "Could you declare the Cold War over?"

Nitze had only a split second to reply: "I hope it isn't over in the sense of becoming hot."

It was a glib comment, of course. It could hardly have been otherwise, coming at the end of a long briefing on abstruse subjects. Thomas and her colleagues were eager to write their stories; they were not receptive to a lengthy disquisition. Yet it was also the perfect response to a valid question— and it was especially perfect coming from Paul Nitze. He did not want to contradict his President's almost euphoric endorsement of Gorbachev's reforms. In the spirit of what was already being called "the Moscow spring," Reagan said that his own description of the Soviet Union as an evil empire in 1983—five years before—had referred to "another era." Yet in replying off the cuff to Thomas's question, Nitze wanted also to be true to his own conviction that the competition between the superpowers, in both its political and its military dimensions, would continue for a very long time to come. So, therefore, must the quest for arms-control measures that would keep that competition, however it was described, from becoming too hot for the competitors to handle.

Paul Nitze worked almost nonstop on the long trip home from Moscow. He alone seemed immune to the sense of letdown that afflicted the airborne deliberations over what to do next in START.

However, soon after his return, he went into an alarming physical decline. He began to suffer from fatigue, insomnia, and sharp pains in his joints, as well as flareups of chronic sciatica and an ulcer. For weeks he tried, with increasing difficulty, to carry on at his normal, vigorous pace. He put in full days at the State Department, drafting papers, attending meetings, working on his memoirs, and writing an op-ed page article for the *Washington Post* in defense of the emerging START treaty. In mid-June, at a dinner dance in honor of Bruce Jackson's marriage, Nitze seemed to be enjoying himself, especially when he had a chance to debate SDI with another guest, Lieutenant General Abrahamson, the director of the program. But even on that occasion, Nitze tired quickly and left early.

At the end of the month, he flew to Nashville, Tennessee, for a speech and an award ceremony; then to Aspen, Colorado, to see his older sister over the Fourth of July weekend; then back to Washington for a National

Security Council meeting at the White House; then to his summer home in Northeast Harbor, Maine, for what was supposed to be a restful and restorative visit with his children and grandchildren.

Much of the time he was in acute discomfort, accompanied by frequent and severe bouts of almost paralyzing exhaustion. Some doctors thought he might have shingles. At the insistence of his friends and family, he went into Johns Hopkins Hospital in Baltimore for a week of tests. His condition was diagnosed as a form of muscular rheumatism caused by a virus and known as Bornholm disease, or "devil's grip."

During this period there was much head-shaking and tongue-clicking around the corridors of government about the seemingly indefatigable and indestructible Paul Nitze finally beginning to "show his age," "lose his grip," and "show signs of giving up the fight." These remarks were often accompanied by suggestions that perhaps to some degree, Nitze's infirmity had been exacerbated if not induced by his discouragement at the prospects for further progress in the few months remaining to the Administration.

There was also muted talk about Nitze's physical condition as a metaphor for the state of the enterprise with which he was so closely associated. Such thoughts were natural enough, for over the decades, Nitze had been not just a practitioner but a personification of American national-security policy. During his latest tour of duty in government, since 1981, he had championed the diplomatic dimension of that policy. He had kept on working the problem of arms control no matter how intractable it sometimes seemed, no matter how intransigent the Soviets on the other side of the negotiating table, and no matter how divided and defiant his own colleagues on the American side. His individual persistence had come to symbolize the hardiness of the arms-control process. Now, quite abruptly, the process had slowed down, and so had Nitze. He suddenly seemed to embody the generalized weariness overcoming the Reagan Administration as it neared the end.

Nitze himself, however, was having none of that. He announced from his hospital bed that he had no intention of giving up on anything any time soon. Among other things, there was still work to be done. George Shultz was scheduled to meet Eduard Shevardnadze in late September for a final push in START. As soon as the virus had run its course, Nitze was back on his feet and at his post, poring over cables from the negotiations that had resumed in Geneva, supervising a steady stream of memos, consulting with Shultz. As long as there was any chance at all of making progress—whether by the removal of even one set of brackets in a single passage of the joint draft text dealing with the smallest detail, or by surprising everyone (including himself) and achieving a finished treaty—Nitze would press ahead.

This never-say-die, it's-not-over-till-it's-over determination was characteristic of the man, but not of the government he served. A grudgingly valedictory mood had long since begun to settle over Washington. Much of the praise for the outgoing Administration was faint, many of the compliments backhanded. Those who saw the Administration as having deserved its setbacks and stumbled into its successes often singled out Nitze's efforts on behalf of progress in arms control as the exception that proved the rule.

The most dramatic example of Nitze's boldness and ingenuity—his once-secret, now-famous venture of 1982—had inspired a successful play, *A Walk in the Woods* by Lee Blessing, about a Soviet and an American diplomat who try to reach a compromise that their home offices do not want. Just before the Moscow summit, the two-man Broadway cast had traveled to Washington and put on a special performance at the Library of Congress sponsored by Senators Sam Nunn, Claiborne Pell, and David Boren. Nitze was the guest of honor. In welcoming him, Nunn casitgated the rest of the exectuive branch: "Paul Nitze has played a major role in developing the sound positions that this Administration has had. He has attempted to get the President to reject the absurd positions. He has also been in the forefront of the effort to get us to work our way out of various muddles toward sensible and creative solutions."

In early August, George Shultz delivered his own testimonial: "Paul Nitze has played all the positions in the game and done so with great skill, grace, and accomplishment. The first INF negotiator, he set in motion the process that led to that historic agreement. In overnight negotiations in Reykjavik, he and Marshal Akhromeyev established the first numbers and counting rules for START. For SDI, he was the first to articulate the criteria that have been adopted to guide the program. Throughout, he has been an articulate spokesman for the Administration in Congress and with the public. So Paul has served this President and this Administration just as he has served their predecessors—in the center of the action on the most important issues. In the Situation Room at the White House, in committee rooms on Capitol Hill, and at the negotiating table, Paul brings a firm sense of the national interest, the keenest of analysis, and integrity to follow the logic wherever it may lead. All of the achievements of the past eight years bear the imprint of Paul Nitze."

Regardless of the follies and failures, the fights and frustrations that had marked its tenure—regardless of what did or did not happen in the short time left—the Reagan Administration would leave its successor the essence of a START treaty. Regardless of how difficult the outstanding differences continued to be, the provisions already agreed on would, as Nitze said in his *Post* article, "reduce the Soviet threat to our retaliatory forces" and thereby buttress the edifice of deterrence on which he had been working for most of his long career. An important legacy was in place.

Moreover, both of the men contending to inherit that legacy, Vice President George Bush and Governor Michacl Dukakis of Massachusetts, had indicated that they would accept, honor, and build on it. In many of their campaign statements, both had kind words for the progress that had been made in START and the broad outlines of the prospective treaty. They cited strategic arms control as one area of foreign and defense policy where there was likely to be a high degree of continuity once a new Administration took office. It would be continuity not just with the previous eight years but with the past forty. In that sense, Paul Nitze was more than the master of the game; he was also a victor.

NOTES

Chapter 1

1. U.S. Air Force Oral History Interview, Albert F. Simpson Historical Research Center, Office of Air Force History, Headquarters USAF, conducted by John N. Dick and James C. Hasdorff on October 25-28, 1977; a second session took place May 19-20 and a third, July 14-16, 1981; p. 5 of transcript (unpublished). Hereafter abbreviated USAF OHI.

The biographical material in this chapter comes from that Air Force interview, augmented by the author's interviews with Nitze and those that Nitze gave to Walter Isaacson and Evan Thomas for their book *The Wise Men: Six Friends and the World They Made* (Simon and Schuster, 1986), pp. 482–483; also, Nitze's reminiscences on being presented the Man of the Year award by the Hotchkiss Alumni Association, at a dinner at the Pierre Hotel in New York on April 18, 1967. Nitze interviews with author hereafter abbreviated PHN and date.

2. Quoted by A. Lavrentyev, "Stroiteli novogo mira" (Builders of a new world), *V mire knig* (In the world of books), cited in David Halloway, "Entering the Nuclear Arms Race: The Soviet Decision to Build the Atomic Bomb, 1939-45," a 1979 working paper (N. 9) for the International Security Studies Program at the Woodrow Wilson International Center for Scholars.

3. Richard Rhodes, *The Making of the Atomic Bomb* (Simon and Schuster, 1987), pp. 524–530 and 753. The Szilard quotation was noted by David Lilienthal.

4. In two articles written in 1954—"Nuclear Weapons: Strategic or Tactical," *Foreign Affairs*, January, and "Unlimited Weapons and Limited War," *The Reporter*, November 18—Brodie argued that the West should explore the limited use of nuclear weapons. By the end of the fifties, particularly in his book *Strategy in the Missile Age* (Princeton, 1959), he returned to his original precepts, once again arguing against the utility of even limited nuclear war.

5. The comments on complementarity come from a letter to J. Robert Oppenheimer written on March 23, 1954; the Groton address was delivered on June 12, 1953; the later references to complementarity came in an interview with Jerry W. Sanders on August 24, 1977, in *Peddlers of Crisis: The Committee on the Present Danger and the Politics of Containment* (South End Press, 1983), pp. 163-164.

6. "Military Power: A Strategic View," *The Fletcher Forum*, Winter 1981.

7. Interview with George Kennan, 12/9/86.

8. USAF OHI, pp. 227-229.

9. Kennan 12/9/86.

10. Rhodes, *The Making of the Atomic Bomb*, p. 646.

11. See, for example, David Mayers, "Containment and the Primacy of Diplomacy: George Kennan's Views, 1947-1948," *International Security*, Summer 1986: Kennan "was more uncertain intellectually and more of a Cold Warrior in the late 1940s than he has wanted to admit"; Michael Novak, "George X. Kennan versus George Y. Kennan," *Washington Star*, December 29, 1977; Edward N. Luttwak, "The Strange Case of George F. Kennan: From Containment to Isolationism," *Commentary*, November 1977; Leopold Labedz, "The Two Minds of George Kennan: How to Un-Learn from Experience," *Encounter*, April 1978. For the defense against "Kennan-bashing," see Barton Gelman, *Contending with Kennan* (Prager, 1984), a sympathetic, even admiring analysis of the "inconsistency" and "alleged contradictions" between "Kennan the hawk" and "Kennan the dove."

12. USAF OHI, pp. 441-442.

13. George F. Kennan, *Memoirs* (Little, Brown, 1967), pp. 458-461.

14. Kennan 12/9/86.
15. PHN 9/26/86.
16. USAF OHI p. 202.
17. PHN 9/26/86.
18. Kennan 12/9/86. Also Kennan, *Memoirs*, p. 472, and *Foreign Relations of the United States* (Little, Brown, 1950), vol. 1, pp. 22–44.
19. Isaacson and Thomas, *The Wise Men*, p. 487.
20. Eben Ayers's diary, January 31, 1950, cited in Gregg Herken, *The Winning Weapon: The Atomic Bomb and the Cold War* (Knopf, 1980), p. 304.
21. Kennan 12/9/86.

Chapter 2

1. PHN 6/4/87. Dean Acheson, *Present at the Creation: My Years in the State Department* (New American Library, 1969), p. 499; Paul Y. Hammond, "NSC 68: Prologue to Rearmament," *Strategy, Politics and Defense Budgets,* eds. Warner Schilling, Paul Y. Hammond, and Glenn H. Snyder (Columbia University Press, 1962), pp. 309–310; Isaacson and Thomas, *The Wise Men,* pp. 496–497.
2. Kennan 12/9/86.
3. Steven L. Rearden, *The Evolution of American Strategic Doctrine: Paul H. Nitze and the Soviet Challenge* (Westview Press/Foreign Policy Institute, School of Advanced International Studies, Johns Hopkins University, SAIS Paper No. 4, 1984), pp. 1–12.
4. *Khrushchev Remembers* (Little, Brown, 1970), pp. 367–368.
5. Voorhees wrote an article that appeared in *The New York Times Magazine* on July 23, 1950, titled "To Prevent a 'Korea' in Western Europe."
6. USAF OHI p. 18, pp. 203–212.
7. PHN 9/26/86.
8. PHN, "Limited Wars or Massive Retaliation," *The Reporter,* September 5, 1957; "NSC 68 and the Soviet Threat Reconsidered," *International Security,* Spring 1980; "a dereliction of common sense" is from a letter to Gregg Herken on July 10, 1986.
9. PHN 9/26/86.
10. "Limited Wars or Massive Retaliation," USAF OHI, pp. 470–472.
11. Stephen E. Ambrose, *Eisenhower, Volume Two: The President* (Simon and Schuster, 1984), pp. 434–435.
12. Desmond Ball, *Politics and Force Levels: The Strategic Missile Program of the Kennedy Administration* (University of California Press, Berkeley, 1980), pp. 39–40. Kennedy was given an early draft of Wohlstetter's article, "The Delicate Balance of Terror."
13. PHN 10/22/86.
14. PHN 12/19/86. Draft Policy Statement for Submission to the NSC: Policy of the United States Toward the Reduction of Tensions and the Limitation of Armaments, March 10, 1951, *Foreign Relations of the United States,* 1951, I: pp. 456–457.
15. Thomas C. Schelling and Morton H. Halperin, *Strategy and Arms Control* (Pergamon-Brassey's Classic, 1985); Schelling, "What Went Wrong with Arms Control?," *Foreign Affairs,* November 1985. Schelling's "Surprise Attack and Disarmament," published in December 1959 in the *Bulletin of the Atomic Scientists,* came out of his part in assisting in the preparations for the conference.
16. This essay was written for the *Saturday Evening Post* but never published.
17. PHN 1/7/87 and 10/22/86.

Chapter 3

1. USAF OHI pp. 113–114, 297–298.
2. USAF OHI pp. 109–110, 389.
3. Nitze's recollection of this episode is recorded in Isaacson and Thomas's *The Wise Men,* pp. 597–598, and was amplified in interviews with the author. Others interviewed on this point were

McNamara, 8/7/86, and Adam Yarmolinsky and Abram Chayes, 1/5/87. The Robert F. Kennedy quotation is from page 121 of his oral history interview at the John F. Kennedy Library.

4. Lloyd Norman, "Top Brass vs. 'Whiz Kids,' " *Newsweek,* May 29, 1961. Nitze made three references to the article in interviews during the spring and summer of 1986 and recalled the encounter with LeMay on July 14.

5. Glenn T. Seaborg, *Kennedy, Khrushchev and the Test Ban* (University of California Press, Berkeley, 1981); and Abram Chayes, 1/5/87.

6. "Was There Ever a 'Missile Gap'—or Just an Intelligence Gap?," *Newsweek,* November 13, 1961, p. 23.

7. McGeorge Bundy 12/8/86.

8. Ball, *Politics and Force Levels,* p. 98 (drawing from a 1973 interview with Nitze).

9. George Ball's comments came during an interview with James Blight and Janet Lang, May 1, 1987, and are included with the October 27, 1962, ExComm transcripts, prepared by McGeorge Bundy and published in *International Security,* Winter 1987/88. Robert Kennedy's account of the crisis is in *Thirteen Days: A Memoir of the Cuban Missile Crisis* (Norton, 1969), esp. pp. 106-109; his further comments on Nitze are from the JFK Library oral history, published in 1988 as *Robert Kennedy in His Own Words* (Bantam Books, New York, 1988); author's interview with PHN 3/17/87; Michael Mandelbaum, *The Nuclear Question: The United States and Nuclear Weapons 1947-1976* (Cambridge University Press, 1979), p. 134 ("The resolution of the crisis short of war was an example, albeit a highly unorthodox one, of successful nuclear diplomacy. And it marked the beginning of successful nuclear diplomacy of a more formal sort").

10. "The Lessons of the Cuban Missile Crisis," *Time,* September 27, 1982. The other authors were Dean Rusk, George Ball, and Roswell Gilpatric. PHN 3/23/86.

11. Charles E. Bohlen, *Witness to History: 1929-1969* (Norton, 1973), pp. 495-496.

12. PHN 3/23/86, and USAF OHI pp. 318-319.

13. Rumsfeld 2/16/87.

Chapter 4

1. Herken, *Counsels of War,* pp. 62-63.

2. "An Alternative Nuclear Policy as a Base for Negotiations," originally an article written for *The Saturday Evening Post* but never published, then circulated as a paper for the Washington Center of Foreign Policy Research in 1959.

3. Alan Tonelson, "Nitze's World," *Foreign Policy,* Summer 1979.

4. PHN 3/19/85, 3/17/87.

5. Robert McNamara, *Blundering into Disaster: Surviving the First Century of the Nuclear Age* (Pantheon, 1986), pp. 55-59.

6. An interview with McNamara in *The New York Times,* September 8, 1968.

7. Clifford 9/9/87.

8. PHN quotations from an interview on August 24, 1977, with Jerry W. Sanders, in his *Peddlers of Crisis: The Committee on the Present Danger and the Politics of Containment* (South End Press, 1983), pp. 141-142, as well as from USAF OHI, pp. 372, 394-395. Warnke 4/23/87. Gelb 10/4/87.

9. Halperin 8/19 and 12/16/86; Brown 9/29/86 and 2/27/87.

10. PHN 3/21/85.

11. John Newhouse, *Cold Dawn: The Story of SALT* (Holt, Rinehart and Winston, 1973), p. 54.

Chapter 5

1. Barry Goldwater, *With No Apologies: The Personal and Political Memoirs of U.S. Senator Barry Goldwater* (Morrow, 1979). Phyllis Schlafly and Chester Ward, *The Gravediggers* (Pere Marquette Press, Alton, Illinois, October 1964). That same year, Schlafly had published another pro-Goldwater book, *A Choice Not an Echo,* with the same publisher.

2. USAF OHI pp. 432-33.

3. PHN 3/19/86.

4. Paula Stern, *Water's Edge: Domestic Politics and the Making of American Foreign Policy* (Greenwood Press, Westport, Conn., 1979), esp. pp. 19-20, 23-27.
5. Kissinger, *Years of Upheaval*, p. 1151.
6. PHN 7/86 and 3/17/87.
7. USAF OHI, pp. 446-447.
8. USAF OHI, p. 464.
9. PHN, "The Strategic Balance Between Hope and Skepticism," *Foreign Policy*, Winter 1974-75, pp. 136-156.
10. William G. Hyland, *Mortal Rivals: Superpower Relations from Nixon to Reagan* (Random House, 1987), p. 45. Kissinger's statement came at a briefing for the press at the State Department on December 3, 1974. However, his own memoirs, *White House Years* (Little, Brown, 1979), stress the validity of his decision not to go for a MIRV ban.

Chapter 6

1. Smith's memoir of the talks, *Doubletalk: The Story of SALT I* (Doubleday, New York), 1980, p. 42.
2. USAF OHI p. 480.
3. See, in addition to Smith's *Doubletalk*, Hyland's *Mortal Rivals*, p. 48, and Raymond Garthoff's *Détente and Confrontation* (Brookings Institution, Washington, 1985).
4. Raymond Garthoff, *International Security*, Summer 1977, pp. 107-108; replying to a letter to the editor commenting on an earlier article Garthoff had written, "Negotiating with the Russians: Some Lessons from SALT," *International Security*, Spring 1977.
5. "An Alternative Nuclear Policy," paper described in n. 2 of chap. 4.
6. USAF OHI p. 437.
7. Smith, *Doubletalk*, p. 42.
8. Teller, "Should the Senate Ratify the SALT Accords?," *National Review*, July 7, 1972, p. 744.
9. Earle and Richardson 3/10/87.
10. For more on Nitze's view on this episode, see his "Essential Equivalence Should Be Arms Talk Goal," *Aviation Week and Space Technology*, July 22, 1974.
11. PHN 3/17/87.
12. PHN 11/5/84.
13. Elmo Zumwalt, *On Watch* (Times Books, 1976), pp. 479-511; Schlesinger 3/12/87.
14. Kissinger, *Years of Upheaval*, pp. 1175-76.

Chapter 7

1. PHN's speech in Los Alamos, quoted in *Aviation Week & Space Technology*, February 3, 1975, p. 74.
2. Hyland, *Mortal Rivals*, p. 171.
3. For more on Team B, see Robert Scheer, *With Enough Shovels: Reagan, Bush and Nuclear War* (updated edition) (Random House/Vintage Books, 1983), pp. 18-22 and 52-65; David Binder, "New CIA Estimate Finds Soviet Seeks Superiority in Arms," *The New York Times*, December 26, 1976; *The National Intelligence Estimates A-B Team Episode Concerning Soviet Strategic Capability and Objectives*, Report of the Subcommittee on Collection, Production and Quality of the Senate Select Committee on Intelligence, 95th Congress (Government Printing Office, 1978); Richard Pipes, "Team B: The Reality Behind the Myth," *Commentary*, October 1986, as well as letter rebutting Pipes's version from Howard Stoertz, Jr., in the March 1987 issue of *Commentary*.
   The Graham quotations come from an article by Murrey Marder, "Carter to Inherit Intense Dispute on Soviet Intentions," *Washington Post*, January 2, 1977, and the Pipes quotation from "Strategic Superiority," *The New York Times*, February 6, 1977. See also his "Why the Soviet Union Thinks It Could Fight and Win a Nuclear War," *Commentary*, July 1977.
4. *Alerting America: The Papers of the Committee on the Present Danger*, edited by Charles Tyroler; introduction by Max M. Kampelman, p. xv.

5. PHN 1/7/87.
6. PHN 1/7/87; the paper "What to Do About SALT?" appears in Nitze's unpublished collection of writings, *Getting from Here to There.*
7. Interviews with Brown, Holbrooke, Blechman, Slocombe, and Davis, 9/6–8/86, Vance 12/9/86, Carter 6/15/87.
8. USAF OHI p. 468.
9. *Foreign Policy,* Spring 1975, pp. 12–29.
10. The National Symposium of the Civilian/Military Institute, February 10–22, 1977, the proceedings of which were published by the institute under the title *Building a Durable Peace, 1977,* pp. 60–62.
11. Sanders, *Peddlers of Crisis, p.* 244.
12. PHN 3/17/87.
13. Charlton, *From Deterrence to Defense,* p. 67.
14. Warnke 4/23/87.

Chapter 8

1. Rostow in testimony before the House Committee on Foreign Affairs subcommittees on international security and scientific affairs and on Europe and the Middle East, February 23, 1982.
2. USAF OHI p. 351.
3. USAF OHI pp. 305–306.
4. The closest Nitze came to expressing in public the view that it would be difficult to reach a meaningful and acceptable compromise in the European arms-control negotiations was in his article "Strategy in the 1980s," *Foreign Affairs,* Fall 1980, p. 98.
5. For a sardonic portrait of Kvitsinsky as a young diplomat in Berlin in the early 1960s, see Nicholas Nabokov's memoir *Bagazh* (Atheneum, 1975), pp. 258–268.

Chapter 9

1. The bishops' report, which had already received considerable publicity, appeared in May 1983: United States Catholic Conference, "The Challenge of Peace: God's Promise and Our Response," *Origins* (National Catholic Documentary Service).
2. Interview in *Newsweek,* March 18, 1985. On Watkins's role in SDI, see his "The Strategic Defense Initiative," *Defense/ 85,* March 1985, pp. 14–18; and "Enhanced Role of Religious Faith at Pentagon Raises Questions, Doubts," December 30, 1984, *Los Angeles Times.*
3. For a detailed reconstruction of the origins of Star Wars, see William Broad, *Star Warriors* (Simon and Schuster, 1985); and Gregg Herken, "The Earthly Origins of Star Wars," *Bulletin of the Atomic Scientists,* October 1987.
4. *Newsweek* interview, March 18, 1985.
5. Gary Wills, *Reagan's America: Innocents At Home* (Doubleday, 1987), p. 280.
6. Yonas, "The Strategic Defense Initiative," *Daedalus,* Spring 1985.
7. *The Wall Street Journal,* December 7, 1983; TV interview, October 22, 1984; *Washington Times,* May 13, 1985; *New York City Tribune,* January 2, 1986; all in *Star Wars Quote Book,* published by the Arms Control Association, July 1986.
8. McFarlane 8/14–15/86; the quotation about "the East-West political dynamic" and SDI being "an initiative whose time had come" is from a July 14, 1986 letter from McFarlane to Gregg Herken, cited in the epilogue to an updated edition of *Counsels of War* (Oxford University Press, 1987).
9. PHN 1/16/85. The interview with Herken appeared in a 1988 draft article.
10. PHN 4/22/87.
11. PHN 3/21/85, 5/6/85, 3/19/86.
12. Reprinted as an article, "To Seize the Moment," in *Naval Institute Proceedings,* February 1985, pp. 13–16.
13. The Daniel Graham quote is from the Herken article cited in n. 9.
14. Kissinger 5/6/85.

Chapter 10

1. For a thorough review of the radar issue, see James P. Rubin, "The Superpower Dispute over Radars," *Bulletin of Atomic Scientists,* April 1987, pp. 34–37.
2. Perle at a discussion at the School of Advanced International Studies of Johns Hopkins University 11/26/84.
3. PHN 3/19/86.
4. PHN 4/17 and 5/7/86.
5. Perle at a dinner meeting with reporters at the first Reagan-Gorbachev summit in Geneva, 11/18/85.
6. At a *Time* magazine symposium on SDI in Washington 6/3/86.
7. Quoted by Herken, "The Earthly Origins of Star Wars," *Bulletin of the Atomic Scientists,* October 1987, p. 26.
8. Perle at meeting with reporters in Geneva, 11/18/87.
9. PHN 3/19/86.
10. Perle's comments come from an interview 11/6/85. See also Don Oberdorfer, "ABM Reinterpretation: A Quick Study: Young Lawyer's New Look at 1972 Pact Triggers Controversy," *Washington Post,* October 22, 1985. For Sofaer's views, see his article "The ABM Treaty and the Strategic Defense Initiative," *Harvard Law Review,* June 1986; the same issue contains a rebuttal by Abram Chayes and Antonia Handler Chayes, "Testing and Development of 'Exotic' Systems Under the ABM Treaty: The Great Reinterpretation Caper." See also Raymond Garthoff, "Policy vs. The Law: The 'Reinterpretation' of the ABM Treaty," published by the Brookings Institution, September 1987.
11. McFarlane 8/14/86.
12. PHN 3/19/86.

Chapter 11

1. Arnold Horelick, "The Return of Arms Control," *America and the World: 1984,* year-end issue of *Foreign Affairs,* Vol. 63, No. 3.
2. PHN 2/14/85.
3. Nixon 4/23/87.
4. Henry Rowen, "Living with a Sick Bear," *The National Interest,* Winter 1985–86.
5. Adelman 7/16/86.
6. PHN 3/19/86.
7. PHN 6/17/85.
8. Perle 11/6/85.
9. PHN 9/12/85.

Chapter 12

1. Schlesinger 8/14/86.
2. Chervov 9/16/86.
3. Kornienko 9/20/86.
4. PHN 10/22/86. This reconstruction of the meeting is also based on other U.S. sources and on a Soviet view provided by Georgi Arbatov on 7/6/87.

Chapter 13

1. Gregory Fossedal, "NSC Minutes Show President Leaning to SDI Deployment," *Washington Times,* February 6, 1987.
2. Arbatov 7/1/87 and Petrovsky 7/3/87.
3. PHN letter of April 22, 1987, to Louis Friedman, executive director of the Planetary Society,

Pasadena, California, who had written Nitze to challenge his comments in the Johns Hopkins speech of April 1.
4. Sagdeyev 7/2/87.

Chapter 14

1. Nunn 5/24/88.
2. Crowe 6/3/88.
3. Nunn 5/24/88.
4. Carlucci interviewed on the Cable News Network in Moscow, 5/30/88.
5. PHN 2/29/88.

INDEX

A NOTE ABOUT THE AUTHOR

Strobe Talbott is the Washington bureau chief of *Time* magazine. He is the translator-editor of *Khrushchev Remembers* and *Khrushchev Remembers: The Last Testament* (1970 and 1974), and the author of a number of other books, including *Endgame* (1979); *The Russians and Reagan,* for the Council on Foreign Relations (1984); *Deadly Gambits* (1984); and *Reagan and Gorbachev,* co-authored with Michael Mandelbaum (1987). In addition, he has been a contributor to two others: *The China Factor,* published with the American Assembly (1981), and *The Making of America's Soviet Policy* (1984).

A NOTE ABOUT THE TYPE

The text of this book was set in a version of Times Roman, designed by Stanley Morison (1889-1967) for *The Times* (London) and first introduced by that newspaper in 1932.

Among typographers and designers of the twentieth century, Stanley Morison was a strong forming influence as a typographical advisor to The Monotype Corporation, as a director of two distinguished English publishing houses, and as a writer of sensibility, erudition, and keen practical sense.

Composed by Creative Graphics, Inc., Allentown, Pennsylvania
Printed and bound by Fairfield Graphics, Fairfield, Pennsylvania
Designed by Iris Weinstein

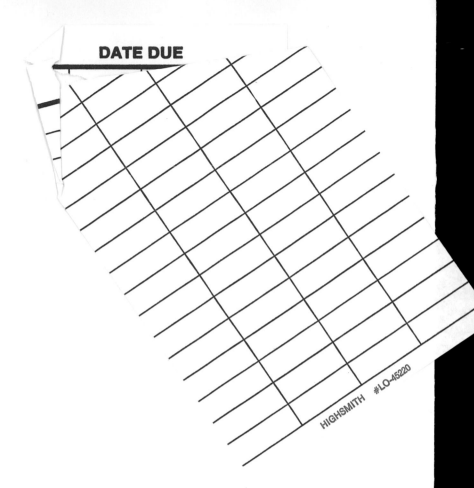

DATE DUE

HIGHSMITH #LO-45220